D0088510

Central Asia's
Second Chance

Other books by Martha Brill Olcott

Kazakhstan: Unfulfilled Promise

The Kazakhs

Central Asia's New States

Getting It Wrong:
Regional Cooperation and the Commonwealth of Independent States
(with Anders Åslund and Sherman Garnett)

Russia after Communism
(edited with Anders Åslund)

Central Asia's
Second Chance

Martha Brill Olcott

CARNEGIE ENDOWMENT FOR INTERNATIONAL PEACE
Washington, D.C.

© 2005 Carnegie Endowment for International Peace. All rights reserved.

No part of this publication may be reproduced or transmitted in any form or by any means without permission in writing from the Carnegie Endowment.

Carnegie Endowment for International Peace
1779 Massachusetts Avenue, N.W., Washington, D.C. 20036
202-483-7600, Fax 202-483-1840
www.CarnegieEndowment.org

The Carnegie Endowment for International Peace normally does not take institutional positions on public policy issues; the views and recommendations presented in this publication do not necessarily represent the views of the Carnegie Endowment, its officers, staff, or trustees.

To order, contact Carnegie's distributor:

The Brookings Institution Press
Department 029, Washington, D.C. 20042-0029, USA
1-800-275-1447 or 1-202-797-6258
Fax 202-797-2960, E-mail bibooks@brook.edu

Composition by Oakland Street Publishing
Printed by Worzalla Printing.
Cover photos by AP Photo/Sergey Ponomarev, AP Photo/Anatoly Ustinenko, Robert Harding World Imagery, AP Photo/Burt Herman.

Library of Congress Cataloging-in-Publication Data
Olcott, Martha Brill, 1949-
Central Asia's second chance / Martha Brill Olcott.
p. cm.
Includes bibliographical references and index.
ISBN-13: 978-0-87003-218-9 (cloth) — ISBN-10: 0-87003-218-6 (cloth)
ISBN-13: 978-0-87003-217-2 (paper) — ISBN-10: 0-87003-217-8 (paper)
1. Asia, Central--Economic conditions—1991- . 2. Asia, Central —Politics and government—1991- . 3. Economic assistance, American—Asia. Central. 4. Peace. I. Title.
HC420.3.O43 2005
320.958'09'051--dc22   2005013327

10 09 08 07 06 05   1 2 3 4 5   1st printing 2005

WIDENER UNIVERSITY
WOLFGRAM
LIBRARY
CHESTER, PA

Contents

Foreword

The strategic importance of Central Asia has been widely recognized since the attacks of September 11, 2001. The subsequent U.S.-led campaign in Afghanistan transformed the region into a front line in the global struggle against terror. But the region's leaders remain strange bedfellows for democratic regimes.

In *Central Asia's Second Chance*, Carnegie senior associate Martha Brill Olcott, an internationally recognized scholar and policy analyst who has studied and traveled in Central Asia for thirty years, vividly depicts the region's many challenges. She writes that renewed international interest in Central Asia is unlikely to resolve urgent social and economic challenges, given the limited level of international engagement and the deeply flawed leadership throughout the region.

Olcott singles out the inward-looking economic strategies adopted by Central Asian countries following the collapse of the Soviet Union, which have impeded regional cooperation. Central Asia's leaders are all men shaped by their Soviet-era experiences, more concerned with exploiting state resources and controlling their populations than with implementing democratic political systems or sponsoring regional cooperation. None has been a serious advocate of economic transparency, and some have refused to support even limited market reforms.

In fact, the region's newfound significance to the rest of the world has emboldened many leaders' sense of personal security. Confident that their support for the war on terror is too valuable to be risked over "secondary" matters, Central Asian leaders have resisted outside calls for political reforms. Not surprisingly, this is particularly true in countries with indigenous energy resources.

Central Asia's population is likely to grow increasingly restive. In March 2005, following a seriously flawed parliamentary election, angry crowds took to the street in Kyrgyzstan, causing their president to flee the country. Especially after the revolutions in Georgia and Ukraine, these demonstrations put other leaders in the region on notice as well.

Olcott highlights a deep contradiction running through U.S. policy toward Central Asia. Partnership with the region's antidemocratic regimes creates long-term security risks in the form of political, economic, and social discontent that can catalyze terrorism. Yet the short-term priority of that same danger argues for continued engagement.

Olcott also faults the international community for using country-specific approaches to development assistance rather than a regional framework. She offers a number of insightful alternative courses to follow.

As the world increasingly comes to view Central Asia as a critical battle-field in the war on terror, Olcott makes an important contribution to our knowledge of a vitally important region still unfamiliar to most foreign policy specialists. Her perceptive analysis of the challenges involved in state building and international development assistance will be of particular interest to scholars and policymakers, but the book's accessible prose is equally suitable for the general reader.

In Afghanistan, we witnessed the devastating effects a failed state in Central Asia can have on people living thousands of miles away. Olcott's expert analysis offers a timely examination of the domestic, regional, and global conditions that contribute to the region's instability and points the way to a brighter future.

Martha Olcott's work is an integral part of the Carnegie Endowment's Russian and Eurasian Program. We are grateful to program support provided by the Carnegie Corporation of New York and the Starr Foundation.

Jessica T. Mathews
President
Carnegie Endowment for International Peace

Acknowledgments

Central Asia's Second Chance was nearly four years in the making, and would not have been possible without the help, guidance, and support of dozens of people in the United States, Russia, Europe, and most important, Central Asia itself.

I gratefully acknowledge the support from the Carnegie Endowment, which not only provided me with the financial resources necessary to complete this project, but also gave me the ideal intellectual settings—its Washington and Moscow offices—to write such a book. I spent hours talking through its major themes with Anders Åslund, Andy Kuchins, Masha Lipman, Lilia Shevtsova, and Dmitri Trenin. George Perkovich, vice president for studies, gave me excellent comments during his careful reading of the text. I am grateful for the assistance of Kathleen Higgs, Chris Henley, and Jill Fox, Carnegie's library staff. I also owe special thanks to Aleksei Malashenko, the codirector of the Ethnicity and Nation Building program at the Carnegie Moscow Center, who traveled with me to Central Asia numerous times during the last four years, and spent hundreds of hours discussing the issues of the book with me.

I give particular thanks to Roger Kangas of NATO's George C. Marshall European Center for Security Studies for his thoughtful comments on the manuscript, and Johannes Linn, formerly vice president for Eastern Europe and Central Asia at the World Bank, who offered comments and criticisms of all the chapters that related to the operation and policies of the international financial institutions in the region.

Some of the material in this book was presented as a draft for comment at international conferences, including the Liechtenstein Institute on Self

Determination at Princeton University, held in Liechtenstein in March 2002; a May 2002 meeting in Istanbul sponsored by the George Marshall Center; and a June 2004 meeting in Oslo, sponsored by the Norwegian Institute of International Affairs. Parts of this book are also drawn from an April 2004 meeting on future directions of Kazakhstan's foreign policy that Carnegie cosponsored with the Institute for Strategic Studies and the Friedrich Eberhardt foundation office in Almaty, and at roundtables supported by the Institute for War and Peace Reporting in Bishkek. Earlier versions of chapters two and three appeared in the National Bureau of Research's Strategic Asia 2002–2003 Asian Aftershocks, edited by Richard J. Ellings and Aaron L. Friedberg, which was presented at a planning meeting in Washington, D.C., prior to publication.

I also thank Ben Slay of the United Nations Development Program Research Center in Bratislava, for sponsoring two of my trips to Central Asia in the immediate aftermath of September 11, from which the idea for this book was originally conceived.

I owe special thanks to a number of friends and colleagues from Central Asia, including Sabit Jusupov and Maulen Ashimbayev in Kazakhstan, and Kuban Mambetaliev, who facilitated my travel throughout the country, and Chinara Jakypova, who directs the Institute of War and Peace Reporting office, in Kyrgyzstan. Abdujabar Abduvahitov, president of Westminster University in Uzbekistan, and Bakhtiyar Babadjanov of the Institute of Oriental Studies in Tashkent, contributed enormously to my understanding of their country. Thanks are also owed to Saodat Alimova and Muzaffar Alimov, who run the Sharq analytic center in Dushanbe, and Chary Annarberdyev and Nadjia Badykova, both from Turkmenistan.

I also would like to thank the staffs of the embassies of Kazakhstan, Kyrgyzstan, and Uzbekistan in the United States. I am particularly grateful for the help that I received from the ambassadors from these countries: Kanat Saudabayev (Kazakhstan), Baktybek Abdrissaev (Kyrgyzstan), and Sadyk Safayev and Abdulaziz Kamilov (Uzbekistan). All were courteous, generous, frank, and giving, as well as helpful in facilitating my travel to each country.

This book came to completion through the labors of the following research assistants, who were responsible for researching footnotes and appendixes: Zhanara Naurazbayeva, Kate Vlachtchenko, Saltanat Berdikeeva, and Lola Ibragimova. All four of these young women are testimony to the kind of intellectual promise that exists with the younger generation in post-Soviet countries. All came to the United States on educational scholarships and earned degrees. I am especially grateful to Caroline McGregor, a former Carnegie junior fellow, who applied her wonderful editing skills to getting this manuscript over its last hurdle.

Finally, this book would not have been possible without the love and support of my husband, Tony, and my daughter, Hillary, both of whom endured my travel, long hours, and weekends in the office, with love and forbearance.

Abbreviations and Acronyms

ADB	Asian Development Bank
AKN	Tajikistan's UN-sponsored drug control agency
bbl	"blue barrel," 42-gallon barrel used as standard for oil trade
BIS	Bank for International Settlements
BTC	Baku-Tbilisi-Ceyhan pipeline
CAAEF	Central Asia American Enterprise Fund
CAC	Central Asia and Center System
CACO	Central Asian Cooperation Organization
CICA	Conference on Interaction and Confidence-Building Measures in Asia
CIS	Commonwealth of Independent States
CPC	Caspian Pipeline Consortium
CSTO	Collective Security Treaty Organization
CTR	Cooperative Threat Reduction
DBK	Development Bank of Kazakhstan
EBRD	European Bank for Reconstruction and Development
ECO	Economic Cooperation Organization
ETIM	East Turkestan Islamic Movement
FSA	Freedom Support Act
GDP	gross domestic product
GEF	Global Energy Facility
IDA	International Development Association
IFES	International Foundation for Election Systems
IFI	international financial institutions
IHROU	Independent Human Rights Organization of Uzbekistan
IMU	Islamic Movement of Uzbekistan
IRP	Islamic Renaissance Party
IOM	International Organization for Migration

KASE	Kazakhstan Stock Exchange
MCA	Millennium Challenge Accounts
NBK	National Bank of Kazakhstan
NGO	nongovernmental organization
OIC	Organization of the Islamic Conference
ONDCP	Office of National Drug Control Policy (U.S.)
OSCE	Organization for Security and Cooperation in Europe
PFP	Partnership for Peace
RAO-UES	Russia's Unified Energy Systems
RRDP	UNDP's Tajikistan Reconstruction, Rehabilitation, and Development Program
PSA	production sharing agreement
SCO	Shanghai Cooperation Organization
SME	small and medium-sized enterprises
SOFA	Status of Forces Agreement
SPECA	Special Program for the Economies of Central Asia
START	Strategic Arms Reduction Treaty
TACIS	Technical Assistance to the Commonwealth of Independent States (EU)
Traceca	Transport Corridor Europe–Caucasus–Asia
UFE	Union for Fair Elections
UNDP	UN Development Program
UNODC	UN Office on Drugs and Crime
USAID	U.S. Agency for International Development
UNESCO	UN Educational, Scientific, and Cultural Organization
UTO	United Tajik Opposition
WTO	World Trade Organization

1

After September 11, An Unexpected Chance

The terrorist attacks on the United States of September 11, 2001, demonstrated what can happen when the international community turns its back on a region—in this case, Afghanistan and its neighbors—and its problems. Yet despite all the money subsequently devoted to the war on terror and to preventing a repeat of the circumstances that allowed Al Qaeda to thrive, the prospect of new failed states developing in Central Asia is greater today than it was then. In March 2005 Kyrgyzstan's president, Askar Akayev, was driven from office by an angry mob, and less than one month later Uzbekistan's president Islam Karimov used force to reassert control in the Ferghana Valley.

For most of the first decade of independence, Central Asia's leaders liked to cite the situation in Afghanistan as the source of many of their problems, claiming it created an environment in which political reform was risky and economic reform needed to take a backseat to political stability. But the population in the region—sparked in part by successful revolutions in Georgia and Ukraine—will no longer tolerate these kinds of excuses.

The situation in Afghanistan shows signs of stabilizing, even though reconstruction there is proving to be a slow and reverse-filled process. The Taliban's hold on power has been broken, the Al Qaeda camps have been largely liquidated, and a national political consensus seems to be developing around the idea that the country should be ruled by a democratically elected government.

Although armed opposition to the government led by President Hamid Karzai remains, fueled in part by a burgeoning drug trade, the ouster of the Taliban substantially reduced a major security risk for these states. And

1

even if Karzai should fall, the threat posed to Afghanistan's neighbors will be mitigated as long as there is a substantial U.S. and international military presence in Afghanistan, logistically supported by the presence of the two U.S. bases in Central Asia: the Manas airbase in Kyrgyzstan and the Khanabad base in Uzbekistan.

This new security environment created an unexpected second chance for the Central Asian states. Alongside the bases came the prospect of increased international assistance to the states of Central Asia as part of a regional strategy to support nation-building efforts in Afghanistan.

The thesis of this book is that much like their first efforts at state building, there is little likelihood that even now the Central Asian states will "get it right." The Soviet-era leaders still in power in these countries show no more— and in some cases even less—inclination to promote democratic political transitions than they did previously, and support for the transparency necessary to sustain economic reform remains virtually absent throughout the region.

Furthermore, the international community has done little to change the mind-set of these leaders. Although funding for the Central Asian states increased, the increases were short term and relatively meager, given the magnitude of economic challenges they face. Donor nations have been unwilling to reevaluate their fundamental approaches to foreign assistance and development needs in the region, so the incentives for reform remain ineffective.

Western interest in Central Asia has been quick to wane, partly because problems have cropped up in other parts of the world. The United States became preoccupied with the war in Iraq, and in general the international donor community became quickly disappointed by the initial results of their efforts at reengagement. By 2004 few outside observers viewed the prospects of reform in much of Central Asia any more favorably than they had three years earlier, and many viewed prospects as even more negative. And when President George W. Bush set the goal of building a community of free and independent nations in his January 2005 State of the Union Address, that was no indication that regime change or democratic institution building in this part of the world be a priority for his administration.[1]

A Fish Rots from the Head Down

Well-thought-out Western engagement is a necessary condition for changing the trajectories of development in this part of the world, but alone, it is insufficient. The outside world can provide foreign direct investment, technical assistance, loans, and grants-in-aid to these countries, but the will for reform must come from within the Central Asian states themselves, as we have seen in Kyrgyzstan. It must come from populations willing to endure the dislocations of economic and political transitions. And even more important, it must come from leaders willing to observe constitutional term limits, willing to hold free and fair elections—even if elections result in their defeat at the polls—and willing to leave office if such a defeat occurs. Democratic reforms can often translate into shorter periods in office than leaders or their families might like.

Reform also requires a kind of selflessness from leaders, a capacity to convince the population that their actions are designed to advance a national interest rather than simply motivated by the ruler's personal gain. This element has been sorely lacking in Central Asia. Even the most nationally spirited of the region's leaders have been compromised by charges that they or their family members have benefited from rigged privatization schemes. The worst behave so outlandishly that they appear as caricatures of greed and personal aggrandizement.

None of the region's presidents was truly prepared for the job of leading an independent state. While we can debate what the ideal training would be, bad training is easy to identify and would certainly include a successful career in the top ranks of the Communist Party of the Soviet Union—an institution that demanded blind obedience and inspired devious behavior. Central Asia's current leaders were all members of the Soviet elite, and the heads of Kazakhstan, Turkmenistan, and Uzbekistan were the Moscow-appointed leaders of their respective republic's Communist Party when the Soviet Union collapsed in December 1991. Kyrgyzstan's Askar Akayev took charge of his republic in 1990 in a coup staged by the local communist elite against the Moscow-appointed boss, who was already a liability to the Kremlin.[2] And the leaders who ousted Akayev in 2005 also served in the Communist Party system. All of these individuals rose through the ranks of the Soviet system thanks to their tenacity and skill as political infighters, not because of any political leadership or original thinking. The challenge of founding new states demands precisely those qualities that the Soviet system chose not to reward.

With the dissolution of the USSR, Central Asia gained independence without having to fight for it. That, in some respects, was a real advantage, for it involved little suffering or loss of life. Yet as a result, Central Asia's presidents generally lack the political legitimacy gained from leading a struggle for national independence.

Tajikistan's Imamali Rakhmonov is a somewhat special case. A former Soviet-era collective farm chairman from a remote region, Rakhmonov was placed in power in 1992 by the commanders who eventually won that country's civil war, which was fought between 1992 and 1997 for political control. A very unworldly man, Rakhmonov built his reputation on a high level of tolerance for brutality, even by local Tajik standards. Rakhmonov's first years in power were a time of bloody payback in the country, marked by vigilante justice against suspected enemies. These traits have made it very difficult for Rakhmonov to expand his power base, which is drawn almost entirely from his native region of Kulob.

In Kyrgyzstan, much changed between the early 1990s when Askar Akayev, the self-styled democrat, was popularly embraced as a nationalist figure and 2005 when Akayev, the increasingly corrupt autocrat, was ousted by members of his own ruling elite.

Akayev, a physicist by training and party functionary by career, had sought to emphasize how different he was from the region's other leaders. In his first years in office, Akayev was eager to cultivate an image of being the Thomas Jefferson of Central Asia, as Strobe Talbott, then Undersecretary of State, referred to him in 1994. His subsequent actions, which included jailing prominent political rivals, such as vice president-turned-opposition leader Feliks Kulov, turned such claims into a source of ridicule, when it became clear that the diminutive Akayev had very little in common with his physically imposing American role model.

Rakhmonov and Akayev, together with Nursultan Nazarbayev in Kazakhstan, Saparmurat Niyazov in Turkmenistan, and Islam Karimov in Uzbekistan have to varying degrees behaved like rulers who are frightened of their populations. Each has used the state instruments at his disposal to hold power, stunting the development of political institutions in the process, though always in the name of greater national gain.

New U.S. Presence

Since September 11, 2001, the expanded U.S. presence in the region has become one of these state instruments stabilizing the Central Asian regimes' grip on power Although the various nations' contributions to the war on terror have varied in strategic significance, each of the region's leaders believed that his efforts should translate into new leverage with the United States.

The Uzbeks were the first to provide a military base to the United States, turning over facilities at Khanabad in Kashi prior to the beginning of the military campaign in Afghanistan. The Tajik and Kyrgyz governments also lobbied for the U.S. military to use their facilities, eager for the boost it could bring their economies. The Dushanbe airport in Tajikistan was used by the United States and France as a "gas-and-go" refueling base during various phases of the military operation in Afghanistan. The United States established a full base facility in Kyrgyzstan, taking over part of the Manas airfield, the country's major commercial airport near Bishkek, and deploying 1,100 military personnel there. In addition, the United States also gained limited landing rights at three airfields in Kazakhstan.[3]

Only Turkmenistan imposed strict limits on its military cooperation with the United States, citing its claim to "positive neutrality." But it did serve as a major transit point for humanitarian assistance bound for Afghanistan, and such cooperation was enough for the United States to reward President Saparmurat Niyazov with a visit from U.S. Secretary of Defense Donald Rumsfeld in April 2002.

The September 11 attacks turned the countries of Central Asia into frontline states for the Bush administration, which previously had given little thought to direct engagement with Afghanistan and placed no priority on increased security cooperation with the Central Asian states.

For years Western analysts had been pointing to the security risks associated with Afghanistan's degeneration into lawlessness and had warned of increasing danger as the Taliban leaders consolidated their hold to include about 90 percent of the country's territory. This theme was frequently repeated in speeches by prominent Russian and Central Asian leaders, almost all of whom believed that anti-regime activists in their own countries had ties to Afghanistan's theocratic rulers.[4]

Central Asia's leaders were eager to link up with the U.S. effort to oust the Taliban because it would rid them of a troublesome neighbor. And many leaders also hoped that direct military cooperation with the United States might translate into security guarantees offered by Washington for their own increasingly less popular regimes.

The Taliban regime had few friends in Central Asia because most rulers saw it as threatening to their secular visions of nationhood and, even more troubling, as tolerating the presence of local and international terrorist groups, such as the Islamic Movement of Uzbekistan (IMU) and the Al Qaeda network. Most of the region's leaders also linked the lawlessness in Afghanistan to a major increase in the opium and heroin trade across their states. But the sense of threat varied, as did the price that the various Central Asian rulers were willing to pay to effect regime change in Afghanistan. By late 1999, however, attitudes toward the Taliban had hardened throughout the region, in large part due to the coordinated series of bombings in Tashkent in February 1999, and an armed incursion into Kyrgyzstan by Afghan-based fighters from the IMU several months later, in which several foreigners were taken hostage.

Cognizant of the deteriorating security environment in the region, the United States increased military assistance to and cooperation with several of the Central Asian states but saw little urgency in the situation, even as the United States became more concerned with the need to contain the threat posed by Al Qaeda.

The U.S. reevaluation of the strategic importance of the Central Asian states struck a responsive chord in the region. Presidents Islam Karimov of Uzbekistan and Askar Akayev of Kyrgyzstan had long been pressing for some form of increased international intervention in Afghanistan, as had Tajikistan's Imamali Rakhmonov. All three men had also been seeking ways to more fully engage with the United States, believing that Washington's preoccupation with oil- and gas-rich states of the Caspian meant that their importance was being eclipsed by Kazakhstan and Turkmenistan.

U.S.–Tajik relations began improving steadily after an internationally led negotiating effort resulted in the introduction of a government of reconciliation in June 1997. But Rakhmonov wanted to further advance this relationship as part of his effort to find strategic counterbalances for Russia's lingering military presence.[5]

Akayev wanted to reverse a deteriorating U.S.–Kyrgyz relationship—and to do so without modifying his domestic policies. Akayev's domestic policies had become a sore point with U.S. policy makers, who were frustrated by restrictions on the role of opposition and independent political groups in Kyrgyzstan introduced in the late 1990s. Akayev's interest in cooperating with the United States was heightened by Uzbekistan's rapid support for the U.S. war effort. An alliance between Tashkent and Washington would change the strategic balance within the Central Asian region, and Akayev did not want his smaller and weaker country to become even more vulnerable to pressure from its more powerful neighbor.

The U.S. military's Enduring Freedom operation in Afghanistan seemed a tailor-made opportunity for Karimov, who saw close ties to the United States as critical to Uzbekistan's ability to develop a defense policy that was fully independent of Russia.

Many in the U.S. Defense Department were pleased with the Uzbek military's performance in a series of programs that grew out of the Partnership for Peace program run by the North Atlantic Treaty Organization (NATO). Military cooperation between the Uzbeks and the Americans increased after the Tashkent bombings in February 1999, in which Karimov appears to have been targeted by religious extremists presumed to have ties to the IMU, though no one has claimed responsibility for the attack.[6]

Karimov's refusal to engage in sustained economic or political reforms had seriously hampered prospects for a close Uzbek–U.S. relationship. At least two U.S. Secretaries of Defense, William Perry and Donald Rumsfeld, had been fulsome in their praise of Tashkent and lauded the prospect of U.S.–Uzbek cooperation. Rumsfeld seemed quite uncomfortable with using human rights—on which Karimov's record is infamous—as a yardstick when evaluating potential strategic partners.[7] But in the end there was too little to be gained in Washington from a close public partnership with remote Uzbekistan for any substantial sea change in relations to occur.

New Chance for Reform

In and of themselves, the pro forma promises Uzbekistan and Kyrgyzstan made regarding their newfound commitment to human rights made these states no less embarrassing allies for the United States, especially Uzbekistan. But the increased U.S. military presence, combined with Washington's claimed willingness to spend more foreign aid dollars in this part of the world, might have served as an opportunity to jump-start their stalled reform process. This book looks at precisely what would have been necessary to do just that.

Chapter two explores whether the regimes in place throughout Central Asia were prepared prior to September 11 to use the renewed international interest in the region the events unexpectedly sparked to resolve pressing economic and social challenges.

Chapter three details the degree of international involvement in the region prior to September 11, and looks at what were the building blocks in place for future engagement.

When the terrorists flew their planes into the World Trade towers and the Pentagon, each of the Central Asian states was in the throes of political or economic crises of varying severity, created in part by a series of bad policy choices on the part of the countries' ruling elite. As chapters four and five show, most of these problems have yet to be resolved, and the security risks posed by the failure to do so are escalating, a subject tackled in chapters six and seven.

Each of the Central Asian states has developed a strong presidential system, and in the most extreme case, Turkmenistan, the president has near absolute power. The political choices that have been made in each of these countries will complicate the inevitable but still-pending transfer of power to a new generation. None of the Central Asian states has developed the political institutions necessary to support a democratic transition. Presidents and parliaments have not been elected democratically, and all too often the latter serve as little more than presidential rubber stamps. In several countries disenfranchised groups in society are growing restive. Violence in Uzbekistan's Andijan province in May 2005 foreshadows future unrest and how easily it may be triggered.

Kazakhstan and Kyrgyzstan are well along in their transition to market economies, but some countries, like Turkmenistan, have not begun, or others, like Uzbekistan, are trying to recreate momentum for a process that was halted in its early stages. Corruption is endemic throughout Central Asia, and there is little protection of private property—a situation that hobbles the performance of even the region's strongest economies. The Central Asian states all have predominantly young populations that are generally growing faster than the opportunities for employment, which creates fertile breeding grounds for recruiters from radical Islamic groups that have been openly operating in Central Asia since the late 1980s.

All the states in the region are engaged in completely revamping Soviet-era education and healthcare systems. Some of these states are doing this far more successfully than others, but in much of the region the patience of the population to withstand the disruptions that accompany even the best grounded of the social reform programs shows signs of strain.

Many political and economic problems created by the collapse of the Soviet Union were exaggerated by the inward-looking policies of state-building strategies, which often had deleterious consequences for the economies of neighboring states. We address this in the following chapter. The international community had little leverage to prevent this, because the United States and other Western governments and institutions used a country-specific approach to the design and delivery of development assistance rather than a framework designed to reinforce regional cooperation.

Five States versus One Region

The international financial community's approach reinforced the unwillingness of Central Asian leaders to give ground in dealing with shared regional problems, which have only been partly addressed, as chapters three and seven explain. Even today, though much less so than in 1991, the Central Asian states remain partially interdependent, which is a legacy of having been part of a single state. All depend in part or in whole on water from the Aral Sea basin, share hydroelectric and other energy systems, and have principal cities linked by highways that crossed largely arbitrary republic boundaries. Although tens of millions of dollars, including a lot of international assistance money, has been spent on reducing these interconnections, the Central Asian states still lack effective bilateral or multilateral institutions to manage the potential conflicts that their intimate geography and shared Soviet history continue to create.

At the same time, for all the complaints about the arbitrariness of national boundaries and all the talk of the relative "newness" of these nationalities, at independence each of the Central Asian states had a distinct titular nationality, with its own culture, language, and history. Although these people had much in common, there were also at least a dozen different permutations of national rivalries, especially when one added into the mix the hundred-odd minority nationalities and ethnic communities also living in the region. Most of these rivalries had their roots deep in history, but all had been further exacerbated by the ways in which scarce resources were allocated during the Soviet period.[8]

Ethnic competition has complicated the state-building process, a theme that appears throughout this book because it has affected foreign policies and domestic strategies in each of these countries. Central Asia's national leaders have consistently sought to demonstrate their uniqueness from their neighbors. Kazakhstan and Kyrgyzstan have always been relatively more open to the recommendations of the international community, and the Tajiks have become receptive too since the 1997 culmination of their civil war in which some 60,000 people died. But to underscore their distinction, the leaders of Uzbekistan and Turkmenistan sought to carve out a model of political and economic development that is said to be in keeping with the specificity of their national culture, rather than to accept strong international direction (and what they saw as inappropriate formulaic strategies).[9]

When the prospect of increased international assistance was raised in late 2001 and 2002, the Uzbek leadership began to reconsider its economic and political strategies. But as we see in chapter four, the Uzbek government has moved much more slowly and introduced fewer reforms than promised. Its introduction of account convertibility was late and incomplete, and the Uzbek government has yet to rescind regulations that restrict the free trade regime.[10] Uzbekistan's go-it-alone strategy has stifled the development of its own small- and medium-size business sector specifically and defeated prospects for regional trade more generally. This strategy has had serious economic consequences for neighboring Tajikistan and Kyrgyzstan as well, contributing to their disappointing economic progress.

Not only has a regional market failed to develop in Central Asia, but an atmosphere of protectionism has been nurtured in its stead. Throughout the Soviet period the Central Asian states were forced into a ghetto of Moscow's making, but regional integration need not be synonymous with international isolation. A regional market would have helped facilitate the integration of these states into the global economy—not inhibit it, as so many leaders of the region mistakenly thought. Given the distance to markets in the United States, Asia, and Europe, the development of a regional market joining Central Asia's neighboring parts of Russia, Iran, Afghanistan, and China would have spurred the development of local businesses. Pooling the capacities, supplies, and markets of these states would have expanded the variety and complexity of medium-size enterprise projects available for investment.

Although the region's leaders have championed the cause of increased cooperation, their deeds have generally belied their words. The Uzbeks, Kyrgyz, and Kazakhs joined together in 1994 to establish a Central Asian Union, eventually renamed the Central Asian Economic Community, and expanded it to include Tajikistan. But, the organization did little to stimulate increased economic cooperation, largely because none of the member states would delegate any authority to it.

Instead, the states of Central Asia began to treat one another as potential rivals or, worse yet, as enemies. This has been particularly true after the rise of the IMU in the late 1990s. Discussions on free trade were overshadowed by the introduction of policies of armed protectionism, stimulated in large part by Uzbekistan's decision to begin formally delineating and even mining its borders with neighboring states in 1999.

Most Central Asians were not terribly concerned that choices being made in their national capitals were adversely affecting those living in neighboring states. After all, their Soviet-era experience with calls to sacrifice national (then termed "republic") interest for a common good had taught them to expect that those making the sacrifice would generally lose more than they would gain.

Each of the states in the region became preoccupied with creating an international identity separate from that of each of its neighbors. The change in psychology seeped down from the leaders to the level of political aspirants and even to ordinary citizens. This is particularly true of those living in the two largest states of the region—Kazakhstan and Uzbekistan. Over time, however, Kazakhstan's leaders began looking to a larger international arena for examples with which to compare themselves, whereas Uzbekistan's elite became even more inward looking, at least with regard to domestic politics.

Turkmenistan had gone one step further; Ashgabat was following a policy of de facto isolationism with its doctrine of "positive neutrality" and nonengagement.

Learning to Live with Independence

It was not surprising that it took a while for the Central Asian leaders to orient themselves to the larger international community, the theme of chapter three. The presidents of these countries were not particularly eager for the dissolution of the USSR, even though following the failed Communist Party coup of August 1991 most realized it was likely to be inevitable and supported resolutions declaring independence drafted by their republic parliaments.[11] Compared with the disturbances in most other parts of the USSR, however, the situation in Central Asia was generally very quiet in the final days of Soviet history.[12] The one exception was Tajikistan, where there was near-revolutionary political frenzy sufficient to force the Gorbachev-appointed head of the republic (Kakhar Makhkamov) to resign under pres-

sure in September 1991, setting in motion a series of events that would cul-
minate in a full-fledged civil war some six months later.

The disturbances in Tajikistan highlighted the dangers associated with
independence. No leader felt exempt from the risk of popular unrest, given
the economic burdens that were created for each new government when the
Soviet Union was dissolved. Each president became the formal master of his
republic's economy but lacked the understanding of how to manage its
assets or how to meet its inherited social welfare burdens.

Though formally independent, each republic was still fully tied to
Moscow, which among other things was still printing all the money to pay
pensions and salaries. All feared that Russia's president, Boris Yeltsin, would
still try to dictate their economic and political choices, while formally recognizing each union republic of the Soviet Union as a sovereign subject of
international law. At the same time there was a deep-seated fear of what
would happen to these countries if Moscow left them to their own devices.
Not only would republic leaders be left to deal with their own increasingly
demanding populations, but they might have to cope with potentially rapa-
cious neighbors, with whom they shared ill-defined borders and to whom
they were still economically linked.

It soon became clear that most of these early fears were exaggerated.
Tajikistan's devastating civil war was not a harbinger of similar unrest in
neighboring states. It proved finite, and eventually, the process of international mediation led to a largely successful process of national reconciliation
in Tajikistan.[13]

The risks associated with independence did not disappear for Central
Asia's leaders but instead took on new forms. Tajikistan's civil war had many
hidden costs, including reinforcing the perception of the region's ruling
elite that the public was prone to uncontrollable violence. Long after the
fighting in Tajikistan had ended, it was still used as an explanation for why
the Central Asian states must move slowly with democratization.

The Tajik civil war also served to reinforce the Uzbek government's economic conservatism, because officials were frightened of what would happen if human security were somehow compromised and social welfare
commitments were not maintained. These fears led to the maintenance of
price supports long after neighboring Kazakhstan and Kyrgyzstan had abandoned them and fostered an atmosphere of economic isolation as Tashkent
was fearful that traders from neighboring states would profit from
Uzbekistan's lower prices.

The disorder in Afghanistan further complicated the process of state building throughout Central Asia. Opposition groups from Central Asia were able to take refuge in Afghanistan, and Islamic groups in particular (from both Uzbekistan and Tajikistan) found this a welcome refuge even in the territories dominated by the Northern Alliance. This was the case even before the Taliban took power in Afghanistan and allowed the Al Qaeda network to establish training camps for international terrorists.

The Central Asian states used both the situation in Afghanistan and the civil war in Tajikistan as excuses for not addressing their unresolved problems of economic and political reform. In reality, however, by the mid-1990s, for all their fears that Islamic extremism might pose a security threat, the region's presidents were also beginning to feel more firmly in control of their countries than they had just a few years previously. Independence began to seem irreversible, but one consequence of this was that there would be no one to bail them out if they faltered, and now more than ever the region's presidents did not want to be turned out of office. Independence had been of enormous personal benefit to these men, especially the four in power in 1991.

The region's rulers and their families began accumulating vast personal fortunes when they figured out how to manipulate the transfer of economic authority from Moscow to the republics. Independence provided Central Asia's presidents with near-total control of all assets of any value in their countries. Given the almost complete absence of private property under the Soviet system, there was enough economic redistribution in even the poorest republics to make their leaders rich. The Soviet system also sharply limited the number of potential political stakeholders in the new Central Asian states. There were no property owners with vested economic interests to deal with, and these presidents' only serious political rivals were former colleagues from the communist elite, who with the dismantlement of the Communist Party now lacked the political instrument that they had previously used to advance themselves.

Learning about One's Friends

With time, the sense of perceived threat from Russia also began to recede, or at least was redefined. Although formally the heir to the USSR, Russia still had to reinvent itself and faced the same economic and political challenges as the other newly independent states. The Kremlin was preoccupied with

Russia's problems, and those that they had helped stir up in the Caucasus. As a result Moscow had less inclination and ability to directly intervene in Central Asia than the region's leaders had originally expected. Russia remained intimately involved in Tajikistan, but its military presence there proved the exception, not the rule.

The leaders of the Central Asian states eventually decided that the biggest threats they faced came from their own citizens, which we address in chapter two. Although the risk that dissatisfied elements would be incited by external forces decreased, the fear that they would be organized by frustrated and displaced local elites remained. The continued independence of their states was not at issue, but the current leaders' capacity to perpetuate their rule was not assured. And if their power were threatened, it was becoming increasingly unclear from whom they might obtain help.

By the mid-1990s, the leadership in Moscow was preoccupied with its own political succession crisis, and after Vladimir Putin took power in late 1999, the new Russian president quickly became mired in Chechnya. As chapter three shows, with the Russian army both overextended and largely unreformed, Moscow's interest in trying to speak for or act in the interests of its Central Asian neighbors was diminishing almost as rapidly as its capacity to do so effectively.

Russia's level of military engagement in Central Asia peaked with the Russian intervention in Tajikistan in late 1992. The Tashkent Collective Security Agreement, signed on May 14, 1992, ceased to be the basis of a regional force when the Uzbeks pulled out in 1999. Russian military cooperation remained quite high with the Kyrgyz and Kazakhs, but when terrorists from the IMU took hostages in the mountains of Kyrgyzstan's Osh oblast, the Russians refused to respond to the Kyrgyz call for help.[14] Bluntly put, Russia's military was not in a position to cover its own needs, let alone the Central Asians'.

Yet there was no other regional power ready or able to fill the gap. Sharing borders with three of the five Central Asian states, China had a strong interest in the region, but the Chinese did not feel pressed to maximize their influence. Their concern was to ensure future strategic advantage while minimizing the risk that the Central Asian states might create immediate security threats for China.

Smaller regional powers, including Iran and Turkey, did see the creation of independent states in Central Asia as potentially shifting the geostrategic balance to their respective advantage. Both states had strong cultural affinities with the Central Asian states, and although both pursued aggressive policies in the region, each lacked the resources to become the deciding influence in any of these countries.

With its substantial U.S. support and NATO membership, Turkey was able to develop a stronger, but by no means commanding presence. The Central Asian states had long seen cooperation with the United States and NATO as a ticket to the future. But prior to September 11, the West had little interest in funding the rapid entry of the Central Asian countries into the global security system, and it seems now that little has changed.

Region Still at Risk

Even without the events of September 11, it was only a matter of time before the Russians were overshadowed in the region by the slowly but steadily growing role of the United States, as well as by the Central Asian states' own broader engagement with the United States and other European and Asian states. This said, the opening of U.S. military bases in the region was a dramatic act, simultaneously an affirmation of the Central Asian leaders' claim of the region's strategic importance and a symbolic end to the Russian and Soviet empires.

It also served as a public demonstration of Russian power in retreat. After years of blustering pronouncements warning Washington not to reach too deep into its backyard, Moscow rather quietly accepted being eclipsed by the United States in areas Russia had long dominated, at least as a temporary necessity. The increased U.S. presence in Afghanistan and Central Asia came in pursuit of a goal—the defeat of the Taliban and the removal of Al Qaeda from Afghanistan—that Moscow desperately shared but lacked the money, military technology, and international support to achieve.

Moscow also recognized that Washington's presence in its backyard was the product of extraordinary events that were wholly unrelated to Washington's attitude toward its former Cold War rival. Although quick to recognize all five newly independent states, the United States initially had been content to take a backseat to Russia in the region.

Prior to September 11, energy policy dominated U.S. strategic engagement in the region, and we address this in chapter three. U.S. policy makers had mixed success in finding ways to maximize the role of U.S. companies in Caspian oil and gas development, but this was not terribly troubling because the exploitation phase of most major projects was still a long way off.

The strategic potential of Central Asia, however, was of growing interest to the U.S. military and security agencies after 1999, which sought increased cooperation with their counterparts in this region. But there was no sense of imperative from the U.S. side about helping these states meet their security needs, reform their militaries, or wean them away from Russia.

This situation has not really changed even with the U.S. bases in the region. Since September 11, the United States has increased the amount of money available for military training and the overall reform of the armed services of the Central Asian states but has not assumed responsibility for supervising and completing the reform process or for ensuring the internal security of these states.

Moreover, the nature of the long-term U.S. commitment to these states is still in question. The arrangements on bases and landing rights give Washington maximum flexibility to remain in the region as long or as short a time as it deems prudent, and the United States shows no evidence of leaving Central Asia any time soon. The United States has signed agreements with the Uzbeks that talk of a long-term security partnership between the two countries, and Washington has laid the foundation for somewhat less inconclusive military-to-military cooperation with Kyrgyzstan and Kazakhstan. Although the United States has promised to keep increasing spending for border security, narcotics interdiction, removal of nuclear materials, and officer training, it has not elaborated long-term commitments or binding security guarantees for any of the states in the region.

As discussed in chapters four and five, neither the promised assistance nor the stationing of U.S. troops in the region will eliminate the security threats that the Central Asian states face. Central Asia remains a region at risk. The change in the status quo in Afghanistan does little more than provide the states of Central Asia with breathing room. Homegrown opposition groups will just have to go further afield for their training and work harder to raise the money to sustain their operations.

The reconstruction of Afghanistan, however, would be of real economic benefit to the Central Asian states. It would allow for the development of new transit corridors across Afghanistan, creating relatively rapid access to the open ports of Pakistan and the possibility of supplying India with Central Asian oil and gas, as well as a host of other economic opportunities.

All of these economic benefits are still somewhat distant prospects, however. Today Afghanistan remains a source of drugs, not jobs, for Central Asia, with no sign that opium cultivation and the heroin trade will diminish. Thus, for the foreseeable future, Afghanistan's neighbors will warily monitor their shared borders. The Uzbek–Afghan border is small and fairly well controlled, but Afghanistan's borders with Turkmenistan and Tajikistan are long and highly porous.[15] With the increase in opium cultivation that followed the ouster of the Taliban leaders, drug traffickers in larger and larger numbers have begun plying the land routes between Afghanistan and Central Asia to reach their markets in Europe.

Even more disturbing is the regular flow of unwanted human traffic, including opponents of the Central Asian regimes, and in particular, those from the remnants of the IMU who have enjoyed safe haven in Afghanistan. And such safe haven is likely to continue to be provided to fighters on an individual basis even by Afghanistan's current rulers. Ties of kinship link Afghanistan's Uzbek and Tajik populations with relatives in Central Asia, and even the most distant of kin will offer refuge to those in political flight. Families who fled to Afghanistan to evade arrest by Soviet authorities in the 1920s are rumored even now to be offering sanctuary to IMU fighters hiding from U.S. forces.[16]

The presence of U.S. troops in Central Asia is of enormous psychological importance, but it does not address any of these problems. Neither do the redefined relationships that are emerging between Russia and the Central Asian states. Limiting Russia's role in the region does not improve the security environment for these states, nor will Russia's reemergence in the region necessarily lead to better risk management. Over the past two years, Russia and China have both signaled an interest in playing a larger role in ensuring the security of the region, but new security arrangements are still largely in discussion stages.

Although it was not the U.S. intent, the Bush administration's renewed engagement with all of the Central Asian states will inevitably redefine strategic relationships in this part of the world. But it will likely do so in ways that will not be readily apparent for quite some time.

The changing security environment in the region certainly helps foster the confidence of leaders of some of the Central Asian states, most particularly President Nursultan Nazarbayev of Kazakhstan, the architect of an increasingly more complex and multivectored foreign policy. Likewise in Uzbekistan, President Karimov has also sought to more aggressively position himself as the close partner of several great powers rather than to align himself with a single country or bloc. The politicians who have positioned themselves as successors to Akayev in Kyrgyzstan have done much the same, signaling their willingness to continue along Akayev's foreign policy path.

Although some of the leaders in the region sought briefly to redefine themselves in ways that were designed to appeal to U.S. authorities in the aftermath of September 11, none has tried to reinvent himself as democratic. If anything Central Asia's rulers now feel more able to be antidemocratic, which we discuss in chapter five. Leaders of the region's energy-rich states in particular feel more invulnerable. Even though they do not say so directly, figures like Kazakhstan's Nazarbayev make clear that they—not the United States or other outsiders—will set the limits of change in their societies, citing cultural imperatives or the dangers associated with empowering the masses in Asian or Islamic societies.

Central Asia's leaders were quick to appreciate that U.S. priorities in the war on terror have been framed by the need to eliminate the current threat. This approach may have made it easier for Washington to deal with the region's present leaders in the short run, but it creates the possibility that current U.S. policies might inadvertently create new security risks down the road.

U.S. policy makers are aware that this contradiction exists and it comes out clearly in every congressional hearing on Central Asia, of which there have been several each year since 2001.[17] Almost invariably, expert witness after expert witness talks about the long-term security risks associated with the failure to reform the economic and political systems of these countries, whereas the parade of U.S. government officials notes the strategic importance of the region and why it is in the U.S. interest to continue to engage with these states.

So while a percentage of U.S. assistance is earmarked to promote the development of democratic societies in this region, in reality Washington has been content to do business with the existing ruling elite, no matter how insecure or grasping it may be. Part of the problem is that most U.S. policy makers give democracy as little chance of succeeding in the region as Central Asia's rulers do themselves. And this very attitude is helping to stimulate the social and economic instability that serves as the breeding grounds for terror.

As this book went to press, the patience of the U.S. government with Uzbekistan was reaching its breaking point. The trial of twenty-three businessmen in Andijan, charged with ties to Akromiya, a splinter group of the radical Islamic Hizb ut-Tahrir movement, had led to an emotionally charged situation in the town. The night after the trial ended, May 12–13, long, peaceful protests turned violent and ended with a siege in which weapons were seized from government stores and a local jail emptied of prisoners at gunpoint. What happened after that is still subject to contention, although unquestionably the government of Uzbekistan's efforts to quell public protest on May 14 was accompanied by a high loss of civilian life.

But while these events were widely reported, and calls for Washington to break off ties with Tashkent frequently heard, the Bush administration had few effective levers of influence at its disposal, to influence the behavior of its fractious ally, President Karimov, and—unlike in Ukraine and Georgia— there were no ready substitutes in the wings to replace him.

In the aftermath of September 11, there really was an opportunity to reshape the trajectory of development in this part of the world. But neither the Central Asian states nor the international community has made good use of this "second chance."

Too many still believe that peace and security in the Central Asian region can be preserved in the absence of economic and political reform in each and every Central Asian state. The problems will not be resolved without the Central Asians' own initiative. If we are to prevent states in this part of the world from descending into chaos, the international community must help them identify solutions to the economic, political, and social challenges with which they are confronted and then help them find the courage to stick to this path. Unfortunately, no one inside this region or beyond it has made this a priority.

2

Central Asia:
The First Ten Years of Independence

If we are to understand what the odds were for the West and Central Asia to make the most of this second chance for renewed engagement, we must understand the ways in which the first chance was squandered in the decade from the collapse of the Soviet Union in 1991 through September 11, 2001.

The debate over whether the first decade of independence in Central Asia was a success or failure is a highly contentious, and it was no less so before the attacks of September 11. In fact, such conflicting evaluations of the economic and political transitions have been offered that it is often hard to believe that observers were all writing about the same group of countries.[1]

Those who took a very short-term view or a very long-term view tended to be the most positive, arguing that after all, Central Asian states got through a decade of existence with relatively little bloodshed. With time, the optimists maintained, the natural wealth in the region would be used to contribute to improved lives for the peoples of Central Asia.

There is much to credit in this argument. The civil war in Tajikistan was not the harbinger of regional collapse that many feared and concluded with a process of national reconciliation that supported flawed but often forward-looking policies of economic and political rebuilding. Moreover, most of the states in the region do have enormous untapped economic potential.[2] In many instances their economic assets are diverse enough to prevent them from falling easy victim to the "Dutch disease," becoming increasingly dependent on natural resource extraction as a source of economic growth, at the expense of investment in other sectors like manufacturing.

Turkmenistan, which sits on vast natural gas reserves, has seemed the most vulnerable in this regard, but the lack of economic diversification is not the result of geography. It comes from state policy developed by a single man, in disregard of the opinion of many in the former ruling elite. Kazakhstan has the largest untapped oil field found anywhere in the world during the last thirty years but also has an abundant and diverse economy with ferrous and non-ferrous metallurgical reserves, and strong agricultural and industrial sectors from the Soviet era. Uzbekistan is energy self-sufficient, has large gold reserves, and potentially enough arable land to grow cotton for export and enough grain to feed its own population. Kyrgyzstan and Tajikistan have the most fragile economies in the region, with metals to export but not enough to sustain the economy, and relatively little arable land. They are, however, the source of water for the region and could develop hydroelectric resources for export.

The pessimists, too, wielded good arguments. These were generally offered by researchers concerned with the region's medium-term prospects, the sustainability of current levels of stability, and the likelihood of economic potential becoming economic achievement. The pessimists expressed considerable doubt that the Central Asian states could cope with the problems that they will inevitably face in this, the second decade of independence: problems of political succession, the transfer of power to a new generation, and growing gaps between rich and poor in what used to be relatively egalitarian societies. This view holds that failure to meet these challenges will eventually create substantial security risks within Central Asia.

This author is included in the latter group, sharing the concern that the state-building strategies of these countries offered little outlet for the expression of elite or mass dissatisfaction that would inevitably develop.[3] Moreover, these shortsighted strategies—sometimes pursued because of the greed of the ruling elite—did little to maximize the ability of these states to provide for their populations or to facilitate a set of conditions that would allow these populations to provide for themselves.

On the eve of September 11, the trajectory of development in much of Central Asia was not very good. This chapter describes the host of factors that had conspired to produce this situation.

International Community Offers Limited Engagement, Not Commitment

From 1991 to 2001, international engagement in the Central Asian region was more talk than action. Russia had far more immediate concerns. China was very interested in developments in Central Asia, as were India, Iran,

Pakistan, and Turkey. China lacked a sense of pressing interest, and the other countries lacked the capacity necessary to engage fully with these states.

This region seemed remote to most Western leaders, despite the fact that the leading Western oil and gas firms and many others in the mineral extractive industries were attracted to the region's natural resource wealth. In September 2001 most of the big oil projects in the region were still in early planning stages, and the difficulty of doing business in the region was tempering Western enthusiasm for engagement. Interest remained high only in the region's largest energy projects, but the frustration level of potential foreign investors was increasing in some of these as well.

Those involved in developmental assistance faced many of the same challenges as foreign investors, which left them convinced that Central Asia's problems were being exacerbated by decisions made by policy makers in these countries. The various bilateral financial institutions were still developing programs for the countries of the region, but the largest of these rarely made it beyond the drawing board, or received only limited funding. Donor fatigue was setting in. Except for the events of September 11, the international community might well have chosen to leave most of the Central Asian countries to their own devices.

Kazakhstan was something of an exception, because its oil and gas industries were attracting billions of dollars in foreign direct investment.[4] Although the country had the region's most aggressive privatization program, most foreign investors in other sectors found it tough going, in large part because of the pervasive atmosphere of corruption.

By contrast, Turkmenistan had been determined to go its own way from the outset and never accepted direction from international financial institutions. Turkmenistan's president, Saparmurat Niyazov, decided to choose investment partners based on the advice of a few trusted foreigners and to use the country's vast gas reserves to fund a new kind of welfare state for its small population, with free utilities, health care, and a six-week paid vacation (all to be provided by the turn of the century). But the turmoil in Afghanistan, combined with Moscow's control of existing gas pipeline export routes, meant that the living conditions of most Turkmen deteriorated rather than improved during this period.

The region's two poorer countries, Tajikistan and Kyrgyzstan, were less in a position to reject the advice of international advisers. In fact, Kyrgyzstan initially leapt at fiscal and other macroeconomic reforms proposed with support from the World Bank, International Monetary Fund (IMF), and other bilateral donors, as a way to secure support for Kyrgyz independence. However, with time, many Kyrgyz politicians—especially those in the opposition—somewhat naively blamed the growing impoverishment of the bulk of the Kyrgyz population on the advice that their leaders had gotten from foreign advisers. Many of Askar Akayev's critics had more difficulty than Akayev in understanding the complexity of economic transition. On the one hand, the country was succeeding—as measured by a host of economic indicators—but on the other hand, poverty rates were increasing, as was public indebtedness. Increased public indebtedness was one of the costs of accepting advice from the international institutions, advice that was designed to help alleviate the increase in poverty that came from the disintegration of Soviet-era economic linkages. Unable to win over his economic critics by persuasion, Akayev altered the rules of the political game to silence them. The Kyrgyz leadership responded by staying within most of the economic guidelines offered by the international community, but absent political controls, the Akayev family and its close associates appear to have been able to increase their personal wealth as well.

The Tajik government, weak and with only incomplete control of the country, turned to the international community for help in rebuilding its war-ravaged economy. But while the government in Dushanbe sought to be cooperative, on one level the environment for reform was compromised by the drug trade from Afghanistan, which continually fueled the further criminalization of the economy that had taken root during the war. Drugs crossing from Tajikistan also undermined the economy of southern Kyrgyzstan and contributed to the severe corruption of law enforcement in parts of both countries.

The Uzbek government invited the IMF into the country in 1994, accepted its stabilization program, and then abandoned it in 1996.[5] From that time on, the Uzbek government was dependent on its own foreign reserves, obtained through the sale of gold and the export of cotton, to support its national currency, the som. This worked for a while, but there was a lot of competition within the economy for foreign credits, and over time government support of the som decreased and the Uzbek currency depreciated sharply in value. By the late 1990s, it was clear to Uzbekistan's leading economists that the country was depleting its assets without finding new sources of economic growth, but there was no consensus on how to end Uzbekistan's growing isolation. Nor was there any concern in Tashkent that

Uzbek economic policies were seriously undermining the economies of Kyrgyzstan and Tajikistan.

Region of Long-Standing Rivalries

Uzbek behavior was reflective of a growing regional trend—one that the international community inadvertently reinforced by economic reform strategies focused on country-specific agendas that emphasized local "ownership" rather than support for overarching regional goals. In their efforts to make these countries unique, the leaders of the Central Asian states were attracted to nation-building strategies that maximized competition and minimized cooperation. Although each of these countries faced similar problems, each leader in the region feared that his personal position would be damaged if these problems were addressed in concert.

This calculation was an unfortunate feature of their shared Soviet bureaucratic legacy and similar fears about the fragility of each of their nation-states. The leaders of all five Central Asian nations publicly embraced independence as a form of restored statehood, but in reality all were quite nervous about what it entailed. Each leader understood that his country was to some degree a Soviet-era creation. National boundaries did not reflect natural geographic divides—nor despite recent claims to the contrary—did they reflect historic patterns of land usage by a group of long-fluid ethnic communities whose histories and cultures were intertwined. Conquerors passed through Central Asia from the east and west, redefining gene pools in their wake and leaving local cultures an amalgam derived from different sources. It was from this mixed heritage that each of Central Asia's presidents set about asserting his country's national uniqueness.

The first settlers were Indo-Europeans, forebears of the Persian population. They were converted to Islam in the seventh century, as a result of Arab conquest.[6] Turkish tribes moving westward into this region then came to dominate it. The Mongols defeated the Turkmen at the time of Chingis Khan (whom many know as Genghis Khan—a different transliteration of his name), adding the last major element to the Central Asian precolonial ethnic mix.[7]

Today's nations began their consolidation in the fifteenth century at the end of Mongol domination. The Russians who came to the edges of the region in the seventeenth century never intermarried with the local population to the same degree, nor did the indigenous Central Asian peoples seek to assimilate with them. Both the Uzbek and Kazakh peoples date from that time; the Kazakhs (like the Kyrgyz) heavily draw from Mongol as well as Turkic stock.[8] The Turkmen were largely consolidated during the time of the Seljuk dynasty, which ruled the area from the middle of the eleventh century until they were displaced by the Mongols in the second half of the twelfth century. The Turkmen (like the Uzbeks) blend Turkic with Indo-European stock, while the Tajiks are descendants of the early Indo-Europeans, although they too intermarried with local Turkic groups.

Tsarist Russia gained control of northern Kazakhstan through treaties signed with the local Kazakh nobility in the first half of the eighteenth century and extended its territory southward by conquest in the middle of the nineteenth century. The conclusion of the Crimean War (1854–56) and the capture of Imam Shamil of Dagestan opened the way for the victorious Russians to complete a process that had been started in the 1840s, namely the reduction of Central Asia and the transformation of its grazing pastures into wheat farms. The Russians first subdued the Kazakh and Kyrgyz tribesmen before going on to defeat the Khan of Kokand (1864), the Emir of Bukhara (1868), and the Khan of Khiva (1873) in modern day Uzbekistan and Turkmenistan.[9]

Ethnic identity remained fluid during the colonial period and of no particular importance. In the Russian Empire, religion was the great divider: The Russian Orthodox had the greatest economic and political rights, but the Muslim community had limited rights of self-government, particularly with regard to questions of family law.

Ethnic identity was formally fixed in the Soviet period. All Soviet citizens had a nationality, as these ethnic identities were termed, registered on line five of their internal passports. So, in the end, Joseph Stalin decided who was who in Central Asia.[10] In the 1920s, in somewhat arbitrary fashion, he carved five Soviet republics out of the Russian colonial acquisitions in Central Asia.[11] The administrative boundaries of the Soviet republics were modified many times and were designed to leave large irredentist populations scattered throughout the region. When independence was granted in 1991, literally millions of Central Asians lived within the region but outside of their national republic.

Like most outside observers, Central Asia's leaders were also fearful that these national boundaries would prove unstable. They worried that multiple claims to certain territories would lead what they believed were inherently fractious populations to take up arms. In fact, however, there has been virtually no interethnic fighting in Central Asia since the collapse of the Soviet Union. Even the competition between the Uzbeks and the Tajiks, who have rival claims to the lands of the former Bukharan Emirate (and its main cities of Samarkand and Bukhara, which are both within Uzbekistan), has been handled relatively well by both sides.

The long-term risk of conflict remains, however. Emblematic of this possible risk, the Tajiks erected a monument to Ismail Samani, the founder of the Samanid dynasty, in downtown Dushanbe and placed a picture of his mausoleum on the one-hundred-somoni bill of their national currency.[12] The problem is that Samani is also a national hero in Uzbekistan, and his mausoleum is the oldest mosque in Bukhara. But there is little evidence to suggest that any sort of direct confrontation is at all imminent. Quite the opposite is true. There has been a strong sense of kinship across national lines, which has helped Central Asia's leaders dampen the interethnic rivalries stirred up by the dissolution of the Soviet empire and the competition for scarce resources, in striking contrast to the Caucasus region.

The civil war in Tajikistan did not become an ethnic conflict despite the fact that it was fought on regional grounds.[13] Moreover, fighting between Uzbeks and Kyrgyz in southern Kyrgyzstan in 1990 was successfully contained, as were smaller clashes between Tajiks and Kyrgyz over water rights in 1989.[14]

For all the talk by Central Asia's leaders of the bellicosity of their peoples, the region has experienced mostly peaceful competition during the early years of independence.

Lurking Nontraditional Security Threats

Risk of Water Shortages

Despite this relative calm, however, the roots of conflict caused by scarcity of resources lie deep. For thousands of years, there has been competition between farmers living in the oasis communities, located between the Syr Darya and Amu Darya rivers in present-day Uzbekistan, and the pastoral nomads who lived in the mountains and steppe lands just beyond in Kazakhstan and Kyrgyzstan.

Much of this competition was over water, and the age-old problem of managing Central Asia's limited water supply took on new significance in the aftermath of independence. Most of the region's water comes from the Aral Sea Basin.[15] Now, instead of nomads and farmers vying for control, upstream and downstream users must work out their conflicting interests.

The region's ecosystem was already under stress for more than a decade before independence. The Aral Sea itself was declared dead in the early 1990s, shrinking dramatically in size and unable to support life. It was destroyed by decades of abusive Soviet agricultural practices, which emphasized high cotton yields of up to three cuttings annually. These yields were obtained through the use of large amounts of fertilizer, which depleted and contaminated Central Asia's water system, leaving vast areas of the region without safe drinking water.[16]

Although independence raised the prospect of greater international engagement on these problems, assistance for remediation came with what most in the region felt was an unacceptable price. The Central Asian states wanted help in purifying contaminated water supplies, but they did not want to be told how to allocate water among themselves or be pressed into developmental solutions that substantially changed water usage patterns.

The Central Asian states still depend on a modified version of the Soviet-era water management system, which was designed to meet the needs of downstream users (Uzbekistan and Turkmenistan), not upstream providers (Tajikistan and Kyrgyzstan), who are interested in diverting large quantities of water to produce more hydroelectric power. The Kyrgyz have begun generating more hydroelectric power since independence—much less than they want, but enough to increase seasonal flooding in Uzbekistan and Kazakhstan.

Water for agriculture is also in greater demand since independence because all five countries went through a process of deindustrialization when Soviet-era interrepublic economic linkages were severed. Industrial productivity dropped by about fifty percent in each of the countries of the region over the period from 1990 to 1998.[17]

As a result, many people in all five countries went into subsistence agriculture. Some of this was spontaneous, but there was also a conscious effort made in each of the countries to use local produce to provide more of the population's food needs. At the same time, the region's major cotton producers tried to keep cotton yields high because it was a major source of export earnings. The amount of irrigated land in Central Asia increased by seven percent between 1995 and 2000.[18]

All the region's leaders recognized that water usage patterns created a potential security risk, but they understood the problem through the prism of their own national interests. It is a textbook case of a problem of the commons, the economic term that refers to the absence of any automatic mechanism or incentive to prevent the overuse and depletion of the commonly held resource: Each leader tried to increase agricultural yields and thought little of the consequences of depleting water supplies needed by other states.

Threat Posed by Extremist Ideologies

Central Asia's leaders also showed the same lack of concern for what might be the fallout across the border in the way that they handled other potential security risks. This was especially true of the risk posed to each of these states by radical or extremist Islamic groups. Some leaders responded by largely closing off their borders; others tried to bury their head in the sand and ignore groups that they could not control, regardless of the danger they posed to their populations.

The risk posed by Islamic extremist groups has varied quite dramatically from state to state, in large part because the Islamic revival has followed quite a different course for the region's long-urbanized Uzbeks and Tajiks than it has for the formerly nomadic Kazakhs, Kyrgyz, and Turkmen. Since the decline of communism, the practice of Islam has been revived everywhere, but radical Islam has made the greatest inroads where traditions of Islamic learning were strongest—that is, in the old oasis cities in what then was known as Mawarannahr.

The formal relationship between Islam and the state is quite similar throughout Central Asia. Travel abroad has become much easier for Central Asia's believers; pilgrimage to Mecca is now an attainable goal, and Muslim missionaries have also reached out to Central Asia. But although contact with the *Umma* (the broader Muslim community) has increased, each of the states has put the Islamic hierarchy under state control in much the same fashion that the Soviets did.

The single Soviet-era bureaucracy that once sought to manage relations between believers and the broader Islamic community in all of the Central Asian republics was divided into five separate national agencies after independence. Each Muslim administration, generally formed around a state committee on religion subordinated to the Council of Ministers, was given the task of appointing the country's leading clerics and licensing the principal mosques and all religious schools.[19]

Many in Central Asia resent the state's continued control of their spiritual worlds. This is particularly true of members of Central Asia's radical Islamic groups, who see themselves as part of a transnational ideological force that pays little attention to national boundaries and that should not be accountable to secular rulers. Some, such as members of the Islamic Movement of Uzbekistan (IMU), which developed out of local radical Muslim vigilante groups in the Ferghana Valley in the mid-1990s, believe this situation must be remedied through force. But Central Asia's leaders find the region's purportedly nonviolent radical Islamic groups equally as threatening. The largest of these is the Hizb ut-Tahrir al-Islami, or the Islamic Party of Liberation, which was founded in Jerusalem in 1953 by Taqiuddin al Nabhani to unite the Islamic community in a new Caliphate and to promote the Islamic way of life. It became active in the region in the mid-1990s, and its influence grew at the end of the decade. Although Hizb ut-Tahrir's roots in the region are among the Uzbek population, it now has members in all five countries. [20]

There was frequent talk of cooperation in fighting these groups during the first decade of independence, but it rarely led to concerted actions. After the bombings in Tashkent in February 1999, attributed to IMU-affiliated extremists, intelligence sharing between the Central Asian states—and with Russia—increased, particularly information on the membership of radical Islamic groups and the whereabouts of key members. Uzbekistan was a strong influence in this regard, pressing hard on the Kyrgyz to extradite Uzbek members of the IMU or Hizb ut-Tahrir found seeking refuge in mountainous Kyrgyz territory, and some of those wanted by the Uzbek authorities were even kidnapped by members of Uzbek state security forces.

Cooperation between the lower levels of neighboring national security organizations went against the existing bureaucratic ethos. In the strong presidential systems characteristic in Central Asia, the atmosphere set at the top is pervasive. Cross-border cooperation on narcotics interdiction brought with it the risk that evidence of collusion by senior officials might be uncovered, since drugs are seen as a funding source for radical groups. As a result, state security officers generally preferred to mind their own business. In the most repressive of these states, Turkmenistan, to give even the slightest appearance of disagreeing with one's superior was to put one's political future, and possibly even one's life, at risk.

Five Unique States

When the Soviet Union first broke up, it made good sense to think of the Central Asian region as a coherent whole, with a single set of problems that might be addressed through a coordinated and integrated single response. Within a decade it was already clear that this was no longer the case. Kazakhstan, Turkmenistan, Kyrgyzstan, Tajikistan, and Uzbekistan were all evolving in different ways, each acquiring a distinct identity, and a unique style of decision making.

Kazakhstan: Unfulfilled Promise

In many ways, Kazakhstan is the most puzzling of the Central Asian republics, because economic growth seemed to provide little incentive for political reform; in fact, the opposite was occurring. Sparked in large part by the promise of its energy sector, Kazakhstan was receiving massive amounts of foreign investment, but legal protections for foreign investors and Kazakh property owners remain inadequate. By the late 1990s, Kazakhstan's strong presidential system had begun to rapidly overwhelm independent political institutions, although President Nursultan Nazarbayev did not behave as autocratically as his Uzbek or Turkmen counterparts.

For most of Soviet history, events in Kazakhstan unfolded in ways that were more similar to those of Russia than elsewhere in Central Asia. In fact, in Soviet times, these five republics were referred to as Middle Asia and Kazakhstan (*Srednyaya Azia i Kazakhstan*), rather than called by a single collective term. Northern and central Kazakhstan were linked to southern Siberia for economic planning purposes, and political events in Russia often had a more rapid resonance here than in neighboring states. Kazakhstan was the most international of the Soviet republics, with the region's largest Russian population and large concentrations of ethnic Germans, Ukrainians, Uzbeks, and Tatars.[21] Soviet resettlement policies left ethnic Russians outnumbering ethnic Kazakhs for most of the post–World War II period.[22] Ethnic Russians began leaving Kazakhstan in the late 1980s, when legislation was passed that dramatically expanded the role of the Kazakh language in public life. The pace of exit increased after independence, and over 1.5 million Russians left the country in its first decade of existence.[23]

The mines, refineries, and factories of northern Kazakhstan were critical to the Soviet Union's industrial output, but these industries virtually ground to a halt when the interrepublic linkages of the Soviet republics were broken in the early 1990s. Northern Kazakhstan was also fully dependent on oil and electricity supplied by Russia, and Kazakhstan accumulated hundreds of millions of dollars of interstate debt trying to keep its factories running and municipal utility services functioning—debt that is still being discharged through the transfer of shares in Kazakh enterprises to designees of the Russian government.

Even though its debt was crippling for the first few years, Kazakhstan has had the easiest economic transition in the Central Asian region, partly because of its vast natural resources and partly because of its human potential.[24] Still, it has not always been easy for the Kazakhs; their economy suffered through a period of sharp economic decline in the early and mid-1990s, and the collapse was most noticeable in the defense-related sectors. Agriculture also went through a period of decline, and by the mid-1990s animal husbandry was in near free-fall, as the population of cattle decreased by more than 50 percent.[25]

The Kazakh economy nevertheless began to display strong growth in the late 1990s, fueled in large part by high oil prices. These also helped Kazakhstan withstand the aftershocks of Russia's 1998 financial meltdown. Kazakhstan also benefited from the rigorous macroeconomic reforms begun in the mid-1990s, including the introduction of freely convertible currency, the development of the most modern banking sector in the region, and the launching of a small but functioning Western-style stock exchange.[26] Kazakhstan partially reformed its tax structure, introduced a professional tax collection service, and cut tax rates to 30 percent for corporate income and to between 5 and 40 percent for personal income.

The Kazakh government also reorganized the pension system to enable Kazakh citizens to choose whether to invest their money in state or private funds. In addition, it began the complete overhaul of both the health-care and education systems, but the implementation process was far from uniform, leaving many poorer regions (where the local tax base is weak) virtually bereft of services and with few opportunities for employment for their populations.

The government also created a new national capital in 1997, Astana (formerly Aqmola—the word *Astana* literally means "capital" in Kazakh), and promoted ambitious plans for creating new highways and rail links between the country's principal cities, which thanks to Soviet centralization were connected to hubs in Russia, not to each other. But these projects are moving forward very slowly, hampered by corruption in the implementation process and the diversion of billions of dollars from transport to construction projects in the nation's new capital. The government had to expend a lot of diplomatic pressure to get foreign embassies to promise to relocate there, and is having an even harder time getting foreign firms to promise to move their headquarters from Almaty.[27]

Most of Kazakhstan's hopes for the future rest with the development of its oil fields, which are likely to make Kazakhstan the fifth largest oil producer in the world. Its oil reserves are estimated to be in the range of 5.4 billion to 17.6 billion barrels, and some optimistic estimates are even twice that.[28] Between 1991 and 2001, Kazakhstan received over $14 billion in FDI, most of it in the oil and gas sector. As this money was largely for the start-up phase of Kazakhstan's major projects, Kazakhstan was virtually guaranteed substantially more foreign investment in the next two decades.

The Kazakh government estimates that its natural resources have a total potential value of $8.7 trillion, with hydrocarbon holdings in the same league as Saudia Arabia, Russia, and Iraq. Kazakhstan has three giant oil and gas fields: Tengiz, Karachaganak, and Kashagan, all three of which have produced money for the state treasury, either from production revenue or large signing bonuses from the firms given exploitation rights.

The Tengiz field, with an estimated 6 billion to 9 billion barrels of recoverable oil reserves, is being developed by the TengizChevroil joint venture. Chevron-Texaco owns 50 percent of this project, ExxonMobil owns 25 percent, KazMunayGaz, the Kazakhstan state energy firm, owns 20 percent, and LUKArco, a partnership between Russia's LUKoil and BP, owns 5 percent.[29] Production from this field began in 1993 but was slowed by difficulties in negotiating terms for the Caspian Pipeline Consortium (CPC) pipeline across Kazakhstan to Novorossiisk in Russia.[30]

Chevron's problems in negotiating with Transneft, Russia's pipeline monopoly, were factors that led the U.S. government to push for alternative routes for Caspian oil. First the Clinton administration and then the Bush administration pressed the Kazakhs to market the output from the Kashagan field through the Baku–Tbilisi–Ceyhan pipeline (which goes from Azerbaijan, across Georgia, then to Turkey).

Like Tengiz on the Caspian coast, Karachaganak is an inland field. Near the Russian border due north of the Caspian, it sits atop proven oil reserves of 2.2 billion barrels and 500 billion cubic meters of natural gas. Forty percent of the country's natural gas reserves are located in that one field. In

1997, an international consortium including Chevron-Texaco signed a $7–$8 billion final production sharing agreement to develop the field for forty years, with a planned investment of $4 billion by 2006.[31]

The country's third main field lies deep beneath the Caspian at the off-shore Kashagan site. It could contain up to 40 billion barrels of oil, three times more than Tengiz, but only about one-quarter of that potential is thought to be recoverable. Kashagan, which is likely to be the largest oil discovery in the past forty years, has two U.S. firms in the Agip KCO consortium that operates the site: ExxonMobil with a 16.67 percent stake and ConocoPhillips with 8.33 percent.

It was initially estimated that the Kashagan field would take at least $12 billion to develop. Exploitation of this project was initially set to begin in 2005 but was subsequently delayed, and project cost estimates were increased as well. Because of the slow timetable for development, the Kazakh government sold off its initial stake in the aftermath of the 1998 Russian financial crisis to raise capital in the form of signing bonuses to meet government pension and salary arrears.

Kazakhstan has several other significant gas-producing areas on land. The primary oil and gas deposits include the Tengiz, Zhanazhol, and Uritau fields, Aktobe in the north, and Kumkol in the Kzyl-Orda region. Undeveloped offshore areas are believed to hold large amounts of natural gas but due to poor pipeline infrastructure linking the natural gas fields in the western part of the country to consumers in the southern part of the country, Kazakhstan still imports natural gas to meet domestic demand.

Much could still happen to derail or delay the plans for development of fossil fuel resources in this landlocked state, but the real challenge for Kazakhstan will be to manage its oil revenues in a way that benefits the country's population more generally. To this end, with World Bank and IMF advice, the Kazakhs created a national oil fund in 2001, a savings account for oil revenues. It is based on Norway's model and funds are regularly deposited. These sums, however, still represent a relatively small portion of the national budget, and its ultimate success will require a degree of economic transparency currently absent from the country's oil industry.

Foreigners frequently complain of their treatment by the government or private contractors. Since the first days of independence, they, like the Kazakhs, regularly faced situations in which they had to pay protection money in one form or another. Failure to do so made it all but impossible to run their businesses successfully, because the courts in the early days, even more than today, were rarely a successful agent of impartial arbitration.

The pattern of corruption reached to the highest levels of government, including President Nazarbayev and his family. Since 1999, stories have circulated of the Nazarbayevs' offshore holdings and bribes successfully solicited from leading Western oil companies. Most of these stories centered around James Giffen, an American citizen and president of the Mercator Corporation, a firm specializing in clinching oil and gas deals on behalf of the Nazarbayev government. Mercator negotiated with Amoco and Texaco the terms under which they could buy the right to participate in the Tengiz and Karachaganak projects, respectively. Mercator was accused of transferring some of these payments it received as a broker in these projects to the personal accounts of the president and other senior Kazakh officials as kickbacks—charges that were eventually sustained in 2004 in grand jury proceedings in New York City.[32]

Nazarbayev has never admitted to any wrongdoing. But many close to him say he was led astray by Giffen, who convinced him that lining one's own pockets is accepted practice among world leaders. The truth of who encouraged whom is unlikely to come to light, but the corrupt practices attributed to Nazarbayev and his family are very consistent with his egocentric ruling style.

Like Soviet party bosses before him, Nursultan Nazarbayev has demonstrated an unwillingness to leave the political scene during his lifetime. He has gone even one step further, moving to set up a political dynasty, either around his oldest daughter, Dariga—founder of a major political party, Asar, or All Together—and her husband, Rakhat Aliyev, or his son-in-law, Timur Kulibayev, who is married to his younger daughter, Dinara, and held a key position in Kazakhstan's oil and gas industry.

With each passing year Nazarbayev seems more determined to make his political mark a permanent one. Nazarbayev has been unwilling to face serious competition in his two formal presidential bids in 1991 and 1999 even though, as the country's most popular politician by far, he probably could have handily defeated any political opponent in a fair fight.

In the 1991 election he faced only token opposition. He then opted out of reelection entirely in 1995, extending his four-year term through a referendum. Constitutional changes in 1998 extended the presidential term to seven years, removed restrictions against his seeking further terms in office, and awarded Nazarbayev extensive political privileges in retirement, including immunity from prosecution.

Nazarbayev successfully ran for reelection in 1999, but only after his major political rival, Akezhan Kazhegeldin, the country's prime minister from 1994 to 1997, was barred from running, ostensibly due to his criminal record, which he gained by holding an unsanctioned meeting to launch his political party, the Republican People's Party. Kazhegeldin fled the country for exile in Europe and the U.S. in 1998—and was regularly threatened with extradition to face charges back home in Kazakhstan. The Kazakhs even issued a warrant for his arrest, which was successfully, albeit briefly, discharged in Italy in July 2000. He was detained at Rome's main Fiumicino airport, kept for two days, and freed only after intervention by Italy's Justice Ministry.

One effort by the Nazarbayev government to get at Kazhegeldin seriously backfired and shows the international financial ignorance of Nazarbayev's close confidantes. In 1999 the Kazakh government formally asked the Government of Switzerland to locate bank accounts of the former prime minister, alleging they contained assets embezzled from the state. But of course Nazarbayev knew that there were accounts in his own name in Switzerland as well as those in the name of Kazhegeldin's successor, Prime Minister Nurlan Balgimbayev. The search for Kazhegeldin's accounts turned up their own much larger accounts as well, and Swiss investigators reported their findings to the U.S. Department of Justice. This sparked an investigation into the source of such money and led to the embarrassing scandal involving Giffen and the ingratiating behavior of certain U.S. oil companies in Kazakhstan.

The Giffen scandal got wider public attention in the United States than it did in Kazakhstan, because by the time this scandal broke in 2002, Kazakhstan's media and its parliament had both been rendered less independent than they had been a decade earlier.

The last Kazakh parliament elected in the Soviet era was disbanded in 1993, almost immediately after Boris Yeltsin forcibly eliminated the Russian Federation's communist-era parliament. But unlike their fractious colleagues in Russia, the Kazakh legislators were a peaceable bunch and were merely seeking to use parliament as a forum for political debate.

The first postindependence constitution was drawn up before elections in 1994. It established a strong presidential system, with limited enumerated powers for the parliament. The parliament chosen in accordance with this constitution served only a year of its five-year term and was disbanded in

1995 on a legal technicality.[33] Most Western observers offered only limited objection to this, because both President Nazarbayev and Prime Minister Kazhegeldin argued strongly that the parliament was a brake on macroeconomic reforms, which the leadership subsequently enacted through presidential decree.

The legislators serving in Kazakhstan's first two parliaments regularly debated legislation with vigor and sometimes even forced their will on a reluctant president. Constitutional changes introduced in 1995 virtually ensured that this would no longer be the case. Kazakhstan's unicameral legislature was replaced by a much weaker bicameral legislature, with an upper house consisting of senators largely handpicked by the president and a lower house with sharply restricted authority.[34] Even so, the parliamentary elections of 1999 were also conducted in a fashion that failed to meet international standards of fairness.

Political opposition became increasingly more dangerous in Kazakhstan. Nazarbayev's family members began gaining control of key media outlets that had been privatized, while truly independent journalists were subject to official and unofficial harassment. Reporters were beaten up in numbers sufficient to make official attributions of the incidents to random street crime seem highly implausible, and editorial offices were destroyed in inexplicable fires. For example, a decapitated dog was displayed outside the *Respublika* newspaper offices with a warning to editor Irina Petrushova, who had pursued the story that Nazarbayev had stashed $1 billion in state oil revenue in Swiss banks, that "there will be no next time."

Well before the war on terror, neither the Clinton nor the Bush administrations seemed to know how to respond to the deteriorating political climate in Kazakhstan and the growing controversies surrounding Kazakhstan's first president. U.S. policy emphasized improving the conditions of investment in Kazakhstan, especially the oil and gas sector. For the most part, U.S. authorities were not overly distressed by the political developments in Kazakhstan, and there was little evidence of reflection by U.S. policy makers on what long-term problems might eventually plague that nation as a result of its government's actions. Kazakhstan came closest to being a success story in the region, and there seemed no reason to antagonize the Nazarbayev regime, especially since it had yet to commit to send its oil from the offshore Kashagan field along the U.S.- supported Baku-Tbilisi-Ceyhan route, bypassing Russia and Iran.

Turkmenistan: Dreams Unrealized

If policy makers in Washington believed that the Kazakhs were managing their resources better than expected and reasonably well, the exact opposite judgment was being made about Turkmenistan, Central Asia's other fossil-fuel-rich state. With proven natural gas reserves of approximately 101 trillion cubic feet, Turkmenistan is second to Russia among the post-Soviet states in the size of its gas reserves. In addition, Turkmenistan has 1.4 billion barrels in proven oil reserves, with possible additional reserves (mainly in the western part of the country and in undeveloped offshore areas in the Caspian Sea).[35] But nowhere had there been a greater contrast between promise at the beginning of independence and achievement a decade later, and nowhere has it been more difficult for Westerners to do business.

Former U.S. secretary of state Alexander Haig was hired by the Turkmen government in 1993 to lobby Washington for increased U.S. investment in Turkmenistan and to soften the position on pipelines through Iran, where he worked up some enthusiasm among potential investors.[36] But in the course of the 1990s, Western plans for development of Turkmenistan's oil and gas reserves were put on hold.[37] Turkmen promises of long paid vacations for the population went unfulfilled, and most who were familiar with the situation in the country (in urban as well as rural areas) reported a steady impoverishment of the population that belied official statistics. Just how badly the Turkmen economy deteriorated in the first decade of independence is hard to know, given that the country has been all but closed to Western financial institutions and all published economic statistics are suspect.

Most troubling was the drop in gas production that Turkmenistan registered from 1994 on, declining from the Soviet-era figure of 81.9 billion cubic meters in 1990 to a low of 13.3 billion cubic meters in 1998.[38] Cotton production also fell, most notably between 1993 and 1996. Gas is a more problematic commodity to develop than oil, as it is completely dependent on the availability of a readily accessible market. Landlocked Turkmenistan's geographic isolation has been a serious handicap in this regard. The two easiest routes to market are through Iran or Russia, both of which are competing gas producers with large reserves that can be used to capture markets through discount volume pricing.

The Iranians tried to ingratiate themselves with the Turkmen, whereas the leading figures in Russia's gas industry considered the Turkmen assets to be theirs, because of large Soviet-era investments that these very people had supervised to develop Turkmen reserves. So Russia's Gazprom and its spin-off companies pursued aggressive tactics to assert control of Turkmen gas, much more so than they applied in either Kazakhstan or Uzbekistan, where supplies were smaller or less readily accessible.

Moscow wanted to feed Turkmen gas into the Russian pipeline system at a low price and sell it to Russia's deadbeat customers within the Commonwealth of Independent States (CIS), leaving Russia's partly state-owned Gazprom in full control of the more lucrative European market. Since 1994, the Russians and the Turkmen have had great difficulty reaching agreement over both price and form of payment for Turkmen gas, and at several points, the Turkmen simply withheld their gas from the market for long periods of time rather than take the heavy compromises Russia was proposing.[39]

The only way that the Turkmen could ship to market bypassing all competitors was to try to ship through Afghanistan, a prospect that interested the Turkmen government from the early days of independence. The idea was to ship gas from the country's giant Dauletabad field in southeastern Turkmenistan, estimated to have reserves of 45 trillion cubic feet, large enough to warrant a proposed investment of over $2 billion for an export pipeline. First the Turkmen government struck a deal with the Argentine firm of Bridas, only to back away from the agreement, shifting in favor of a pipeline proposal from California-based Unocal, which signed an agreement with the Turkmen government in October 1994 to market gas from this field through an international pipeline consortium that included Delta Oil, a Saudi firm that boasted a good working relationship with the various factions vying for control in Afghanistan.

The consortium promised to market Dauletabad gas through a pipeline that went through Afghanistan to markets in Pakistan and, hopefully, India.[40] There was also a proposal to build an oil pipeline through Kazakhstan and Uzbekistan, into Afghanistan, and out to open seas in Pakistan. But the Turkmen government knew that it would be impossible to get international financing for such a pipeline unless there was peace in Afghanistan, and they believed that the Taliban clerics offered the best chance of a rapid restoration of order. Although the Turkmen government never provided de jure recognition, they did allow Turkmen officials to formally champion the Taliban cause, and Foreign Minister Boris Shikhmuradov came to Washington in 1996 to press the Clinton administration to recognize the Taliban regime.

There was very limited payoff for the Turkmen policy, which among other things further distanced the government in Ashgabat from its counterparts in the rest of Central Asia. Worn out by waiting for a seemingly endless civil war in Afghanistan to conclude, and unwilling to do business with the Taliban regime, Unocal walked away from the pipeline projects in 1998.[41] Difficulties in doing business in Turkmenistan played some role in the decision as well, as the Turkmen government had unrealistic expectations of the value of their project, given that it held the rights to the Dauletabad field, not Unocal, and the rights to the export pipeline itself were disputed.[42] Other investors have also privately confided their relief at being out of the country.

In 2001, as now, Turkmenistan was almost wholly lacking a legal infrastructure. Its large multitiered administration was often assigned conflicting responsibilities, which ensured bureaucratic deadlock as all appointees tried to clear all actions with the country's president. And Niyazov had very strong opinions as to how things should be done, including what priority should be accorded to various forms of tribute to him, both public and private. The former is easier to document than the latter, because by the mid-1990s Niyazov had committed his government to spend billions of dollars in rebuilding the main avenues of Ashgabat. Public and private palaces were erected, and at one point government ministers were each allowed to build a small palace-style hotel whose proceeds were theirs to keep. Some of the money came from public sources, and some from extortion, which was used to line pockets as well as to fund officially sponsored projects. An unspecified amount of illegally obtained income is rumored to have come from the drug trade.[43] Much of it also came from successful arm-twisting of potential foreign investors.

On small investment projects, foreigners had to deal with the gatekeepers designated by the president (who have included some prominent Turkish and Israeli businesspeople). But on large projects, virtually all the decisions must be made during face-to-face consultations with President Niyazov, who is blunt about the cost of doing business with him.[44]

Niyazov, who dubbed himself Turkmenbashi (head Turkmen) the Great, has created a cult of personality that outstrips that of Stalin in its extremes. Over the first decade of statehood, Niyazov went from being an average Soviet-apparatchik-turned-president to become an omnipresent figure in Turkmenistan. Declared president for life in 1999, his face is everywhere, appearing on everything from yogurt containers to the national currency. A rotating gold-plated statue of the president, shown on the cover of this book, dominates the skyline of the capital city of Ashgabat. For several years his picture has been beamed instead of a logo in the corner of all the national television stations, regardless of what is being broadcast.

Like Stalin, Niyazov has periodically admonished the sycophants he appointed to serve in key state posts for their excessive enthusiasm in the honors bestowed on the president. But in reality, no criticism of Niyazov is possible in private. It is not simply bad judgment to criticize the leader, true anywhere in Central Asia, but an instant way to stunt a career. In Uzbekistan, too, prudence dictates silence in most settings where President Karimov is present. But Uzbek officials have admitted in private that Karimov has been occasionally guilty of bad judgment, something that no civil servant in Turkmenistan has dared do since the early 1990s.

Any public disapproval of the president has been impossible in Turkmenistan. The development of independent media was thwarted from the outset, as was the development of informal or formal independent political organizations. Those who sought to create them were subject to arbitrary arrest, as were the human rights activists who tried to monitor the government's treatment of its critics.[45]

To criticize Niyazov is to criticize the foundation of the Turkmen state. He casts himself not as a mere president, but as the nation's spiritual leader, and for a time Niyazov even floated a rumor that he was immortal, like a prophet. He dropped the claim when some of Turkmenistan's Muslim neighbors objected to this as blasphemous. Yet at an international conference in 1997 the author of this book was attacked by a vice minister from Turkmenistan for having said that each of the region's presidents would someday die and have to be replaced.

Though certainly mortal, Niyazov is also supremely self-confident, and since the mid-1990s his actions have been predicated on a belief that he is capable of reshaping how the international system functioned, or at least with regard to newly independent states such as his own. It was for this reason that Turkmenistan has pursued a Niyazov-inspired doctrine of "positive neutrality" since 1995, opting for nonengagement in most of the regional and superregional initiatives, but never explaining that certain aspects of his behavior bar Turkmenistan from joining some organizations and not others.

Working around the confines of this inadequately articulated policy was quite frustrating for U.S. policy makers. Adherence to positive neutrality seems to have fueled Niyazov's refusal to commit its gas to a U.S.-backed

Trans-Caspian Pipeline, to run under the sea and join up with the proposed Baku–Tbilisi–Ceyhan pipeline system. Supporting the U.S. project, however, would have helped give Niyazov the improved access to markets that the Turkmen president was so desperate to obtain, which is why the Turkmen leader's behavior seemed so incomprehensible to U.S. leaders.

Kyrgyzstan: Western Planning Gone Awry

The leaders of the richer states in the region may have felt comfortable distancing themselves from Western advice and financial counsel, or in the case of Kazakhstan, erecting large filters for determining what advice would or would not be tolerated. Those running Central Asia's poorer states, however, did not always believe that they had the same luxury.

Kyrgyzstan was a case in point. In the first several years of independence at least, the country's president, Askar Akayev, embraced the causes of economic and political reform with seemingly genuine enthusiasm, vowing that Kyrgyzstan would become the Switzerland of Central Asia—a financial center, a transport hub, and a popular destination for international tourists. Cynically, it can be argued that Akayev was probably turning necessity into advantage, as he sought to distinguish his country and its leadership from that of the other states of the region. Lacking the wealth of many of its neighbors, Kyrgyzstan had little more than the personality of its president to serve as a magnet for attracting Western investments, loans, or grants in aid.

Loans and grants proved easier to attract than investment. The international development community rushed in with long-term credit and aid when Kyrgyzstan agreed to be the first state in the region to engage in a macroeconomic reform program. In May 1993 Kyrgyzstan was the first in Central Asia to introduce a national currency with the support of an IMF macrostabilization program. The Kyrgyz government also introduced a liberal trade regime and in 2000 was the first of the post-Soviet states (excluding the Baltic nations) to enter the World Trade Organization.

For the Kyrgyz, there was little benefit to be gained from a protectionist policy. Absent a regional market, they had few prospects for foreign investment in the manufacturing sector, and this held true for both food processing and textiles, sectors that were partially developed in the republic during the Soviet period. Although Kyrgyzstan's trade policy was economically sound, they couldn't get support for it from their neighbors. Neither the Uzbeks nor the Kazakhs were interested in opening their markets to

Kyrgyz goods, which had a devastating effect on the tiny economy of Kyrgyzstan and further cut off the Kyrgyz from easy access to the larger, traditional market of Russia.[46]

As a result, over the course of the first decade of existence, Kyrgyzstan went from a country that the international development community felt was a promising service center and regional hub to a place that the donor community used for experimenting with poverty-alleviation strategies, which were necessitated in part because of Kyrgyzstan's large international debt.

From 1995 to 2001 the Kyrgyz government borrowed $1.4 billion. By June 2001 the annual cost of debt relief was 130 percent of the national GDP, making Kyrgyzstan a prime candidate for debt relief. [47] Kyrgyzstan only attracted $382.1 million in FDI.[48] Moreover, much of the FDI went into a single project, the gold mine, Kumtor, a joint venture with Canada's Cameco. The Kumtor Gold Company was established in 1992 to develop the Kumtor mine, which had estimated reserves of 9.3 million ounces of gold. The project, which went into production in 1997, was quite controversial in Kyrgyzstan, because critics argued it benefited the investor at the expense of the government. In the early years there were allegations that Akayev family members were benefiting from the international sale of the project's gold.[49] Later, Kumtor was sharply criticized following a cyanide spill into Lake Issyk Kul.[50]

The Kumtor project made Kyrgyzstan's economy appear more robust than it actually was. For example, Kyrgyzstan's industrial output grew 6 percent in the first half of 2001, but when companies developing the Kumtor gold field were factored out, industrial output actually fell 5.4 percent during the period.[51] In much of the country, agriculture went into decline, and the size of the Kyrgyz cattle herd fell precipitously in the 1990s.[52] By late 2001 the Kyrgyz economy had bottomed out. Pockets of new economic activity could be spotted in the capital of Bishkek and even in some villages and towns, but most Kyrgyz were living in more dire straits than in the previous decade.

As a result, opposition to President Akayev was growing. Akayev's open support of Boris Yeltsin in August 1991 (at the time of the failed Communist Party coup) was seen as a daring act in the Kyrgyz political environment. But by the mid-1990s the country's political elite had accepted the idea that the country would make the region's speediest transition to a democratic political system. And this made many angry with their president when he sponsored—or, if not, certainly tolerated—policies that limited the range of acceptable political activity in the country.

Many of the country's independent media outlets were fined or even closed in the second half of the 1990s, in some cases precisely because they made allegations of presidential corruption. The editor of *Respublika*, Zamira Sydykova, the country's best known independent journalist, served twelve months in a woman's penal colony after having been found guilty of libeling the president in 1997.[53]

Nevertheless, Akayev remained the most willing of the region's leaders to subject himself to his country's electorate. Akayev ran in contested elections for the presidency three times, in 1991, 1995, and 2000.[54] Kyrgyzstan was the only country in the region to hold presidential elections in 1995 when Akayev's counterparts in other Central Asian countries extended their terms through referendum.

Washington's expression of displeasure played a major role in helping Akayev make up his mind to hold the 1995 election, but by the late 1990s political pressure from the United States was less frequently employed and less effective. In fact, the United States sat quietly by while a way was found for Akayev to run for a third term in 1998. This was accomplished through a ruling of the constitutional court that the two-term rule of the Kyrgyz constitution did not apply to the president, because his first term in office began before independence.

The country's first postindependence constitution, adopted in 1993, established a parliamentary-presidential republic, but this was modified by referendum in October 1994, which established a two-house legislature with sharply curtailed powers to replace the Soviet-era unitary body. As in Kazakhstan, the intent was to make the legislature more malleable and increase the strength of the president and his administration. Even after these changes, Kyrgyz parliamentary elections held in 2000 still fell short of accepted international standards, because the government remained fearful that it would not be able to control a freely elected popular body.[55]

The conduct of the 2000 Kyrgyz presidential election was even more troubling and was criticized by the Organization for Security and Cooperation in Europe (OSCE) for failing to meet international standards.[56] The campaign was flawed well before the balloting; several candidates were eliminated because they failed to pass a behind-closed-doors exam in Kyrgyz, including some who were trained philologists.[57]

Most celebrated was the case of Feliks Kulov, the leader of the opposition Ar-Namys (Dignity) Party. Kulov had been dubbed "the People's General" for his behavior while commandant of Frunze (as the capital city of Bishkek was known during the Soviet era) at the time of the civil unrest of 1990. The charismatic Kulov was the only politician whose popularity came close to that of Akayev during the 1990s.

After independence Kulov went on to serve as vice president of Kyrgyzstan, head of Chui province, minister of national security, and mayor of the capital city of Bishkek, a post from which he resigned to create Ar-Namys. Kulov was arrested in March 2000 and accused of abuse of power, forgery, and complicity in committing a crime. In August 2000, a military court released Kulov, a decision public prosecutors appealed, leading the military court to repeal the not-guilty verdict.

Many thought that Kulov was arrested to scare him off from running for president. Kulov opted not to leave the country, in an effort to remain a viable political figure, although he declined to run in the 2000 presidential election.[58] Even so he was arrested soon after its conclusion, in January 2001, and sentenced to seven years of imprisonment in a maximum-security prison including the confiscation of his property and loss of his military rank.

Tajikistan: Climbing Back from Civil War

Like Kyrgyzstan, by late 2001 the Tajikistan government was in a serious debt crisis. Tajikistan had been one of the poorest republics in the Soviet period, and like Kyrgyzstan, Tajikistan has only a limited asset base with which to draw potential foreign investment. But after years of civil war, Tajikistan was viewed as a much riskier business climate than its neighbor to the north. So the government of Imamali Rakhmonov had little choice but to invite in the experts from the World Bank, the IMF, as well as the European and Asian bilateral financial institutions, to help his advisers devise an economic reform strategy.

The Tajiks introduced their national currency, the somoni, in 2000 and with it the beginnings of a private banking sector. But there has been much less transparency here than in Kyrgyzstan, and IMF assistance has been periodically suspended because of allegations of Tajik officials deliberately manipulating official statistics. Some of this manipulation was certainly sheer negligence, but the negligence has helped conceal the economic impact of the narcotics trade, which throughout the 1990s was presumed to have been equal to between 50 and 100 percent of Tajikistan's GDP, depending on the size of each year's Afghan poppy harvest.

Tajikistan's drug trade was in part fueled by the economic desperation of its people. After a decade of independence, over 80 percent of the population was living below the poverty line.[59] Tajikistan's industrial output had fallen dramatically, and its agricultural production was sharply off as well.[60]

Tajikistan suffered a triple blow in its first decade of statehood. Soviet-era cross-border ties dissolved, creating immediate economic hardship. Then almost immediately after independence the country plunged into civil war, and fighting spread over much of the country in 1992 and 1993.[61] This war remained a frozen conflict until international mediation led to a largely successful process of national reconciliation nearly five years later.[62] Finally, even after the civil war ended, the Uzbeks refused to open their borders to Tajik goods, for either sale or transit.

The civil war had an impact on virtually all aspects of life in the country and has been the defining event of Tajikistan's independence. It is believed that 60,000–100,000 people died during the fighting between 1992 and 1994 and that about a tenth of the population became internally displaced. The war is estimated to have cost about $7 billion in lost revenue, leaving the economy of Tajikistan in virtual ruin.[63]

Although Tajikistan received its de jure independence at the end of 1991, it did not begin functioning as an independent state until several years later. Political life in Tajikistan spiraled out of control right after the failed August 1991 Communist Party coup, which was supported by the republic's leader, Kakhar Makhkamov, who was serving as both Communist Party secretary and president.

A number of seemingly antithetical political forces wanted to see Makhkamov ousted, including an active pro-democracy movement in the republic's capital city of Dushanbe that had been gaining support since early 1990. There was also a very ambitious but frustrated former Communist Party leader, Rahmon Nabiyev, who had been removed from office by Mikhail Gorbachev, and who represented powerful Soviet-era economic interests in Khujand in northern Tajikistan (in the Tajik part of the Ferghana Valley, which was an important part of the Soviet-era political power bloc centered in Tashkent).[64] Finally, Tajikistan had a group of charismatic Islamic leaders, who had come to public prominence as part of the state-permitted religious revival of the late 1980s and who believed that state policy should be shaped by Islamic values.[65] All three groups—the pro-democracy activists, Nabiyev's circle, and the Islamic leaders—were able to mobilize large numbers of people from Dushanbe and beyond against Makhkamov, with the clerics able to call on religiously devout villagers from distant parts of the country.

In the face of public pressure, Makhkamov resigned in 1991 and was replaced by Nabiyev, who quickly fell out with both the pro-democratic and pro-Islamic groups. Large demonstrations the next spring turned into factional fighting, along regional as well as ideological lines. Khujand and Kulob provinces had always been competing pro-communist strongholds, with Nabiyev from Khujand and current President Imamali Rakhmonov from Kulob.[66] By contrast the pro-Islamic forces drew much of their support from Qurgan-Teppe and the democrats from Dushanbe. Nabiyev was forced to resign in May 1992, and a coalition government was formed, headed by Akbarsho Iskandarov, a Khujandi, who served as chairman of the parliament. The country then was engulfed in fighting, until the Iskandarov government was overthrown in November 1992, with the support of Russian troops based in the country.[67]

Imamali Rakhmonov, a former Soviet farm head, seized power at the time, gradually expanding the geographic reach of his power. Elected president in 1994, in what most outsiders viewed as a flawed procedure, Rakhmonov continued to be viewed by most Tajiks as a factional leader, a man who would favor the interests of his native Kulob region (and particularly the men who fought with him) over those of the nation. This made the power-sharing arrangement formalized by the national reconciliation agreement so critical, as it brought other groups into the government, including a few members of Tajikistan's Islamist groups, who were part of the United Tajik Opposition, or UTO.[68] But pro-Tashkent entrepreneurs from Khujand, so powerful in the republic during Soviet times, continued to be excluded, which further alienated the Uzbek government of Islam Karimov from that of Imamali Rakhmonov.

The presence of Islamists in Tajikistan's government also made the leaders of neighboring Uzbekistan, Kyrgyzstan, and Kazakhstan nervous, almost as nervous as the armed Islamists in the Tajik mountains did. The ruling elite in the region believed that there were still strong ties between both groups of Islamists and that they would seek to threaten these regimes from within and without in coordinated fashion.

The leaders of neighboring states held the Tajik government responsible, when the activities of the IMU became more violent. IMU fighters invaded

Kyrgyzstan's Batken region in 1999 and 2000, just over the mountains from Tajikistan.[69] They also infiltrated into mountainous areas of Surkhan Darya region, just over the Tajik border in southern Uzbekistan, during the spring and summer of 2000, and in the most remote areas they fought off Uzbek government forces for almost six weeks.[70]

On the eve of the U.S. military campaign in Afghanistan, control over Tajik territory by the Rakhmonov government was still far from complete, which is why the IMU had been able to seek sanctuary in and passage through Tajikistan. Pushed by Karimov in particular, the Rakhmonov government increased pressure on the IMU in 1998, forcing them to abandon their center of operation from the Tavildar region of Tajikistan. The IMU set up new camps near Balkh and Mazar-i-Sharif in Afghanistan in 1999 and 2000, using funds obtained from Al Qaeda. The fighters, and their families who lived with them, a few thousand strong, came mostly from Uzbekistan but included other Central Asian nationalities and ethnic groups as well, and many of the individuals in the IMU fought with the Islamic forces—the UTO—during the Tajik civil war.[71]

Although Central Asia's leaders were exaggerating its scale and immediacy, the threat posed by the IMU to the security of the region was growing during the final years of the Taliban government in Afghanistan, given the enhanced training and equipment available in the Afghan camps.

Uzbekistan: Fear in the Heart of Central Asia

Much like the other Central Asian states, Uzbekistan's government reflects the personal stamp of its first and, to date, only president. Born in Samarkand, the capital of Tamerlane, the 14th century Turkmen-Mongol conqueror also known as Timur, and of Tajik and Uzbek heritage, Islam Karimov saw Uzbekistan as the center of Central Asia's culture and civilization. He believed that with him at the helm, the country would fulfill its historic destiny to lead in the region. So clear was his sense of mission that Karimov saw no reason to seek public or international approval for his choices.

Although Karimov is often compared with Niyazov in Turkmenistan, the comparison is not a fitting one. Karimov is a strong and autocratic figure, but he is not all-powerful. Key advisers have limited discretionary power and much administrative responsibility, as do key regional leaders. Also, unlike Niyazov he has not created a cult around himself.

Karimov made Timur, not himself, the national hero. There is an enormous statue of Timur in a main square of the capital, Tashkent, and a large museum, with exhibits that detail his philosophy of strong but enlightened rule. Karimov's reasons for celebrating Timur are much debated. Obviously, one intention was to use historic precedent to justify Karimov's decision to establish an authoritarian political system. Uzbek officials have explained the cult of Timur as a means of weaning Uzbeks from the Russian-dominated Soviet-era versions of their history and to confirm for them that independence was a return of statehood and not an accidental and temporary historic aberration. But Uzbekistan's neighbors understood it differently and saw it as raising the specter of Uzbek hegemonic behavior.

Although he may not have accurately predicted the collapse of the Soviet Union, Karimov, like virtually all of the Uzbek ruling elite, saw independence as both a positive development and an opportunity to settle some historic scores, particularly with the Russians. But while Karimov attacked Soviet-era decisions for distorting and damaging his country's economy and environment, Karimov's worldview was shaped by his Soviet-era training and experiences. He promised to carve out a model of political and economic development that was attuned to Uzbekistan's nationally specific needs, but the economic and political system that developed was little different from the past, except that the ruling elite lacked the ideology and organizational structure of the Communist Party to legitimate their rule.

Karimov remained a strong supporter of a command-and-control-based economy and was attracted to Chinese-style models of economic reform, in which one part of the economy was liberalized but the larger part remained under strong state control. Karimov believed that the Soviet-era system of price supports and subsidies could be preserved if Uzbekistan's two primary export-earning commodities—cotton and gold—would remain under state control. This, Karimov believed, would be a formula for preserving social and political stability, especially if new responsibility were devolved to traditional local institutions, such as the *mahalla*.[72]

Karimov's economic strategy was a logical complement to his political program. In the last years of Soviet rule, Uzbekistan was beginning to develop a culture of political participation with two pro-democracy political parties: Birlik (Unity) and Erk (Liberty), whose founder, well-known poet Muhammad Salih, ran against Karimov in the 1991 presidential elections. There was also a growing Islamic revival, fueled in part by the appointment of a dynamic young *Mufti*, Muhammad-Sadyk Muhammad-Yusuf, to head the country's religious establishment.

The Communist Party elite was also becoming far less monolithic in its worldview than previously, and many of the country's more reformist figures supported the leadership of Shukrulla Mirsaidov, a onetime vice president, than the more rigid and authoritarian Karimov.[73]

Fearing his lack of popularity, Karimov began moving against his rivals. Mirsaidov was dismissed in early 1992, and following that the leaders of Birlik and Erk were soon forced into exile or subjected to officially sponsored harassment.[74] Since then the only legal political parties have been those created by the government.

The civil war in Tajikistan also fueled the Uzbek government's fear of a violent popular uprising. Throughout the region, the Tajik war was offered as justification for a go-slow approach to democratization. Many Uzbeks accepted the government's political policies, dreading the upheaval they saw across the border in Tajikistan, or worse yet, Afghanistan.

The country's Islamic revival proved more difficult to contain than the secular opposition had. Muhammad-Yusuf was removed in November 1992, but radical Islamic groups centered in Andijan and Namangan continued to gain support from the thousands of young underemployed men who lived in the densely populated Ferghana Valley. There were several charismatic Islamic figures preaching in these years, men who had gotten their first training in underground schools in the 1970s, and then in the looser conditions of the late Soviet era were able to travel to and study in other Muslim countries.[75] Even though the most prominent of these were arrested or driven into exile by the mid-1990s, radical Islamic ideas continued to be propagated in the absence of the popularly acclaimed religious leaders.[76]

Although the Uzbek government had been targeting leaders of radical Islamic groups since the mid-1990s, they did so even more ruthlessly after the explosions in Tashkent in February 1999.[77] Not content merely to confine themselves to members of the IMU, the Karimov regime set out to eliminate potential as well as actual religious opposition. In the next two years, over 7,000 "religious extremists" were arrested, and those rounded up included people with known associations with seditious groups, those reputed to be devout, and those who were seemingly devout, such as bearded men or women wearing extremely modest dress.[78]

The largest of Uzbekistan's radical Islamic groups, the Hizb ut-Tahrir, experienced a dramatic increase in its membership in the mid- and late

1990s.[79] Although outlawed throughout the region, its leadership maintains that their call for the creation of a new Caliphate is still in its peaceful phase—returning Muslims to the true faith. Following massive arrests, adherents of the movement went underground in Uzbekistan, and Hizb ut-Tahrir cells began mushrooming beyond Uzbekistan's borders.

The Tashkent bombings further hardened the Uzbek government's determination to both delineate and defend its national boundaries. It began mining some of the border areas shared with Tajikistan and Kyrgyzstan to keep IMU insurgents from getting in.[80] This did not stop the IMU, but ordinary people paid a large price: Farmers and their animals have been blown up, and trade has been seriously disrupted.[81]

Contacts between friends and family members were also sharply restricted by the introduction of new visa requirements. Turkmenistan was actually the first, in 1999, to introduce visa requirements for visiting the country—a requirement that applied to all foreign visitors including CIS citizens. But the decision by Uzbekistan to introduce a visa regime for citizens of neighboring countries later that same year brought about even more serious hardships, given the much larger numbers of people who were used to traveling via Uzbekistan to get between points within Tajikistan, Kyrgyzstan, or Kazakhstan. Only those living right on the border were exempt, and even they were restricted as to their visa-free point of entry.

The international environment in which the Uzbeks found themselves reinforced their economic conservatism because the government was frightened of what would happen if human security were somehow compromised and social welfare commitments were not maintained. Uzbekistan stuck to price supports long after Kazakhstan and Kyrgyzstan had abandoned them, but the trade restrictions introduced to sustain this policy stifled Uzbekistan's own entrepreneurs, who were made all but extinct after Uzbekistan closed its borders in early 1999.[82]

It is hard to measure the price Uzbekistan paid for Islam Karimov's economic choices. Defenders of the regime point to official figures that report a growth in the GDP during the 1992–2001 period.[83] Much of this growth is a reflection of the profitability of state-owned and state-exported commodities such as gold and cotton and does not reflect real growth in the size of Uzbekistan's domestic economy. And figures provided by the state statistical services are of questionable accuracy. Moreover, the Uzbek economy remained highly dependent on the cotton economy and its vicissitudes, a point discussed further in chapter four.[84]

For all their public praise, even close supporters of the Uzbek president privately admitted that Uzbekistan was in a period of economic crisis as it approached its tenth anniversary of independence. The multiple exchange rates for the som, the national currency, created strong disincentives for the kind of economic diversification that the Uzbeks needed. Private ownership was expanding very slowly, a tragic irony given how entrepreneurial the Uzbeks had proven themselves to be in the gray economy of the Soviet period.

As this survey of the Central Asian states shows, the first decade of independence led to increased differentiation among the states of the region—economically more so than politically. None of the countries were evolving into democratic political systems. But two states, Kazakhstan and Kyrgyzstan, made a strong commitment to pursue macroeconomic reforms, as key to their strategy for dealing with the economic chaos that developed in all the post-Soviet states as a result of the collapse of the USSR and its unified economic system. Although this strategy may have heightened social dislocations in the short run, it also led both countries to develop economies in which private ownership plays a sustaining role.

The leaders of Tajikistan, who supported macroeconomic reforms, lost a critical five years due to the civil war, whereas Uzbekistan and Turkmenistan sought to minimize social dislocation at considerable cost to the long-term development of the private sectors of their economies. Although much reduced, Soviet-era dependencies still continued to make all these economies vulnerable. The economic recovery in all five countries was affected to varying degrees by Russia's 1998 financial meltdown, a crisis which reinforced countries' preexisting tendency to either look outward or withdraw inward in pursuit of their goals. Each country set its policies independently of each other, but inevitably all are affected by the decisions their neighbors made, as they are by the interdependencies of geography and the problems of shared resource management. All of this made the geopolitical choices of these states of at least as much importance as their domestic economic and political ones, and we turn to the subject of foreign relationships in the next chapter.

3

The Geopolitics of Central Asia
prior to September 11

The Central Asian states did not anticipate independence, and the international community never envisioned it for them. It is not surprising then that relationships between these states and their more powerful neighbors had a tentative quality in the decade following the collapse of the Soviet Union. For all the hype about the potential of Central Asia and the Caspian region, most of the international community spent the better part of the 1990s trying to figure out what priority to assign these newly independent states. Likewise, the Central Asian states were themselves uncertain how to prioritize the offers of the foreign actors who came calling.

The calculus of decision making was complex, involving potential economic benefits and the advancement of general security needs. Although members of the world community talked of their uniform "Central Asian policy," most of them were developing policies that differentiated between states, with preference for engagement with the more energy-rich states of the region.[1] Even those countries that gave Central Asia priority status because of geography or history—countries like Russia, China, Turkey, and Iran—still had a hard time deciding at what cost to advance their interests, and in which countries.

Russia's policy makers defined Central Asia as a region of primary strategic importance. To Moscow, the granting of independence to these states, especially Kazakhstan with its long shared border and large Russian population, felt like an arm that had been ripped off from the body of the nation. The Commonwealth of Independent States (CIS) failed to develop into an effective mechanism for advancing Russian interests, and Moscow's efforts to develop asymmetrical bilateral relationships with each of these states also fell far short of its goals.

52

The Central Asian states were fearful of Russian hegemony but even more wary of China's long-term intentions, given the potential power of the Chinese state and the seeming ease of its expansion into the region. At the same time, they were in awe of China's success at economic reform and wanted to learn from it. During the decade following the collapse of Soviet rule, China sought to protect its national interests in the potentially critical border region. The authorities in Beijing were mostly interested in positioning themselves to fill any void that might develop, not in pushing Russia out.

The United States was drawn to the region by the oil and gas reserves of the Caspian, which Russia and Iran were eyeing as well. Estimates of the Caspian Sea region's proven crude oil reserves vary widely by source. The U.S. government's Energy Intelligence Administration has estimated proven oil reserves in the Caspian Region as a range between 17 and 33 billion barrels, which is comparable to OPEC member Qatar on the low end, and the United States on the high end. Prior to September 11, Washington was slow to shift from rhetorical to strategic engagement because U.S. policy makers were unsure how to rank the relative strategic importance of the area.

Turkey and Iran both saw the independence of these states as an opportunity to fulfill their respective senses of historic destiny, but unlike the United States, both lacked the resources to effectively advance their national interests in the region. Of the two, Turkey had the best chance of influence, as Washington toyed with using Turkey as a surrogate. This strategy began to fade when U.S. policy makers came to better understand that "playing the Turkish card" provided no simple fix, both because of Turkey's own domestic problems and because of the ambivalent attitudes shown by Central Asia's leaders toward Turkish state and nonstate actors.

A number of other states also made strong diplomatic forays into the region, often hand-in-hand with their potential investors. The United States briefly considered using Israel as something of a surrogate in the region. That strategy was quickly abandoned, but the Israelis developed a visible presence of their own in much of the region, as Russian Jews who emigrated from these republics became an important source of capital investment.

Korean businessmen were also interested in the area, in part because descendants of populations deported in the 1930s by Joseph Stalin to the Central Asian region still lived there.[2] In the first years of independence, Koreans were an important source of capital and business know-how in Kazakhstan and Uzbekistan in particular. Japanese business interests also quickly appeared in search of investment opportunities, and the Government of Japan targeted the Kyrgyz government for foreign assistance. Investors from Singapore also briefly considered the region.

The Central Asian states were all admitted to the Organization for Security and Cooperation in Europe (OSCE), as successor states of the USSR. Although the leaders of key European states felt certain that they wanted to occupy a position of commercial importance in these countries, they placed no priority in maximizing their direct involvement except in the energy sector. Most European leaders were far more preoccupied with the impact that the end of communism had closer to home—the rebirth of Central Europe and the collapse of Yugoslavia—than they were with events in Central Asia, although they were happy to receive visiting Central Asian leaders with great pomp and ceremony.

All this international interest in their countries provided a tantalizing array of choices for the leaders of the Central Asian states. After decades of being cooped up behind the iron curtain, all were eager to head diplomatic missions, seeking a unique international presence for their nation, and to solidify their hold on power. Askar Akayev vowed to make Kyrgyzstan the Switzerland of Europe; Nursultan Nazarbayev claimed that Kazakhstan was a bridge between Europe and Asia; Saparmurat Niyazov tried to create a new international status for Turkmenistan; and Islam Karimov strove to make Uzbekistan a valued military partner of the West. Only Imamali Rakhmonov, hobbled by years of civil war, faced very limited choices. Each of the Central Asian leaders also believed that an enhanced international profile would make him the first among equals in the Central Asian region.

Russia: Would Neoimperialism Replace Imperialism?

Failure of Russian-Dominated Multilateral Efforts

The initial foreign policy challenge for all the Central Asian states was managing relations with Russia. In the first few years of independence, the leaders of these states feared that Moscow would mediate between them and the rest of the international community.

Russia's President Boris Yeltsin quickly asserted that Russia was heir to the power of the Soviet Union and demonstrated this symbolically by occupying Mikhail Gorbachev's Kremlin office and apartment. In the same way that controlling the Kremlin defined Russian leadership, Russian dominance over the vast territories that had once formed its empire was critical to maintaining Russia's great-power status. The peaceful dissolution of the USSR was part of the price that Russia's new leaders paid for taking control of the Kremlin.

To maximize the value of their prize, Yeltsin and the senior Russian leadership sought an instrument that would allow Moscow easy control of the former Soviet republics. Even the most pro-Western "liberals" in the Moscow political establishment, such as Foreign Minister Andrei Kozyrev, believed that Russia's national interest had to prevail over the efforts of its new neighbors to define and advance their own domestic and foreign policy agendas.[3] Initially, it was expected that the CIS would serve this end.[4] The formation of the CIS was the instrument of dissolution for the USSR, allowing for the transition from a single country to twelve separate states (the three Baltic republics having effectively attained their de jure independence in September 1991). But Russia's leaders hoped to turn the CIS into something more. They urged the creation of a host of coordinating bodies in which Russia would have weighted votes to ensure Moscow's control of key sectors of the economies of all member states and to institutionalize Russia's role in their foreign investment strategies.

The nationalists heading Azerbaijan, Georgia, and Moldova refused to take part in the CIS precisely because of their fear that the organization would turn itself into a mechanism of Russian neoimperialism. The communist-era figures in charge of the Central Asian republics were less nervous about this. These men had embraced independence reluctantly, in part because of the magnitude of challenges associated with it, and the leadership councils of the CIS allowed the familiar Soviet form of collegial decision making to be used as a tool in this transition.

Unlike their less experienced colleagues in Azerbaijan and Georgia, who had come to power from the political opposition, Central Asia's party stalwarts recognized that there was no running from Russia's ambitions, which were best confronted head on.[5] It must have seemed obvious to them that Russia's leaders would use brute force, even if only in masked fashion, to advance their claims. Developments in Transdniester (Moldova), Abkhazia (Georgia), and Karabakh (Azerbaijan) provided object lessons as to what happens to states that turn away from the CIS. By early 1994, Moldova, Georgia, and Azerbaijan had all become full participating members of the CIS, in part to freeze the ethnic and civil wars that their nonmembership had helped stimulate.[6]

The CIS never became an effective tool of Russian domination, because most CIS state leaders strongly opposed the transfer of national sovereignty, in large or in small measure, to a Russian-dominated multilateral organization. The Ukrainians were adamant on this point, as were Georgia's President Eduard Shevardnadze (1993–2003) and Azerbaijan's President Heydar Aliyev (1995–2003), both formidable figures with long Soviet-era experience. This position was also strongly endorsed by the presidents of both Turkmenistan and Uzbekistan.

For their part, the leaders in the Kremlin were unwilling to seriously consider any restructuring of the CIS that would make it an organization of equal partners. The most vigorous effort in this regard was the campaign by Kazakhstan's President Nursultan Nazarbayev in 1994 to have the CIS replaced by a Euro-Asian Union (EAU), which was to function much along the lines of the European Union.[7]

With time Yeltsin's administration began to tire of pressing for revitalization of the CIS. By the mid-1990s they understood that Russia's own transition problems were much larger than their original reckoning, and that there was no easy way to harness the energies of the former Soviet republics to serve Russia's needs. However, this did not mean that Moscow abandoned the CIS; summits of the CIS presidents were held regularly, at least until Boris Yeltsin's ill-health limited his participation. Even then, for a brief period from April 1998 until March 1999, the Russian magnate Boris Berezovsky was given the job of CIS executive secretary to revive what was becoming an obviously moribund institution. After taking over Russia's presidency, Vladimir Putin again tried to use summitry to reinvigorate the organization, but to little avail. By late 2001 the CIS was a bureaucratic shell of an organization, a sinecure for those in the Russian elite who were incapable of climbing to the top of more competitive ladders.

The Kremlin, however, did not abandon the cause of "integration," as they liked to term it, and explored the creation of other multilateral organizations with smaller numbers of more willing partners. Belarus was the most eager and in 1996 entered an agreement that was designed to achieve its full integration with Russia, a prospect that many in Moscow elite circles have been determined to delay indefinitely.

There was also a customs union of five states, originally a union of four—Russia, Belarus, Kazakhstan, and Kyrgyzstan—that formed in 1995 and expanded in 1999 to include Tajikistan. But it did virtually nothing to regulate trade and tariffs between its member nations.[8] Its lack of vitality was partly the result of the influence of the multilateral financial institutions, which sought to wean these economies from dependency on Russia through the conditions for financial assistance that they introduced.

Kazakhstan, Kyrgyzstan, and Tajikistan also remained part of the Collective Security Treaty Organization (CSTO), along with Russia, Armenia, and Belarus. The CSTO, initially known as the Tashkent Collective Security Agreement, was renamed after Uzbekistan withdrew from it in 1999, leaving the organization to function more as an instrument of divorce than as an institution capable of meeting the security needs of member states.

By the late 1990s, none of the states in the region saw Russia as able to do much to help them meet their security needs, including, most pressingly, reversing Taliban victories in Afghanistan. Russia was funneling arms to several Northern Alliance commanders, using the Central Asian states as the conduit, but this only slightly slowed the Taliban's advance.[9]

Russia, bogged down in the quagmire of Chechnya, was unable to do much to help these states meet their internal security concerns. Russian officials said no to the Kyrgyz when asked to provide military assistance during the Islamic Movement of Uzbekistan (IMU) incursions of 1999 and 2000 and countered by calling for an increased role for the CSTO to improve common security. To this end, in May 2001, a 1,500-man rapid deployment force for use in Central Asia was created, which held field exercises in the region but was never fully deployed.

None of Moscow's institutional creations served their intended purpose, which was to harness the successor states' potential to fulfill Russia's own national needs. Nor did they do much to help the Central Asian states cope with their own problems. They did, however, serve one positive purpose: Bringing together the leadership of various groupings of CIS states helped make the dissolution of the Soviet Union a smoother process than many in Central Asia had anticipated.

Russia's Other Tools of Control

The Russian leadership also had many noninstitutional levers to use in pressuring its newly independent neighbors. Given the interconnected nature of the Soviet economy, all the post-Soviet states were dependent on Russia economically. Each of these states also inherited large Russian populations, whose fate could be used as a club to gain important concessions by Moscow. Shared borders required management. Only Tajikistan and

Uzbekistan do not share a common border with Russia, and the Turkmen border is in the Caspian Sea.

Control of energy supplies was and remains a potentially effective Russian tool. In the first years of independence Russia used its position as energy supplier to squeeze concessions from a number of post-Soviet states, most prominently Kazakhstan, which was almost wholly dependent on Russia for electricity used in northern Kazakhstan and for most of the oil and gas used in the country as well. Eventually Kazakhstan gave equity stakes in some of its own hydroelectric stations to Unified Energy Systems, or RAO-UES, Russia's partly state-held national energy grid, in return for debt forgiveness and slowly relations between the two states in the energy sector shifted to a more market-driven foundation. But in the early years Kazakhstan was often forced to make unwanted concessions to Russia because of Moscow's use of its energy debts.[10]

The Russian government used its control of the Soviet-era oil and gas pipeline system that passed across its territory to seek concessions from Kazakhstan, Turkmenistan, and Azerbaijan, although not always to the intended effect. Russia, through its state pipeline operator Transneft, was a tough negotiator over terms for the Caspian Pipeline Consortium (CPC) to move Tengiz oil from Kazakhstan to the Russian port of Novorossiisk. Russia's actions seemed to substantiate alarmist claims made by powerful former cold warriors in Washington, leaving U.S. policy makers convinced that as much Caspian oil as possible should reach market through routes that bypassed Russia.

The Russian gas industry tried hard to retain control of the Turkmen gas industry, creating Turkmenrosgaz in 1995 as a vehicle for doing this.[11] However, President Niyazov quickly became disenchanted with the terms offered by the Russians for the transit and sale of Turkmen gas and fired the officials responsible for bringing him this deal, deciding that their loyalty lay with those now running Russia's gas industry and not with the new Turkmen state.[12]

When Turkmenrosgaz failed, Gazprom used its control of the gas pipeline system as a lever to keep Turkmen gas out of the European market and allocating it to poor-paying CIS customers, such as Ukraine and Georgia.[13] Citing difficulties of payment collection, Moscow offered Ashgabat barter transactions and a low purchase price at the Turkmen border and refused to improve the terms when the Turkmen walked away from the bargaining table in 1997. But in the case of Turkmen gas, there was no foreign partner on whom to displace costs, and as a result Turkmen gas production atrophied by three-quarters from 1992 to 1998 because the government in Ashgabat could not move it to potential markets.[14] These two cases represent Russia's most aggressive behavior in the region.

The Russian military also had strong views about what policies should be pursued in Central Asia. Russian officials gave Tajikistan's leadership little choice about the continued presence of the 201st Motorized Division, which Moscow declined to turn over to Dushanbe or remove from the country, despite repeated allegations that Russian officers facilitated the drug trade and that the troops largely consisted of local Tajiks serving on contracts.[15] Russia also provided border guards to protect the Tajik–Afghan border, even after Moscow began turning over full control to the other Central Asian countries, citing Russia's own security needs for their continued military presence in Tajikistan.[16]

Russia's limited military presence in Central Asia was strongly supported by ordinary Russians as well as by military officials. Russian nationalists, in particular, had strong opinions about how the Russian government should comport itself in Central Asia, and they developed a vocal lobby in the Duma.[17] These people kept accounts of the hardships faced by Central Asia's ethnic Russian minorities in the news. The coverage included everything from the poverty-stricken elderly Russian population who were just about all that remained in Tajikistan after its civil war, but also ordinary Russians trying to adjust to their newly acquired status of ethnic minority. Such misfortune was depicted in such dire terms that Uzbek, Kazakh, and Turkmen state-controlled regulatory agencies began cutting back on the air time made available to the Russian television stations to keep local Russian passions from being further inflamed.

In the early 1990s, the Russian government lobbied hard but unsuccessfully for rights of dual citizenship for the ethnic Russians living in all of the post-Soviet states. Central Asia's Russians were eligible for Russian citizenship, but if they opted out of local citizenship they lost their personal share in the privatization process, which included ownership of their physical residence. Only Turkmenistan's government acceded to the idea of dual citizenship, in a ten-year agreement signed in 1993.

To little avail, the Russian government also pressured the Central Asian countries to grant the Russian language the same legal status as the national languages of these states. Eventually, in 2001, the Kyrgyz government agreed to do so, and the Kazakhs provided it a lower but special legal status as the "language of international communication." (In 2004, however, the public role of the Russian language was sharply cut back.) The remaining three states continued to provide Russian language education but with dramatically diminished funding, and fluency in the national language became mandatory for anyone with political or economic ambitions.

Public grumblings aside, Russia basically left the local Russian population to sort things out for themselves on a family-by-family basis. Millions of Russians left the region, most bound for Russia.[18] Kazakhstan incurred the largest absolute loss of ethnic Russians of all the post-Soviet states. A total of 1.5 million Russians left Kazakhstan between 1992 and 2000. Untold numbers of Russians (and many non-Russians) who remained found ways to acquire Russian Federation passports and in defiance of local law made themselves dual citizens. When Russian citizens got arrested on political charges, as several purported separatists did in Ust-Kamenogorsk, Kazakhstan, in 1999, Moscow restricted its response to quiet protests.[19]

Russia's move toward a market economy promoted an attitude of realism toward the former Soviet republics. From the early 1990s, reformers like Yegor Gaidar and Anatoly Chubais pressed Moscow to cut itself off from the economic burdens posed by these states. Moscow initially tried to keep all CIS members in the ruble zone as a means of regulating their economies. But in July 1993 Russia sharply limited the supply of rubles to these countries, all of which were still in the ruble zone.[20] Russia's economic reformers were more interested in controlling inflation than in attaining more ephemeral neoimperialist goals, and this decision hastened the untangling of the economies of the Soviet successor states.

Even in areas of the economy such as Caspian oil and gas development where they tried hard to hold their own, the Russian government and Russian firms had to take a backseat to more powerful U.S. and Western economic interests. Russia hoped to assert its influence through the demarcation of the Caspian Sea into national sectors with provisions for common development to compensate states such as Russia (and Iran) that lacked large untapped undersea deposits if strict national boundaries were observed. Russia and Iran originally proposed that each Caspian nation be awarded equal shares of 20 percent. If the waters were allocated according to each country's coast, Kazakhstan would have 33 percent, Russia 19 percent, Azerbaijan 18 percent, Turkmenistan 17 percent, and Iran 13 percent. Unwilling to wait for formal demarcation, Kazakhstan, Azerbaijan, and Turkmenistan each began seeking investors to develop their declared national sectors.[21]

Russia took an essentially pragmatic approach to these developments and began developing its own national sector. Moscow also reached an agreement on the terms of demarcation with both Azerbaijan and Kazakhstan and made progress toward agreement with Turkmenistan.[22]

In contrast to the nationalists, intellectuals, and policy advisers who argued that Russia's historic destiny is inextricably tied to its former colonies, Russia's leaders slowly came to realize that they were not in a position to implement policies predicated on notions of national destiny. Changes in the makeup and nature of the Russian leadership helped produce this more pragmatic approach. Boris Yeltsin was a condescending and ineffective leader at the end of his presidency. The relative void at the top of the Russian state created increased room for Central Asia's leaders to maneuver in their dealings with Moscow.

When Vladimir Putin came to power in 1999, he faced a group of men in Central Asia who felt confident in their ability to represent their national interests. By then, each of the ruling Central Asian leaders had far more high-level diplomatic experience than did Putin. He decided to turn this into a Russian asset, winning favor with his Central Asian colleagues by treating each of the region's presidents more like his equal than Yeltsin had ever done. And, as we see in chapter six, eventually this strategy considerably benefited Russia.

Under Putin's leadership, Moscow was prepared to admit that Russia had limited resources and had to make difficult choices about where and how to assert Russian influence. Many of these decisions were made through the prism of the seemingly endless war in Chechnya, which further reinforced Russia's natural inclination to see developments in the Caucasus as more intimately tied to the core of Russian security interests than those in Central Asia.

China's Eyes on the Future

Sharing borders with three of the five Central Asian states (Kazakhstan, Kyrgyzstan, and Tajikistan), China was nearly as interested in the independence of the Central Asian states as Russia was, although Beijing was far less prepared than Moscow to aggressively assert its national interests. Chinese authorities accepted, for the moment at least, that the Central Asian states lay within Russia's sphere of influence, but Beijing's leaders

wanted to secure their long-term interests in the region and position themselves to parry any short-term security threats that power voids in the
region might produce. For this reason, by and large, the Chinese leaders
did not believe that they were in a competitive relationship with the
Russians, because a strong hand exercised by Moscow was generally consistent with preventing the power void that the Chinese feared. The Chinese looked warily, however, at the expanding economic presence of the
United States and other Western countries as creating potential limits to
China's own future engagement.

Senior Chinese officials were quick to embrace these states. In the last
years of Soviet rule, the Central Asian republic leaders had been developing bilateral relationships with their regional counterparts in China. Upon
independence, Beijing rapidly signaled that it was far more appropriate for
Central Asia's newly sovereign presidents to forge direct relations with their
counterparts in Beijing. Official invitations were issued, and Central Asia's
presidents and foreign ministers went to the Chinese capital eager to satisfy
their curiosity about the nature of the economic miracle that the Chinese
were experiencing.[23] Chinese Prime Minister Li Peng made a much heralded
tour of Central Asia in 1994, visiting all five countries in twelve days and
signing a number of bilateral agreements.[24] Peng's visit was designed to
indicate that Beijing viewed its new neighbors with some regard, but it was
more a publicity effort than the creation of a foundation for a close cooperative relationship between these states.[25]

The formation of independent states in Central Asia created new security
threats for the Chinese by increasing the demands for greater autonomy or
independence by Uighurs and other Turkic Muslim minorities who lived
just over the border in China. These groups had been energized in the 1980s
by the growth of ethnic politics in the USSR.[26] Pro-separatist Uighur groups
in Kazakhstan and Kyrgyzstan enjoyed strong support from Kazakh and
Kyrgyz nationalists. After a burst of initial activism in the early 1990s, authorities in Kazakhstan and Kyrgyzstan sharply curtailed their activities after
being pressured strongly by China to do so. The Chinese government
claimed that virtually all organized Uighur groups were real or potential terrorists. After a spate of bombings in China in 1997 (both within and outside
of Xinjiang), the Central Asian governments began to accede to the Chinese
request. Exiled Uighur groups based in Kazakhstan were blamed for three
bus bombings in Urumchi in western China in February 1997, and none of
the Central Asian leaders wanted armed groups living on their soil.[27]

The Kazakh and Kyrgyz borders with China also became more closely regulated, in part because of the ease with which Uighurs had been able to pass from Afghanistan into Tajikistan and then further north. This changed somewhat after the successful Taliban campaign of winter-spring 1997, when Chinese authorities instituted a "special regime" on their own border with Afghanistan.

The Central Asian leaders took seriously Chinese claims that Uighur terrorists were receiving terrorist training in camps supported by Osama bin Laden. Although many Western sources discounted this at the time, journalists covering the U.S.-led bombing campaign in Afghanistan recovered Uighur-language documents from bombed out and abandoned Al Qaeda camps, which proved the presence but did not date the arrival of Uighurs in these camps.[28]

By the time of the 1997 bombings, the Chinese were able to press their position through the Shanghai Cooperation Organization (SCO), formed in 1996.[29] This organization began as a confidence-building measure developed to coincide with the delineation of the former Sino–Soviet border. The government in Beijing questioned the legitimacy of the border in 1963, and although there was progress in negotiations in the mid-1980s, the formal boundaries had not been fully delimited when the Central Asian states inherited them in 1991.

The five-state agreement of April 1996 set up the framework for bilateral negotiations for the delineation of outstanding disputed regions.[30] The agreement also included plans for a demilitarized zone, which some wanted set at 20 kilometers and others at 100 kilometers from the border. It placed strict limitations on the stationing of troops and the numbers of men and equipment that can be brought in for military exercises, plans that were implemented in April 1997.

In 1998, there was considerable progress in delineating both the Kazakh and Kyrgyz borders with China. A joint statement by President Akayev and President Zhiang Zemin made during Akayev's April 1998 trip to Beijing kicked off a period of intensive negotiation. In July 1998, Kazakhstan and China also signed an agreement dividing 944 square kilometers of disputed border territories, with nearly 60 percent of the land remaining in Kazakh hands.[31] Critics of the agreement, however, say that China got the most valuable bits.

In both cases, it became clear that negotiations over borders were more complex than earlier public fanfare implied. The formal delineation of the

Kazakh–Chinese border was largely completed in 1999, but the Kyrgyz–Chinese border was not finalized until May 2002.[32] As we will discuss in chapter five, the 2002 treaty between Kyrgyzstan and China turned into a major political crisis for President Akayev, with opposition figures accusing him of treason for signing it.

Confidence-building measures notwithstanding, the existence of the SCO did not mitigate Chinese pressure for the ceding of territory by the Central Asian states. According to Azimbek Beknazarov and a committee of other Kyrgyz legislators who have studied the transfers,[33] Akayev turned over 125,000 hectares of land to the Chinese government beyond that which was disputed during the Soviet period.[34] In 2003, there was also an additional land transfer made by the Tajiks.

The concession of territory by Kyrgyzstan and Kazakhstan was recognition of China's potential for hegemonic power in the region. The leaders of both countries have also tried to ingratiate themselves with Beijing in more subtle ways. Kazakhstan and Kyrgyzstan have had foreign ministers who speak Chinese and have sent ambassadors to Beijing who were fluent in Chinese as well. By contrast, the Uzbeks, who lack a shared border with China, have dealt with Beijing in a more tempered fashion, pursuing a relationship more rooted in principles of mutual advantage.

All of Central Asia's leaders recognized that China's booming economy made it an increasing economic force, and it was already a major trading presence throughout the region. China's share of trade is not always reflected in official statistics, which do not include the exchanges of illegal shuttle traders, or those who engage in small-scale and unregistered import and resale of Chinese goods. Although the Central Asian countries steadily increased the barriers against this kind of trade, shuttle trade has been an important source of capital accumulation for small Central Asian entrepreneurs, who then reinvest their profits in more permanent enterprises. In the first years of independence, there was also a certain amount of illegal immigration from China, when Chinese citizens (often those with relatives in Central Asia) brought capital across the border to buy factories or farms in Kazakhstan or Kyrgyzstan and simply took up permanent residence. There are no official or even good unofficial estimates as to the size of the new Chinese communities, but there is no evidence to suggest a calculated policy of encouraging emigration on China's part.

The Chinese government does have calculated long-term economic interests in the Central Asian states, most particularly in the energy sector. In

1997, the Chinese National Petroleum Company, or CNPC, won a tender—and a 60 percent stake—in the Zhanazhol and Kenkiyak fields in Aktobe, Kazakhstan.[35] The Chinese committed to building a $9.6 billion pipeline, but then scaled down the project; by late 2001, less than $200 million had been authorized.[36] From then on, China's role in the Central Asian energy sector has steadily increased.

The Chinese government is also interested in the development of transit links that would allow the Central Asian states to better use the Chinese highway and railroad system and ports to shift transit trade away from Russia—an interest they share with the Central Asian states. But the major rail link across the region (from Druzhba in Kazakhstan to Urumchi in China), opened in 1992, was severely handicapped by the lack of storage facilities both on the Kazakh and Chinese borders.[37] Plans call for an ambitious 20 million tons of freight to pass through Druzhba annually, but only 6 million tons crossed from Kazakhstan into China in 2001.[38]

Highway connections through Central Asia into China remained problematic, despite efforts throughout the 1990s to improve them, including upgrades of the Karakaroum highway, which extends from Urumchi to Pakistan. In March 1995, a quadripartite trade agreement on the transport of freight was signed between China, Kazakhstan, Kyrgyzstan, and Pakistan calling for a uniform customs policy along the highway, and a ceremonial four-nation truck convoy in October 1996 launched the upgrade designed to make the highway fit for year-round travel, as opposed to the May through October regime of the past.

The Karakaroum highway, which is shown on the map provided in this book, is the foundation of regional linkages with China. A linkup from Bishkek to the Karakaroum highway through Torugart already exists, and the EU-initiated Traceca program (an abbreviation for Transport Corridor Europe–Caucasus–Asia) helps pay for upgrades to the road from Osh through Sary-Tosh to meet a road that the Chinese are cutting through to the border at Irkeshtam.[39] In July 1997, the prime ministers of Uzbekistan and Kyrgyzstan as well as senior Chinese officials attended a ceremonial opening of the new customs point, where a centuries-old trade route has been widened and resurfaced for truck traffic to serve primarily southern Kyrgyzstan, southern Kazakhstan, and Uzbekistan. Moreover, a highway link connects (as weather permits) Bishkek to Kashi (via Naryn to Torugart) and then on to the Karakaroum highway, which is the shortest way to get from Almaty to China. This route lacks freight storage facilities, however, and so is used primarily by local traders.

In February 1998, China, Uzbekistan, and Kyrgyzstan signed an automobile transportation agreement, pledging to complete upgrades on the highway by October 1998. There are two other crossing points for Kazakhstan, at Pakhtu (from Semey) and Khorgos (from Almaty). The Chinese also announced plans to build a major freight storage and forwarding facility and to establish a free enterprise zone designed especially for joint ventures with Kazakhstan.

Links and spurs to the highway were added, and plans for further additions were made. In September 1998, Tajikistan's president opened a 54-kilometer stretch of Qurgan-Teppe–Kulob broad-gauge railway that will link up with the Karakaroum highway. In November 1998, Kazakhstan, Kyrgyzstan, Pakistan, and China signed a cooperative agreement to upgrade roads connecting Almaty in Kazakhstan with Karachi in Pakistan.[40]

For all these agreements, progress on these highway and storage projects has been slow and has done nothing to modify the realities of geography. Mountain passes that top out at nearly 10,000 feet, road closings due to snow, and glacial erosion are certain to remain commonplace. In transport, as in so many other areas of the Chinese relationship to the Central Asian states, the emphasis of the first decade after independence was in laying the foundation for future closer ties. Although transport links were improved, the Chinese adopted a wait-and-see attitude, leaving the construction of international standard freight terminals until there was an economic breakout in at least a major part of the Central Asian region.

The United States Extends a Lukewarm Hand

Prior to September 11, U.S. engagement with the Central Asian states consisted of policies designed to protect against potential long-term security risks rather than to secure the United States against imminent dangers originating in the region. The one exception was the U.S. engagement in nuclear diplomacy with Kazakhstan, which was a priority of both the George H. W. Bush and Clinton administrations to ensure that all Soviet-era nuclear weapons were removed from the newly independent states. Policies in the oil and gas sector, however, began to take center stage in the relationships of the mid-1990s and were intended to diversify Western long-term reserves, rather than to cope with near-term energy issues.

On the surface, U.S. policy makers seemed eager to maximize their influence in the region. The United States was quick to send diplomatic representation to these states, establishing full embassies in Kazakhstan and Kyrgyzstan immediately after independence and everywhere else shortly thereafter. But there was far more show than substance in these early bilateral relationships. U.S. foreign assistance to all five countries from FY1992 to FY2002 was less than $3 billion, as data in the appendix show. Spread thinly across more than a dozen categories, the United States offered the Central Asian states little more than symbolic help in meeting the tasks of economic, political, and social restructuring.

U.S. policy makers, of course, helped shape the priorities of the International Monetary Fund and the World Bank, as well as the European Bank for Reconstruction and Development and the Asian Development Bank, all of which were providing technical assistance for economic restructuring and investing in infrastructure projects. The main instrument of direct U.S. policy was the Freedom Support Act, whose funds were designed to support a slow process of civil society building, which was anticipated to take generations.[41] This was not considered troubling, because in the years following the collapse of the Soviet Union, U.S. priorities in Eurasia lay elsewhere, in coping with the potential security risks that this could lead to in Europe and Russia.

By contrast, each of the Central Asian leaders was anxious to secure close ties with the United States, both because of the international prestige that this brings and because such ties help further distance these states from Russia. Central Asia's leaders came to Washington with these hopes. Some were received at the White House; others were not.[42] When Turkmenistan's President Niyazov was shunned by the Clinton administration in 1993, he faked photos of a White House meeting and disseminated them. Few in Turkmenistan ever learned that the meeting was simply never held.

Although invitations have been frequent, no U.S. president has yet traveled Central Asia. U.S. Secretary of State James Baker traveled to Kazakhstan in December 1991 and again in February 1992 when he traveled to Kyrgyzstan and Uzbekistan as well. Later, in November 1997, First Lady Hillary Clinton visited the same states, as did Secretary of State Madeleine Albright in April 2000. Vice President Al Gore went to Kazakhstan in December 1993. Gore's trip in particular reflected the Clinton administration's new realization of the importance of the Caspian Sea basin's oil and gas reserves, disproportionately located in Azerbaijan, Turkmenistan, and Kazakhstan.

This change in approach was signaled in Deputy Secretary of State Strobe Talbott's "Farewell to Flashman" address of July 1997, which elaborated a new U.S. policy for Central Asia and the south Caucasus. Talbott invoked George MacDonald Fraser's dashing fictional hero Lieutenant Harry Flashman, who fought to advance the interests of the British Empire in much of this region, to argue that these countries would no longer be pawns on the chessboard to be moved at will by great powers.[43]

Central to the new U.S. policy was the reevaluation of Russia's role in the region, which the Clinton administration saw as more heavy-handed and less stabilizing than previously thought, and as a result the administration began promoting the idea of multiple pipelines for the export of Caspian oil. This idea was first mentioned in 1995 but was not translated into an action plan until 1998 when the U.S. government began to pressure Western oil companies and local governments to develop a pipeline running from Baku (Azerbaijan) through Tbilisi (Georgia) to Ceyhan (Turkey), or the BTC pipeline.[44] With the exception of the CPC pipeline, which was a requirement for Chevron's development of Tengiz oil, the Clinton administration did not support the development of new export routes for Caspian oil through Russia.

Washington was also against Caspian oil reaching market through Iran, leaving the Caspian states very few new options other than BTC.[45] But U.S. policy makers were unwilling to underwrite any of the construction costs involved in the oft-promoted BTC pipeline and largely confined their spending to feasibility studies and loan guarantees to U.S. firms engaged in the development of Caspian oil, gas, or related service sectors.

For all the talk about the importance of Caspian oil and gas, U.S. interest in these states was nothing like that shown to Persian Gulf oil producers, or even smaller producers closer to home like Mexico or Venezuela. The energy reserves of Kazakhstan and Azerbaijan made these countries of particular concern to U.S. policy makers, but they were content to demonstrate their interest through photo opportunities at the White House and by a willingness to turn a relatively blind eye to human rights violations and reversals in democratic political institution building in potential oil- and gas-producing states, including those dutifully reported by the State Department.

With time, U.S. interest in Kazakhstan, in particular, began to grow, as word began to spread of the gigantic oil reserves in the offshore Kashagan field.[46] This increased attention also helped stimulate corruption in Kazakhstan. Former Soviet-era communist officials understood the mechanisms of corruption in their own system and served as eager students for Western businessmen offering lessons on navigating the gray areas of market economies.

Although the U.S. government was not a direct party to this corruption and made clear that U.S. firms understood that they were bound by the provisions of the Foreign Corrupt Practices Act, it was incurious about the ethics of U.S. courtiers in Caspian presidential "courts." In fact, the U.S. government seemed to favor the use of U.S. middlemen, because this meant that U.S. firms were more likely to get big contracts. The case of James Giffen, president of the Mercator Corporation, is quite instructive. U.S. officials must have been uncomfortable with Giffen's boasting of his Kazakh passport and formal status as part-time adviser to President Nazarbayev, but no one seems to have suggested that he ever give up his U.S. passport (which he was eventually forced to surrender to the court in New York City as part of a bail agreement), and Giffen enjoyed good access to senior policy makers in Washington.[47] This access, however, began to dry up after a grand jury in the southern district of New York began investigating Giffen and a number of former Mobil Oil officials.

Despite the allegations of corruption surrounding the Kazakh president and his family, it was seen as possible (although not always easy) to do business in Kazakhstan, so pragmatically most people tolerated the court around Nazarbayev, or tried to penetrate it for their own advantage.

At the same time, politics in Turkmenistan was becoming more opaque and less amenable to Western business interests, and most U.S. firms did not view investing in the country as a tempting prospect—despite Turkmenistan's enormous gas reserves, the best efforts of Alexander Haig, secretary of state in the Reagan administration,[48] and lobbying by Turkmenistan's very articulate Foreign Minister Boris Shikhmuradov, who conveyed an impression to Westerners that he understood their concerns.[49] Limited transport opportunities for energy resources made the inhospitable business environment even less attractive, particularly after the Taliban's takeover effectively cut off the option of transport across Afghanistan.

U.S. interest in Turkmenistan peaked when it looked like California-based Unocal would get access to gas from the Dauletabad field and build a pipeline through Afghanistan. In 1996 and 1997, the project was regarded by many as a tool for forging a new national consensus in Afghanistan. The

Unocal-sponsored project—and the training and infrastructure repairs that were ancillary to it—was a frequently cited incentive offered up by U.S. government officials and participants in UN-sponsored peace negotiations in Afghanistan. But after intelligence linked Al Qaeda camps in Afghanistan to the August 1998 bombings of U.S. embassies in Kenya and Tanzania, Washington's retaliation included a cruise missile attack against Al Qaeda bases in Afghanistan.[50]

Changing assessments of the security situation in Afghanistan temporarily killed the Trans-Afghan pipeline, because Unocal suspended its operations immediately after the bombing raids.[51] Even then, policy makers in Washington continued to hold out hope that the Turkmen government would lend its support to the U.S.-sponsored Trans-Caspian gas pipeline project to augment supplies shipped through the BTC. But with no major U.S. investor actively working to develop Turkmenistan's assets, dealing with Ashgabat proved much harder for Washington than negotiating with Astana, because without Kazakh oil the BTC route would be only marginally profitable. Although the Kazakhs were willing to commit to the idea of shipping some oil through this route in principle, they were not willing to specify amounts. The Turkmen government was even less forthcoming, and by 2001 Washington had already written off Ashgabat and Turkmen oil and gas, at least for the near term.

The Kazakh government's unwillingness to neither firmly commit to nor reject sending oil through the BTC pipeline became an important lever for the Kazakhs to use in their relationship with Washington. By the late 1990s most senior policy makers in Washington viewed Kazakhstan as the most important state in Central Asia. The bilateral relationship was managed through the Gore–Nazarbayev commission, which technically accorded the Kazakhs the same level of access in the Clinton administration that the Russians enjoyed through what began as the Gore–Chernomyrdin commission, renamed with the appointment of subsequent Russian prime ministers. By contrast, the bilateral commission with Uzbekistan was set at the level of the CIS coordinator, an ambassadorial appointment, and his Uzbek counterpart was the foreign minister.[52]

As democracy-building efforts were faltering everywhere in the region, some prominent members of the Clinton administration felt that little would be gained by pressing the Kazakhs too hard for what were increasingly becoming much-needed political reforms. The potential costs of doing so were made clear during Albright's April 2000 trip to Kazakhstan, which turned into a diplomatic embarrassment when President Nazarbayev answered her public criticism of his domestic policies with an equally public and highly critical interpretation of the history of U.S. race relations.

The growing sense that these states were failing at political institution building further strengthened the position of those in the policy-making community who argued that Washington had to put security concerns at the top of the agenda. The United States had already successfully done this with regard to Kazakhstan. The cornerstone of U.S.–Kazakh security cooperation was a seven-year agreement signed in December 1993 to destroy Kazakhstan's nuclear silos, in which the United States helped facilitate the return of Kazakhstan's inherited nuclear arsenal to Russia.[53] By 1995, all nuclear warheads had been returned, and 147 missile silos had been destroyed.[54]

The U.S. military presence in the region began to grow in 1999, and U.S. military assistance increased sharply in 2000 and 2001. Cooperation with the United States and the North Atlantic Treaty Organization (NATO) was already the most effective way for these states to modernize their militaries. But the United States and other NATO countries did not consider funding the rapid entry of the Central Asians into a global security system a priority. The focus of NATO expansion lay elsewhere, well west of the Urals. Even the most vigorous Pentagon defenders of increased engagement with the Central Asians were unwilling to push for anything more than a go-slow process with these states, in which U.S. military reforms would take at least one or two generations to complete.

The Central Asian states joined NATO's Partnership for Peace (PFP), and all fell under the operational control of the U.S. Central Command (Cent-Com).[55] Its commander-in-chief, General Tommy R. Franks, visited the region in September 2000 and then again in May 2001. U.S. interest in the region was also marked during the command of his predecessor, General Anthony Zinni (August 1997–August 2000), but it proved difficult to translate this high-level interest into improved delivery of U.S. and NATO military assistance to these countries. There were problems of coordination between CentCom and U.S. military officials with responsibility for PFP, as well as between the various NATO nations seeking to assist the Central Asian states. All this was further complicated by the difficulty of getting the Central Asian states to work in concert. In short, there was no single Western plan, and no shared view of regional imperatives by the states whose militaries needed to be reformed.

Uzbekistan, Kazakhstan, and Kyrgyzstan were all active members of NATO's Partnership for Peace and participated in regional cooperation exercises with the United States annually. The United States initially planned to form a single regional peacemaking force, Centrasbat, to be dispatched in some distant future in the event of ethnic conflict. But in the U.S.-led training exercises held in the region in 1997 and 1998, the various Central Asian militaries competed against each other to such an extent that following these exercises U.S. assistance to the Central Asian states became more bilateral in focus. But this contributed only marginally to better coordination of U.S. military assistance and did nothing to better rationalize the assistance being offered by other NATO states.

Uzbekistan was emerging as the most important U.S. security partner in the region, though still not a major one. Nonetheless, U.S. policy makers realized that they might need to call on Tashkent for strategic support, especially given the now recognized security threat posed by Al Qaeda camps in Afghanistan. In May 1999, the U.S. Department of Defense and Uzbekistan's Defense Ministry signed two different cooperative agreements. The U.S. officials stated that they had no interest in gaining basing rights.[56] But in 2000, the United States made use of the provisions of these treaties to deploy unmanned Predator drones equipped with missiles into Afghanistan to try to kill Osama bin Laden.[57] In addition, U.S. Special Forces conducted a training mission in Uzbekistan, and in August 2001, a small group of U.S. Special Forces was also sent into Tajikistan as part of an anti-Taliban operation.[58] Washington was already looking to the Central Asian states to help it close serious security gaps, but the scale of U.S. military engagement in the region was designed to begin a long-term reform process and only make marginal contributions to improving the current security environment of these states.

Near Neighbors and Big Hopes

While geography is a constant, history defines and redefines how we understand geopolitical divisions. Many of Central Asia's nearest neighbors saw the collapse of the Soviet Union as an opportunity to regain historic advantage and expand their geopolitical reach through exerting disproportionate influence on these five newly independent states. But most exaggerated how much benefit their influence would bring, and underestimated the reluctance of Central Asia's leaders to have their foreign policies shaped by external forces.

Turkey: Hoping to Play a Guiding Role

Turkey and Iran both viewed the creation of independent states in Central Asia as offering them enormous opportunities for expanding their geopolitical influence. Ankara and Tehran saw little downside to granting independence to the Central Asian states. Leaders of both countries were eager to use arguments of historical and cultural affinity to advance their economic and geopolitical interests.

The Turks fared much better in this than the Iranians, becoming a more important economic partner for these states. This was partly due to strong U.S. support of their efforts, combined with Washington's assiduous efforts to isolate Tehran. Turkey also had the stronger economy, and Turkish businessmen were eager to invest in projects in Central Asia. They were also not as daunted by corruption as many of their U.S. and European counterparts and in particular sought a foothold in the region's construction industry, food processing, and textiles.

Turkey's president Turgut Ozal (1989–1993) was an especially strong supporter of partnering with the newly independent Turkic states (Azerbaijan, Kazakhstan, Kyrgyzstan, Turkmenistan, and Uzbekistan) and gathered the leaders of these states for a series of summit meetings, which he hoped would lead to a more formal organization. The first such meeting was held in Ankara in 1992, and Ozal also made a well-publicized trip to the region in 1993. After Ozal's death, President Suleiman Demirel continued the initiative, holding summits in 1994, 1995, and 1996 and traveling to the region in 1996. His successor, Ahmet Necdet Sezer, held a summit for the Turkic presidents in 2001. The Central Asian leaders also frequently visited Istanbul and Ankara, and several were rumored to use the intermediary services of Turkish businessmen to help them develop their personal fortunes. These ties were especially important for the Turkmen president, who used Ahmed Calik, head of Calik Holdings, to market substantial amounts of Turkmen fine cotton and other commodities. There are also rumors of the Karimov family using connections in Turkey as well, as apparently did Nazarbayev in the period immediately following independence.

The Turks, who never ruled in Central Asia, still see themselves as natural leaders in the region. The Turkish government and private benefactors in Turkey offered scholarships to tens of thousands of students from the region.[59] Turkish educators offered technical and financial support for replacing the Cyrillic alphabet with the Latin one that is used in Turkey, and Turkish media made television programs available at preferential rates.[60] U.S. policy makers approved of and occasionally helped fund these efforts, which were seen as diminishing the role of Russia and thus strengthening the independence of these states.

Nonetheless, as the 1990s advanced, the Central Asian leaders understood the limitations to Turkey's international influence. While all were eager to keep Turkey as an important partner of their respective states, they were not willing to grant the Turks a role as mediator. Most believed that one big brother had been enough.

Relations with Russia were a complicating factor for all concerned. Russian policy makers did not want to see the Central Asians trade Moscow for Ankara (or worse yet, for a partnership with Ankara and Washington) and put considerable pressure on the region's leaders to keep a balanced policy toward Turkey—a policy in which relationships with Ankara were not at the exclusion of older and more traditional friendships. The Russians also put considerable pressure on the Turks to keep their proper place, pressure that Ankara could not ignore because the turnover of trade between Turkey and Russia was larger than between Turkey and all the Central Asian states combined.

Iran: Geopolitical Ambitions But Little Success

Central Asia's leaders were committed to making up their own minds about whom to be friends with and whom to shun and were unwilling to give either Moscow or Washington veto power on these issues. All five Central Asian states established diplomatic relations with Tehran, but Iran has faced an uphill battle in obtaining what it sees as its natural geopolitical role in Central Asia. For the last several hundred years, the Turks have generally overshadowed the Persians, and the ideological nature of the Iranian regime further disadvantaged Tehran in its dealing with Central Asia's secular elite.

The Iranian leadership has consistently maintained that its interests in the region are those of a traditional nation-state. They have sent ambassadors to the region with secular backgrounds who have emphasized the commercial aspects of their diplomatic missions. Iranian officials have by and large managed to convince the Central Asian leaders that Iran's Islamic revolution poses no direct threat to them. Kazakhstan and Turkmenistan have not been willing to endorse Washington's oil and gas pipeline strategy that bypasses Iran. Turkmenistan is shipping gas through Iran and would like to be able to obtain international financing to ship even more gas along that route, while President Nazarbayev regularly reaffirms Kazakhstan's interest in eventually shipping part of its offshore oil to market through a new pipeline that linked these fields with Iran.

Only Uzbekistan's Islam Karimov continues to remain suspicious of the motivations of Tehran's rulers. From the Uzbek perspective, Iran, unlike Turkey, has the capacity to upset the power balance in the region in a number of negative ways: by serving as a champion of religious values, by favoring the interest of Tajiks, with whom they share a cultural heritage, over Uzbeks, and by generally overshadowing Uzbekistan, a country with whom they are practically neighbors. Although Karimov has kept his country's relationship with Iran more formal than friendly, Tehran is an important trading partner for Tashkent, buying up cotton that does not go to Russia.

There is little religious affinity between Shia Iran and Sunni-dominated Central Asia. None of the Central Asian nations have Shia Muslim populations, with the exception of Tajikistan's minority Ismaili population, who live in the isolated Badakhshan region and are not recognized as true Muslims by the Shia Twelvers of Iran.[61] Tajikistan's ruling elite was suspicious of the Iranian actions during the civil war, because of the close ties to Tehran of several in the leadership of the Islamic Renaissance Party. Many of these concerns faded after the Iranians used these relationships to help negotiate Tajikistan's national reconciliation agreement.

Since the mid-1990s the Iranians have enjoyed a close relationship with the government of Tajikistan, whose population speaks an Iranian dialect that is very closely related to the Persian spoken in Iran. The government in Tehran has served as a source of cultural and educational materials, especially for the revamped Tajik education system, which is shifting from writing Tajik in Cyrillic to Arabic characters.[62]

Turkmenistan is the only Central Asian state to share a border with Iran, and its dependence on transit through Iran has helped foster close ties between Ashgabat and Tehran. But economic relations between these two states are not as close as either side had hoped, because U.S. sanctions against Iran thwarted a planned Turkmen–Iranian–Turkish pipeline to market Turkmen gas. Iran's inability to obtain international financing for a proposed $2.5 billion pipeline that would carry 30 billion cubic meters meant that the Turkmen had to settle for a $190 million pipeline that ran from Korpedzhe to Kurt-Kui and had an initial capacity of 4 billion cubic meters. This pipeline was completed in December 1997 and now carries over 6 billion cubic meters per year.[63] Because the Iranians have the least valuable sector of the Caspian, their only real hope of receiving substantial new income from Caspian oil and gas would be from its transit. In general, Iran's initial high hopes of benefiting from improved transport and communication routes through Central Asia were not realized.

India and Pakistan: Biding Their Time

India and Pakistan also welcomed the independence of these states. The Central Asian states sought close diplomatic relations with both these states, but they looked to India with particular interest. All of Central Asia's leaders are aware of the economic and geopolitical power that New Delhi would come to exercise as its economy continues to grow, and so visits to the region by senior Indian political figures have been treated as occasions of particular note.[64]

India was a high-profile state in the region well before independence because of its long-standing special relationship with the Soviet Union. Tashkent was an Aeroflot hub, and India even had a diplomatic presence in the region, giving them a real leg up had they wanted to take advantage of it. But from the point of the Indians, the Central Asian market is still small, and the difficulties of working in it are magnified by the transport and political problems associated with moving goods across Afghanistan and Pakistan, respectively. The Indians had virtually no control over the former, and easy access to Central Asia's markets was of such marginal importance as to almost be disregarded in the Indian calculations concerning their relationship with Pakistan.

By contrast, Pakistani leaders initially viewed trade with the Central Asian states as a partial solution for their own serious economic problems. They had vain hopes that the revitalized Economic Cooperation Organization (ECO) could serve as an effective instrument for creating multilateral projects encouraging economic ties. This was a goal that they shared with the government in Tehran, where ECO was headquartered.[65]

Many in Islamabad also hoped that the promise of new transit routes across Afghanistan could become an effective incentive for all parties in Afghanistan to come up with a workable power-sharing formula. Quite obviously, even more powerful interests in Pakistan were at work pushing for a Taliban victory, which they saw as opening the same commercial prospects and having desirable domestic consequences. More moderate Pakistanis saw India as the market at the end of these new commercial routes, which would be unobtainable if Pakistani Islamists pressed successfully for a Taliban victory, and so sought to use these commercial opportunities as an incentive to dissuade fellow Pakistanis from pursuing such extremist politics. Although there were a few optimistic peaks in Indian–Pakistani relations in the 1990s, the goal of opening trade between the two countries remained an elusive one.

As was true of the Indians, Pakistani entrepreneurs found doing business in Central Asia more difficult than anticipated, and both Indians and Pakistanis found it difficult to apply lessons learned at home to the Soviet-style economies that were being transformed in these countries.

The Middle East: Disappointing Co-religionists

At the time of independence, there was considerable expectation that the leading Islamic states, especially the Arab states, would play a large role in Central Asia. Their role too has proved to be much smaller than many expected, although all five Central Asian states eventually joined the Organization of the Islamic Conference (OIC).[66] The Caspian market simply proved too small and unattractive for most businessmen in the wealthier Muslim states. The economies in these countries have been generally less vigorous than local economists had forecast, which reduced the amount of investment capital available to mid-size entrepreneurs. Those with large amounts of capital to export have generally had far more attractive opportunities than investments in Central Asia. Small- and medium-sized entrepreneurs from the Gulf states, in particular, have gotten involved in the region, and trade originating in and through the United Arab Emirates has played an important role in helping Central Asian entrepreneurs to acquire capital.

Ties with the Arab world have also had a strong imprint on the religious life of the Central Asian states, although much less so than Saudi Arabian philanthropic organizations, in particular, would have liked. Much of the money for building hundreds of large mosques and religious schools in Central Asia has come from abroad, mostly from the Arab world, but also from religious groups in Turkey. At first, virtually all such contributions were welcomed by Central Asia's rulers, but with time, and particularly from 1999 on, they became concerned with regularizing the influence of foreign Islamic missionaries and restricting their activities exclusively to official channels, which would allow the respective Central Asian governments to better control the money spent for religious purposes.

The presidents of all five Central Asian countries accept that they are ruling over large communities of Muslim believers, and each realizes that he must try to make himself credible to believers. All have traveled widely in the Arab world, and Kazakhstan's Nazarbayev and Tajikistan's Rakhmonov have traveled to Saudi Arabia, generally fulfilling some of the rites of pilgrimage during their visits.[67] The annual pilgrimage to Mecca is observed with official involvement in all the Central Asian countries, and the privilege of organizing pilgrimage tours is a major source of income for clerics who enjoy their regime's favor.

At the same time, in contradictory fashion, one Middle Eastern state has begun to play a much larger role than was initially expected. Despite the fact that some of their Arab supporters disapprove, the leaders of Kazakhstan, Turkmenistan, Uzbekistan, and Kyrgyzstan have all traveled to Israel, in part to court potential investors.[68] As the home of tens of thousands of Jews who left Central Asia beginning in the 1970s, Israel has become a major source of capital in a number of these countries. For example, Israel's Merhav Corporation has invested more than $1.3 billion in Turkmenistan's economy, mainly in the energy sector.[69] In Kazakhstan, Aleksandr Mashkevich and his Eurasia Group are prominent in the country's mineral sector, and Mashkevich's organization of the Jewish Congress of Kazakhstan has played an important bridging role between Kazakhstan and the American Jewish community.[70]

Unlike their occasional opposition to the opening of new mosques, the region's rulers have supported the opening of synagogues and Jewish cultural centers, because the region's Jewish population is law abiding, small in number, steadily diminishing, and therefore poses no threat. Moreover, the relationships being forged with Israel also often serve Russian interests in the area, as some of the investors from Israel are deeply involved in the Russian economy as well. The good relationship between most Central Asian leaders and the Israeli government, however, has done little to slow the pace of Russian Jewish outmigration from the region.

Cautious Probes by European and Asian Friends

Despite high levels of interest and close proximity, Turkey, Iran, Pakistan, and even the countries of the Middle East were never as influential in Central Asia as were Western Europe, Japan, and Korea. Only entrepreneurs from the latter groups of states had the capital and technical expertise necessary to turn the Central Asian economies around. Although none of the highly industrialized countries placed real priority on Central Asia, they nonetheless began to collectively dominate the economies of these states. Most of their influence has come through the operation of the various international financial institutions they support: the World Bank, the IMF, the EBRD, and the Asian Development Bank (ADB).[71] National foreign assistance programs have also been very important, offering loans, grants-in-aid, and lines of credit to the five Central Asian states. In the case of the neediest of these states, Kyrgyzstan and Tajikistan, international donor groups have been formed to coordinate this assistance.

The Japanese have played a major role in Kyrgyzstan and have been a principal international donor for its reconstruction program. Japan (directly and through the ADB) has played a large role in the modernization of Kyrgyzstan's transportation sector. The Japanese sometimes say that their interest in Kyrgyzstan and Kazakhstan comes from the physical resemblance between Kazakhs and Kyrgyz and the Japanese, but the strategic resources that these states have are even more important. The Japanese joke is that they were aiding the Kyrgyz because they felt an ethnic affinity because some of the communities that form part of the Japanese people are said to have initially come from the same part of the Siberian landmass as the early Kyrgyz. Japanese enthusiasm for the Kyrgyz waned, however, after a group of Japanese geologists were taken hostage in the mountains of Kyrgyzstan during summer 1999, and the Japanese government was rumored to have paid several million dollars to obtain their release.[72] This led to a brief Japanese withdrawal from the assistance business in Kyrgyzstan, but they were back as a major donor by 2001.

The South Korean government and Korean investors took a keen interest in Central Asia because of the ethnic Koreans who live in the region. Korean industrialists have made use of local Koreans as intermediaries and by doing so have improved their relative status throughout Central Asia.

The most important Korean investment in the region is that of Daewoo, which invested a total of $1.4 billion in making automobiles in Uzbekistan for sale throughout the region. The Daewoo factory depends on components made in neighboring states, so these cars have preferential tariff status in most Central Asian countries as products of joint ventures. After a relatively strong start, the project ran into difficulties—some the result of Daewoo's own diminished position following the Asian meltdown of 1998, and others caused by toughening terms of trade relating to the project introduced by the Uzbeks in 2000.

For their part, the Central Asians are very pleased by the interest shown in their countries by Japan and Korea, in particular, as well as the smaller scale involvement of firms from Singapore, Malaysia, and Indonesia. Such activities help cement the idea—most forcefully argued by Kazakhstan's President Nursultan Nazarbayev—that this region is the future bridge between Europe and Asia.

Particularly in the early years of independence, Germany played a very active role in Kazakhstan and Kyrgyzstan, because of the presence of a large ethnic German population, who had been deported from the Volga region (where they had lived for nearly 200 years) at the start of World War II. According to German law, this population was eligible for repatriation to Germany.[73] After German reunification, it became increasingly difficult financially for German authorities to continue to absorb the cost of repatriating ethnic Germans from the former Soviet Union, and so they began targeting investments that would simultaneously create employment opportunities for this population and improve the local economy more generally, in the hopes that this would encourage the Germans to stay. However, these investments did little or nothing to slow the departure of the region's German population.

One important collective effort of both the Europeans and the Asians has been to support improving transportation links through the region that bypass Russia. The EBRD is an important source of funding for Traceca, the new Europe–Caucasus–Asia transport corridor project, which envisions a new system of trade routes from Europe, across the Black Sea through the Caucasus and Caspian Sea to Central Asia. Slow but steady progress is being made on the project, which consists of building new connections and improving existing transport links. When this is completed, transit time from China to Europe will be cut by several days. The main driving force for Traceca is the European desire to take advantage of the growing Chinese market and to serve the developing market in the Ukraine and the Caspian states, allowing European goods to substitute for Russian ones. The slow pace of this project allows the Europeans to stage their investment according to how market conditions develop and to keep the project on a back burner if market recovery slows and conditions of turmoil develop. Europe already is an important trade partner for the Caspian states, but the volume of trade is quite small by European standards. Similarly, the ADB is also investing in transportation improvements in the region.[74]

In the end, however, oil and gas (and to a lesser extent other mineral deposits) stimulate much of the European and Asian interest in the region. BP has been a major investor in Azerbaijan and initially had a major stake in Kazakhstan. British Gas was a partner in Kashagan, Kazakhstan's largest gas field, from 1997 when the production-sharing agreement for the site was signed, until April 2005, when it sold its stake to the Agip KCO consortium, the site operator. Both France's TotalFinaElf and Italy's Agip (which was incorporated in Italian state energy firm ENI, adopting the ENI name in June 2004) have large stakes in Kazakhstan; Agip/ENI was named operator for the Kashagan field in 2001. The Chinese state oil firms have considerable holdings in Kazakhstan and are pushing forward with plans to pipe Caspian oil eastward across Kazakhstan to their refineries. The Japanese, via Inpex, a stakeholder in Kashagan, are also engaged.[75] Western firms like the U.S.-based Newmont Mining have been involved in exploiting Uzbek gold, namely from the Muruntau mine, the world's largest open pit gold mine. Both British and French banks are agents for the sale of that country's considerable annual gold output.[76]

The Central Asian states have tried to parlay their economic ties to Europe into membership in a variety of European and Asian institutions. All are members of the OSCE. Kazakhs are also engaged with the European Parliament, which like the OSCE has been quite critical of political developments in Kazakhstan. In fact, the OSCE has condemned a whole host of political developments throughout the region, rarely with much consequence. Although the Europeans often pay lip service to the importance of democracy building in this region, commercial politics drives their behavior even more forcefully than Americans'.

The British feted Kazakhstan's Nursultan Nazarbayev, and in November 2000, Queen Elizabeth II awarded him the Order of the Knight of the Grand Cross of St. Michael and St. George at the very time that the international press was filled with accounts of the offshore holdings of the Nazarbayev family and the U.S. Department of Justice was investigating allegations of wrongdoing by American oil companies engaged in Kazakhstan.

In a decade of independence, Central Asia's rulers traveled much of the world, toured European and Asian capitals, and accumulated honorary degrees, awards, and prizes. But despite these travels, by September 11 none had managed to carve out a set of enduring alliances or a role for himself or his nation that had more than a tentative quality. Perhaps most or even all of these men were satisfied with what they and their various foreign ministers had managed to achieve, for despite the potential impermanence of their new international positions, to enormously varying degrees, each had become a global actor, something that was beyond his wildest expectations in December 1991.

4

Meeting Social and Economic Burdens

Most of the bleakest predictions involving the future of the Central Asian states assumed that these governments would be unable to meet the social burdens posed by their populations, causing public dissatisfaction that would undermine political stability. This chapter examines the social and economic challenges that these countries face, the risks that the challenges pose, and whether developments subsequent to September 11, 2001, have reduced those challenges.

From the late 1990s observers of the region began warning that growing unemployment, increasing poverty, and fraying health-care and education systems (especially in densely populated rural areas) were making most of the Central Asian region vulnerable to ethnic conflicts, the spread of radical ideologies, and general social upheaval.[1] Prior to September 2001, the international development community placed no priority on responding to these mounting problems. Money was generally available to study the problems in this region, but the amount of assistance money available to help these states respond to these challenges was generally declining. As already noted, the one exception was in the area of security, where U.S. and other NATO funding was increasing.

Few donors, however, seemed inclined to substantially increase assistance in the area of political and economic institution building. Few outside observers saw much evidence to suggest that the governments in the region would substantially alter their policies, and most saw substantial increases in allocations as "throwing more good money after bad." Nor was there any particular sense of alarm about this. Western aid circles showed no interest in examining the assumptions that underlay the allocation and distribution of foreign assistance to try to better effect outcomes in this regime.

In fact, there was initially a great deal of pessimism about the economic prospects of the Central Asian states and real uncertainty as to what kinds of developmental strategies were appropriate for them. Despite their relatively well-educated populations, the heavily resource-based nature of their economies led many to view these republics as underdeveloped, mirroring the Russians' view of the "backwardness" of Central Asia. But fears that these states would fail in their transitions to market economies began to be replaced with far more optimistic projections when several states reached out for international expertise. Kyrgyzstan's leaders agreed to turn their country into a virtual guinea pig of reform, while Kazakhstan seemed set on an ambitious privatization program. Even Uzbekistan appeared to be seriously flirting with measures that, if pursued, would free up its economy.

But within a few years, pessimism again slowly set in, as states like Uzbekistan and Turkmenistan rejected all meaningful international direction and the distortions of Tajikistan's economy remained almost unmediated despite considerable international engagement. Even in Kazakhstan and Kyrgyzstan, considered relative success stories, the lack of transparency was fueling a disproportionate shift in assets to the ruling families and their closest supporters, setting limits on further reform.

Although many regional experts were preaching doom and gloom about what might lie ahead, most developmental economists were not panicking about the situation in the region, not because things were going so well, but because they were not going as poorly as in other places, such as many parts of Africa.[2] To be sure, the percentage of the population generally accepted as living in poverty had increased, but there were no reports of famine anywhere in Central Asia. However idiosyncratic the state-building strategies of some of these states may have been, none seemed about to implode from within. And although tensions along selective borders were increasing, increased technical assistance targeted for border security seemed likely to diminish the prospect of interstate conflict.

Given this scenario, prior to September 11, Western policy makers may not have liked the decision-making frameworks with which the leaders in the Central Asian states seemed most comfortable—a universally high tolerance for corruption accompanied in some cases by a tortoise-like pace of reform. Yet the aid and assistance industry did little more than merely criticize the way that the Central Asian regimes were implementing the internationally sponsored reform programs was not possible.

Some Western specialists even began echoing of the arguments of Central Asia's leaders: These countries were not really ready for economic and certainly not political reform, given their long experience under the Russian and Soviet colonial yoke.[3] These versions of the past were no less simplistic than the earlier sociological and historical renderings of Soviet scholars, long mocked by the very Western analysts who were now content to hide behind their own historical claptrap.

Evidence that got in the way was conveniently forgotten, such as the fact that Kazakhstan and Kyrgyzstan were outperforming Russia in many macroeconomic indicators. Kyrgyzstan was the first post-Soviet state to engage in financial restructuring, and Kazakhstan had the strongest banking sector in the Soviet successor states. Both countries had introduced private ownership of land, albeit with some restrictions, and both had reorganized pension systems, health-care systems, and education systems to make them financially self-sustaining. But making them self-sustaining was not synonymous with maintaining the same standards of living that those who are dependent upon the social service sector for their survival had enjoyed during the Soviet era.

Despite their areas of economic accomplishment, however, Western observers frequently were unwilling to hold any of the Central Asian nations to the standards that were applied to the countries of Central Europe. The former were allowed to hide behind a curtain of Asianness and excuse failures through their lack of a history of prior statehood. After September 11, the international community began to revisit some of their earlier assumptions about Central Asia, questioning whether their passivity in the face of faltering economic and political reform strategies was creating previously uncalculated security risks.

This reevaluation has not produced any particularly dramatic results. Some additional assistance money has been made available to states that demonstrate their reform-mindedness, but no untoward pressure has been applied to states that do not seek to comply with recommended guidelines. Although the international financial community is much more concerned with the problem of debt relief in this region than it was a few years ago, the earlier models of reform have not been subject to any thorough reexamination.

While foreign policy makers may not feel that conditions in Central Asia warrant their immediate attention, Central Asia's citizens find little consolation in knowing that things will have to get a lot worse before the outside world devotes focused attention to trying to make them better.

Uzbekistan, Kyrgyzstan, and Tajikistan all meet many of the World Bank's criteria for low-income countries under stress. Although Turkmenistan's government reports average wages and per capita gross domestic product (GDP) that are high enough keep them off the list of troubled states, these official statistics are highly dubious. Oil- and gas-rich Kazakhstan is the only potential success story in the region, but even it is underperforming, a point reinforced in a 2002 World Bank study on the impact of systemic corruption on the Kazakh economy.[4]

Who is to blame for the disappointing performance of many of these states? Is it the leaders who failed to follow the advice of the international community, and either rejected the macroeconomic stabilization programs proposed to them or failed to implement them in a conscientious enough fashion, closing a blind eye to the corruption that surrounded them? Or is it the fault of the international financial and assistance community who dashed into a region they knew little about with many preformed assumptions about how best to move these societies from point A to what the outside world saw as the desired point B? The following chapter details how economic policy has been implemented in these states since 2001.

Is Kazakhstan an Economic Success?

Kazakhstan should have the brightest future in Central Asia, because of its vast natural resources and human potential and because it has gotten right some of the economic decisions made over the past decade.

Kazakhstan has experienced one of the most rapid recoveries from the economic collapse caused by the demise of the USSR. Although its GDP had not yet recovered to pre-1990 levels, Kazakhstan had begun to experience steady growth by 2004, and its average per capita income rose to $1,780 in 2003, making it second only to Russia in the Commonwealth of Independent States (CIS).[5] Kazakhstan fared far better than Russia in 1998 and was able to contain fairly successfully the impact of the Russian and Asian financial crises that occurred that year. In recent years, the value of the local currency has held relatively stable, and the Kazakh tenge has effectively been a freely convertible currency.[6] Kazakhstan has a strong national bank and internationally rated private banks, led by Kazkommertsbank, which has entered the list of the world's top 1,000 banks.[7] All banks have to adopt international banking standards, including the risk-weighted 8 percent capital-adequacy ratio set by the Bank for International Settlements. The scheme has cut the number of banks from 130 in 1995 to 35 in 2004, of which 16 are in a National Bank of Kazakhstan-sponsored deposit insurance scheme.[8] Public savings amounted to 9.0 percent of GDP by final use in 2003.[9]

The country has a functional stock exchange, whose regulations are modeled after those of the U.S. Federal Exchange Commission, but which suffers from a paucity of blue chip stocks being traded.[10] The stock exchange is held back by modifications in the government's timetable for privatization of the country's largest and potentially most profitable state-owned enterprises. The Kazakh government is also reconsidering its earlier decision that all state assets should be eventually turned over to private ownership and is contemplating whether some of the oil and gas reserves in particular should remain in permanent public trust.

Privatization of small and medium-sized enterprises is virtually complete, but the process by which this occurred was semitransparent at best. Currently, the private sector employs approximately 50 percent of the population. Agriculture remains a mainstay for over 40 percent of the population in rural areas. Although agriculture provides employment for 35 percent of the total population, it accounts for only 7.7 percent of Kazakhstan's GDP.[11] Private ownership of agricultural land was introduced in Kazakhstan in June 2003 over the objections of most of the Kazakh population, who view it as violating the traditions of their former nomadic culture. The land law, which contains many caveats as to who can own land and how much they can own, sank the political career of Prime Minister Imangaliy Tasmagambetov, who was dismissed after a parliamentary vote of no confidence on this question.[12] The performance of the agricultural sector has improved in the last few years but still requires substantial investment, especially if independent farming is to survive. Right now the biggest beneficiaries of the new land law are successful industrial entrepreneurs who are buying up land to engage in agribusiness.

The Kazakhs reformed their tax structure and increased its tax collection rates. They reduced value-added tax (VAT) and mandatory social service payments to a manageable 15 percent and 7–20 percent range, respectively, as a result of reforms introduced in 2003.[13] At the same time, there is also growing concern that further reforms to the tax system could leave foreign investors vulnerable to having existing contracts renegotiated and their total tax burdens increased.

The Kazakhs reorganized the pension system, introducing new state and private pension plans, and are in the process of reforming the old state-funded health-care and education systems to put them on sounder financial footing.[14] These changes, combined with the unexpectedly high prices of oil, have led Kazakhstan to go from budget deficits to a small budget surplus in 2002, to a tiny deficit in 2003, and to projected small surpluses through 2006.[15]

Although currently considered a low-end, medium-income country, Kazakhstan has the capacity to develop a strong economy and already has the fastest growing GDP in the region, in both percentage and real terms.[16] Not all of this can be explained by high global oil prices and increased production. The country's real GDP growth in 2003 was 9.2 percent.[17] Although the energy sector made the largest contribution to the budget in 2002 (accounting for 33 percent of total revenues), it has not yet overwhelmed the other sectors of economy.[18]

Kazakhstan's Oil Sector

Most of Kazakhstan's hopes for the future rest with the development of its oil and gas assets. Kazakhstan currently produces just over 1 million barrels a day, but U.S. government projections expect the country to produce 8 million barrels a day by 2020.[19] Even recognizing that much could still happen to delay or even derail some of the plans for developing Kazakhstan's oil sector, the country is certain to be a significant oil producer in the second and third decades of the twenty-first century.

Kazakhstan anticipates a total investment of $52 billion in its oil and gas sector by 2015.[20] Initially the Kazakh government saw foreign investment as the sole way to fund the development of its oil reserves. But as Kazakh officials gained a greater realization of how the global oil industry operates, they demanded a larger share of the ownership of assets, in existing as well as in new projects, and pressed investors for a greater role in determining the speed and conditions of asset development.

The Kazakh government issued new guidelines in a state program for development of the Kazakh sector of the Caspian Sea. The new regulations for the sale of licenses for the development of untapped onshore and offshore reserves now stipulate a requirement of 50 percent Kazakh ownership of the project, either in the form of partnership with a private Kazakh firm or with the Kazakh state oil company.[21] The government also increased pressure on consortium members in both the TengizChevroil and Kashagan projects to renegotiate loopholes and other terms of their contracts, at the very time when Kazakhstan's three largest projects are increasing or at least gearing up for production.

Starting in 2002 there has been a lot of talk by senior government officials about the need for rebalancing oil contracts. In one often-quoted address, Kazymzhomart Tokayev (who served alternatively as prime minister, state secretary, and minister of foreign affairs during this period) talked about how this was fair recompense for Kazakhstan's support of the United States in the war on terror. This comment created a furor and led President Nazarbayev to issue a series of statements in which he tried to reassure Kazakhstan's foreign investors that the terms of the existing contracts would not be renegotiated. However, the Kazakhs went so far as to demand the right to purchase a share in the consortium developing the Kashagan field, threatening changes in the legal system that would effectively force changes in the terms of the existing contract had the consortium developing the field continued to refuse them.

Although the Kazakhs seem to understand the subtleties of the shifting geopolitical sands, it is less clear that they understand the potential fragility of such leverage. Oil prices vary sharply from year to year, and oil from Kazakhstan's offshore deposits is technically challenging to extract and expensive to transport, given the distance to open seas. Companies that have already committed vast resources to projects in Kazakhstan will certainly show real staying power, even if the conditions of developing their assets become more difficult, but new capital must be attracted if the Kazakh government is going to reach its investment targets. Projects in Kazakhstan will compete with those in other countries where there may be higher projected returns on investment or easier working conditions. When Western oil firms were first drawn to Kazakhstan, it was nearly impossible for them to do business in Russia or begin new projects in Libya, Iraq, or Iran, all countries where the investment climate might improve substantially.

Many in Kazakh decision-making circles are willing to take these risks and trade a slower pace of development for increased Kazakh ownership. Delays are easier to tolerate when oil prices are high, and existing production yields good income streams. And Kazakh reformers, in particular, do not mind slowing the income stream until there is greater legal transparency in the Kazakh economy.

Despite their new toughness, the Kazakh officials maintain that the government has become more investor-friendly. They point to the fact that in February 2002, Kazakhstan's oil industry was reorganized when the state oil company, KazakhOil, was joined with the state oil transport company, Kaztransneftegaz. They defend this reorganization as a way to bring new professionalism to their activities. The new entity, KazMunayGaz, has also become an advocate for greater Kazakh ownership, seeking to retain their holdings while keeping supervisory responsibility for the investments in which they partner.

Lazzat Kiinov, an oilman who had served as the governor of Mangistau oblast, or region, was named KazMunayGaz's first president, and Nazarbayev's son-in-law Timur Kulibayev (formerly of Kaztransneftegaz) was given the number two post in the organization. [22] There was a further reorganization in 2003, when Kiinov was replaced by Uzakpai Karabalin, a change that seemed to further enhance the power of Timur Kulibayev in particular, and the role of the Nazarbayev family in the oil industry more generally.[23] Some supervision of KazMunayGaz is exercised by the Energy and Natural Resources ministry, which is headed by an atomic energy specialist, Vladimir Shkolnik, who serves as a spokesman for the industry, defending the decisions that are made in KazMunayGaz and in the office of the president.

On the positive side, the Kazakhs can point to improvements in the transport situation. Kazakhstan inaugurated the Caspian Pipeline Consortium (CPC) pipeline in late 2001, and the "quality bank" required to maximize Tengiz profits became operational in mid-2002. The first quality bank to be created in the CIS, it provides compensation to the Kazakhs for the differential value of their crude oil, which is higher than the value of the crude mix that goes through the Russian-controlled pipeline.

Opening the CPC decreased export costs of Tengiz oil by roughly 50 percent and created unused capacity for Russia's Transneft, prompting Transneft to offer Kazakhstan an increase in its annual export quota. Construction of the Baku–Tbilisi–Ceyhan (BTC) pipeline began in 2003 and is set to be completed in 2005.[24] The BTC would allow the Kazakhs to transport up to an additional 20 million tons of oil per year by tanker across the Caspian to Baku. The Azerbaijan government has been lobbying the Kazakhs to take an equity interest in the project, but to date the Kazakhs have resisted.

The improvements in prospects for the transport of Kazakh oil have further emboldened the Kazakh government. The $3 billion second stage of the

TengizChevroil project, which is designed to raise production to 440,000 barrels per day, was supposed to begin just after the CPC pipeline became fully operational. The second stage of the Tengiz project was delayed until late 2003 because of a dispute between the government of Kazakhstan and the major consortium partners over the accelerated depreciation schedule and the financing of the investment program. A settlement, which was reached in stages, slows the pace of development in favor of producing more tax income for the Kazakh government, which in turn has committed to a more aggressive government reinvestment program in the project.[25] The threatening tactics used by the Kazakh government, which included allegations of tax code and environmental violations by Tengiz consortium members, served as a warning of the new toughness with which Western investors would be treated.

This toughness was also applied to companies in the Agip KCO consortium that is developing the Kashagan field. Unlike Tengiz, where the Kazakhs have a 20 percent share in the consortium, the Kazakh government sold its one-seventh share for $500 million in the fall of 1998 to cushion the Kazakh budget from the aftershocks of Russia's financial meltdown. Many members of the elite were quite critical of this decision, arguing that government was selling its assets to foreigners too cheaply. As Kazakhstan's income from the project is to come exclusively from royalties and tax payments, this makes the timetable of production critically important to them. The project was originally slated to begin production in 2005, but the commercial development plan submitted by the Agip KCO consortium to the Kazakh government in 2003 called for production to start in 2006, with the first large flows of oil slated for 2008-2009.

This timetable was also seen as unrealistic by the consortium members, who reached an agreement with the Kazakh government on a new production schedule in 2004; the Kazakh government was to receive $150 million in compensation for accepting a delay in the start of production until 2008.[26] Initial output is to be 75,000 barrels per day, ramping up to 450,000 barrels per day.[27] But having resolved the timetable issue to mutual benefit, the Kazakh government put the consortium on notice in June 2004 that it was interested in purchasing British Gas's 16.7-percent stake in the Kashagan project, which had become available the previous year. The government also made clear that it would not be deterred by the consortium agreement, which gave project partners first rights to available stakes, an option that the Agip KCO members had publicly announced their intention to exercise. As background noise, a group of legislators threatened that parliament would reexamine the entire consortium agreement because of constitutional provisions governing government control of subsoil rights, which they said the agreement could be considered as having violated. A compromise was reached in early 2005, where the Kazakh government would purchase an 8.33 percent share for approximately $700 million.[28]

Some of the increased assertiveness of the Kazakh government is part of an inevitable learning curve that occurs in newly independent states. In the early 1990s Kazakh officials understood little about how the international oil industry worked and what kind of bargaining position the size of their assets could gain them. The Kazakhs now view their economic potential in new ways and are beginning to realize that nonrenewable resources have to be treated with respect, precisely because they cannot be replaced.

The Kazakhs are also becoming more cognizant of the value of their gas reserves; the oil in the Caspian shelf has considerable amounts of gas that can be developed as the oil assets are retrieved. Some of the gas must be reinjected into the oil deposits to maximize oil production, but excess gas either has to be flared (which has ecological consequences for offshore deposits) or captured, and this captured gas can be marketed. The Kazakh government now estimates that Kazakh gas production could rise to 20.5 billion cubic meters per year in 2005 (up from 13.14 in 2002), to 35 billion cubic meters in 2010, and even to 70 billion cubic meters by 2015, depending on how much of the Kashagan gas must be reinjected.

In addition, Kazakhstan has some giant fields, which are primarily gas producers. The largest of these—the Karachaganak gas and gas condensate field in the northwest corner of Kazakhstan—is also completing its second phase of development, which has led to the doubling of condensate output.[29] The Karachaganak Integrated Organization has already invested $4 billion in the development of the deposit, and investments are now expected to reach $16 billion over the next forty years, a considerable increase over original figures.[30] In July 2003, the Karachaganak oil field, owned by the same consortium, also began shipping its first oil along the CPC pipeline through a newly constructed 600-kilometer linkup.

Some of Kazakhstan's hopes in the gas sector rest with its improved relationships with the gas industry of Russia. Some Western energy observers argue that the Kazakhs have given too great a role to the Russian state monopoly Gazprom in transporting and marketing their gas, which will be done through KazRosGaz, an equal-share joint venture between Gazprom and KazMunayGaz. KazRosGaz plans a sales volume of approximately 5 billion cubic meters by 2004.[31] By agreeing to these terms the Russians have agreed that Kazakh gas will be sold in the European market (a concession that the Turkmen have failed to gain), albeit at a discounted purchase price.[32] It also guarantees the Kazakhs some market access at the expense of competing Central Asian producers. The Kazakhs also hope this will lead to greater cooperation with Russia on the processing and marketing of gas from the giant Karachaganak field.

Managing Windfall Profits

The oil and gas industry has soaked up over 80 percent of the investment dollars coming into Kazakhstan since 1999, making the successful management of energy income the government's number one economic challenge.[33]

A National Fund was created in 2000 to shelter income from taxes earned through the sale of the country's oil, gas, and other mineral resources.[34] The fund is intended to help protect Kazakhstan from fluctuations in the price of oil, gas, and other raw materials it exports. The income from the investment is intended to be used to bolster the budget, including social service expenditures and support for the country's economic policy.

The creation of the National Fund is a small step toward transparency. Its focus is limited, restricted to the management of tax generated from the sale of resources. Fund managers have no say in the conditions governing the production or sale of oil, which remains largely in the hands of the president and his family, although, as noted, formal authority is divided between various state agencies, including most prominently the ministry of energy and natural resources and KazMunayGaz.

The management of the oil industry still provides many potential points for siphoning off income. The Kazakh state oil company is subject to limited outside scrutiny, so they are able to write off very high management and reinvestment costs with little consequence. This is also true of other state enterprises managing natural resources, not only in Kazakhstan, but in Kyrgyzstan and Turkmenistan as well. The selling and reselling of oil, both for transport, and to "customers" who are little more than intermediary purchase points, are both forms of transfer pricing and create opportunities for those with ready access to Kazakhstan's oil to profit from the difference between the local purchase price and the world market price of oil. For example, in 2002, Bermuda was Kazakhstan's second largest trade partner, accounting for 20 percent of the country's exports and virtually all of this trade was oil sent out for resale and reshipment.[35]

Rumors hold that some of the money from this goes to the offshore accounts of President Nazarbayev and his family, who have already been tied to a number of offshore companies in ongoing bribery and corruption investigations into Kazakhstan's oil industry.[36] Despite the fact that documents presented in a U.S. district court create a clear chain of transfer from U.S. oil companies to Nursultan Nazarbayev and former prime minister Nurlan Balgimbayev, the Kazakh government maintains that its president has never personally profited from the country's oil industry. After the Kazakh corruption scandal broke in New York City, the newly appointed prime minister, Imangaliy Tasmagambetov, admitted the existence of a $1 billion secret oil fund that had been deposited in Swiss banks in 1997.[37] Kazakh authorities maintain that much of this money went to pay off pension arrears and to support the national budget, and that the remaining $212.6 million has been returned to the country's new National Fund.[38]

It is interesting to speculate where the money that was returned to Kazakhstan actually came from, as most of the accounts referred to in the indictments handed down in the U.S. Southern District Court in New York City were frozen as part of the investigation. Tracking down the money from Kazakhstan's international oil transactions is probably an impossible task, given the number of offshore companies involved in the oil trade.

And whatever the truth of the president's own involvement, or that of the former prime minister, many unsanctioned individuals clearly profited from the large margin between the Kazakh internal and the world market prices. The government's periodic restriction on oil exports from Kazakhstan attest to the illicit flow being only partly regulated by the president and his family.

Although the National Fund is not intended to address any of these problems, it does capture some of the income from oil revenue. But the makeup of the National Fund, its relationship to the Kazakh government, and the decisions that the government made about the use of the fund's income (which is largely being invested abroad) have all generated criticism from the International Monetary Fund (IMF), as well as from a group of independent experts with the Open Society Institute's Caspian Revenue Watch.

The fund has been criticized within Kazakhstan as well, from those who hoped the Fund money would be directly invested in the country, either through funding specific development projects or by encouraging the development of Kazakh investment funds. Many complained that the government's decision to invest all of its money outside the country was as telling an indictment of Kazakh economic reform as was possible.

The choice to use foreign fund managers and invest abroad, however, does help insulate the fund from at least some degree of political interference. There is no question that there would be a vicious fight between various Kazakh interest groups if the National Fund were to invest in domestic projects. For example, the lingering power of local remnants of the Soviet military-industrial complex was demonstrated in the Kazakh government's industrial policy. Issued in 2003, it promised state investment in heavy industry, the very sector that most reform-minded economists in the country believe cannot operate profitably under market conditions.[39]

Need to Diversify the Economy

The government of Kazakhstan recognizes that it has to diversify the country's economy to provide long-term prosperity for its citizens and gain a place of importance in the international system. However, achieving this goal will be more difficult than offering pronouncements as to its worthiness. Like many other resource-rich states, Kazakhstan must resist the temptation to fund its state solely on economic rents and must instead invest these rents in projects designed to produce new sources of employment for the population, which will in turn generate new sources of taxation for the government. Kazakhstan has targeted several nonenergy-based sectors for investment, including machine building, light industry, furniture production, pharmaceuticals, and paper mills. But the government's long-term policy is vague despite the lengthy industrial strategy document issued in 2003 that was supposed to translate it into concrete and realizable goals.

A new law on foreign investment put forward in 2003 did little to boost investor confidence.[40] The law streamlined the investment process by reducing the number of bureaucratic agencies that a potential investor needed to go through and the number of special licenses that foreigners needed. But many Westerners fear provisions in the new law that seem to force foreign investors to seek adjudication of disputes in Kazakh courts rather than in international ones and feel that leveling the playing field will serve to increase the advantage of local Kazakh entrepreneurs, who are better able to navigate in the largely nontransparent environment of Kazakhstan. The country is only moving very slowly to increase transparency in economic transactions, and those branches of the economy that are closest to the remnants of the Soviet military-industrial complex remain the least transparent.

The question of how closely Kazakhstan should coordinate its economic policies with those of Russia remains a topic of debate for Kazakh economists and politicians. Economic cooperation between the two countries has been increasing over the past few years, sometimes for geopolitical reasons, a point discussed in chapter six, but much of the explanation is economic. Russian capital finds Kazakhstan an attractive investment site, both in heavy industry and light industry, so much so that the two countries are likely to enter the World Trade Organization (WTO) in tandem, even though tariffs between these two countries have yet to be fully harmonized.[41] In purely economic terms, Kazakhstan's economy is now sufficiently robust to keep from being overwhelmed by the larger Russian economy, and Russian capital may serve as a spur for the return and reinvestment of Kazakh offshore capital, without which the goals of economic diversification are unlikely to be achieved.

Outside of the area of oil and gas, Western firms often find it difficult to compete with Russian firms that have targeted particular sectors. This has been particularly true in nonferrous metallurgy and in the power sector. In ferrous metallurgy, India's Lakshmi Mittal has become the dominant force in Kazakhstan. Mittal's London-based Ispat International controls Kazakhstan's giant Karaganda steel works and has been so successful that in 2004 it reorganized as Mittal Steel and went on a global buying spree.[42]

Western companies seeking to develop Kazakhstan's power sector also experienced problems.[43] Cooperation with Russia and Russian firms has been of increasing importance in this sector, with Russia's state-run electricity firm RAO-UES playing an increasing role in harnessing Kazakhstan's resources to meet their global marketing strategy.

However, while these projects may be very good for their investors, in the end, Kazakh economic reform will only be judged a success if the country is freed from dependence on the export of natural resources as the primary source of its GDP.[44] Oil and gas income can only be expected to fund some of this diversification. The National Fund will supply some funds to be used in national development programs, but the period of windfall profits is still several years away, and unless the pace of democratic political institution building is dramatically increased, there will be no safeguards in place to ensure that this revenue is handled in a fully transparent fashion.

The challenge is not simply to create jobs. The Kazakh government predicts a shortage of some 100,000 workers by 2006, given the current age structure of the Kazakh population and the projected growth of the oil and gas sector. The government fears that most of these jobs could be filled by foreign workers, so it is pressing Western firms hard to hire and train local workers as part of their contractual obligations. But this strategy will not succeed unless the Kazakh government improves the primary and secondary education systems while sustaining its investment in higher education. The problem is particularly acute in rural regions, which have experienced very uneven paces of recovery from the crises of the early 1990s. Kazakh government spending in the social sphere currently accounts for 5.4 percent of the national budget, and in a 2004 report the IMF welcomed higher outlays for education, health, and development of physical infrastructure, which could be accomplished through the use of rising oil revenues that entail effective budgetary institutions and budgetary reforms.[45]

The long-term challenge for the Kazakh government is to make sure that part of the population is not left behind as the economy continues to grow. To frequent visitors, it appears that the gap between rich and poor is growing, although according to its Gini index Kazakhstan has done fairly well; Kazakhstan has a Gini index of 31.3, a relatively good score for a developing nation, compared with 33.1 for Canada, and 40.8 for the United States.[46] Similarly, a Swiss study reports that some 28 percent of the population of the country lived below the subsistence level, again making poverty less of a problem in Kazakhstan than in most of the neighboring states.[47]

Judged by key economic indicators, the government of Kazakhstan's economic policy has been more successful than that of any other country in the region; nonetheless, the expectations of many of its people have not been fulfilled, creating political risk for its nondemocratically elected government. In the end, popular perception is more important than the statistical record of a government's performance. Although the government has worked hard to dispel popular myths about early windfall profits from the country's oil and gas, the majority of Kazakhs still find it difficult to understand why natural resource wealth does not translate into quick improvement in popular standards of living.

The existence of a large underclass (people living in or close to poverty), small by Central Asian standards, but large enough to be of real political significance, helps explain why Kazakhstan's leaders have refused to expand political participation except in a controlled fashion.

Kazakhs also expect their government to apply public earnings to address festering ecological problems from the Soviet era: some caused by the gradual death of the Aral Sea, which has shrunk to 20 percent of its 1960s size, leaving behind a salty desert, others by decades of Soviet weapons testing in the republic. Many Kazakhs also complain that the government should be doing more to combat the new social blights such as AIDS, drug addiction, and tuberculosis, all of which have grown exponentially since independence.[48]

It will be years before Kazakhstan has a chance of being anything approximating a rich state with vast new resources to apply to addressing existing social problems. This gap between public expectations and government capacity should be creating new incentives for the government to stamp out corruption and increase opportunities for economic participation, as a means of gaining revenue to help them solve these problems. But as discussed in chapter seven, the growth of corruption in Kazakhstan, as elsewhere in the region, remains virtually unchecked.

Similarly, the international community has found it increasingly difficult to lobby for continuing reform in Kazakhstan, thanks to the country's diminishing need for international assistance. In 2003, the IMF closed its country office in Kazakhstan because the government had discharged its principal loan obligations and does not seek to borrow further money.

Turkmenistan: Still Squandering Its Potential

Turkmenistan offers contrasts and similarities with Kazakhstan. It is also a resource-rich state, with smaller but still considerable oil reserves and much larger gas reserves than Kazakhstan. Like Kazakhstan, Turkmenistan has only limited reason to borrow from international financial institutions. So it can usually pick and choose which international advice it follows. But unlike those of Kazakhstan, Turkmen reserves are not finding their way to Western markets, nor are they likely to any time soon. In many ways, Turkmenistan is the one Central Asian country that has deliberately chosen to have been left behind.

The government of Turkmenistan holds out extraordinary hopes as to the prospects of foreign investment, expecting $63 billion to be invested in its oil sector alone by 2020. But by 2004, only about $1 billion had been invested in new extraction projects, and no major investment commitments were pending.

At one time, major Western energy firms Unocal, Royal Dutch Shell, and Mobil all signed agreements with the Turkmen government for the development of oil and gas fields, as did a number of smaller companies including

Bridas, Itochi, and Larmag. But these firms eventually decided that it was not worth their while to see these projects through to full exploration. Their departure has left only a handful of foreign oil and gas firms doing business in the country: Petronas, Maersk Oil, Dragon Oil, and of course Russia's Gazprom, which remains Turkmenistan's dominant foreign partner.[49]

Similarly, Turkmenistan has the most inhospitable investment climate in the region, with absolutely no transparency in its hypercentralized economy. No foreign investment can be arranged without the president's approval, and no goods can be exported and no foreign reserves dispersed without his signature,[50] which is especially critical as the country's currency, the manat, is effectively worthless. The manat was introduced without an internationally supported stabilization program, and although initially set at 1:1 with the dollar, it has now fallen to an official rate of 5,200 manat to the dollar (with a street rate of four to five times that), with the government doing little to eradicate the black market trade in currency.

International expert opinion is not sought and goes unheeded to such a degree that it is now rarely offered. Those running the international financial institutions mince no words in describing their frustration in dealing with the Turkmen and complain that government officials are rotated in and out of office so frequently that few develop any expertise in foreign economic matters. The World Bank's country brief on Turkmenistan includes a note that although ten pieces of policy advice were prepared over a ten-year period, they had virtually no impact. As a result, the country received only three relatively small World Bank loans and has been disqualified from further borrowing because of its refusal to report external debt.[51]

Similarly, the European Bank for Reconstruction and Development (EBRD) considers Turkmenistan a country for what they term baseline or minimal engagement, and its small lending program is focused exclusively on the country's beleaguered small and medium-sized business sector, which is crippled by currency and export restrictions and further hampered by the very limited privatization of the key sectors of the country's economy. The slow pace of privatization virtually dribbled to a halt in 2001. The current legal structure precludes the privatization of oil and gas deposits. Plans for widespread privatization of agriculture have been regularly delayed, most recently in 2004.[52]

But the Turkmen government has no interest in making the changes necessary for engagement with international financial institutions. This leaves them with little leverage to exercise in Ashgabat.

Turkmenistan is an economic statistician's nightmare. Virtually nothing reported by the government can be believed, including the size of the population of the country, which is placed at 5.73 million by official sources, a figure some informed observers see as an overestimation of 25 percent.[53] In fact, those who have tried to substantiate Turkmen government claims in most social and economic sectors have come to the conclusion that Turkmen statistics represent the world that Turkmenbashi would like to exist, not the one in which most Turkmen actually live. Figures on average life expectancy, infant mortality, and prevalence of infectious diseases are all dubious.[54] In fact, in 2004 it was made illegal for doctors to record a whole series of infectious diseases, including plague and hepatitis—a novel but dangerous means of "eradicating" disease, and then in 2005 most hospitals outside of the capital were simply closed.[55]

Turkmenistan's government reports paint a rosy picture of the country's economic progress, claiming increased output of 23.1 percent in 2003, the third straight year of growth exceeding 20 percent. But the EBRD believes that a more realistic estimate of economic growth for 2003 would be 11 percent, largely the product of high energy prices.[56] Moreover, Turkmenistan was the most poorly performing Central Asian state on EBRD's transition indicator index for 2003, having a total improvement rating of one on a five-point sale, which indicates little or no progress.[57]

Even economic statistics that are subject to partial international verification are problematic, given the terms under which Turkmenistan sells its natural gas to Russia. Gazprom has become more aggressive in dealing with Turkmenistan in recent years because policy makers seem to feel that the Kremlin's acceptance of the U.S. military presence in Central Asia increases Russia's freedom of action in other areas. Gazprom currently purchases 45 percent of Turkmenistan's gas. According to the most recent arrangement signed in April 2003, Gazprom paid $44 per thousand cubic meters for Turkmen gas (half in cash and half in barter).[58] When the real value of the bartered "goods" is calculated, the effective purchase price is between 22 and 28 cents per thousand cubic meters.[59] In early 2005, Ashgabat tried to play hardball with the Russians, demanding $60 per thousand cubic meters rather than $44, as previously agreed. Gazprom refused to agree to the price hike, and Turkmenistan turned off the spigot.[60]

About 6 billion cubic meters per year are now going out through Iran, and the Korpedzhe to Kurt-Kui pipeline could carry 10 billion cubic meters per year if enough supply were available. Turkmenistan is compensating Iran for its share of the cost of this pipeline through transit revenues.[61]

Fossil fuel and cotton are Turkmenistan's principal exports. Increases in Turkmenistan's GDP were the result of the resumption of gas sales to Russia in 1998. But accurate information about exports from Turkmenistan is impossible to obtain and is viewed by the Turkmen government as no one else's business. Turkmen economists with access to information provided by foreign partners are sworn to secrecy and told that their well-being and that of their relatives is at risk if they divulge any of it. It is so widely rumored that trade in oil and gas directly benefits the president and his family that this supposition can virtually be treated as fact. Some of the profit is said to come from fuel sales to Afghanistan during the years of Taliban rule, reported to involve millions of dollars annually, and done without a paper trail.[62]

It is virtually impossible to know how serious a problem presidential corruption is in Turkmenistan because Niyazov exercises direct control over the country's Foreign Exchange Reserve Fund, through which the earnings of most foreign investments are managed. He also sets the priorities in how the foreign exchange is to be spent, which has gone disproportionately to large construction projects, rather than for investments in national infrastructure.[63]

President Niyazov and his family managed to penetrate into nearly every sector of the country's economy. One Turkmen exile, Murad Esenov, even referred to Niyazov as "Mr. 33 Percent," a reference to the share of every foreign transaction that is said to go to the president or his designated recipient.[64]

The same small group of foreigners has influence in both the textile and energy sectors. These investors include most prominently Yosef Maiman of Israel and Ahmed Calik of Turkey—each with considerable personal holdings and each rumored to have helped Niyazov and his family members extend their own personal holdings.[65] Both are understood to be intimates of the president, and Calik, who holds dual Turkish and Turkmen citizenship, even served briefly in Turkmenistan's cabinet.

Since 1997, the Merhav Group, led by its president and chairman of the board, Yosef Maiman, has been the government's official contractor for a $1.6 billion upgrade of the country's largest oil refining complex at Turkmenbashi, the port town on the Caspian seacoast. The upgrade calls for new facilities and the revamp of existing facilities. Niyazov also asked Merhav to plan the modernization of Turkmenistan's second largest refinery, the Seidi Refinery. Ahmed Calik similarly came to Turkmenistan in the mid-1990s. He has built textile factories and luxury high rises, along the way becoming Niyazov's senior adviser on economic affairs and energy sales and a close confidante, rising to the rank of deputy minister of the textile industry. In Turkmenistan, Calik is suspected of financial machinations and the abuse of his access to Turkmenbashi. It is difficult to measure Calik's holdings in the country, but one textile factory, for example, built with Japan's Mitsubishi in Ashgabat cost $169 million.

Turkmenistan's cotton trade is rife with corruption. The sale of raw cotton within Turkmenistan and its export are still done almost entirely through state-set purchase prices, and personal fortunes are made and sustained on the difference between the state-set prices and those of the international market. Here too, the president and his family are rumored to benefit through trade conducted by Turkish intermediaries.

There are also a number of other privileged families who have been awarded quotas for the growing and private sale of cotton outside of quota. Soviet-era collective farms have been renamed more than reorganized, although many farms have been forced to shift to or add the cultivation of cereal grains, the production of which has increased tenfold since independence.

In Turkmenistan, as elsewhere, there has been an increase in the overall acreage under cultivation, which puts substantial stress on the country's already beleaguered water system. Ashgabat's partial solution for this, the creation of a giant reservoir, Grand Turkmen Lake, in eastern Turkmenistan has further exacerbated the tension caused by competition over water with Uzbekistan.[66] Although water resource management is one area where the Turkmen have been willing to take very limited international direction, they have not been willing to consider modifications to the planned reservoir.

Overall, the leverage of the international community in Turkmenistan has decreased since September 11 because Niyazov believes that his country's increased geopolitical importance means that he can get away with further centralization of power. He hoped that the fall of the Taliban regime would lead to an increase in his country's strategic importance and to an improvement in Turkmenistan's economic circumstances by allowing the trade of Turkmen gas and even oil across Afghanistan.

However, there is little evidence that changing geopolitical conditions will translate into substantial economic gains anywhere soon. The creation of an international donor group to help fund Afghanistan's reconstruction created renewed interest in a Trans-Afghan pipeline, which was formally endorsed by the leaders of Afghanistan, Pakistan, and Turkmenistan at a meeting held in Ashgabat on June 26, 2003. The Asian Development Bank assumed responsibility for the preparation of a feasibility study for the project, with $1.5 million in funding coming from Japan's pledges to Afghanistan. Similarly, Japanese firms, Indonesia Petroleum, and Itochu Oil Exploration have expressed possible interest in developing Turkmenistan's Dauletabad field and participating in the project, but they have done little more than send senior executives on fact-finding missions to the area, and they seem more interested in long-term access to these assets than in near-term investment.[67]

Several factors weaken the attractiveness of the Trans-Afghan Pipeline project, including the fragile security situation in Afghanistan, doubts about prospects for India–Pakistan cooperation (if gas is not sold in India as well as Pakistan, then the economics of the project are problematic), and the continued challenge of doing business in Turkmenistan.

In April 2005, the ADB finally announced, after considerable delay, that their feasibility study concluded that the Trans-Afghan pipeline was in fact commercially viable. But until a strong commercial partner is found for the project, and the supply of Turkmen gas insured, the project is likely to be slow to develop into a steady source of income for any of the countries involved.

Although geography and geopolitics have hindered the development of Turkmenistan's gas industry, the Turkmen themselves have played a major role in dampening interest in their oil. Unlike most oil producers, Turkmenistan is in a buyer's market rather than a seller's market. Neighboring Azerbaijan and Kazakhstan have more attractive assets and more favorable investment conditions. Turkmen oil still is shipped through the Soviet-era pipeline network that is controlled by Transneft (Unocal's plans to build a new oil pipeline from Turkmenistan in a companion project to their gas pipeline flopped). But despite considerable U.S. efforts at persuasion, Niyazov refused to commit Turkmen oil and gas to a U.S.-sponsored system of Trans-Caspian pipelines to feed into the Baku-Tbilisi-Ceyhan export route. His refusal doomed the Trans-Caspian underground gas pipeline project. This leaves Turkmenistan still stuck between competing producers such as Russia and Iran, both of which are able to undersell Turkmen gas if necessary to protect their respective markets.

In part because of the challenge of arranging new oil pipeline routes, the Turkmen government has decided instead to favor expansion of a domestic refining industry. The cost of the refining projects has further added to Turkmenistan's indebtedness.[68] The initiative for this decision came directly from the Turkmen president, acting on advice from foreign investors like Maiman and Calik who are profiting from the decision.

In the area of oil and gas, Turkmenistan has suffered from the failure to delegate responsibility or develop competent leadership. Those in senior positions who were promoting creative solutions in these areas have been pushed from power.[69] From a technical viewpoint, their departure makes conducting economic reform increasingly more difficult, even if President Niyazov should decide to reverse his policies. In general, the country has suffered from a hemorrhaging of talent, which began with the departure of Russian specialists when Turkmenrosgaz collapsed in 1993. With time, the local Russian population has become increasingly unwelcome in Turkmenistan. Russian-language education was sharply cut back in 2001, the use of Russian in official life was reduced in 2000, and finally in 2003 the Turkmen government refused to extend the ten-year treaty on dual citizenship with Russia signed in 1993 and effectively expelled all dual citizens who chose not to accept Turkmen citizenship.[70] This led to a new brain drain of Turkmen residents of all nationalities, so severe that the country restored the requirement for exit visas in 2003, having only eliminated them in 2002. This measure requiring visas, justified as necessary to prevent relatives of the increasing numbers of political prisoners from fleeing "justice," was designed to force local Russian speakers to remain in the country.[71]

In any case Niyazov's policies have done little to prepare either Russian or local Turkmen speakers to fill leadership roles in the economy. Primary and secondary education has been reduced from eleven years to nine, and university education from five years to two, plus the number of places in institutions of higher education for all Turkmen citizens has been cut by about 90 percent. The curriculum at all levels has been redefined to emphasize the history and culture of the Turkmens and the guiding rule of Turkmenbashi rather than the teachings of math or science. *Rukhnama*, a moral code written by Turkmenbashi himself, is part history, part philosophy, part patriotic primer. This rather inchoate text is mandatory reading for students, and a second volume was published in September 2004.

In 2004, the state began to enforce an earlier decree that granted recognition solely to educational degrees attained in Turkmenistan, or as a result of Turkmen government-sponsored educational exchanges.[72] The decree covered only those degrees granted since 1993, so Soviet degree holders are exempted. But now anyone choosing to study abroad (be it in the United States, Russia, or Turkey, the three most common destinations) on their own initiative will effectively be barred from employment in their specialty upon their return. And if they do not return from abroad, then their relatives become politically suspect and could lose their jobs or worse. In addition, in 2002 mandatory state service was introduced for all men aged 17 to 49, further delaying access of trained young people to the economy.[73] This measure helps soak up some of Turkmenistan's burgeoning youth population, but it occupies them for only two years and is not designed to give them any applicable skills, making it likely that they will simply contribute to the country's population of able-bodied poor.

There is no reliable information available about the percentage of the Turkmen population living in poverty. The Turkmen government categorizes only 1 percent of the population as such, but the EBRD estimates that 58 percent of the Turkmen are poverty stricken.[74] The World Bank estimates that 44 percent of the population live on less than $2 per day, a larger share of the population than in Kazakhstan (where the figure is under 10 percent) and nearly identical to the percent of poor and working poor in Kyrgyzstan.[75] Income figures are not an effective measure of poverty in Turkmenistan as they are in some other Central Asian countries because of the allocation of free or low cost communal services such as electricity and gas.[76] But current accuracy aside, the percent of the population living in poverty in Turkmenistan seems likely to increase.

Kyrgyzstan: Eager to Reform but Failing to Thrive

Kyrgyzstan has been the most receptive country in the region to international advice, yet it has failed to develop a sustainable economy. The World Bank classifies the Kyrgyz Republic as a low-income, highly indebted country. That definition remained consistent throughout the rule of Askar Akayev, and popular frustration with economic stagnation helps to explain his ouster as president in March 2005.

Sadly for Central Asia, Kyrgyzstan may represent the best that the region can hope for. Kyrgyzstan was listed in the third quintile in the World Bank's 2001 Country Policy and Institutional Assessment of International Development Association countries. By contrast, both Uzbekistan and Tajikistan were placed in the fifth quintile.[77]

Specialists in the international financial community generally find it fairly easy to work with the Kyrgyz, who often bring a high degree of professionalism to their work. There has also been a very supportive attitude between the government of the Kyrgyz Republic and these multilateral financial institutions, which encourages the international financial community to help Kyrgyzstan with debt restructuring and to develop new borrowing strategies to help them fund various aspects of their poverty-alleviation program.

Kyrgyzstan has the highest debt-to-income ratio in Central Asia. This stems in part from energy debts, but most of the debt is repayment obligations from borrowing to support economic and social reforms. Debt became burdensome for the Kyrgyz because their economy did not recover as rapidly as the international financial experts initially projected. So as the international community helped lead Kyrgyzstan into its current crisis, they are also assisting the Kyrgyz to get out of it.

In March 2002, the Paris Club began rescheduling Kyrgyz debt, in return for the Kyrgyz government working out a new poverty alleviation program in consultation with the World Bank and its other primary lenders.[78] These lenders in turn have offered substantial additional funds to the Kyrgyz on generally improved terms.[79] These funds also give the international financial institutions new leverage in pressing the government into greater fiscal responsibility.

Even though the Kyrgyz government has not met all the agreed targets, in March 2005 the Paris Club agreed to forgive another $124 million of debt and reschedule $431 million.[80] Current assistance money is under closer international supervision than were earlier aid packages, to prevent the kind of pilfering of assistance money that is generally assumed to have occurred in the first seven or eight years of independence. Unfortunately, nothing but anecdotal evidence is available on how much of the early assistance money went astray through out-and-out theft, favoritism, or simply misguided projects.

Kyrgyzstan has a very small economy, with little prospect of significant expansion. It experienced a net decline in its GDP for 1990–2001 but it has had a faster rate of recovery than some of its neighbors.[81]

Privatization of small and medium-sized enterprises (SMEs) has been effectively completed in Kyrgyzstan, and by January 2004, the overall level of privatization had reached 70.7 percent.[82] Approximately 60 percent of the population is engaged in the private SME sector, which produces 85 percent of GDP, and 93 percent of agricultural production comes from the private sector.[83] There is still only limited legal protection of private property, something that the Kyrgyz government has pledged to improve as part of its poverty-reduction strategy for 2003–2005.[84]

But the withdrawal of the state from the economy in Kyrgyzstan has not been sufficient means to produce a speedy recovery from the economic shocks associated with the collapse of the Soviet Union. According to the Kyrgyz government, 50 percent of the population was living in poverty in 2003.[85] The economy in and around the capital of Bishkek performed much better than that of the rest of the country.[86] And according to the UNDP, 88 percent of the population of Kyrgyzstan lives on under $4 per day.[87]

Unemployment is less than 10 percent, which makes clear that Kyrgyzstan's poverty problem is caused by the working poor. The standard of living of the poor does seem to be rising as the poverty gap and severity figures have declined. Poverty is believed by the World Bank to have peaked in 1999, according to its Kyrgyz National Poverty Reduction Strategy for 2003–2005.

The government of Kyrgyzstan needs to close the gap between the country's north and south, a gap that is cultural and economic as well as geographic. This was a task that the Akayev government set for itself, but one that it could not accomplish quickly enough to retain the confidence of most of the population in the south. While some of the regions in northern Kyrgyzstan are actually poorer than most of the communities in the south, in absolute numbers there are more poor people living in southern Kyrgyzstan, given the density of population in this region. And since Kyrgyzstan's leaders have traditionally come from the northern part of the country, many southerners believe that their economic problems are the result of government neglect.[88] The government strategy for poverty alleviation developed under President Akayev, however, was sensitive to these regional factors, and poverty levels in the south were being reduced faster than the republic average at the time that he was pushed from office. Unemployment is also a more serious problem in the southern oblasts of the country, and this seems certain to continue to plague Akayev's successors. They too will find it difficult to eradicate poverty quickly, unless the structure of foreign assistance is dramatically transformed, a point we return to in the conclusion. The population density in southern Kyrgyzstan, as well as its youthful age structure, is likely to continue to make poverty and unemployment problems of national security.[89] The region is an area of potential ethnic and ethnoreligious conflict, because Uzbeks compose over a third of the population in the south, living largely in ethnic enclaves in the border region. There are still memories of the interethnic fighting in Osh and Jalal-abad that took place in 1990, but tensions have mostly been defused, largely because local Uzbeks (and Kyrgyz) in Kyrgyzstan enjoy a much higher standard of living in Kyrgyzstan than their kin across the border in Uzbekistan. Although the formal statistics of the two countries do not bear this out, visitors to the region observe that the standard of living on the Kyrgyz side of the border is much higher than that on the Uzbek side.[90]

In addition to being generally poorer, the population in the south also tends to be more religious than in the north. This is partly because of the presence of a larger Uzbek population, which tends to be more observant than the Kyrgyz, but even the Kyrgyz of the south tend to be more observant Muslims than their northern counterparts. Radical Islamic groups like the Hizb ut-Tahrir are gaining members much more quickly in the south (among Kyrgyz as well as Uzbeks) than they are in the north.

The population in the north and the south each think that the other half of the country has been favored by the government's economic policies. Overall, the Kyrgyz government had little choice but to allow the international community to experiment with the Kyrgyz economy, given the inability of the government to reverse the country's economic decline. But the sums allocated—and most of the guidelines as to how this money was to be spent—were set by the international institutions funding projects in the country. Bilateral financial institutions offer very limited grant financing and the Kyrgyz leadership had very little bargaining clout to press even more willing sources for more grants-in-aid and fewer loans. The size of the awards to Kyrgyzstan were determined in large part by international advisers' expectations about how rapidly Kyrgyzstan's economy would grow, and their expectations further fueled the naïveté of the Kyrgyz, who had no comparative basis for judging their country's economic potential.

The assumptions that Kyrgyzstan's economy would grow faster than in fact it did were not irrational, however. There was reason to hope that by being "first through the gate" on questions of economic investment the Kyrgyz would attract foreign capital. In conditions of freer trade, Kyrgyzstan would have had a smoother economic recovery, though not an easy one. Initially international advisers had no reason to anticipate the pattern of border closures and trade disruptions that occurred within Central Asia. And both the Kyrgyz and their international advisers underestimated the inherent fragility of the Kyrgyz economy and overestimated the country's capacity to reach the global market with its goods. Unfortunately, not all of the current economic planning is better grounded in reality.

Food security is currently an important priority, and the Kyrgyz government deserves credit for having introduced the most wide-reaching agricultural reforms in the region. Despite how critical improving performance of the agricultural sector is for ensuring food security, both IDA and the IMF feel that Kyrgyzstan could do more to stimulate private sector participation in agriculture.[91] But there are real limitations as to how much growth in the agricultural sector Kyrgyzstan can hope to achieve, regardless of whether the sector is fully privatized. Kyrgyzstan's food production index has improved considerably since independence—the only country in the region for which this is the case (with the exception of Turkmenistan, whose figures are suspect). The amount of cropland available per person is very limited (0.28 hectares), however, and cannot be substantially increased without the Kyrgyz diverting water from downstream user states.

Kyrgyz economists still see the expansion of light industry as a source of additional employment. Some further expansion of light industry is possible, and an improved legal environment, combined with favorable tax regimes (under 20 percent), will give Kyrgyzstan an edge should regional trade restrictions ever be reduced. But it is hard to envision Kyrgyzstan's industry developing a strong regional presence, given the increasingly commanding position occupied by new or substantially reorganized Kazakh and Russian enterprises in the region. The Russians and the Kazakhs are at least as market savvy as the Kyrgyz and are generally better capitalized.

While Kyrgyz government economists offer both optimistic and less optimistic scenarios for future growth, they recognize that the former would require a dramatic change in the trade and investment climate of the region. Realistically, even the more pessimistic scenarios of 4.9 percent annual GDP growth will be difficult to achieve, not to mention the 7 percent growth rates in the more optimistic alternative scenarios. The lower figures are predicated on a volume of investment of 20 percent of GDP, but investment patterns in the past few years make this target appear quite unrealistic.[92]

The country's principal economists also continue to hope that Kyrgyzstan will develop into a regional transport center. The government has used substantial amounts of foreign assistance money, particularly from the EBRD and the Asian Development Bank, to improve transport linkages within the country to the Tajik and Chinese borders, yet failure to develop a strong regional demand for trade has meant that these road improvements have led to little new revenues for transit traffic through Kyrgyzstan.[93] Although no longer dreaming about becoming the Switzerland of Central Asia, the Kyrgyz still hope to be a doorway to China, as these countries are the only World Trade Organization (WTO) members in the region. However, when Kazakhstan and Russia join the WTO, as is likely to occur in the next few years, this advantage too will be lost. The old Soviet rail and highway systems favor both of these states over Kyrgyzstan.

Until Russia and Kazakhstan are close to WTO membership, they will continue to penalize the Kyrgyz for their go-it-alone policies with regard to the WTO. Both Russia and Kazakhstan favor the continuation of a uniform tariff system of partner states over a free trade regime, at least into 2005, and both of these states are important trading partners for Kyrgyzstan.[94] In 2002, Russian and Kyrgyz tariffs were reported to have been harmonized to only 14 percent.[95] For now, Kyrgyz goods are subject to high fees and bribes that must be paid to move goods across borders and through international checkpoints in Kazakhstan and Russia. IMF economists estimate that road transport costs from Kyrgyzstan average 10-15 percent of total costs, of which only about one-third are associated with fuel.[96]

Kyrgyzstan also has overly optimistic plans to substantially expand its gold mining sector. These plans are effectively dependent on the price of gold exceeding $400 an ounce, given the high extraction costs for most of Kyrgyzstan's untapped large deposits. Working many of these deposits would also entail substantial environmental risks. The Kyrgyz population has become increasingly more ecologically risk averse in the aftermath of several cyanide-related deaths caused by working the country's large Kumtor field.[97]

The Kyrgyz government took steps to improve the investment climate in the gold industry in spring 2004. The Kumtor project, now in its second phase of development, was transferred to a new legal entity, Centerra, a joint venture between Cameco and the Kyrgyz government.[98] Centerra then sold 70.2 million shares (about 9 percent of the company), all from the Kyrgyz government packet through an initial public offering on the Toronto stock exchange. This transaction earned the Kyrgyz government about $115 million and left them with a 16 percent stake in the project. Although the government has pledged that the money will go toward poverty alleviation, the sale produced a legislative outcry, as it was accomplished through government decree and not through legislation.[99] There were also complaints that the share price ($15.50) was too low and much speculation as to who might have benefited from this.

Plans to seek major international investment to expand Kyrgyzstan's hydroelectric industry are also controversial. Kyrgyz economists are pressing for the government to implement Soviet-era plans for the development of supersized hydroelectric power stations that would substantially increase the country's export potential. But plan proponents are less concerned with the potential geopolitical fallout from downstream users. The main objection would likely come from Uzbekistan, because the Kazakhs have some interest in the Kyrgyz expanding energy production, as a way to help shift Soviet-era linkages into more market-driven relationships. Russia's state-run electrical company, Unified Energy Systems (RAO-UES), is keenly interested in harnessing Kyrgyzstan's hydroelectric potential in their effort. As discussed at greater length in chapter six, in recent years RAO-UES, already active in Kazakhstan, has been investing in Kyrgyzstan and elsewhere in the region to enable Russia to sell its surplus energy in Europe. Although investment by this quasi-governmental Russian entity may provide a secure environment for the expansion of Kyrgyz hydroelectric industries, it does not maximize local income potential.

A similar situation exists in the gas sector, where Russia's Gazprom is making a bid to acquire assets throughout Central Asia and promising to reinvest regional profits into improving local transport networks. Gazprom's role in Kyrgyzstan is increasing but is unlikely to lead to significant new economic opportunities for the Kyrgyz. Plans for developing new Kyrgyz oil and gas fields are relatively capital intensive, given the small size of these deposits and the abundance of energy in neighboring states.

The Kyrgyz government sees tourism as an area of major economic potential, but there is very little prospect that growth in this sector will achieve targeted goals. The Kyrgyz are in direct competition with Kazakhstan's larger and better developed leisure industry, which depends on revenues from that country's large expatriate business community. Tourism currently accounts for only 3.9 percent of Kyrgyzstan's GDP. The Kyrgyz would like to expand adventure tourism by Westerners and middle-class tourism by Indians, but the country has few international connections and a real dearth of first- and even second-class tourist facilities. Currently, there is only one real luxury-class hotel in the country, and it has very low occupancy rates. It was partially owned by the president's wife, who took over the project to keep the Hyatt Corporation from withdrawing from the country, rather than because the Akayev family saw this as a lucrative investment.

Finally, the poverty-alleviation strategy is undermined by the pervasive atmosphere of corruption in the country. Corruption is allegedly being attacked through an improved legal infrastructure and judicial system. Although this effort has always claimed to target everyone, in reality, while Akayev was in power, the president, his family, and the families of his close associates were all effectively immune from prosecution. Many fear that Akayev's successors will simply replicate earlier behavior. Unless there is a serious modification of presidential power, those who are above the law will continue to meddle in the economy without constraint.

Whether or not President Akayev and his close relatives had personal holdings on the scale that was rumored will take a long time to establish. Certainly the public actions of the presidential family fueled these perceptions.

In the early years of independence, Askar Sarygulov and Dastan Sarygulov, both cousins of first lady Mairam Akayeva, headed the state privatization committee and the state-owned gold company, Kyrgyzaltyn, respectively. In more recent years, the grown children of the president and their spouses have come to represent the family interests, and Akayev's son Aidar and his Kazakh son-in-law Adil Toigonbayev were said to monopolize fuel oil distribution, liquor sales, real estate, local cabarets, casinos, and the media, and popular resentment of that helped to erode Akayev's popular support.[100] Opposition politicians' claims that the first family had a stranglehold over Kyrgyzstan's economic life may be exaggerated, but it seems to have been fairly common practice for people with clear title to desirable properties to be forced to sell them at below market price after "expressions of interest" from members of powerful families.

The popular perception that Akayev was corrupt certainly fueled public support for his ouster. So too did popular resentment, particularly in the south, that the Kyrgyz government had not devoted enough resources to poverty alleviation. But it is not clear that successor regimes will be any more honest, or any more able to deliver economic assistance and reconstruction to the densely populated communities of the south or the poverty-stricken but remote regions in the north.

As elsewhere in the region, economic statistics tell only part of the story. Leading local economists believe that the income of the Kyrgyz population is twice as large as indicated by the official statistics, given how much of the population hides income to avoid taxation.

Certainly, life in and around the capital city of Bishkek reflects the existence of a small but growing middle class, as well as a very small upper class. The city enjoys oblast status, which has allowed the city residents to further profit from the local economic recovery. But the downside of this is that the city is serving as a magnet; internal migrants account for 83 percent of the new population in Bishkek, contributing to a growing housing, employment, and crime problem in the capital.[101] The effects of Kyrgyzstan's uneven economic recovery are most pronounced in the south. It has made the region prey to the drug trade and a fertile area for Hizb ut-Tahrir to recruit new members. In addition to railing against the corruption of Kyrgyzstan's secular regime, Hizb ut-Tahrir pays its members between $50 and $100 per month for distributing leaflets, creating a new source of employment in an area where competition for jobs is acute.

While the ouster of Askar Akayev may have bought his successors some breathing room, especially if a southerner like Kurmanbek Bakiyev, a native of Jalal-abad and former governor of the Chui oblast, is elected the country's next president. But the risk of serious social or political unrest emanating from Kyrgyzstan's south is going to remain a long-term one.

Tajikistan: Can Its Failing Economy Be Helped?

Six years after the Tajik government began to work closely with international economic advisers, the country remains the very poorest of the post-Soviet states and has the smallest gross national income in Central Asia at just $1.3 billion in 2003.[102] It also suffers from crippling foreign debt. Reconstruction projects have added substantially to Tajikistan's civil war–era debt owed to neighboring states.[103] Over 80 percent of the country's population is reported to live in poverty, and most who have seriously studied the economy on the ground have little confidence in the government's capacity to achieve even the very modest goals of decreasing poverty levels to 75 percent by 2006 and 60 percent by 2015.[104]

Only 56 percent of all able-bodied citizens in Tajikistan were reported to be employed when the country's poverty reduction strategy was drafted, but employment statistics are, of course, unreliable. The three top sources of income for the population of Tajikistan are participating in the illegal drug trade, working for foreign-sponsored nongovernmental organizations (NGOs), and surviving on remittances from migrant laborers working largely in Russia.[105] Although the relative ranking of the three varies some-what from year to year, of the three groups, only those working with NGOs would be recorded as being employed.

Tajikistan is also crippled by the enormous outflow of talented people of all nationalities, who began leaving during the civil war and continue to do so. Even today ethnic Tajiks with economic alternatives remain reluctant to return home, which creates a substantial developmental barrier for Tajikistan.

All the other Central Asian countries were able to begin the process of state building with complex administrative structures intact. The presence of functioning administrations that penetrated down to the most local level made the delivery of social services much easier, even though bureaucrats were often unprepared for the new financial challenges they faced. Because Tajikistan's civil war was a contest between regions, the winners chose to redefine the country's administrative units, firing talented people who had supported the losing side.[106]

The war destroyed public trust in the government, and the contempt with which it is held has further exacerbated its difficulties in collecting rev-enues, even from legitimate businesses. Even Tajik officials privately admit that much of Tajikistan's commercial revival is linked to the drug trade, especially in the capital city of Dushanbe. Those engaged in construction, the service industry, and retail trade generally keep two sets of books to hide employees and revenues from government inspectors. Because of its civil war, the Tajik government has been more vulnerable to the pressures of patronage than elsewhere, making officials very wary of privatization. According to a January 2004 interview with a deputy chair of the Tajik state committee, 7,500 companies had been privatized from 1991 to the end of 2003, of which 6,900 were small with only the remainder being medium or large companies, in part because the government was incapable of creating a transparent tender process.[107] Privatization has also been hampered by unrealistically high prices, the paucity of solvent bidders, and the almost total unavailability of credit.[108] But many of Tajikistan's state-held assets have little appeal to a commercial buyer.

As with so many of these poorer countries, agriculture has become a great mainstay of the population, but the country is trapped in the conundrum of whether to grow cash crops (mostly cotton) or food.[109] Tajikistan has not demonstrated the ability to become an increasingly efficient food producer, partly because of the deterioration of agriculture during the civil war years, but mostly because of the almost total lack of reform in the agricultural sector.[110] A number of civil war–era commanders serve as collective farm leaders and profit disproportionately from the country's cotton crop.

The Soviet-era industrial base is also in disarray. Factories have closed, and the country's major export facility, the Turzunsade aluminum smelter, requires considerable investment to maximize its profitability. During the Soviet years, Tajikistan was one of the main aluminum producers. Its Turzunsade plant, built in 1975, employed about 11,000 people and had a capacity of 517,000 tons per year, making it one of the largest smelters in the world. In 2002, the plant produced 309,000 tons of aluminum. The plant currently accounts for up to half of Tajikistan's export revenue and consumes around 40 percent of the country's electricity. The plant sells mostly to corporations in China, Iran, Greece, Netherlands, Russia, Switzerland, Turkey, and Turkmenistan.[111]

Most of the supervisory class has left the country, and the skills of the labor force are deteriorating. Given the current state of education in the country, the skill level of the work force seems certain to deteriorate even further. Attracting new investment to Tajikistan will be extremely difficult.

A generation of Tajiks is largely being abandoned to manage as it can, with far less access to education and social services than the preceding generation, but there are very few international projects designed to address these problems.[112] Nearly 80 percent of children of the poorest families lack any material assistance from the state. The educational system of the country is in complete disrepair; over 50 percent of all schools nationwide require capital investment, and not surprisingly the worst schools are found in rural areas. Since 1990 enrollment rates in primary and secondary schools have been declining, and the gender balance in the schools is changing as well, because when forced to choose parents will buy winter clothing to send sons to school in preference to daughters. This same pattern is said to exist in much of Turkmenistan and Uzbekistan, and even in parts of Kazakhstan and Kyrgyzstan. But in Tajikistan, the problem is exacerbated by the fact that the number of places in secondary schools is also dropping, with fewer available in 1999 than in 1990, while the high school-age population has increased by 12 percent during these same years.[113]

Tajikistan is the most isolated of the Central Asian countries. Before independence, over 80 percent of Tajikistan's freight left the republic through Uzbekistan. But the government of Uzbekistan has made the movement of road freight across its territory quite difficult, forcing the Tajiks to ship through Kyrgyzstan, a more arduous route, and to sell their goods in the much smaller and well-saturated Kyrgyz market. This has been especially bad news for Tajikistan's formerly prosperous Sughd (previously Leninabad or Khujand) province, which used to be economically fully intertwined with Uzbekistan. Allegedly, the Uzbek policies are in response to security concerns, but it is clear that the Uzbek government also wants to eliminate competition from Tajik goods in Uzbek markets.

Trade transit within Tajikistan is also a real physical challenge. Tajikistan's highway system is in the worst repair of any of the Central Asian countries, and some 90 percent of its freight moves out of the country by rail. Tajikistan is served internationally by CART Tajikistan, the state-owned airline, which offers regular service to Russia and very limited service to neighboring countries, Turkey, Iran, and Germany.

Much like Kyrgyzstan, Tajikistan has unrealized potential as an energy exporter. Currently, Tajikistan meets part of its energy needs by importing gas from Uzbekistan (paid for in part through barter arrangements in which the Uzbeks get Tajik hydroelectric power), which is a constant source of debt for Tajikistan and the cause of domestic electricity shortages.[114] Like the Kyrgyz, the Tajiks are working closely with Russia's RAO-UES in the hopes that a consolidated Russian-dominated electric grid will give a weak state like Tajikistan more clout to transform water into hydroelectric power. But the end result is likely to be a Tajik hydroelectric system that is under Russian control, with even less profits remaining in country than current Tajik calculations call for. The Iranians also are potential investors in hydroelectric projects in Tajikistan.

The Tajiks would also like to encourage foreign investment in telecommunications. But the density of telecommunications in Tajikistan is the lowest in the CIS: some 9.3 telephone lines exist per 100 urban residents, and 0.6 percent for rural residents. There has been virtually no investment in television relay and broadcast facilities and very limited use of satellite dishes, leaving Tajik viewers and listeners with very little choice. The number of listeners is declining as well; as Soviet-era television sets and radios break, many people, especially those in the countryside, do not have the money to buy new foreign electronics. This situation is common in the poorer areas of each of the Central Asian republics but is a particular problem in an isolated country such as Tajikistan.

The situation in Tajikistan is ripe for the spread of extremist ideologies, as well as the further criminalization of the economy. Tajikistan already has many of the features of a narco-state. With the revitalization of the opium and heroin production in Afghanistan, heroin trade across Tajikistan has been steadily increasing, and with it the economic and political impact of Tajikistan's drug lords. As much as 4,460 kilograms of heroin have been seized along the Tajik border since the start of 2004.[115] A year before the total amount seized was 5,600 kilograms, and there is no evidence of a dramatic improvement in interdiction rates.[116]

Finally, as long as Rakhmonov is in office, there is likely to be little serious effort to attack the economic corruption that is at the core of the Tajik state, which is bad news for those who would like to use legal means to address Tajikistan's poverty.

Uzbekistan's Refusal to Reform

Years of nearly draconian restrictions on trade, combined with the government's policies of import substitutions, have distorted many aspects of Uzbekistan's economy, including the magnitude of the country's debt burden, which was 40 percent of the GNI in 2001.[117] At the center of the problem was Uzbekistan's decision to maintain Soviet-era state purchase and price support systems in agriculture and a multiple exchange rate system for its currency. The latter was an explicit violation of the terms of its economic stabilization agreement with the IMF and led to the program being abandoned in 1996. But Uzbekistan's president maintained that he better understood the nature of his country's economy than foreign specialists did, and he and they spent the next several years talking past each other.

The Uzbek government's own step-by-step program of exchange rate reform had not led to a single rate of exchange by December 2001, when a new letter of intent outlining agreed upon structural reforms was signed with the managing director of the IMF. The agreement was designed to cover a six-month period, ending on June 30, 2002, by which time the Uzbek government promised to introduce a series of structural reforms, including exchange rate unification and a stage-by-stage elimination of the state procurement system for raw cotton and grain. In these two sectors, Uzbek farmers (who are still largely organized in collective or communal farms) have production targets set and are offered seriously deflated purchase prices for their harvest.[118] In return, the IMF and World Bank would help the Uzbek government meet projected budget deficits if the latter kept to the timetable for structural adjustments.[119]

The Uzbek government also committed to liberalize the country's highly restrictive trade policy.[120]

However, the Uzbek government never qualified for the additional assistance, having failed to meet the agreed targets. Moreover, by late 2002, the IMF and World Bank had reached new levels of frustration in dealing with the Uzbek government, in large part because of the introduction of a series of new tariffs and other trade restrictions, which led to the virtual collapse of the fledgling wholesale trade network in the country and further hampered trade with neighboring states (leaving millions of dollars in goods on trucks that were blocked en route to Uzbekistan).

Much of this drama played out against the backdrop of strong international criticism at the May 2003 EBRD annual meeting, which the Uzbeks had fought hard for the privilege of hosting and for which they had invested tens—if not hundreds—of millions of dollars in facelifts for their capital city. The EBRD meeting set a number of political and economic targets for the Karimov regime to meet and gave them a year to do it. But when Uzbekistan finally introduced exchange rate unification in October 2003, international confidence in the Uzbek economy was almost nonexistent.[121] This measure, introduced without substantially easing individual or enterprise access to hard currency, did more to bolster the position of the critics of Karimov's regime than of its supporters. As their May 2004 EBRD deadline approached, criticism of Uzbek policies (its human rights record as well as its economic reform track record) increased, leading to a decision by the EBRD's board of governors to stop lending to the Uzbek government and its state-owned enterprises.[122]

For all of President Islam Karimov's public assurance that he knew what was best for the Uzbek economy, the question of whether or not to sharply quicken the pace of structural reforms was increasingly divisive among the Uzbek ruling elite. Those favoring more rapid reform were increasing in number and outspokenness. Yet, even these pro-market reformers were frightened about what a unified exchange rate would mean for the standard of living of ordinary Uzbeks, although they also believed that delay could prove more costly than immediate implementation.

In 2002, Uzbekistan's per capita GDP of $1,670 was slightly better than that of Kyrgyzstan ($1,620) and Tajikistan ($980), but much less than that of Kazakhstan ($5,870) and Turkmenistan ($4,250).[123] Although government policies have kept income low, a 2003 EBRD country strategy report argues that Uzbekistan has avoided the extreme levels of poverty prevalent in some of the other poor CIS countries, with a government-reported national poverty rate of 27.5 percent.[124] The EBRD expectation, like that of the Uzbek government, is that this rate will increase if economic reforms are pursued aggressively. However, it is hard to know the actual poverty rate.[125] Anecdotal information, including this author's own considerable travel experience in Uzbekistan, indicates a sharp deterioration in the standard of living in the past few years. Although official statistics report continued economic growth, the U.S. Department of State explicitly rejects these figures, claiming that Uzbekistan's GDP increased by only 0.3 percent in 2003.[126] And increasing public restiveness seems directly linked to deteriorating economic conditions of at least part of the population. There were demonstrations in markets in Kokand and Kashi in November 2004.[127] Moreover, some see the motivation for the bombings of March-April 2004 as more economic than religious.[128]

Many blame the increasing restrictions on the illegal shuttle trade between Uzbekistan and neighboring states, which used to supply the countries' bazaars and stalls with cheap goods, as well as on new regulations governing the operations of small vendors. These regulations have put many small merchants and traders out of business and left most consumer goods priced beyond the means of the average Uzbek family—this despite the Uzbek government's strong emphasis on maintaining the social welfare net, spending a relatively large 7 percent of GDP in 2001 on health and education and 6 percent on social transfers.[129]

There is substantial controversy about the use of local councils of elders, the *mahalla*, to distribute relief aid to poorer families. Although they are seen as doing a good job in identifying those families with genuine need, some Western experts argue that poverty assistance could be more equitably managed through a state-supported professional social service.[130] These experts also argue that too much money is spent on salaries and that many benefits are extended to rich and poor alike, including family subsidies, cheap gas, electricity, and subsidized rent.

Schools are also used to target assistance to children. At the beginning of the school year books, backpacks, and even boots and winter coats are distributed to certain grades nationwide. School lunches are also an important source of nutrition for Uzbek children, as meager as they sometimes are. The high overhead costs of Uzbek schools, however, are yet another source of criticism for the government.

It is hard to know then why Uzbek reform was further delayed during 2001–2003. One explanation may be the rumored ill-health of the country's president. Believing that a succession was relatively imminent, most of the leading contenders for power may have tried to keep the economic playing field frozen in place to maximize their own potential for patronage and personal wealth.

Corruption is as serious a problem in Uzbekistan as elsewhere in the region, although detailed information about it is more difficult to come by than in the less repressive states.[131] There is no question that decisions made about the pace of privatization and other economic reforms are shaped in part by the personal interests of President Karimov, his inner circle, and a small group of other privileged regional elite. The partial state purchase of cotton, and to a lesser extent grain, at less than world market prices is a source of enormous benefit to those who manage the country's export trade. Similarly, fortunes have been made on the disparity between the different values of the Uzbek som and by the small groups of people that control the major commercial retail outlets.

Part of the answer for the delay in reform lies in the visceral and somewhat irrational fear among older members of the elite as to what freeing the Uzbek market and privatizing key sectors of the Uzbek economy would mean for social stability in general and employment in particular. Official unemployment in Uzbekistan in 2001 was 0.6 percent, and the EBRD estimates that the introduction of a unified exchange rate would lead to the loss of between 150,000 and 250,000 jobs and create an official unemployment rate of 3 to 4 percent of the work force. They also estimate that Uzbekistan would be able to maintain positive per capita growth rates, given the country's rich resource base.[132]

Uzbek critics argue that economic reform would inevitably lead to the introduction of private land ownership, something that many in the country believe would create near revolutionary levels of public dissatisfaction, given population density in the rural areas, where over 60 percent of Uzbekistan's population lives. Many fear that private ownership would lead to feuds over land and access to water, because agriculture in Uzbekistan is almost entirely dependent on irrigation. Some 88 percent of the cropland is currently irrigated, one of the highest irrigation rates in the world.

There is nothing in the current environment in rural Uzbekistan, however, to suggest that these fears are warranted. The land available per capita is tiny, only 0.5 acres, water rights have been an age-old source of conflict in the region, and Soviet-era overcultivation of cotton has left a legacy of salinated soil and polluted water supplies.

Uzbeks missed the opportunity to cut back on the cultivation of cotton in the first years of independence, when it would have been relatively easy to introduce a lot more crop diversification than has occurred, because Uzbekistan's supply of cotton for Russia's textile industry was subject to negotiation after independence. Uzbekistan could have moved to a different balance between the cultivation of food crops and cotton and sought the development of a much strengthened agribusiness and textile sector of its own. Instead, Uzbekistan's nascent industries were crippled by the state's refusal to grant them free access to hard currency. Linkages to Russia's textile industry were reaffirmed through long-term contracts on market terms that benefited those engaged in the trade and provided the Uzbek state with hard currency earnings.[133]

Uzbekistan is likely to remain the major source of supply to Russia's textile industry for the foreseeable future, but many Uzbek economists are coming around to the idea that the staged privatization of agriculture is necessary, and that it is fully possible to achieve even with Uzbekistan's dependence on cotton cultivation. The key, in their opinion, is that farmers are able to sell their cotton for something close to world prices and have ready access to hard currency to allow them to purchase seed and agricultural equipment.

This, however, is still not the case, and in 2003 and 2004 some farmers destroyed the cotton grown on private plots rather than accept the price offered for it.[134] Their dissatisfaction helped to fuel the violent protests of May 2005. But even these did not produce a rapid change in Uzbek government economic policy, either toward agriculture or for small- and medium-sized enterprises.

Uzbekistan's private sector has received little benefit from the government's introduction of currency convertibility, largely because of the difficulty in actually gaining access to money since Uzbek tender and hard currency are both in short supply. This situation affects entrepreneurs and consumers alike, because the introduction of a national credit card banking system, to which wages may be paid and purchases charged, severely disadvantages small traders and bazaar merchants. According to a report prepared jointly by the Swiss State Secretariat for Economic Affairs (SECO) and the IFC, 99 percent of smaller Uzbek firms are engaged in no form of private trade, [135] and this was before the national credit card system was introduced and their access to cash further curtailed.

Much of the enthusiasm has been beaten out of Uzbekistan's entrepreneurial class in the past decade, and many have abandoned the idea of doing business in Uzbekistan. The World Bank estimates that SMEs account for only 15 percent of the country's GDP but provide 41 percent of the total employment.[136] These figures are at sharp variance with official Uzbek statistics that claim that SMEs account for 29.1 percent of the country's GDP, and that 89 percent of Uzbekistan's population is employed in the private sector, 88 percent of which is engaged in SMEs.[137] This last figure, however, includes mainly those employed in agriculture.

The lack of security of private property dissuades potential entrepreneurs from starting businesses. Many of those engaged in the private sector lost their property between 1993 and 1995 when some of the early privatizations were rejected as illegal, and they fear this could happen again. A November 2002 decree, signed well after the Uzbek government recommitted itself to meet the goals of macroeconomic reform, sent shudders through the Uzbek small business community. This decree seemed to open the door to renationalization of any enterprise that has changed its principal line of economic activity since privatization occurred. It also made it easier for state officials to use extortion to try to force the sale of successful businesses to local "insiders," which may have been what was tried unsuccessfully in Andijan to cause the arrest of twenty-three businessmen for supporting illegal Islamic groups. When one adds to this high (and varying) levies on both the import and the export of goods, high-profit tax, and how hard it is to maneuver through the multitiered Uzbek bureaucracy, it is surprising that anyone has the energy or patience to run a privately owned enterprise in the country.[138]

Under the prevailing economic conditions in Uzbekistan, it is hard to gauge how much of the earlier entrepreneurialism of the Uzbeks remains and how successful the Uzbeks will be in penetrating a Central Asian market that initially they could have dominated, but that now is filled with competitors' goods. Some Uzbek capital fled the country in the early 1990s, and Uzbek entrepreneurs do play a role in Kyrgyzstan, Kazakhstan, and Tajikistan, but those Uzbeks who have invested in neighboring countries may find Uzbekistan's own market difficult to penetrate.

Reformers in the Uzbek government understand that there are no quick fixes for the economic stagnation created by a decade of vacillating on questions of economic reform. Establishing a single exchange rate for the Uzbek som opens the door to the strengthening of the country's private sector and will stimulate the development of a local entrepreneurial class whose existence might stimulate necessary political reforms. However, the relative impoverishment of the population over this same period, and the growth of radical Islamic forces in their midst, makes the outcomes less predictable and the process of reform riskier than it would have been if started earlier.

The quick survey found in this chapter of the economic and social developments in the region from 2001 through the first half of 2005 records few encouraging developments.

Kazakhstan's economy is by far the strongest in the region, and has been further bolstered by the high price of oil. The Kazakhs recognize that windfall profits in natural resource extraction could fund long-term economic development that would secure the country's future. But it is unclear if they have identified the right formulas to do this, or have the will to see the projects through.

Turkmenistan faces all the challenges of structural reform that it did five years ago, and shows fewer signs of being capable of modifying the political power structure that cripples the bureaucracy, and the elite is no more competent in managing the geopolitical challenges that also prevent them from marketing their gas at competitive prices.

Uzbekistan, like Turkmenistan, has yet to modify the state command structure of the economy, which has seriously retarded the development of agriculture in particular, as the cotton sector is still largely unreformed. Uzbekistan's continuing tight trade policy continues to cripple the development of small- and medium-scale enterprises in the country, and hampers their development in both Tajikistan and Kyrgyzstan.

There, in Tajikistan and Kyrgyzstan, developments underscore the slow nature of economic transition in resource-poor countries that accept macroeconomic reforms. The situation in both these countries attests to the difficulties of balancing the need for reform with the risk of indebtedness, and how the latter eventually defines the pace of the former.

The economic progress of all five states continues to be held back by the failure of the Central Asian states to deal with their common problems: the absence of a regional trade regime, the competition over water, and the lack of a regional understanding of how to allocate energy resources most efficiently.

As the ouster of Askar Akayev in Kyrgyzstan and the unrest one month later in Uzbekistan testify, the Central Asian population is no longer willing to sit by in silence as they are denied what they see as their economic due.

5

Failures of Political Institution Building Create the Challenge of Succession

Since September 11, 2001, policy makers in Washington have sought ways to use increases in foreign assistance money to jump-start the process of democratic reform in Central Asia, initially as part of a regional strategy for rebuilding Afghanistan. But the war in Iraq shifted the attention of U.S. nation builders, leaving them little creative energy and diminished resources to apply to Central Asia. And even after Georgia's Rose revolution, when democratic change in post-Soviet states became a prospect with real likelihood, U.S. priorities rested with those countries that seemed better prepared for such democratic transitions.

The need for the Central Asian states to improve their human rights record had long been reaffirmed as a U.S. goal, as Undersecretary of State Strobe Talbott eloquently stated in his 1997 "Farewell to Flashman" address on U.S. policy in Central Asia and the Caucasus.[1] Even after September 11, State Department officials charged with oversight in these areas, including two assistant secretaries—Lorne Craner, head of the Bureau for Democracy, Human Rights, and Labor, and Elizabeth Jones, head of European and Eurasian Affairs—continued to goad Central Asia's leaders to strive harder to make their nations embody democratic goals. And the Central Asian states were all still being nominally held to the good governance objectives that had increasingly come to dominate the rhetoric of the George W. Bush administration after Saddam Hussein was overthrown by U.S. forces in Iraq.

The U.S. government tried to stay impartial throughout the political crisis of late February-early March 2005 that led to President Askar Akayev's ouster in Kyrgyzstan. State Department officials condemned the conduct of the election, but unlike the case of Ukraine when Viktor Yushchenko was treated as an aggrieved party, in this instance Washington preferred negotiated compromise.[2] They also gave Uzbek president Islam Karimov ample opportunity to explain the use of force to quell protests in May 2005.

But the way the United States went about trying to improve human rights and governance issues attested to the relatively low level of strategic importance that the Bush administration accorded to the region.

Secretary of State Colin Powell's refusal to certify Uzbekistan in December 2003 as making sufficient progress in the protection of human rights and the implementation of democratic reforms was a very telling act, of more rhetorical weight than substantive importance. The State Department could have asked the White House for a waiver for Uzbekistan on the grounds of U.S. national security but opted not to. When the aid cutoff came, only $18 million of direct U.S. assistance to the Uzbek government was affected, and ways were even found to transfer some projects relating to penal system reform to programs not affected by the certification process.

When Central Asia was of critical importance to the United States, as in the first year of the war on terror, the agenda of the U.S. Defense Department overshadowed those of the U.S. State and Energy departments. The view from Defense was quite straightforward: The Central Asian states' strategic importance was defined first by what they brought to the war on terror, and second through their contribution to U.S. energy security. Questions of long-term security, such as democracy building, were of no real priority.

If gaining the Central Asian leaders' cooperation required persuasion, the administration was willing to provide incentives in the form of increased foreign assistance. But in the early days of the war, when the Defense Department sought to overcome logistical problems relating to military operations in Afghanistan, the concern was that aid recipients got what they wanted if possible, and the Central Asian states wanted increases in security assistance. However, in part to mute some of the criticism of congressional critics who complained that the war on terror was being used to bolster dictatorial regimes, the administration also included increases in funds devoted to political institution building in the supplementary funds allocated for FY2002.[3]

U.S. and Uzbek authorities realized the importance of Uzbekistan changing its international image if the relationship between Washington and Tashkent were to develop into a strategic partnership, because Uzbekistan's government had frequently been cited for serious human rights abuses. To this end, President Islam Karimov, who traveled to the United States in

March 2002, went so far as to pledge to carry out systemic political reforms introduced over a five-year period that would result in democratically contested parliamentary elections in 2004 and presidential elections in 2007.

However, it did not take long for President Karimov, as well as the other Central Asian leaders, to realize that U.S. officials had limited, and very focused, interest in their countries. Washington, at least at the highest levels, was not going to deeply concern itself in their internal affairs, as long as their Central Asian partners proved dependable in the areas of shared concern. If anything, the Central Asian leaders rather quickly figured out Washington's new interest in their countries would translate itself into a freer hand to pursue their own domestic agendas. As long as they gave periodic lip service to the idea of shared goals while serving a vital role in the war on terror, they could set their own timetables for their achievement.

Initially, some in Western capitals believed that Central Asia's leaders might be receptive to political reforms, because the risk posed by terrorist groups was diminishing. The U.S.-led bombing campaign in Afghanistan had largely destroyed the camps used by the Islamic Movement of Uzbekistan (IMU) and killed many of its leaders. Increased and better targeted security assistance offered by the United States and its North Atlantic Treaty Organization (NATO) partners would make new extremist groups easier to detect and eliminate.

It did not take long for Western hopes to fall, and as they did, U.S. groups pushing for funding of projects relating to political institutional reform in the Central Asian states found it increasingly more difficult to secure support. There were more pressing demands for U.S. foreign aid dollars, and U.S. policy makers sought projects that would yield more immediate results or directly benefit American taxpayers.

The "carrot" being offered was small, and the "stick" brandished by U.S. policy makers was so light as to be of no threat. When the leaders of the Central Asian states showed little interest in seriously engaging in political reform, the size of the carrot was reduced even further, making the strategy of "planting seeds" even less likely to yield a harvest.

Although U.S. policy makers criticized negative developments, until the limited aid cutoff to the Uzbek government in 2004, there have been only minimal consequences for Central Asia's offending leaders, except that the money earmarked for democracy assistance in FY2004 was substantially less than that provided in FY2003, or in FY2002 after supplemental funds were allocated. U.S. assistance money was cut back again in the planned budget for FY2005, and there is with little prospect of it being increased in the near future.[4] Although Central Asia's leaders do not like the appearance of a slap in the face, they do not feel punished by diminishing resources available for civil society–building projects in their region. Much of the increase in funding for the Freedom Support Act (FSA) funding in 2002 and 2003 went to activities that the region's governments begrudgingly accepted, because these activities were seen as benefiting critics of the regime more than supporters.[5]

There is very little evidence to suggest that the Bush administration ever saw nation building in Central Asia—that is, strong support of either political or economic reform—as much more than a vague long-term goal. The best evidence for this is how little new money was made available to the region. The funds allocated to these states increased, and these increases were large in relative terms but small in absolute terms. This is particularly true of FSA funds that were allocated for democracy-building programs, which netted the Kyrgyz $1.16 per person for 2002—and they were the best funded state in the region on a per capita basis.[6] The Central Asian states were getting a larger percent of the monies being allocated to the former states of the Soviet Union, but the amount of money going into these countries was much smaller (both on per capita and absolute terms) than aid to closer allies such as Israel or Egypt.[7]

The relatively small sums were justified as part of a philosophy of using assistance money to plant the seeds for the development of civil society, rather than as a subtle form of bribery, to help Central Asia's leaders find solutions to some of their economic problems, with the caveat that at the same time they had to escalate the pace of developing pluralistic political institutions.

By 2001, gold-plated bribery of the kind described above might no longer have been effective in energy-rich Turkmenistan and Kazakhstan, although it would have worked in Kazakhstan in the early 1990s. But in Kyrgyzstan, Tajikistan, and Uzbekistan, substantial increases in FSA funds might well have yielded changes in both local government and national political life, especially had they been coupled with large increases in economic assistance.

The popularly led ouster of Askar Akayev in March 2005 was to a large extent made possible by long-standing U.S. support of nongovernmental civic groups in Kyrgyzstan, and facilitated by the presence of a U.S.-funded independent press center. But civic society institutions were still poorly articulated in many of the rural regions of the country, making the task of ensuring and sustaining a democratic transition of power a precarious prospect. More work with local elites could well have served as a stabilizing factor in Kyrgyzstan, not to mention in Uzbekistan, where state failure is a growing risk.

The Central Asian states all had a considerable absorption capacity for foreign assistance, with well-educated populations and professional bureaucracies. Most policy makers believed that the Central Asian regimes could make effective use of far larger sums of money than were being allocated to them and would have accepted them. This was especially true of funds targeted for teacher training and curriculum reform in the natural sciences, health-care reform, and even reform of the penal system. In these areas host governments might have locked horns with their foreign advisers on selective questions, but they were willing to take a great deal of direction from the outside world, especially if in the process the changes that were possible were more than those of just a demonstration effect. Nor did U.S. policy makers see corruption as so endemic as to make increases in foreign assistance seem a bad investment.

Some assistance money clearly went astray, sometimes because of the incompetence of those administering the projects, by choosing inappropriate partners, or being unaware of malfeasance by foreign nationals or grant recipients working on these projects.[8] Nevertheless, much of the money went to the projects and audiences it was intended to serve, and as USAID became more accustomed to working in the conditions of Central Asia, its monitoring of projects improved as well.

The problem was one of priorities. The administration did not direct Congress to allocate the kind of money necessary to make the U.S presence an effective one, which would only have occurred if the threat of the withdrawal of funds would itself serve as strong incentive for a recipient government to modify policies. The foreign assistance monies at risk would have needed to be large enough to create unfunded mandates in areas that the local population had grown used to receiving.

But U.S. policy makers saw solving the problems of the Central Asian states as an unrealistic goal, given the complexity of reconstructing the fragments of the command economy and the remnants of authoritarian vertical hierarchies that formed the framing structure of these states. Having opted for smaller sums and the use of a demonstration effect, the question of appropriate partners as recipients became more critical.

In the area of political reform, in particular, this served to further limit U.S. leverage, because much of this assistance focused on trying to create alternatives to the remnants of the Soviet-era elite that continued to dominate in each of these countries. USAID funds were dispersed through U.S. nongovernmental groups that worked in partnership with local groups, most of whom were politically unaligned and some of whom were openly in opposition to the regime.[9]

These activities were largely predicated on a model that sought to address long-term security risks that might emanate from Central Asia. The potential for short-term security risks radiating from these states began fading in importance for the Bush administration. The bases in Central Asia had largely served their purpose by late 2003, and with a much larger military presence in Afghanistan itself, the administration was thinking about shifting them from "hot" to "warm" status.

Yet, as this chapter describes, the risks associated with failures in political institution building throughout Central Asia continue to increase, although the potential security threats associated with these failures vary from country to country. Nor does the ouster of Akayev bode well. It is more likely to signal a new wave of political instability than the beginning of a smooth transfer to accountable democracies in this region. Economic dislocations of the transition to independence are beginning to appear more permanent. Radical Islamic groups appear to have little trouble attracting new members. All of this makes the future in Central Asia difficult to predict and often frightening to ponder.

Kyrgyzstan: The United States Missed Its Chance

U.S. policy makers could have used the opening provided by the events of September 11 to push for further political reforms in Kyrgyzstan, because here the goal of good governance was potentially attainable. Had they done so Akayev might have been enticed into presiding over a final term in office that created the preconditions for a democratic transfer in the fall of 2005 when his term was set to end. Instead, the ripple effects of the March 2005 parliamentary elections he felt bold enough to rig continue to be felt. Discontent over results that favored his cronies led not only to his ouster, but will likely lead to destabilization even beyond Kyrgyzstan's borders, as opposition groups in other countries grow more restless and ambitious.

Until the mid-1990s, Kyrgyzstan was developing into a democratic society, along a timetable that was not dissimilar from Central European states such as Romania, Bulgaria, and Slovakia. But then, partly under pressure from leaders of neighboring states, not to mention from his own family, President Akayev lost his enthusiasm for democratic reform and began to behave more like the other Central Asian rulers.

Kazakhstan's President Nazarbayev and Uzbekistan's Karimov resented the high esteem U.S. policy makers had for Akayev, whose state seemed to them insignificant. Each believed his own nation should be the U.S. favorite in the region and both sought ways to make Akayev pay for his popularity in the West. Both were able to use trade and energy issues as an effective lever to demonstrate Kyrgyz insignificance. Akayev was able to assuage his sense of powerlessness, and even the growing disapproval of the West, when he balanced these off against the new ease with which his family and friends could accumulate wealth. In the end, feelings of personal loyalties overwhelmed Akayev's idealism.

The conditions of the early 1990s lent themselves to idealistic values more than those of the end of the decade. By the late 1990s potentially powerful rivals to the president were emerging within Kyrgyzstan, who used the fragility of the Kyrgyz economy to challenge Akayev's state-building acumen. At the very time that his hold on power was being challenged, Akayev seems also to have become increasingly more aware of his relative weakness and came to the realization that no matter how democratic Kyrgyzstan was, it would always be overshadowed by more powerful— though less democratic—neighbors.

The U.S. decision to open a military base in Uzbekistan was a bitter pill for Akayev to swallow, because it demonstrated that his was not a special relationship with the United States. Within a month of September 11, Uzbekistan had clinched an exclusive partnership with the United States.[10] Here again, another window of opportunity to nudge Akayev toward greater democracy was missed. The Kyrgyz president would have accepted most preconditions imposed by the United States to get his own base to balance Uzbekistan's new strategic preeminence. Unlike in Uzbekistan, where the use of conditionality would have slowed U.S. access to an air base without producing any easy solutions for moving the country toward democratic reform, in Kyrgyzstan conditionality would have served as an effective tool for political change—and done so without compromising the U.S. goal of immediate access to Central Asian airfields.

This is especially true if conditionality had been used with some subtlety. As the leader of a sovereign state, Akayev would not have been willing to accept and fulfill a list of political demands. Some changes he likely would not have acquiesced to regardless of the rewards on offer, such as exonerating former vice president and opposition leader Feliks Kulov and releasing him from jail. But if the sums involved might have allowed for problem solving in sectors that the Kyrgyz themselves viewed as necessary, then the United States could have pressed them to speed up and expand plans for political reform in a number of sectors and could have gotten good cooperation from the Kyrgyz government. There were a large number of political reforms spelled out in the poverty-alleviation strategy that the Kyrgyz government had agreed to with the World Bank in 2001.[11] These reforms included projects for improving the efficacy of local government and the gradual transformation of many senior local government posts from appointment to election. There were also plans to overhaul the remnants of the Soviet-era election system, replacing it with new technology.[12] The introduction of a multifaceted anticorruption policy was also an important part of the poverty-alleviation program, which outlined reeducation and retraining of local judicial, investigative, and police officials programs.

The Kyrgyz had arranged for low levels of funding for all of these projects through their major international assistance partners, but they easily had the capacity to absorb several hundred million dollars of grant assistance (not loans) to expand these projects.[13] They did not have the capacity to absorb and repay debt, however, making it critical that any additional assistance be offered in the form of grants. Major increases in funding in even these three areas of reform (local government, election system reform, and anticorruption policies)—of an additional $100 million to $150 million per year—could have created a more stable playing field to anchor the country as it moves forward from the upheaval of Akayev's ouster.

Even if the United States and other Western donors had concentrated on one single area, such as helping the Kyrgyz with electoral reform, they could have influenced developments to favor advocates of civil society. The German government had failed to provide transparent ballot boxes in time for the October 2004 local government elections.[14]

Just three months before the scheduled February 2005 parliamentary elections Kyrgyz authorities were complaining that U.S. authorities still had not delivered on a promise to help fund the $320,000 national fingerprinting drive to prevent multiple voting. But the United States had other priorities and in 1991 wanted to concentrate its assistance money for the region on Afghanistan. The United States also lacked the administrative capacity to disperse and supervise tenfold increases in assistance money in any of the Central Asian countries, given the prevailing model of assistance that dispersed most democracy assistance funds through U.S.-based (or at least U.S.-supported) NGOs, which absorbed large portions of these funds in salaries for U.S. personnel and overhead for their home offices.

Had the United States been willing to make a substantial investment in the political reform process in Kyrgyzstan, Akayev might have agreed to many otherwise unpalatable measures, such as ending harassment of certain political opposition figures. The United States could have further sweetened the prospects for political reform by promising Kyrgyz suppliers substantial contracts to provide humanitarian and technical assistance reconstruction projects in Afghanistan. This would have given Kyrgyz light industry a real boost.

In such an atmosphere of expanded U.S. political and economic engagement with Kyrgyzstan, Washington could have put Bishkek on notice that the conduct of the 2005 parliamentary elections had to meet democratic norms, and that Akayev needed to convince the political opposition that he would in fact leave office at the end of his term in October 2005. The cost of failing to do either of these two things would put continued U.S. assistance at risk, and that would leave Akayev and his successor regime vulnerable. But U.S. assistance was not sufficient to influence Akayev's behavior.

U.S. officials serving in Bishkek understood just how desperate Akayev was to restore the balance of power within Central Asia. But instead of thinking creatively, the United States chose not to make the development of democratic political institutions a priority in its bilateral relationship with the Kyrgyz Republic and made only modest increases in foreign assistance.

A modern printing press, funded by the State Department, was unveiled in Bishkek in November 2003 as a way to prevent governments from being able to use the state chokehold on printing and distribution to put independent newspapers and publications out of business, a common trick.[15]

The printing press, run by Freedom House, the U.S. democracy promotion organization, is being used to print publications of independent groups in Kyrgyzstan and Tajikistan, and played such an important role in the first round of the 2005 parliamentary elections in Kyrgyzstan that the government arranged a convenient loss of electricity to the building which houses it between the first and second rounds. Power was eventually restored through portable generators located with the help of the U.S. embassy.[16]

The existence of the center will contribute to the training of a future generation of journalists, but it provides little assurance that the current generation will be allowed to work in an unfettered fashion.[17] In fact, over the past three years quite the opposite has been true. Independent newspapers have been forced into bankruptcy, and several journalists who are highly critical of the government have been threatened with arrest, one died mysteriously, and an independent media center in Osh was vandalized.[18]

Still, Kyrgyzstan's press remains the most boisterous in the region, and the country's newspapers and electronic bulletin boards have seen wide-ranging discussions of the sort that do not appear elsewhere in Central Asia. Some of the government's claims of opposition press irresponsibility are grounded in reality, but the pro-government press has been no more responsible, offering biased and fawningly flattering coverage of Akayev and his wife Mairam. Within days of Akayev's ouster, government and opposition press were again sparring, in part over which groups would get to control the government press.

Political opposition and honesty are not synonymous. Some of the charges of corruption around the first family are certainly true, but many of the president's supporters have come by their money honestly, as has most of the opposition.[19] Nevertheless, there are rotten apples found throughout Kyrgyz public life, in the government and among the opposition. And allegations of corruption are not clear cut. For example, Kyrgyz human rights leader Ramazan Dyryldayev rejects the well-publicized claim that he used funds given by foreign donors to buy property abroad, even though charges stem from an independent audit of his organization.[20] Similarly, the arrest of the country's most celebrated prisoner, Feliks Kulov, was certainly politically motivated, but it is also plausible that he was guilty of some abuses of office of which he was accused, and his exoneration in April 2005 was done in a wave of euphoria and without any real examination of the original charges against him.[21] It is also plausible that Akayev knew about and may have even condoned some of Kulov's purported weapon sales.

When a culture of corruption permeates a political system, everyone is compromised. The corrupt nature of Kyrgyzstan is unlikely to change quickly even with Akayev's ouster. But corruption certainly grew worse during Akayev's last few years in office, giving no incentive to pro-opposition or the pro-government groups to be more honest, temperate, and mature in behavior. Instead, they are likely to want the part of the pie they feel they have been denied.

The distance between the government and opposition tended to grow, as the president felt more able to deal effectively with his critics. This is partly the product of increased cooperation between Russia and Kyrgyzstan on questions of internal security. Such cooperation was designed to help shape Kyrgyzstan into a "guided" democracy, rather than a society that is recognizably democratic according to Western norms. Simply put, Russian–Kyrgyz cooperation on internal security issues is intended to teach the Kyrgyz how to make more skillful use of threatened force and political intimidation and how to shape political reforms to create the illusion of participation. But neither the Kyrgyz population, nor most of the Kyrgyz elite were satisfied with this form of virtual participation.

Kyrgyzstan is the one Central Asian country in which public opinion has been able to force changes in government policy. Akayev's increasingly autocratic behavior fueled unrest as early as the spring of 2002, shortly after 2,000 coalition troops were stationed at the Manas airfield and stability became of primary importance. The arrest of a popular politician, Azimbek Beknazarov, in January 2002 led to the shooting of five protesters in March. This sparked mass demonstrations which continued despite the resignation of the entire government in May. It was only when the appeals court lifted the charges against Beknazarov that the protesters went home. Akayev never fully regained political legitimacy.

Beknazarov, as chairman of the Jogorku Kenesh (parliament) committee on judicial and legal affairs, had called for Akayev's impeachment after the government decided to cede 125,000 hectares of territory to Chinese control during border negotiations.[22] Beknazarov, who went on to serve as the general prosecutor in the interim government following Akayev's resignation, claimed that these lands contained valuable water resources, as well as the graves of people who died fleeing to China to avoid arrest by Russian troops in the 1916 uprising.[23]

Shortly afterward, on January 5, 2002, Beknazarov was arrested and charged with exceeding his official powers as an investigator in the Toktogul regional prosecutor's office seven years earlier. Beknazarov was put on trial in January 2002, and his supporters began to picket and some even began a hunger strike.[24] When one of the fasting demonstrators died of a stroke, tempers flared even more, and demonstrations in his hometown of Aksy in the province of Jalal-abad grew in size, so that by March hundreds, if not more, were participating. [25] Intimidated by the size of the demonstration, on March 17 and 18, 2002, the local police used force to break them up, leaving five unarmed people dead. Their deaths quickly became the cause of nationwide protests leading to calls for Akayev's resignation.

Akayev tried to defuse the crisis by appointing a team of special investigators. [26] He himself flew to Jalal-abad, which created more criticism than it quelled. People complained that he, the president, who confined his stay to the airport, failed to honor the dead by visiting their graves. Akayev also sought scapegoats. At first the district administrator of the village where the demonstrations took place, Shermamat Osmonov, was saddled with all the blame, and Akayev fired him almost immediately, although Osmonov and his superiors maintained that the police opened fire in self-defense, a claim that proved impossible to sustain. Eventually, in May 2002, Osmonov's superiors were removed, although both were quickly named to prominent positions elsewhere in the government. [27] Several local police officers, however, faced prosecution, including the former Jalal-abad province police chief, Kubanychbek Tokobayev. [28]

The deaths in Aksy and the government's response to them unified Akayev's political opposition for the first time. The scale of public protests grew, and people from provincial cities started marching to the capital. Advisers close to the president feared that if a way out of the crisis were not found, Akayev would be forced to resign. [29] In May 2002, in an unsuccessful effort to satisfy the opposition, Akayev fired Prime Minister Kurmanbek Bakiyev and named Nikolai Tanaev, a Russian who had long worked in the republic, to replace him.

In the weeks that followed, Akayev demonstrated his political mastery. He promised to meet with the legislature while simultaneously threatening to disband the very same parliament, which would strip the current members of all privilege. [30] When this did not defuse the demonstrations, Akayev's new friends from Russia's Ministry of Internal Affairs were on hand to help show their Kyrgyz colleagues some new tricks. Meeting halls became impossible to rent, and marchers were turned away from Bishkek.

Akayev also sought to open new channels for political dialogue, inviting the whole country to debate what changes to the country's constitution should be made to open up the political process. [31] At the president's behest, a committee of jurists, politicians, and political activists was organized, and they recommended restricting the power of the presidency, enhancing the independence of the prime minister and the cabinet, and converting

Kyrgyzstan's two-house legislature back into a one-chamber body with enhanced powers. But the version of the constitution put to the voters on February 2, 2003, was not that offered by the committee, but one rewritten by the office of the president, which left the presidency stronger than the committee of specialists had envisioned and made it almost impossible for the president to be impeached.[32] The referendum, which also included a call for President Akayev to serve out his term of office, passed overwhelmingly. Just to make sure that Akayev would do this without undue public pressure, in the run-up to the referendum, the Kyrgyz authorities added a number of constitutional amendments that made it permanently more difficult for opposition groups to get permits for large public meetings.

This experience convinced Kyrgyzstan's opposition—-and many who had previously been politically apathetic—that Akayev was not to be trusted, that he would always find a way to cheat or outmaneuver his opponents. It explains why they were so fearful that Akayev would use the newly elected parliament to propose a constitutional amendment that would have allowed him to continue in office after his term expired in 2005.

The parliamentary elections of February 27–March 13, 2005, became Akayev's testing ground, and rather than relying on help from Washington and technical assistance from OSCE instructors, the presidential entourage decided to make these elections a testing ground for "managed democracy." But Akayev received bad political advice from his Russian advisers, and even with extra training, Kyrgyzstan's security forces proved unreliable in crowd control.

While the actual process of voting was judged more transparent than in the previous parliamentary election, the violations of democratic norms were rarely random.[33] Dozens of people who got on the ballot were pressured into withdrawing their candidacy, generally to allow an Akayev supporter an easy election victory. Several prominent critics were denied places on the ballot due to legal loopholes, including three former ambassadors, who failed to meet the residence requirements for parliamentarians because of their diplomatic service.

Included in their number was former foreign minister Roza Otunbayeva,[34] who returned to the country in 2004 to join the opposition. Otunbayeva was excluded from running against Akayev's daughter Bermet in the February parliamentary elections. A former ambassador to the United States and UN envoy in Georgia, she was disqualified under the law that says candidates must have resided in Kyrgyzstan for the previous five years.

Political independents and opposition figures were targeted for defeat, and most of the reports of vote buying came from their districts. A half dozen opposition figures, though, received a majority of votes during the first round of balloting, when under half the seats in the legislature were filled. Even more effort was put into defeating opposition candidates in the second round—it was then that the U.S.-government-funded independent printing press found its electricity cut without explanation, starving opposition candidates of the means to print materials and reach voters.

Two key opposition figures, Adakhan Madumarov and Kurmanbek Bakiyev,[35] who most thought would be reelected easily, went down to defeat in the second round, each claiming they were the victims of fraud. The defeat of Bakiyev in particular seems to have been a rallying point. This former prime minister and declared presidential candidate had strong support from both the public and the elite in the populous and impoverished south, his home region. After his defeat, Bakiyev joined forces with other discontented southern politicians, solidifying the United Opposition, which then sought to wrest control of the southern half of the country from Akayev. This goal was achieved in only a few days. The speed with which they stabilized their new popular or interim executives and legislative councils undoubtedly gave confidence in the ability of the opposition to make a smooth transfer of power, as thousands of unhappy residents in Bishkek—a town in the north—took to the streets on March 24. The organizers did not anticipate that participants in the march—mostly young people—would break off and storm the president's office. Yet when Akayev fled they were only too happy to pick up the pieces and assume authority.

Akayev brought little honor to himself in the way he retreated. He swore in the newly elected parliament even as events in the south were devolving out of his control. He is rumored to have fled his office rolled up in a carpet as protesters converged. Outside the country, he tendered his resignation by videotape but only after days of declaring via e-mail that he had no intention of doing so.[36]

The uncertain void at the country's helm exacerbated the constitutional crisis. Kurmanbek Bakiyev was named prime minister and acting president by the old legislature—the legislature elected in 2000 and ostensibly replaced by those elected in 2005, though their legitimacy was under dispute. As a compromise, to stave off the prospect of having neither a president nor a parliament, Bakiyev recognized the legitimacy of the 2005 parliament (except in 20 disputed districts), which in turn affirmed him as prime minister, but not acting president.

Bakiyev in turn named Roza Otunbayeva acting foreign minister, and temporarily brought in Feliks Kulov, the former security minister, to coordinate security, but Kulov resigned after one week to position himself to run against Bakiyev in presidential elections scheduled for July, 10, 2005. In mid-May Kulov made an alliance with Bakiev, and he will become prime minister if there is a Bakiev victory. This led outside observers to be worried about the openness of the contest and whether it would be compromised by continued behind-the-scenes bargaining among political factions.

Askar Akayev, like his colleagues throughout the region, introduced political institutions that were intended to create an illusion of political participation. They were designed to assuage foreign and domestic critics and not to facilitate the sharing of power by the president and his entourage with other groups in society. When demands for real power emerged Akayev's first instinct was to try and stifle protest and when that failed he sought to push the offending groups from political life. But over time the Kyrgyz population and the opposition elite learned to anticipate his behavior, and in March 2005, they simply outsmarted him.

To his credit, Akayev did learn one thing from the events in Aksy: that firing on an unarmed crowd could lead to civil war. For all his unwillingness to resign, he nonetheless opted for restraint. Unfortunately, as the May 2005 violence in Uzbekistan shows, there is no reason to assume that other Central Asian leaders would make the same choice.

Kazakhstan: Can Nazarbayev Hold On?

The United States discovered it had little leverage during the last months of Akayev's rule, and little ability to press for the 2005 vote to be free and fair. As is similarly the case with Uzbekistan, Washington's hands were tied when the airbase at Manas became a reality.

If it has been difficult for international actors to influence the process of political institution in Kyrgyzstan, it is even more difficult in Kazakhstan. Given Kazakhstan's natural resource wealth, Western leaders are reluctant to apply "sticks." And given Kazakhstan's financial solvency, there are few potential "carrots" that can be offered.

Given the key role of Western firms in developing Kazakhstan's strategically important oil and gas reserves, Western leaders will not press hard for democratic reform in Kazakhstan until they believe that the non-democratic nature of the Kazakh regime is undermining its own short-term security.

Because Kazakhstan has been benefiting from the high price of oil, there are few positive incentives available. The Kazakhs have no need to borrow money from the International Monetary Fund (IMF) or the World Bank. They are able to raise money on international capital markets, so they can pay for technical assistance if necessary. The Asian Development Bank (ADB) and the World Bank continue to operate in the country, but their focus is on cofunded technical assistance programs.

The international community can influence political institution building in Kazakhstan, but it is difficult to find potentially effective levers. The good news is that many key figures in Kazakhstan realize that political institution building must accompany economic growth if their country is to exert international influence and secure the long-term welfare of its people. But Kazakhstan is unlikely to introduce democratic political reforms without the cooperation of the current president. This does not doom the prospect of democratic reform, but it does complicate it, and anyone interested in trying to reform Kazakhstan's political system must take as a given that President Nazarbayev will remain in office until 2013, assuming he stays in good health.

Nazarbayev has already announced his intention to run for reelection in December 2006, and the 1998 constitutional reforms allow him to hold a second seven-year term. The challenge in the 2006 campaign will be to ensure a transparent voting process, prevent voter fraud, allow potential candidates to collect voter signatures, and ensure candidates are not barred from running through some form of judicial or administrative intrigue, as was the case with former prime minister Akezhan Kazhegeldin, who was struck from running for parliament, the Majilis, from the Republican People's Party of Kazakhstan in 1999.

Kazakhstan's citizens are patient, provided the standard of living in the country continues to improve and the president's family reduces rather than increases its hold over the country's economy. But in the wake of the Rose, Orange, and Tulip revolutions, Kazakhstan's opposition is determined to turn this January 2006 presidential election campaign into a real fight.

Developments in Kyrgyzstan, Georgia, and Ukraine also make it less likely that Nazarbayev will be able to further consolidate political power in his own hands and continue choking off economic opportunities for those outside of his family while ruling extraconstitutionally. All eyes are on him.

The political system in Kazakhstan most resembles that of Kyrgyzstan, in that in both countries there is already a strong penetration of civil society institutions, the political and economic elite is partially fragmented, and the president has been associated with a pattern of corruption. But there are important differences.

Kazakhstan is a much wealthier society than Kyrgyzstan, with a much larger economy. Both countries have pursued relatively similar policies of economic reform, but Kazakhstan attracted vastly greater sums of foreign investment due to its large oil and gas reserves, which also have allowed the Kazakhs to benefit from high global oil prices. As a result, poverty is much less of a problem than in Kyrgyzstan, and Kazakhstan's poor are relatively dispersed across the country's enormous territorial expanse, making them much more difficult to organize and mobilize.

Some might argue that civil society institutions are not as well dispersed in Kazakhstan, but the biggest difference is that the majority of the political elite is still unwilling to break with the country's president. There are powerful members of the elite who are supportive of political reform, but most of the elite are young enough to be content with a gradual opening of the political system. The ethnic Kazakhs who dominate the nomenklatura come from a culture in which a premium is placed on respect for one's elders. The challenge for Nazarbayev will be to retain their support.

Most members of the elite believe that despite all his flaws, Nazarbayev has been a very positive force for the country, securing Kazakhstan's independence under difficult conditions and maximizing Western support without alienating Russia. The goal of these people is not to embarrass the president, nor drive him from power, but to ensure that when Nazarbayev departs in 2013, or earlier due to ill-health or demise, Kazakhstan is left with an open and competitive political system, with a functioning legislature, at least a quasi-independent media, and a political party system or some other effective means of funneling potential members of the elite into the political system.

The elite advocating this approach is growing increasingly more numerous and more effective over time. Its membership is drawn heavily from the economic sector and from those in the state and other professional sectors who have benefited from the opportunity to study abroad or in Kazakhstan's

Western-style training institutions.[37] Their emergence serves to strengthen the claim that the introduction of market reforms facilitates the development of democratic societies, because those who acquire economic power are interested in gaining political power as well, if only to protect their holdings.[38]

Although the economic vitality of Kazakhstan has helped to create a vocal and visible group lobbying for greater transparency in economic and political decision making, it is still too early to predict whether they will be successful in advancing their reform agenda. While the supporters of democratic political reform in Kazakhstan have been increasing in number, the president is still able to silence his critics at will. The past few years provide ample evidence of this. In late 2002 a group of key reformers left the government and formed a political movement called Democratic Choice of Kazakhstan (DMK), which sought to expand the reach of participatory government in Kazakhstan, improve the judiciary, and increase economic security through better protection of private property. Their plans to transform the movement into an opposition party were thwarted, but the process showed the limits of the power of the regime as well as that of the opposition.[39]

Since Akezhan Kazhegeldin resigned as prime minister in late 1997, Kazakhstan's young entrepreneurs and economic pro-reformers have become increasingly frustrated. These people are a relatively tight social group, none of whom formally supported Kazhegeldin's subsequent efforts to create an opposition within the country, but all of whom were disturbed at the increasing consolidation by the president and his family members in the aftermath of Kazhegeldin's removal. They believed that the case for reform had to be made within the confines of the political establishment and by enlisting support of those close to the president.

These people have not sought to oust Nazarbayev or strip his family of their vast economic holdings. Their intent, rather, was to increase their own assets and expand their own political influence, and they believed increased transparency offered them the best chance of doing this. However, Nazarbayev's son-in-law Rakhat Aliyev tried to gain control of some of the DMK backers' holdings, including media outlets and the import and export of alcohol and sugar. Aliyev, deputy head of national security, wanted to further expand his economic empire, in part to enhance his own power base within Kazakhstan's security organs.[40]

In retaliation, the independent Tan TV (owned by DMK member Mukhtar Ablyazov) aired footage that charged Aliyev with using his office to acquire personal assets. The exposé was embarrassing for Nazarbayev and made a mockery of his anticorruption policy, because Aliyev had formal supervisory responsibilities in that sector. Nazarbayev "exiled" Aliyev, naming him ambassador to Austria. Aliyev temporarily lost control of his media holdings, Karavan and Kazakh Commercial TV, and his diplomatic posting to Austria disadvantaged him in his struggle for political succession within Kazakhstan.[41] Aliyev was one of the fiercest opponents of democratic reform in Kazakhstan. Ironically he was assigned the task of pressing for Kazakhstan to receive the OSCE presidency in 2009 and therefore responsible for detailing for Astana the kinds of political reforms Kazakhstan must undertake to make the OSCE presidency a reality.

The fates of those who opposed Aliyev are far worse. The momentum behind the creation of the DMK movement quickly began to peter out when two of its organizers, Mukhtar Ablyazov, former minister of energy, industry, and trade, and Ghalymzhan Zhakqiyanov, former head of the northern Pavlodar oblast, were arrested on several charges relating to abuse of office.

Zhakqiyanov's arrest almost created an international incident, when he took refuge in the French embassy in Almaty and was released only after the French and German ambassadors were assured that he would remain under house arrest throughout the course of the investigation into his alleged misconduct. Zhakqiyanov, however, was taken off to jail, tried, convicted, and sentenced to a seven-year prison term.[42] Ablyazov, also convicted of all charges, was sentenced to a six-year prison term but was granted amnesty in May 2003, when he promised to abstain from all further political activity. Zhakqiyanov refused to accept these same terms and remains in jail, although he was transferred to a penal work colony in August 2004.

The treatment that Zhakqiyanov and Ablyazov received gave some DMK founders pause. Both Nurlan Smagulov, president of Food Corporation, a grain export company, and Yerzyan Tatishev, chairman of TuranAlem Bank, left the movement after Nazarbayev cautioned that the country's business executives should confine their efforts to the economy, much as Russian President Vladimir Putin had done with the "oligarchs." By backing out of politics, both Smagulov and Tatishev were able to retain their holdings.

Two other organizers—former first deputy prime minister Oraz Zhandosov and Alikhan Beymanov—broke with DMK to create the Ak Zhol (White Way) Party and were joined by Bulat Abilov as cochairs of the new party, a move designed to preserve an impetus for reform while simultaneously avoiding the fates of Zhakqiyanov and Ablyazov.[43] The current strategy of Ak Zhol reflects the decision by its leadership to seek a measured approach to political change, rather than to proceed hastily and promote political backsliding through governmental retaliation instead of reform.

Members of Ak Zhol are hopeful that while the president will move against individuals, he will not purge the pro-reform economic elite in its entirety, because it is already strongly represented in key positions in the government, banking sector, and business community. The goals of Ak Zhol are privately endorsed by many of these people, but few with direct ties to the Nazarbayev regime are willing to be publicly identified as Ak Zhol supporters.[44]

A change in the law in July 2002 forced all the political parties to reregister, and not all the parties met the tougher terms of required membership necessary for legal recognition.[45] Ak Zhol did gain registration and ran candidates in the 2004 local and parliamentary election campaigns as part of an opposition bloc with DMK and the Communist Party. This enabled the latter two groups to participate, as they had been denied registration as political parties.

The fact that these people continue to survive and play a role in Kazakh political life makes it clear that Kazakhstan is not an authoritarian country. Although Kazakhstan is certainly not a democracy, its people enjoy a large measure of personal freedom and control over their private space, which is applied to all the ethnic communities living in the country. Ordinary citizens do not fear that the hands of the security forces will reach down to touch them, even if they criticize the president and his family in private settings. Those who try to enter politics, however, are made aware of the long reach of the state. Although he is a dictator—a term Nursultan Nazarbayev is increasingly uncomfortable about using in public, preferring to be thought of as a sort of modern-day khan—the Kazakh president also recognizes that there are restraints on his power.

Nazarbayev believes that political power is partly defined by the society that he governs. Kazakh society, like Kyrgyz society, has always been more open than Uzbek or Tajik society. The Kazakhs like to say that this is because of their nomadic past, which made their culture more adaptive, more receptive to foreign influence. Certainly in recent centuries the traditional Kazakh society took more from its contact with Russian culture than it did from the settled oasis cultures of the peoples who lived in Uzbekistan and Tajikistan. The process of cultural blending began well before the years of forced assimilation of Soviet times, and it may be for this reason that the Kazakhs (and Kyrgyz) have found the transition to independence easier than have the other peoples of Central Asia.

The organization of Kyrgyz and Kazakh nomadic society along clan and tribal lines has encouraged a spirit of openness, because throughout Kazakh history clan and tribe elders met and discussed the important political issues of the day. This was true even in the sixteenth and seventeenth centuries in which the three hordes of Kazakhs were united under a single ruler. None of the Kazakh khans had the power of a figure like Timur (Tamerlane), the Uzbek national hero.[46]

Nonetheless President Nazarbayev does not tolerate people who damage his image. His family's dominating role in media has helped create an atmosphere of more restrained political discourse than in Kyrgyzstan. Journalists who cross the line have been brutally persecuted. In May 2002, Irina Petrushova, editor of the outspoken newspaper *Respublika*, who had written scathingly of Nazarbayev's cronyism, received a warning note attached to the body of a decapitated dog.[47] Also that month, when Kazakh opposition journalist Lira Bayseitova was out of the country, her 25-year-old daughter Leila died after receiving terminal injuries while in police custody.[48]

Another example, the treatment of journalist and human rights advocate Sergei Duvanov, who was arrested and found guilty of statutory rape, was widely reported in the West—charges that an independent European commission concluded were politically motivated.[49] Duvanov had been reporting about the ongoing grand jury investigations in New York into corruption in Kazakhstan's oil industry and had published articles that linked the Kazakh president to these investigations.[50] Continued international attention to the case led to Duvanov being transferred to house arrest in January 2004.[51]

Duvanov's case emphasizes the contradictory messages that the Kazakh president has sent in recent years. Nazarbayev wants Kazakhstan to be accepted in the community of serious states, one that accepts European norms. That is why he is pushing for Kazakhstan to be the first post-Soviet state to serve as chairman of the OSCE. (The choice for 2009 will be made in 2006.) Yet Nazarbayev's own behavior or the actions he permits to be taken in his name make the achievement of this goal seem improbable.

OSCE officials made it very clear to Kazakh leaders that they would have to move quickly to reform their political system, if they want the chairmanship. To advance their candidacy they must conduct free and fair parliamentary elections, allow the political opposition to exist without harassment, create the preconditions necessary for independent media to function, and create an independent judiciary.[52]

However, the Kazakh government has been willing to go only part way to meet objections of its international critics. Some small steps have been taken over the last few years. For example, in 2001, Kazakhstan began choosing some local legislatures and officials on the basis of competitive election, and the intent is to gradually substitute election for executive appointment.[53] In November 2002, the Kazakh president announced the founding of a permanent consultative body that was convened in part to provide a scorecard on how the government was doing.[54]

The September 2004 parliamentary and local elections were conducted according to a new election law that made it easier for independent candidates to compete and provided for political parties to be represented on local election commissions.[55] The passage of a new media law on December 25, 2003, was roundly criticized by U.S. and OSCE officials for failing to meet international standards and then vetoed by the president with great fanfare at an international media forum (sponsored by his daughter Dariga) in Almaty in April 2004.[56]

But candidates from pro-presidential parties enjoyed extraordinary advantage in the electoral contests, and then when they failed to perform up to expectation, the actual conduct of the election was skewed to produce more favorable results. Nobody knows whether or not this was done at Nazarbayev's command, but what is clear is that Nazarbayev did not press his subordinates to conduct elections that met European norms. Had he done so, the final results would have come much closer to exit polls than was the case.

But chicanery on the part of the government seems to have been responsible for denying members of the coalition a fair share of seats in the parliament. While exit polls reported coalition candidates receiving 22.9 percent of the vote, the official tabulations gave them only one seat. The coalition was also handicapped by the arrest of Bulat Abilov, Ak Zhol cochair, on the eve of the election, making his candidacy illegal.[57] Another surprise was the relatively poor showing of Asar, Dariga Nazarbayeva's party, which got only 11.38 percent of the vote, against 19.1 percent as recorded by exit polls. The big winner in the election was Otan, the party closest to the president, which took 60.62 percent of the vote in the official results but only 40.1 percent according to exit polls.[58]

The OSCE strongly criticized the conduct of these elections. Ak Zhol refused to take the one seat it won, claiming that the entire electoral process had been illegitimate, but the Kazakh election commission rejected its call for a nationwide referendum to annul the results.[59] Ak

Zhol's leadership then began to press for change in the structure of government and seek support from other prominent figures who have broken with Nazarbayev. These include, most prominently, the former leader of Otan and parliamentary speaker Zharmakhan Tuyakbai, who resigned in protest of the elections, as well as Zamanbek Nurkadilov, former mayor of Almaty and most recently emergencies minister, who formally fell out with Nazarbayev in 1999 after Kazhegeldin was sent into exile for speaking out regarding the Giffen kickback corruption scandal. Nurkadilov accused the president of corruption and "wasting the country's rich mineral resources."[60]

In the aftermath of the Ukrainian revolution, most political opposition groups in Kazakhstan organized as a bloc called For a Just Kazakhstan, which threw its support behind a single candidate, Tuyakbai, at a convention in Almaty on March 20, 2005.[61]

The opposition hopes to turn the next presidential elections into a Ukrainian style landslide. They do enjoy popular support, particularly in Almaty, the country's largest city. They have managed to hold demonstrations of as many as 2,000 people,[62] but the police have easily dispersed the crowds, and the Tuyakbai campaign has been harrassed when trying to hold events in the region.

Nazarbayev has a lot of discretionary power, and a lot of real options. He maintains that he is committed to real, albeit gradual, political reform accompanied by concrete steps to improve the social and economic conditions of the Kazakh people.[63]

In a February 2005 address to the nation, he offered a series of social promises. For example, that the number of young people sent to the West for master's degrees at the state's expense would increase tenfold, to 3,000 annually. If he fulfills this concrete promise, it will boost his popularity.

The process of political reform in Kazakhstan is highly regulated and designed to create the impression that democracy is being bestowed on the Kazakh people by its benevolent president, who is doing so in a way that is consistent with the country's culture and history.[64] Although Nazarbayev desperately wants to lead Kazakhstan onto a world stage, he is determined to do it in his own way, preserving what he sees to be the perquisites and prerogatives of office. Take for example his management of relations with James Giffen, whose arrest has been discussed in earlier chapters. Nazarbayev could—and should—have cut his ties with Giffen, or claimed ignorance of any illegal actions in which Giffen may have engaged, but instead he rehired Mercator Corporation, now being run by Giffen's son.

If Kazakhstan is going to evolve into a democratic society, it is incumbent on U.S. and European leaders to make clear that rich and poor states are held to the same norms. In the nearly six years since the investigations into the source of Nazarbayev's Swiss bank accounts began, he has been a welcome official visitor in many European capitals and has been received warmly by the Queen of England and the president of France. Nazarbayev's wish to have his country chair the OSCE provides a golden opportunity to hold the Kazakh leadership to international standards.

It is obvious that Kazakhstan cannot become a mature democracy in the span of a few years, but if the Western leaders accept the assertion that the best Kazakhstan can become is a "guided" democracy, the Kazakh president will guide the Kazakh people not only to six more years of Nazarbayev's rule but to the transfer of power to a candidate of his choice.

Opposition party leaders believe the president and his family see the successful transfer of power in Azerbaijan as an invitation for them to do the same, although they recognize that the failed efforts to transfer power of Shevardnadze, Kuchma, and Akayev have created new and more powerful precedents.[65] Nazarbayev has no sons, and only one of his three daughters, Dariga, seems to have any political ambitions, and she is his daughter by marriage, born to Nazarbayev's wife before the couple met. Two sons-in-law, Rakhat Aliyev and Timur Kulibayev, also dream of becoming president.

Although Dariga seems to have the inside track, the race to the finish line may be bumpy. Asar's failure to win more seats in the 2004 election suggests the only tepid backing of her father.[66] Timur Kulibayev, the son of a regional communist boss from oil- and gas-rich western Kazakhstan, has acquired valuable experience and skills in his post as second in command in the Kazakh state oil and gas company and could be a formidable opponent.

Over the next several years many new contenders are likely to emerge from outside the family, and they will try to make the 2006 presidential race a real contest. Even if Nazarbayev has an easy time in 2006, the 2013 contest will be hotly contested. Kazakh society is going to become more complex over time, and with that, the prospects of Nazarbayev establishing a dynasty grow more unlikely.

Uzbekistan: Failed Promises to Reform

The political system of Uzbekistan is fundamentally different from that of Kazakhstan and Kyrgyzstan, and much less responsive to influence from outsiders. This makes it all the more frightening that most observers believe that Uzbekistan is becoming ripe for political change and see virtually no evidence that the country's elite or population is able to sustain a democratic transformation.

While observers can squabble over the degree of political participation afforded the citizens in Kazakhstan and Kyrgyzstan, Uzbekistan is without question a modern-day authoritarian political system. But while the power of the president and the security organs reaches down into even remote localities of the country, successful exercise of this control requires public cooperation, which has become more difficult to attain.

Uzbekistan has not been immune to the forces of globalization. The impact of technology means that this country is quite unlike the totalitarian states of the 1930s; independent sources of information do penetrate to the Uzbek population, at least the portion that makes an effort to access them. News broadcasts on the state channels are closely monitored for content, but it is estimated that almost half of the households in Tashkent have access to satellite-relayed programming, which includes Russian, English, and Turkish language services. Similarly, although user privacy is not as well protected in Uzbekistan as in Kyrgyzstan and Kazakhstan (the Uzbeks use Chinese technology to block access to "offensive" sites), there are Internet cafes in almost every part of the country. Many young Uzbeks have become cyber-sophisticates, finding ways to gain access to materials that are intended to be inaccessible in Uzbekistan. In the end, economics more than politics defines how much access a person has to unfettered sources of information.

Political discourse in Uzbekistan grew steadily more relaxed. Although the call to appear in the local procurator's office still strikes real fear in the heart of normal citizens, such summons can also be wholly innocuous. In private and semiprivate settings, ordinary Uzbeks now venture to discuss political themes and to speculate on the future of their country. Even before the large-scale protest in Andijan in May 2005, they had begun grumbling publicly—in stores, in markets, and when they are delayed in traffic. Less common were formal public protests, but they too were occurring with increasing frequency. Women led these demonstrations more often then men because police were more likely to disperse such crowds without arresting the participants.[67] Moreover, after a series of suicide bombings in March–April 2004 were blamed on Islamic extremists, many ordinary Uzbeks seem to have sympathized with those who felt so aggrieved as to resort to such desperate acts, rather than with their victims.[68] And it seems to have made other kinds of groups more willing to demonstrate as well, which is in sharp contrast to public reaction after the explosions in 1999. [69]

All this suggests that the citizens of Uzbekistan will continue to press for political change, even if force is used by the state to try to control them. The challenge is to get Uzbek authorities to open up the political system in the face of increasing public dissatisfaction rather than close it further. If the government clamps down, they risk civil war.

There was a honeymoon period of about six months, in late 2001 to early 2002, when observers hoped that increased U.S. engagement might lead to much-needed political reforms. But so little reform occurred that in late 2003 the U.S. Department of State formally condemnned Uzbekistan for its failing human rights record.[70]

Could the United States have made a major difference in Uzbekistan's political evolution in these years? Unlike in Kyrgyzstan, there was a limited capacity in Uzbekistan to absorb large increases in foreign assistance designed for political projects. The elite support base for such reforms was much more limited, because there was virtually no independent entrepreneurial class seeking protection of legally acquired property. Over the long term, however, increased levels of assistance would have had some positive effect by raising the level of professionalism throughout the judicial and penal system and in all sectors of public administration. It also would have stimulated the development of a group of independent entrepreneurs, who could have lobbied for further political reforms.

The improvement of the security environment in Afghanistan in late 2001–2002 created an opportunity for the Uzbek government to engage in political reform, if they had wanted to. But these events did little to modify the personal ambitions of most of the key members of the Uzbek elite. Most of the close circle surrounding Karimov had constructed political careers that were strongly identified with a top-down style of political decision making that ensured control through the threat or use of force.

That Karimov wanted a strategic partnership with the United States was clear, but discussions of political reform in Uzbekistan proceeded from a very different basis than those on economic reform. Many senior policy makers in Tashkent believed that the country had made a mistake to proceed so slowly with the introduction of a market economy, but few defended the need for political reform on any grounds other than those of expediency to gain credibility in the United States and Western Europe.

As already mentioned, during Karimov's March 2002 visit to Washington, he made a lot of promises and also signed five separate agreements between the U.S. and Uzbek governments. The agreements included most importantly a broad-based "Declaration on the Strategic Partnership and Cooperation Framework," covering political, security, economic, humanitarian, and legal cooperation, which committed the Uzbek government to support democratic reforms.[71] The United States promised support for Tashkent in the face of external threat or risk to the territorial integrity of Uzbekistan. In return, to quote the official communiqués: "Uzbekistan reaffirmed its commitment to further intensify the democratic transformation of its society politically and economically...and to build in Uzbekistan a rule by law state and democratic society...to develop a law-based government system, [and] further reform the judicial system and enhance the legal culture."[72]

Paradoxically, the strong wording may have been the result of pressure from the Uzbek side. One version of events holds that the State Department originally suggested a somewhat weaker text, which would have allowed for more realizable goals being set. But, according to this account, in discussions held parallel to the official negotiations, some members of the Uzbek delegation pressed for tougher language, arguing that unless nearly impossible goals were set nothing would be achieved.

Even if Karimov was sincere in his promises to support political reforms, he saw Uzbekistan's journey toward becoming a participatory society as a long one and not threatening his personal control. He had already extended his term of office to 2007, in a referendum held in January 2002.[73]

The hand of fate need not endorse the timetable of dictators, and by mid-2002 rumors began spreading about the president's ill health, and with them came signs of jockeying for position among the putative godfathers of Uzbekistan's leading political families. These men had little understanding of how a democratic system operated, and no confidence in it (one cannot manipulate what one does not understand).

The government made some largely symbolic steps to introduce a few of the promised political changes. Karimov supported the gradual transformation of the parliament from a body that provides a rubber stamp on all decrees and draft laws emanating from the president and his cabinet, to one capable of debating and eventually even independently drafting legislation.

Legislators chosen in 2004 serve in a new bicameral body, but despite Karimov's glib promise of 2002, they were not freely or fairly elected. Tentative steps have been made to begin the development of political parties that represent different interests, but virtually all the parties participating in the 2004 election are pro-regime, and most were organized for the purpose of making these elections appear democratic.[74] Political parties not organized by government initiative have not been able to receive registration.[75] This includes new political parties, as well as Erk and Birlik, both of which have been able to hold organizational meetings but have not met the formal and sometimes whimsically applied legal conditions for registration.[76]

State censorship has been formally eliminated, but the government retains control over the content of media. They do this through registration, the requirement for state-registered media to file annual broadcast and publications plans, and by how they release news. Journalists who violate the unwritten codes are either beaten or arrested for "defaming the image of Uzbekistan abroad," a threat to which those working for Western NGOs are particularly vulnerable.[77]

Much the same strategy has been applied to human rights activists. Some previously banned groups were registered, and conferences have been held on a number of political themes that had previously been taboo, although sometimes such forums are solely for the benefit of specially invited foreign guests.[78] The activities of human rights groups are still closely monitored, and those organizations that go beyond the bounds of government-determined acceptability remain subject to harassment, losing their accreditation and having their leadership arrested.[79]

A similar pattern of slow and problematic progress emerged toward prison reform and the protection of the legal rights of the accused. In a few instances, police officials have been charged, found guilty, and received prison terms for the use of excessive force in interrogating suspects arrested on the suspicion of being religious extremists.[80] The government has made some improvement in the conditions of prisoners of conscience, including granting them increased opportunities for prayer and some amelioration of what in many cases are dire conditions.[81] The Uzbek government even permitted the UN special rapporteur on torture, envoy Theo van Boven, to visit its prisons.[82] Since then there have been a handful of independent investigations of alleged police brutality in the deaths of prisoners, and the police were exonerated in one case.[83] Official cover-ups of the use of torture at every level of the judicial system remain commonplace, and the Uzbek government refused requests for an international inquiry into the use of deadly force in Andijan in May 2005.

The regime in Tashkent insists that Hizb ut-Tahrir poses an armed threat to the state and is more adamant about this since the siege in Andijan, laid to Akhromiya, its splinter group. Although some religious prisoners have been granted amnesty, several thousand people remain in jail for allegedly seditious activities linked to religion.[84] Religious activists tend to be subject to the worst abuses of authority.[85] Courts treat confessions as proof of guilt, so extreme measures are frequently used to gain confessions. The government campaign against Hizb ut-Tahrir entered a new phase after the bombings in March, April, and July 2004.[86] The latter explosions coincided with the trials of thirteen defendants being tried for the former attacks.[87]

In addition to searching for survivors from the IMU, the government has continued to arrest people with ties to Hizb ut-Tahrir. There are small cells active in much of the country, and their numbers are enhanced by new recruits, by government amnesties of small numbers of religious prisoners, and by the release of activists who have completed their prison terms.[88] Hizb ut-Tahrir members also continue to cross back and forth from Tajikistan, Kazakhstan, or Kyrgyzstan, bringing materials printed in these neighboring countries back to Uzbekistan. Although Hizb ut-Tahrir is illegal in these countries as well, the local authorities there perceive less of a threat from their activities, are less vigilant in their supervision of suspected members, and give shorter jail terms to those convicted of proselytizing.[89] The general state of nervousness about the dangers posed by Hizb ut-Tahrir is increasing in the region, especially since the organization has been able to recover the momentum of recruitment, which was substantially slowed in the immediate aftermath of September 11, when the United States led a global international campaign to cut off funds to potentially suspicious Islamic charities. But it did not take too long for the money chains through Central Asia to be restored, given the relative ease with which Islamic groups can raise small sums of money from believers in the region.[90]

In the Uzbek case, as elsewhere throughout the region, the supervision of religious life is in the hands of secular authorities, and for most of Central Asia at least, many of these authorities were tied to the atheistic regime. The country's senior cleric, the *Mufti*, is nominally chosen by a gathering of religious elders, but in reality he serves at the explicit behest of the state committee that supervises Islamic affairs. While the individual mosques are now easily able to raise money and conduct services with only minimal intrusion by state-appointed authorities, the opening of religious schools is still strictly regulated by the state, and it is very hard to secure permission to open new schools, something that was not true in the early years after independence.

To cast itself as supportive of "good" believers, the state committee includes some believers in its membership who are loyal to the Uzbek state. In recent years, it has given some new authority to the *Mufti* and his administration and has returned some property to its control.[91] But the committee has also done things that have angered believers, such as trying to limit the opulence of *ifta* (breaking the day's fast) celebrations during Ramadan and weddings. These steps were so unpopular that they led to rumors that some of these believers are in fact members of radical Islamic groups who are interested in sabotaging the state's policy toward religion from within, by pressing the state to support policies that go against the values of the Uzbek community.

Restrictions on adopting religious dress in schools and public places initially introduced in the late 1990s remain in effect. They appear to be less rigorously enforced, largely because they have had their desired effect of forcing women in *hijab* (headscarves) to withdraw from public life, and getting bearded men to either shave or go underground. These were actions that enjoyed some public support, which highlights the complexity of religious life in Uzbekistan, where secular, traditional, and radical Islamic forces have longed vied for influence within the community. But the majority of Uzbeks, who practice at least some of the rituals of Islam, seem to support the idea that religious life should be regulated by the community of believers, within a civil framework provided by the state. On most other questions, there seems to be very little consensus, including what should be the attitude toward extreme Islamic groups (those who reject the dominant Hanafi legal tradition). Support for the Hanafi tradition of Islamic jurisprudence is deeply rooted in Uzbekistan, and the growth of Hizb ut-Tahrir (which rejects all four of the traditional Islamic schools of law) is a reflection of the absence of secular and religious options.

The Central Asian elite, of course, is not formally against Islam but is very wary of revivalist or fundamentalist Islam, which seeks to regulate modern life according to the teachings of the Quran. The elite wants to keep the republics secular and prevent devout Muslims from forcing all of their co-religionists into the public observance of the faith, which is becoming more and more commonplace everywhere in Central Asia.

Although the heavy hand applied by the Karimov regime to "extreme" Islamic groups creates genuine discomfort in Washington, the official Uzbek attitudes encouraging "good" or tolerant Islam while attacking "bad" or extremist Islam is very much in keeping with official U.S. thinking on these questions. If not for its human rights record, Tashkent would be a good example of a state embracing the Bush administration's view of moderate Islamic ideas to defeat the spread of radical ideology.

Even now, the U.S. embassy in Tashkent invites both moderate clerics and members of the state council on Islamic religion to the United States as part of the international visitors program. The U.S. government has also made fellowship money open to Uzbek scholars of Islam to come to the United States and pursue research projects in comparative Islam that are designed to encourage greater religious tolerance. Although there is reason to question the practicality or likely success of the U.S. approach in general, in the case of Uzbekistan, at least, it has helped sharpen the discussion over the proper relationship between religion and the state. Those who come to the United States draw few practical examples that are easily applicable in the Uzbek context, but they do seem to come away with a sense of how atypical the current Uzbek relationship between religion and the state is in the greater global community, despite the fact that it is wholly ordinary in the Central Asian context.

The international community has been much less concerned over interethnic relations within the country than it has over the treatment of human rights activists or the Islamist minority. Ethnicity has proved more fluid in Uzbekistan than in any other place in the Central Asian region. Those who choose to identify themselves as Uzbeks and who learn the language are viewed as Uzbeks, even if they come from ethnically mixed families or from families who in earlier times may have identified themselves as Kazakh, Kyrgyz, or Tajik.[92] Although the percentage of ethnic Tajiks is a question of great controversy, they are without question Uzbekistan's largest minority, especially given the large outmigration of ethnic Russians since independence.[93]

Over the past eighty years much of the Tajik-speaking population in Uzbekistan has gradually reidentified themselves and their families as Uzbeks on their passports and official documents. But some of this reidentification is just political expedience, and an untold number of Uzbeks still identify as Tajiks and would prefer to be living in a Tajik-dominated state.

The Uzbek–Tajik split continues to have real impact on Uzbek political life. Tajiks, especially those living in the border regions, are seen as potentially disloyal. There has even been the forced resettlement of residents of some Tajik villages along the mountainous spine that Uzbekistan shares with Tajikistan (in Uzbekistan's provinces of Kashkar Darya and Surkhan Darya), the site of the summer 2000 IMU incursion.[94]

Similarly, any time a Tajik is the beneficiary of political favor, rumors begin to spread that he will use his new position to advance Tajik interests. When Shavkat Mirziyayev, a Tajik from Samarkand, was appointed prime minister in November 2003, many Uzbeks began to complain that this was just the first step in the Tajiks "stealing away" the cities of Samarkand and Bukhara, both of which Tajikistan believes rightfully belong in their republic.

Regionalism is also a very important political factor in Uzbekistan, and the lingering power of regional elites is another reason why Tashkent has been reluctant to engage in widespread political or economic reforms. As elsewhere in the region, the president appoints provincial leaders, and Karimov has made steady use of this power, replacing officials whose loyalty was in doubt. But there has been a great deal more stability at the middle and lower levels of the provincial government, and regional elites use their political and economic levers to extract rents from the local population, in return for delivering rents to the ruling elite in the capital.

As political conditions normalized during the first decade of independence, these subnational identities, which were stimulated in the tumultuous conditions of the final years of Soviet rule, have receded to some degree. But in a time of political transition, the country's social and political cleavages will inevitably become more important. Even before the protests in Andijan in May, 2005, the signals of impending transition were becoming increasingly apparent in Uzbekistan. The average man on the street was already talking about how it was time for the president to leave. Although it is difficult to predict whether this transition will come in a few months or a few years, the political system will be difficult to transform until it is completed.

Unlike in some of the other countries of Central Asia, the competing political forces in Uzbekistan are unlikely to want to use parliamentary or other Western-style participatory forms of government to mobilize political support. None of the Uzbek contenders feel that they have mastered such styles of political infighting.

However, the absence of formal political institutions to moderate elite competition means that the period of political transition will be a time of great instability in Uzbekistan. Excluded political groups seeking to expand their influence are likely to appeal to regional and subnational groups as they seek ways to expand their potential power bases. For much the same reason, the role of religious opposition groups may expand as well, particularly the least radical of them.

One of the real tragedies of recent Uzbek history is that while the government claims to better understand its population than foreign observers do, its instincts about how to achieve both political and economic reform while maintaining stability seem woefully flawed. Over the past two years the Karimov regime has grown more wary of accepting foreign assistance in the area of political institution building than ever before, seeing U.S. nongovernmental organizations as little more than well-dressed revolutionaries. Foreign groups have found it harder and harder to get their registration renewed, and if the current trend persists, by 2006 there will be virtually no Western organizations actively working in the field of elections or rule of law. One tragic corollary is that foreign assistance in the area of education, a parallel function for many of these groups, is also being slashed.

Despite rising public dissatisfaction in Uzbekistan, there is a slim chance that the transfer of power will be accomplished peacefully. But it is impossible to imagine that it will occur through democratic means. The political system of Uzbekistan may appear simple to the casual outside observer, with a powerful president and a strong security system able to dictate the terms of political and economic engagement to a country of some 25 million people, but in reality, the political system is quite complex. It is governed by an internal logic and rules of engagement that are opaque to ordinary citizens but transparent to those who need to know them.

Such a complex system is quite slow to be transformed, especially if the transformation is coming at the hands of outside actors who do not fully understand where the levers of power lie, let alone how or by whom they are exercised. This was a lesson that the Soviet rulers of Uzbekistan were slow to learn. They—like the U.S. and Western democracy builders—believed, or at least argued, that they were pressing for change in order to introduce a more just and equitable political system, one that would benefit the people and not the rulers.

The ouster of President Akayev in Kyrgyzstan changed the political equation in neighboring Uzbekistan, for a frustrated Uzbek population are now less inclined toward patience. The Karimov government's use of force to maintain its control has heightened the risks that it faces. Given the hard road Uzbekistan faces, most secular opposition groups—both democratic activists and the largely mute critics of Karimov, who serve in the regime—still hold out hope that timely political reforms will be introduced, but few have much insight on how to induce Karimov to create more public space for civic society institutions.

Turkmenistan: Stalinism in One Country

Turkmenistan is a totalitarian system, no less so than Germany under Hitler or the Soviet Union under Stalin. Western leaders, however, have not sought to oust or isolate the Turkmen leader, largely because they do not believe his actions create strong security risks for other states. But that does not make him any less odious a political figure.

The behavior of President Saparmurat Niyazov raises the question of how the international community should respond to a totalitarian ruler who lacks global ambitions, as the inattention to the plight of the Turkmen nation is coming at a time when dictators elsewhere are being ousted or targeted for removal. Instead Turkmenbashi has been able to continue brainwashing his population through his far-reaching cult of personality. By choosing to recognize the legitimacy of Niyazov's authority and granting him the minimal amount of respect due to the leader of a sovereign state, the international community has effectively become complicit in Turkmenbashi's cult.

Ironically, U.S. officials justify the policy in Turkmenistan as a necessary complement to the war on terror—the same justification that was responsible for the decision to go to war in Iraq. Washington defends its decision to seek cooperative security relations with Turkmenistan despite the country's egregious human rights record because the Turkmen leader has allowed the shipment of large quantities of humanitarian assistance to pass through en route to neighboring Afghanistan and has provided limited landing rights and other support services for the allied forces active in the region.

Turkmenistan's security cooperation with the United States is inversely proportional to its commitment to political liberalism. When the political situation in Turkmenistan began to deteriorate seriously in 2003, Niyazov raised the prospect of closer security cooperation with the United States to fight drug trafficking and other transnational threats. In the fall of 2004, the Turkmen leadership discussed furthering military-technical cooperation and border protection issues when Lieutenant General Lance Smith, deputy chief of U.S. Central Command, visited Ashgabat, following General John Abizaid's visit. Given the lack of professionalism and the pervasiveness of corruption in the Turkmen military and security services, it is hard to believe that increased cooperation between Ashgabat and Washington will have much effect.

For a far smaller contribution to the war on terror than that being made by Uzbekistan, the U.S. administration tolerates a regime in Turkmenistan that is far worse and that is unlikely to change as long as Niyazov is in power. U.S. officials like to point to small victories, such as how draconian restrictions on Turkmen citizens' freedom of movement were relaxed some-what due to strong U.S. pressure and the threat to invoke the Jackson–Vanik amendment.[95] The Turkmen government gets virtually no direct U.S. assis-tance, outside of the area of security, and policy makers in Washington defend the small sums that go to nongovernmental groups in Turkmenistan as keeping the tradition of civic initiatives alive, no matter how few in num-ber and how apolitical in content the funded projects may be.[96]

Anyone who has contact with Niyazov knows how little interest he has in supporting the development of participatory political institutions in his coun-try. Most foreign assistance for civic institution building in Turkmenistan goes to foreign-based activities or opposition groups.[97] But this money, which is only devoted to peaceful forms of political capacity building, is relatively small, reflecting both the low level of international interest and the limited capacity of Turkmen opposition groups based abroad.

Turkmenistan's political system is increasingly a one-man show: In 2003, the fifty-member parliament (the Majilis), already a mere rubber stamp for the president, was completely stripped of its powers. These powers were then turned over to the Halk Maslahaty (the 2,507-member People's Coun-cil), which Niyazov has termed a more authentic representation of Turkmen traditional culture, a modern substitute for the gathering of tribal elders. But the tribal elders of traditional Turkmen society had considerable power, whereas the current Halk Maslahaty is filled with delegates from the various branches of the government and other public institutions as well as sectors of the economy.

Niyazov has always defended his choices as providing the Turkmen peo-ple with the kind of political system they want. Although he talks of hold-ing presidential elections in 2008–2009, no one believes that there will be competitive elections held in Turkmenistan during Niyazov's lifetime.[98] He sees himself as an all-knowing benevolent khan, able to reach his decisions after only the most cursory consultations with his advisers. He prefers to be guided by formal audiences with the Turkmen people, held in Ashgabat or in well-publicized tours of the more distant parts of the country—some of which are even undertaken in disguise, as if there could be any mystery about the identity of any short Turkmen traveling with a large security detail.

As long as Niyazov is in power, there will be no possibility of building or even "planting the seeds" of any democratic society. What was highly unlikely before became virtually impossible following the failed coup led by former foreign minister Boris Shikhmuradov, on November 25, 2002. Niyazov escaped unhurt after, as he claims, gunmen opened fire on his motorcade. Niyazov launched a fierce police crackdown against the suspected perpetrators. Some human rights watchdogs claim that more than 100 people have been arrested following the alleged assassination attempt, including Shikhmuradov, who was sentenced to twenty-five years in prison for treason. The same sentence was given, in absentia, to two other accused plotters, the exiled former Central Bank chief Khudaiberdy Orazov and former Ambassador to Turkey Nurmukhammed Khanamov.[99] Property belonging to them and their relatives was seized according to provisions of the "Betrayers of the Motherland Decree."

The details of the coup are still incomplete. U.S., Uzbek, and Turkish diplomats based in Ashgabat do not share what they know. One alleged participant, Leonid Komarovsky, a naturalized U.S. citizen who was a business associate of Shikhmuradov, was arrested and then released because of substantial pressure from Washington.[100] His version of events is much like that of Shikhmuradov's supporters: that the former foreign minister returned to Turkmenistan to talk the president into resigning, which Shikhmuradov hoped to do by demonstrating that he had the support of the rest of the government.[101] According to other accounts, some of the disloyal security forces may have been involved in the attack on Niyazov's motorcade as it was making its way from his residence in Ashgabat due to the lack of open opposition in the country.[102] It is hard to imagine that Niyazov could have been convinced to resign or that Shikhmuradov believed that he could take power without the use of force. But the real intention of the plotters is unlikely ever to be known, even if Shikhmuradov manages to survive his twenty-five-year prison term.

The Turkmen elite faced a stark choice: endure their president or try to overthrow him. It was clear that Boris Shikhmuradov was publicly pressing for his removal, and he sought support from the governments in Russia, the

United States, Turkey, and Uzbekistan to achieve this end.[103] Some in the Uzbek government seem even to have facilitated Shikhmuradov's return to Turkmenistan. The governments of Russia, Turkey, and the United States seem to have had prior knowledge of Shikhmuradov's plans and may have promised support in the event of his success.

All had observed that Niyazov's behavior was becoming more erratic. During a presentation to a Washington audience in the spring of 2002, Shikhmuradov talked about how fearful he always was about reporting to work on Mondays, because, he maintained, Niyazov always offered his most absurd policy recommendations on that day, having been left to his own devices on the weekend.[104] The goal, the former foreign minister said, was to talk Niyazov out of an idea before he signed it into law by mid-day. Clearly, much slipped through, including things like renaming the days of the week or the months of the year to commemorate Niyazov's life as well as the history of independent Turkmenistan.[105]

Privately, Shikhmuradov admitted that he bore some responsibility for the political excesses of Niyazov's regime, because he had acquiesced to them.[106] Publicly, he described himself as having initially been swayed by Niyazov's charisma, which he was eventually able to see through. Niyazov did not take kindly to competition, and Shikhmuradov, a Soviet foreign correspondent (a widely assumed cover for the state security services), was held in high regard.

Shikhmuradov's ability to influence the Turkmen president had been declining since the mid-1990s, as the Turkmen president began turning to a number of key foreign business partners for advice. Shikhmuradov was removed as foreign minister in 2000, and when he resigned from his post as Turkmenistan's ambassador to China in October 2001, he was rumored to be only days away from arrest, having been accused of illegally selling to Russia five Sukhoi fighter jets along with 9,000 Kalashnikov submachine guns and 1.5 million bullets, charges that Shikhmuradov vehemently denied.[107]

The former diplomat had enough contacts to live comfortably abroad but chose instead to form his own political party, the People's Democratic Movement of Turkmenistan, and to become a very vocal and public opponent of the regime.[108] However, because he was half Armenian and half Turkmen, he was not viewed as having any real presidential ambitions.[109] He feared that Niyazov's support for the war on terror gave him a freer hand to pursue ever more repressive policies. Now an "ally" of Washington, and rumored to be suffering from hardening of the arteries, Niyazov felt empowered to move against any real or potential future enemies. He has always feared disloyalty on the part of his government and as a result has rotated state officials in and out of office. But in the months after September 11, Niyazov turned on a number of high-ranking officials that he believed had independent political power bases.

The most public attack was made against former security chief Muhammad Nazarov, dismissed in March 2002, and charged with "premeditated murder, procuration of women, abuse of power, bribe-taking, illegal arrests, the manufacture and sale of counterfeit documents, seals, stamps and blank forms, embezzlement and the abuse of power." Nazarov received the maximum sentence of twenty years in prison.[110] Twenty-two men formerly under his charge also faced prosecution.[111]

In March 2002, Major General Tirkish Tyrmyev, the head of the border guards, was also dismissed. In May 2002, the head of the Central Bank, Khudaiberdy Orazov, was fired, and the Turkmen government has regularly sought Orazov's extradition, on charges of being a traitor of the fatherland. With these arrests, Niyazov assumed sole control of all decisions involving Turkmenistan's foreign exchange. Former defense minister Kurbandurdy Begendjev was also arrested, in December 2002, and charged with four counts of corruption.[112] In addition, Shikhmuradov's successor, Batyr Berdyev was arrested on December 8, 2002.[113]

But only Shikhmuradov, arrested on November 25, 2002, earned a Stalin-style show trial. An obviously beaten and seemingly drugged Shikhmuradov was put on display to the republic's legislature and then found guilty of treason, only to have his life sentence commuted to twenty-five years of hard time. Niyazov offered this as a personal gesture of generosity, and in return the former foreign minister praised the spiritual guidance of Turkmenbashi during a broadcast confession in which Shikhmuradov claimed that he had been led astray through his addiction to drugs. This confession, which was broadcast in part on Russia's TV1 and then archived on Shikhmuradov's website, appeared scripted by someone in the president's office, if not by Niyazov himself.[114]

The lives of ordinary citizens were affected as well when exit visas were reintroduced. Exit visas were abolished in January 1, 2002, but reinstated in modified form in February 2003. Further limitations on the registration and range of activities permitted to NGOs also were imposed, making it much more difficult for them to receive foreign funding.

The OSCE, with strong U.S. support, was sufficiently alarmed about the human rights situation in the country in the aftermath of the 2002 failed coup attempt to invoke the Moscow Mechanism.[115] But the rapporteur, Emmanuel Decaux, a professor of international law at the University of Paris, was denied a visa to enter Turkmenistan.[116] OSCE officials have also requested, and been denied, access to political prisoners—a refusal that has fueled rumors that prominent prisoners are dead or seriously ill. Niyazov has explained that according to Turkmen law, prisoners must serve five years of their term before they can receive visits.

Discrimination against Turkmenistan's two largest minority populations, the Uzbeks and the Russians, also increased after the failed coup attempt, as Niyazov believed that the leaders of both countries were complicit in the planned coup against him. The Uzbeks in Turkmenistan are treated worse than Uzbek minority populations in any other part of the region. Although disputes over water were likely more important, their plight was probably a reason why the Uzbek government may have facilitated Shikhmuradov's return.[117]

In 2003, the Turkmen government introduced further cutbacks in Uzbek-language education and media, leaving it no real role in the country's public life.[118] Increased travel restrictions for entering and leaving the country were also introduced. This had the desired effect of making it financially onerous and often logistically all but impossible for Uzbeks living on both sides of the Turkmen border to visit their relatives and family graves. Some have speculated that the Turkmen president expected Uzbeks in the border regions to turn their displeasure on President Islam Karimov. Niyazov also wrested control of the country's Islamic administration from the Uzbek clerics who previously ran it, and in 2004, former *Mufti* Nasrullah ibn Ibadullah was even arrested for his opposition to the use of *Rukhnama* in mosques and was charged with treason for his alleged involvement in the 2002 coup attempt.[119]

The impact on Turkmen–Russian relations has been more complex. In the aftermath of the coup Niyazov felt compelled to turn to Moscow as a protector, to prevent the Kremlin from supporting any new Shikhmuradov figure that might come along. Niyazov saw agreeing to a long-term contract with Russia's Gazprom as the best way to do this, and the twenty-five year agreement negotiated in 2002 was signed in the presence of Russian President Putin when Niyazov visited Moscow in April 2003.[120]

Nothing ever leaked about the understandings reached between Putin and Niyazov in their private sessions, but Niyazov was left feeling both insecure and angry that he had ceded so much control of his economy for so little economic return. In April 2003, he turned on the Russian population of Turkmenistan, refusing to extend the treaty of dual citizenship with Russia and giving local dual citizens until June 22, 2003, to choose Turkmen citizenship or leave the country. But new exit requirements effectively closed off the latter option, because those opting for Russian citizenship needed to go to Moscow to get the visa support to leave Ashgabat legally but of course were barred from leaving the country to get to Moscow. And even those with the proper documentation to exit were confronted with a new sharply curtailed Turkmen Air schedule of flights to Russia. Russian citizens found in Turkmenistan after the deadline risked having their property expropriated. It was reported that several thousand Russians were literally thrown out of their apartments and their possessions put on the street.[121]

These events caused an uproar in Moscow. Protestors marched on the Turkmen embassy, deputies in the State Duma demanded retaliation, but the Russian government took no concrete actions. The whole episode was quite embarrassing for Putin and the Russian government. As the Russian press wrote, they were trading gas for people. Ironically, the agreement between Turkmenistan and Gazprom proved relatively short lived, as the Turkmen stopped delivering gas to the Russians in late 2004 and sent the agreement back for renegotiation in early 2005.[122]

The decision by the international community—or more particularly by both the United States and Russia—to tolerate the behavior of the Turkmen president closed whatever small window of opportunity there might have been to push for political reform. Reform would never have been an easy sell with Niyazov, but had Washington and Moscow been more aggressive in their courting of the Turkmen opposition prior to the November 2002 coup attempt, Niyazov might have been pushed to make some very tentative steps toward opening up his country's political system. Easing restrictions on NGOs and allowing Turkmen citizens freedom to exit their country for travel and study would have strengthened linkages between the Turkmen community and the outside world.

The United States had potential leverage in Turkmenistan, particularly, if they had exercised it in concert with Russia, because the Turkmen regime cannot survive without being able to sell its resources internationally, and cooperation between Moscow and Washington would be enough to isolate Turkmenistan. So when a credible opposition emerged in the person of Boris Shikhmuradov they could have collectively pushed Niyazov to make political concessions or face the risk of international embargo. But neither country was concerned enough about the political situation in Ashgabat to do this. Moscow's main concern was to secure Turkmenistan's gas, which was obtained on better terms from a frightened Niyazov, whereas Washington wanted no small ripples to disturb the execution of its geopolitical priorities.

Developments in Turkmenistan show how rapidly the ruling elite can turn on its president. By November 2002, many members of the Turkmen elite had decided that their country's hyperpresidential system put their very existence at risk, as well as the political and economic future of their country and its citizens. But it also showed how hard it is to achieve regime change in Central Asia.

Whether Boris Shikhmuradov and his supporters would have carried through on their promises to introduce a government that promoted economic reform, a functioning parliament elected in a free and fair fashion, and establishment of freedoms of speech, press, and assembly will likely never be known. But as long as Niyazov is in power, the country's very small political elite will remain terrified to speak out at home, and even the small group that survives in emigration will be cautious given that their extended families are hostages of the regime.

As long as Niyazov lives, Turkmenistan is likely to enjoy at least the semblance of stability, albeit one that is obtained at great cost to the personal freedom of the Turkmen people. Although scattered protests do occasionally occur—for example, in summer 2004, there were reports that anti-Niyazov political leaflets had begun to circulate in parts of the country—Niyazov believes that his day of final reckoning is still a long way off. In a pronouncement on the "ages of man," he decreed that the age of wisdom begins at 73.[123] And he behaves as if he has decades left to decree a wise alternative to his own near-divine rule. Someday, however, Niyazov will pass from the scene. Although Article 61 of the constitution concerns presidential succession, providing for the speaker of the People's Council to take over, by definition this is a post that is only given to someone who is seen as wholly lacking in political ambitions.[124] The longer Niyazov lives, the more unlikely it is that those currently in jail or in exile will be able to play a major role in the succession, leaving the struggle for power to be played out by sycophantic courtiers who still enjoy Turkmenbashi's favor.[125]

But unlike those who gathered to inherit the remains of Stalin's power, those in Ashgabat will immediately confront powerful foreign patrons, and those who control the flow of Turkmenistan's commodities are likely to prevail over the most ambitious of the Turkmen pretenders.

Tajikistan: A Step Behind

Tajikistan is the only place in Central Asia where the president did not spend the first half of the 1990s consolidating his political power and his family's control of the economy. Unique to Central Asia, Tajikistan is a post-conflict society, headed by a president who consolidated power because his side emerged on top in a divisive civil war. Although Tajikistan came out of that war territorially intact, its political and economic power structure was substantially modified, with shifts in power between regional actors, and naturally all the power at the national level was transferred to the winners.[126] Power shifted from Khujand (now Sughd) to Kulob and from an older generation accustomed to the soft life of the top layers of the Soviet elite to a younger generation with hands dirtied in the field or in battle (in many cases, literally so, and in other cases those who supported and financed the battle).[127]

There was some power sharing provided for in the General Agreement on the Establishment of Peace and National Accord in Tajikistan reached in June 1997.[128] The accord provided for the demobilization of fighters from the losing side, the United Tajik Opposition (UTO), and set terms for their reintegration into governmental structures.[129] The best opportunity for the United States and other Western nations to influence developments in Tajikistan came in the period shortly after the signing of the reconciliation agreement. Tajikistan, which had qualified for very little Western assistance previously, was desperate for funding to rebuild its wartorn economy and the atrophied remains of its Soviet-era bureaucratic infrastructure. But Western assistance agencies did not link political and economic reforms, which enabled President Imamali Rakhmonov's government to consolidate power in ways that limit the prospects of those who seek to challenge it.

Although Rakhmonov and most of his colleagues might not have understood how a market economy functioned, or had much idea of how Tajikistan could maximize its contribution to the global economy, they did understand that their prize was of limited value without some degree of economic reform and that with economic reform would come increased transparency. They also understood that Russia lacked the resources to make this investment. Although Moscow would continue to exert a chokehold on security relations, it would not inhibit Western interventions in many sectors of the economy or in the country's political life.

But the United States and the western European nations had no real interest in increasing their leverage in Tajikistan. They were pleased that the country's civil war was drawing to a close, but ending it had never been an international priority, in part because it was playing out under the shadow of the much greater, partially interconnected, and seemingly irresolvable conflict in neighboring Afghanistan. In fact, ongoing security concerns within Tajikistan itself led several nations to reduce or even withdraw their missions.[130] Neither the United States nor Western European nations were willing to invest in the rapid overhaul of Tajikistan's security system.

Funds were scarce, and there was real question as to the capacity of Tajiks to absorb this money. The one exception was the area of narcotics interdiction, where the international community made a commitment to capacity building, but through 2001, funding for these programs averaged less than $1 million annually. So dire was the situation that the Tajik Agency for Narcotics Control (AKN), created in 1998, was nearly forced to close on several occasions, even though it was viewed as a highly professional operation.[131] The narcotics trade across Tajikistan limited prospects for political and economic reform, but dealing with it required curbing opium production in Afghanistan because "rents" from the drug trade were a major source of personal income to a number of Tajikistan's key political figures.

After September 11, the United States also had the opportunity to influence developments in Tajikistan, by using new funding for reform of Tajikistan's security system to pave the way for political change. U.S. funding in a number of security sectors increased, and Tajikistan joined NATO's Partnership for Peace Program in February 2002, adding yet another source of funding.[132] But the increases were relatively small or one-time allocations. For example, Tajikistan received $21.5 million for security and law enforcement reform in 2002 and only $1.2 million in 2003.[133] That same year the United States announced a $2.4 million grant to help Tajikistan fight drug trafficking, despite the fact that many experts believed that opium production in Afghanistan was up by about 6 percent in 2003.[134] U.S. diplomats serving in Tajikistan pressed hard for more money, arguing that the Dushanbe regime not only could successfully absorb such increases but had earned them by bringing its civil war to conclusion and engaging in a modicum of structural economic reforms. Neither their arguments nor

Tajikistan's strategic location (sharing a long and largely unprotected border with Afghanistan) had much impact.

The U.S.-led military campaign in Afghanistan did little to increase the relative importance of Tajikistan for U.S. policy makers. Fearful of undermining their support for the government of Afghan President Hamid Karzai, U.S. officials did not want to move against Afghanistan's Northern Alliance warlords. Many of these men were Afghan Tajiks and partnered with their ethnic brethren in Tajikistan to move their contraband supplies. And the Tajik government had much less to offer in a strategic partnership than the Uzbek or Kyrgyz governments. Nor did Tajikistan offer much in the way of potential cultural or political congeniality to spark the interest of policy makers in Washington who might argue that the country was worth supporting as a nascent or fledgling democracy.

Awareness of his country's increased strategic importance also seems to have made Rakhmonov less willing to engage in political reform; rather than moving to embrace democratic principles, he began moving more firmly away from them. This partly reflected his greater ability in manipulating the powers of the presidency, which seems to have taken him about five years to understand, roughly the same amount of time it took for Central Asia's other presidents to consolidate their power. The constraints of the 1997 National Accord have proven relatively easy to circumvent, and Rakhmonov feels secure in his control of the levers of power. While willing to give lip service to the need to preserve democratic forms, he is consolidating power in the office of the president, a position he has made clear that he has no intention of vacating any time soon.

In fact, he felt confident enough to press for a constitutional referendum in 2003 that, following Nazarbayev's example in Kazakhstan, changed the term of office of the president to seven years and made him, who comes up for reelection in 2006, eligible to serve two additional terms in office. According to current law, Rakhmonov would then be forced to retire in 2020 at age 68. The clumsy way the referendum was conducted showed his relative lack of concern for international opinion. Voters could cast their ballot "yes" or "no" for a group of fifty-six amendments, and many Russian voters complained that they were handed Tajik-language ballots with no translation provided.[135]

Few international observers were present, so it is likely that the 93.13 percent approval rating was the product of old Soviet-style voting, where a single person bearing numerous passports of family members could cast all their votes.[136] Or it may just be that Rakhmonov accurately judged Tajikistan's citizens' overwhelming support. But one thing is certain: he quite correctly judged that the United States would put no real constraints on his behavior; all the referendum earned him was a rejoinder that Tajikistan was expected to choose its parliament and president by means of free and fair elections.[137]

The Rakhmonov government is more interested in imitating a democracy than being one. Like Kyrgyzstan, Tajikistan has a very large NGO sector, sustained by the international community, which collectively serves as the second or third largest employer in the country. Rakhmonov and his team understand that to place sharp restrictions on this sector would simply exacerbate the country's economic problems. Moreover, any dramatic change in the legal regulatory environment that controls the NGO sector would certainly provoke an international outcry and put Tajikistan's sizeable foreign assistance at risk. But Tajikistan has not made sufficient progress in either political institution building or in economic reform to get the degree of foreign debt relief that Kyrgyzstan has gained.[138]

The Tajik government has confidently increased pressure exerted on independent media, and the number of independent media outlets is decreasing. Critics of the government can find the size of their print runs reduced, greater difficulty in distributing their publications, or even revocation of their licenses.[139]

Opportunities for political participation are diminishing. The Democratic and Social Democratic parties both opposed the June 2003 election, causing the leadership of these parties to be further marginalized. Members of the formerly powerful political families in Khujand have been barred from leading roles in national politics for so long that they now set their sights on just retaining some influence in their home region.

While relations between Rakhmonov and the Islamic Renaissance Party (IRP) are souring,[140] Rakhmonov no longer fears the mobilization potential of the IRP, whose leadership is now divided between those who are willing to serve in the regime, those who are interested in using Tajikistan's laws on political parties to serve as a loyal opposition,[141] and those who believe that cooperation with the regime threatens their religiously inspired political agenda.[142]

The government has used the existence of this third group, as well as a seemingly small but obviously increasing presence of the Hizb ut-Tahrir movement on Tajik territory, to justify the increased state control over the

Islamic establishment. As part of the compromise reached in the aftermath of Tajikistan's civil war, Tajikistan's Islamic establishment was allowed a greater degree of self-government than elsewhere in the region. But in 2003 the Rakhmonov government began to take control of the process, appointing new imams, and generally seeking to regulate the content of sermons being preached in the country's mosques.[143]

The writ of the national government extends over the distant Badakhshan province more in name than in fact. The provincial capital of this mountainous region, which has two peaks over 7,000 meters, is linked to the capital city of Dushanbe by a road that is effectively impassable for much of the year. In the immediate aftermath of the civil war, the Kulob-led government sought to break the independent spirit of the Pamir people (who speak a dialect of Tajik and who are Ismailis, a sect of Shia Islam that advocates human dignity and compassion—a minority in a country with a Sunni majority). Pamiris who traveled outside their home region did so at risk of death.

A relatively peaceful status quo was eventually restored, in large part through the auspices of the Aga Khan, a leader of the world community of Ismailis who is embraced as a descendant of the prophet Muhammad.[144] The Aga Khan has been a major benefactor in the Badakhshan region of Tajikistan, in particular, but his educational, agricultural, and technical assistance programs are open to participation from all parts of the country. The Badakhshan region also contains Tajikistan's most remote borders with Afghanistan and has been an entry point for the transit of drugs and other forms of illicit trade, as has the 125-mile stretch of border that extends throughout Katlon province (the combined Kulob and Qurgan-Teppe regions).

Constant rumors persist about how intimately the government is connected to the drug trade, with unsubstantiated allegations ranging from the corrupt behavior of low-level police officials up to and including the mayor of Dushanbe. This is obviously a topic about which it is all but impossible to collect reliable information; the few written sources that exist are quite contradictory. Some authors describe a network of loosely or even unconnected traders who bribe various levels of government officials to get their goods across the country, whereas others see a well-organized criminal structure at the core of the trade, which has been closely connected to local Russian military forces and senior Tajik government officials.[145] The Tajik government has shown no real enthusiasm for rooting out government officials tied to the drug trade;[146] in 2004 it even briefly replaced the country's "drug czar" with someone allegedly tied to organized crime, only to remove him after public outcry.[147] Despite the varying theories on its course, most informed observers agree that the complicity of Tajik government and security officials in the drug trade, from the lowest regional to the highest national levels, is sufficient to greatly complicate the task of anyone, local or international, eager to engage in systemic political reform.

Political life in Tajikistan will be influenced by events in Kyrgyzstan, but it is hard to know whether it will serve to increase the chances for democratization or to exacerbate the countervailing processes of political and social decay.

Tajikistan had parliamentary elections on February 27, 2005, the same day as the first round of elections in Kyrgyzstan. The vote was criticized by the OSCE for falling far short of international norms. The ruling People's Democratic Party got 80 percent of the vote, while the Islamic Renaissance and Communist Parties got only 10 percent of the vote collectively, and they together will hold only 6 of 63 parliamentary seats.

The four opposition parties—Democratic, Communist, Islamic, and Social Democratic—have strongly protested the election results, and pressed for a new election. But unlike their Kyrgyz counterparts, they have not been able to translate these protests into large popular demonstrations against the Rakhmonov government.

The opposition believes that they have a better chance of defeating Rakhmonov in 2006 than in getting the recent parliamentary results overturned. But their confident optimism should be tempered by their countrymen's continued political apathy, stemming from dread of another wrenching civil war.

If Kyrgyzstan's "tulip revolution" succeeds, and a new regime that is democratic in reality, not just rhetoric, puts down roots, it will reverberate positively throughout a region that many have written off as hopeless from the point of view of building democratic societies. The Kyrgyz example has put all other leaders in the region on notice that they too must take seriously the need for popular political enfranchisement or risk being driven from power.

If however it fails, and the new regime creates itself in mirror image to Akayev's, different in name only, it will have failed not because the masses in Central Asia are unreceptive, but because the ruling elite in Kyrgyzstan managed to sabotage the process of political change. Thus even the failure of the Kyrgyz revolution will not leave Central Asia's other leaders feeling more secure.

Events in Kyrgyzstan provide strong evidence that sustained Western support for grass-roots political organizations can prove effective. Some freshly organized student groups played a pivotal role in mobilizing the final demonstrations in Bishkek that brought down Akayev. The foundation needed for the creation of these groups was laid over the course of a decade by human rights groups, independent press and journalists, and political monitors at work in the country. The established groups proved there was a niche in Kyrgyz public life that would make the formation of newer groups possible as they established citizens' right to organize independently of the government.

This natural foundation of nongovernmental political groups is absent in both Uzbekistan and Turkmenistan, and increased U.S. assistance will not succeed in creating it overnight. In neither country can NGOs be expected to organize or channel public opposition in peaceful ways. In Uzbekistan in particular, where the risk of anomic violence is already palpable, there is reason to fear that secular groups will have only minimal impact on creating what the United States would see as desirable political outcomes. Here, too, there is the growing risk that the use of force by the regime will not quell protest, but instead plunge the country into civil war. And what is going on underneath the surface in Turkmenistan is largely terra incognita, so impenetrable has this society been to outside influences and observers.

Tajikistan, meanwhile, is more difficult to predict. Civil society groups have penetrated more deeply in that society than in either Turkmenistan or Uzbekistan, but the population has already paid a huge price in the civil war that developed as part of the aftermath of the political mobilization of the early 1990s, and may choose to remain politically unengaged despite the presence of both secular and religious groups seeking to engage them.

Kazakhstan is much more of a conundrum. Civil society institutions have penetrated quite deeply in the society, and a vocal opposition both inside and outside the ruling elite exists to challenge the power of President Nazarbayev. But it is less clear how much of a priority the United States should place on influencing outcomes. Obviously, the United States should strongly support the conduct of transparent and competitive elections in

Kazakhstan, and offer technical assistance to both the government and opposition to help make this a reality. But, in sharp contrast to Kyrgyzstan, the Kazakh opposition is much more capable of funding their own activities, and there is no need to create a perception that they are U.S. puppets by pumping in too much aid.

Much like in Kyrgyzstan, a regime change is unlikely to produce a foreign policy shift toward the United States. Just like in Kyrgyzstan, any successor government is likely to seek to sustain close ties with both Russia and China, as well as maintain the support of the U. S. government.

6

Changing Geopolitics:
Less Has Changed than One Might Think

The war on terror has increased the strategic importance of the Central Asian states for Washington, but it has not led to dramatic changes in the security environment in the region. None of these states is likely to follow the path of Latvia, Lithuania, or Estonia into the North Atlantic Treaty Organization (NATO), and none is likely to be admitted into any of the key European political and economic associations. The reason for this is not their location east of the Urals, but rather their governments' failure to progress toward European economic and political norms. While the Kyrgyz may claim that the ouster of Askar Akayev is like the revolutions in Georgia and Ukraine, positioning them for the West's warm embrace, in reality the only state that has any chance to be accepted as a full-fledged member of European institutions is Kazakhstan, and it still has a long way to go before its leaders have a hope of achieving the sought-after presidency of the Organization for Security and Cooperation in Europe (OSCE).

The limited U.S. military presence, combined with ensured access to the region's oil reserves, defines the strategic importance of Central Asia to the United States, and concerns about the region's stability have been secondary to Bush administration strategists. In late 2001 and most of 2002, U.S. leaders and those from other Western governments talked a great deal about the importance of increased engagement with the Central Asian states and the need for international financial institutions to work more closely with these countries to help them cope with the unresolved developmental challenges that the breakup of the Soviet Union and independence brought them. In the end, however, this proved to be little more than talk. And even with the

Georgian and Ukrainian revolutions, where freedom and democracy were hailed as being "on the march," little if nothing was done to spur on the trend; regime change in Central Asia did not become a U.S. priority.

Plans for a regional strategy for rebuilding Afghanistan were largely shelved when the magnitude of the challenges in Afghanistan became clear and were almost entirely forgotten after the war in Iraq was launched. Although the overall amount of international assistance coming into the region has increased in recent years, these increases have been relatively small and have not bought the international financial institutions any real increase in their leverage. Added to this is the general sense of donor fatigue, as the U.S. Agency for International Development, the International Monetary Fund, the World Bank, and the Asian Development Bank were all tied down by more pressing commitments in other parts of the world.

From the point of view of the international donor community, the Central Asian region was divided into states that had no pressing need for help because they were either doing well (enough)—Kazakhstan, Kyrgyzstan, and Tajikistan—and those that were difficult to engage effectively—Uzbekistan and Turkmenistan. But this meant that the region's states were largely left to their own devices to cope with failures of their own developmental strategies and the nontraditional security threats these helped stimulate, and few contingency plans were developed for extraordinary events that might develop, such as the ouster of a sitting president.

New Role for the United States

The launching of the war on terror made many U.S. policy makers divide the world into friends and foes, but even those Central Asian countries that were quick to demonstrate their support for U.S. military campaigns in Afghanistan and Iraq have found out that improved relations with the United States fall far short of a strategic partnership.

For both sides, the interest, naturally, has been more in what they can do for us than in what we can do for them. The United States has no interest in making the investment to turn any of the Central Asian states into reliable security partners, and a state like Uzbekistan, which is truly interested in developing such a relationship with the United States, has been unwilling to engage in the systemic economic and political reforms necessary to become full partners of the United States and its European allies.

The scale of increased U.S. security assistance in the region was designed to respond to immediate U.S. security needs. In the aftermath of September 11, 2001, the U.S. Department of Defense was the lead actor in defining the priorities of the U.S. strategy. U.S. military assistance increased quite strikingly in 2002 and 2003, only to drop sharply in FY2004 and FY2005, when the relative importance of these bases began to diminish.[1]

The decline in assistance reflected the fact that the priority of senior officials in the Department of Defense had shifted, although they continued to try to strengthen bilateral military relations with these states.[2] It also was the product of views held by other policy makers, such as those in the State Department, as well as those charged with congressional oversight of foreign policy (both congressmen and their staffs), that the U.S. relationship with the Central Asian states could not mature into anything resembling a partnership unless the leaders of these countries committed themselves to more far-reaching economic and political reforms than even the most liberal-minded of them was willing to consider. Nor was it a priority of U.S. policy makers to try to figure out how these leaders' attitudes might be changed or whether new kinds of engagement or greatly increased funding might produce different outcomes in the region.

There was no powerful constituency in the United States willing to take up Central Asia's cause. The energy lobby was not seriously concerned about the political or economic status quo. The U.S. oil companies active in the region were generally quite satisfied with the U.S.–Kazakh relationship and were pleased by the increased U.S. security presence. Those concerned with the nation-building aspect of the war on terror were far more concerned with how allocations for Afghanistan would be spent, and then after the invasion of Iraq they were drawn to the much larger pot of money for rebuilding efforts in that country.

Unlike Armenia or Ukraine, the Central Asian states lack sizeable diaspora communities in the United States. The existing communities are small, and their most vocal elements are political exiles whose agenda often overlaps with those of U.S. human rights groups. They also rely heavily on congressional support but lack the lobbying potential to press for their concerns on an ongoing basis. So although the Senate has passed amendments to the Foreign Operations Appropriations Act reflecting displeasure with developments in various Central Asian countries, such as the incarceration of former vice president Feliks Kulov, the arrest of a prominent journalist in Kazakhstan, or the persecution of independent Muslims, such resolutions have little bite.[3] In general, since September 11, Congress has been disinclined to take actions that would impede the U.S. international security posture in Central Asia and elsewhere. The Bush administration has not sought to use the threat of funding cutoffs as an effective tool of foreign policy. Funding to states in the region has only been at risk when the State Department has denied certification, and that has only been done once in Central Asia, with a small aid cutoff to Uzbekistan in 2004.

Uzbekistan: Central Asia's Frontline State

The Uzbek government has become an increasingly more embarrassing ally for the United States, but Washington has yet to find effective levers to successfully influence Tashkent's behavior. When this book went to press, the White House and State Department were trying to figure out how to respond to Karimov's refusal to allow an international investigation into the use of deadly force in Andijan in May 2005.

By late 2003, the Department of State's frustration with the Uzbek government's lack of progress in the area of human rights had grown to a point where the Secretary of State declined to issue a certification of progress, putting continued foreign assistance to the country at risk, including assistance in the area of cooperative threat reduction, though there, a presidential waiver was issued.[4] Six months later Secretary of State Colin Powell again denied certification, cutting the Uzbek government off from about $18 million of FY2004 foreign assistance.[5]

Secretary Powell's action showed the change in the official U.S. attitude toward Uzbekistan that occurred over a relatively short period of time. Readying itself for the upcoming presidential election in which its commitment to democracy building in Iraq would be a point of contention, the Bush administration was sensitive to charges that it was soft on dictators, and Uzbekistan seemed a place where an example could be made without damaging U.S. strategic priorities, and even without too badly damaging the U.S.–Uzbek relationship.

The State Department sought ways to cushion Tashkent's disappointment over its diminished status. Elizabeth Jones, Assistant Secretary of State for European Affairs, was in the Uzbek capital when the decision was announced, presumably in part to counsel the Uzbeks on what specific changes would facilitate receipt of FY2005 foreign assistance funds targeted for the Uzbek government. Nongovernmental recipients were not affected;

their funding was not linked to certification. That the administration showed such concern for the Uzbek reaction suggests that the aid cutoff was intended more for a U.S. audience than an Uzbek one.

Yet the State Department's actions, which the Defense Department made no effort to block, showed Uzbekistan's diminishing strategic importance. Although Secretary of Defense Donald Rumsfeld flattered Tashkent with talk of "a strong relationship that was growing stronger," the Pentagon believed that Washington had a sufficient military presence in the Central Asian region to protect U.S. interests.[6] The U.S. facilities in Central Asia were no longer frontline, and the Pentagon began to step down their state of readiness, turning them from "hot" to "warm" facilities, and was considering even downgrading them to "cold" readiness.

Although the new pattern of U.S. military global deployment was clearly still in flux, the Central Asian pillars of it seemed firm. A large U.S. military presence there was less important than long-term basing rights, especially for Kashi-Khanabad, where 1,000 troops are stationed and which still serves as a forward deployment area for the U.S. Central Command.[7]

The decision by the Bush administration to create a very limited alliance with the Central Asian states has proved to be a new real disappointment for Uzbekistan. In the immediate aftermath of September 11, Uzbekistan jumped at the chance of close military cooperation with the United States, knowing that this would anger Moscow.[8] The increased U.S. presence in the region was worth the near-term problems to Uzbek authorities, because it met so many foreign policy priorities simultaneously. The United States would bring both military might and moral rectitude to bear in crushing the terrorist groups in Afghanistan. Tashkent believed that the presence of U.S. bases would make it easier for Uzbekistan to manage its relationship with Russia and believed that a U.S. military presence would put Moscow on better behavior in the region more generally. Tashkent also hoped it would help balance China's exercise of influence as well. Most important, the Uzbeks hoped that the enhanced security partnership with Washington would lead to funds to speed the pace of military reform and result in Uzbekistan's ability to manage regional security challenges.

Until 2005 Tashkent's priority was with the U.S. relationship, moving to improve relations with Russia and China only after it was clear that Washington planned to limit its strategic engagement with Tashkent. For example, Uzbekistan was the only Central Asian state to join the U.S.-led coalition that invaded Iraq, despite the fact that this damaged its relations with Russia and China. Since May 2005, Uzbek foreign ploicy as tilted toward Beijing and Moscow.

While the U.S. government would like to maintain its military partnership with the Uzbeks, it must be on U.S. terms. U.S. military assistance to Uzbekistan has increased and has focused on border security and enhancing counterterrorism capability and interoperability—projects that could eventually help make Uzbekistan a reliable regional partner for the United States. But the level of support offered by the United States is predicated on a very-long-term process of military reform. It is designed to assist the Uzbeks in becoming better able to meet the security challenges they face but does not offer the Uzbeks any security guarantees in the event that they are unable to do so.

U.S. policy makers are quick to talk about the shared goals with Uzbekistan in the war on terror, but Washington made only the most tentative first steps to help Tashkent address the internal conditions that produce support for Islamic extremist groups. Relatively little money is being spent on judicial or prison reform, compared with that spent on training in the area of general military or border security. For example, in FY2003 the United States only spent $1.3 million on projects related to judicial reform in Uzbekistan, compared to $9.7 million in military assistance that year.[9] More money is being spent on programs designed "to moderate" Islam than to change the behavior of a legal system that abuses the civil rights of religious believers.

Although increased U.S. funding cannot undo the legacy of Soviet-era penal system brutality in which prisoners were routinely beaten to obtain confessions, it could help create an atmosphere more conducive to change. Corruption and abuse in the legal system is a problem throughout the region, in part because most of Central Asian law enforcement officials must meet formal goals set for "closed cases," much like they had to do in the Soviet era.

Reports from both the State Department's Bureau of Democracy, Human Rights, and Labor and reports from Human Rights Watch detail the pattern of abuse found in Uzbekistan's judicial system. They show that it is made worse by the high level of corruption in Uzbekistan's law enforcement and judicial systems, where evidence is often planted on innocent people in order to collect bribes to secure their release.[10] Police and judges often seek bribes in compensation for what they paid in bribes to get their jobs, again a practice that is characteristic of the region as a whole.

But the Uzbek government has shown an interest in pursuing legal system reform, and their agenda even overlaps what U.S. democracy promoters advocate, though it is certainly less inclusive. In September 2003, London's Westminster University opened a branch in Tashkent, partly supported through government funds, that offers a degree in legal studies. Scholarships are limited and many qualified young people cannot afford tuition, but there are few alternatives. At the current pace it will be a dozen or more years before there is a critical mass of Uzbeks with Western-style legal training. The Uzbek government is also interested in professional retraining programs for police officers and criminal investigators. There have been a number of successful USAID-funded programs in this area, as well as programs in Turkey, but here too funding problems limit their reach.

In general it has been much harder to get USAID to commit foreign assistance money to legal system reform in Uzbekistan than in Kyrgyzstan.[11] Many democracy activists argue that it is not suitable for the United States to fund legal reform programs in partnership with a repressive government, and they advocated working solely with independent groups. They argue that supporting government initiatives makes the United States appear a guarantor or partner of the current regime. But to support only independent groups while advocating political reforms makes the United States appear to be a deliberate agent of regime change.

In reality, the United States has been neither. After a series of bombs went off in Tashkent and Bukhara over a period of a few days in March–April 2004, the United States offered Tashkent help in identifying possible perpetrators, who were presumed to be linked with domestic as well as Afghan- or Pakistani-based cells of the Islamic Movement of Uzbekistan (IMU).[12] But the United States offered little else, and only sent special investigators to Tashkent after the July 2004 bombings because the U.S. embassy was one of the targets successfully attacked.[13] By contrast, Russia offered the Uzbeks the opportunity to participate in joint antiterror operations.

The question of how the United States is perceived in Uzbekistan is a critical one, but one that is impossible to gather firm evidence to answer. Public support in Uzbekistan for the U.S.-led war on terror seems to be diminishing with time.[14] But public opinion polling in Uzbekistan is problematic given the overall political environment, which makes it very difficult to assess the linkage between Uzbek–U.S. relations and what seems to be a decline in public support for President Islam Karimov.

It seems clear that the Uzbek leadership has not been able to capitalize on their new strategic partnership with the United States and the signs of increased international prominence that have come with it. For example, warm receptions in some Western capitals and well-reported visits by leading Western statesmen did not translate into increased popular support for the president.[15] But it is quite another thing to argue that the U.S.–Uzbek relationship is a source of the growing domestic unrest, or that it fuels the spread of Islamic radicalism, or that it will poison U.S.–Uzbek relations under subsequent Uzbek governments.[16]

Long before September 11, Islamic radicals criticized the Uzbek president for his pro-American, and in their words, pro-Zionist policies, but this notwithstanding, most observers see the appeal of these movements as largely rooted in deteriorating socioeconomic conditions.[17] And it is these conditions that are much more likely to affect the conditions of succession in Uzbekistan than are Uzbek foreign relations.

Kyrgyzstan: A Nonexclusive Friendship

By contrast in Kyrgyzstan, the site of the other U.S. air base in the region, public opinion about the U.S.-led war on terror *did* have an impact on the country's political life. The U.S relationship with Bishkek is even more complex than with Tashkent. The initial U.S. presence in Kyrgyzstan was the result of a one-year renewable agreement.[18]

As with the base in Uzbekistan, the role and staffing of the U.S. military facility at Manas airport has also changed. The base now serves as a major logistical hub for U.S. operations in Afghanistan.[19] The U.S. Department of Defense sees advantages in the base, but there is no way that the relationship could transform the country into a linchpin state for the United States in the region, given its small population, the limited potential of its economy, Kyrgyzstan's relatively isolated location, and the size and condition of the Kyrgyz military. [20] The United States nonetheless had a strong commitment to help the Kyrgyz develop a more effective defensive capacity, and much of the focus of U.S. assistance is on improved border security.[21]

The opening of the new base gave the United States instant visibility in Kyrgyzstan, whereas the U.S. base in Uzbekistan was effectively hidden away in Kashi-Khanabad, whose remoteness kept the U.S. presence out of sight. The Peter J. Ganci air base in Kyrgyzstan is an extension of the country's principal airport, and those serving at it are frequently seen in the city.[22] The Kyrgyz were disappointed the United States did not make more use of local help to supply relief aid and manpower in Afghanistan, but even without this, the basing agreement with the United States was advantageous. Most important, it helps neutralize some of the strategic gain Tashkent accrued when it briefly hosted the sole U.S. base in the region. It has also provided about 100 local jobs and revenue for the government and local suppliers.[23] One of those to benefit most, however, was Adil Toigonbayev, son-in-law of ex-president Akayev, who supplied jet fuel for the base. As a result, the United States seemed complicit to the corruption of the ruling family in the eyes of many ordinary Kyrgyz.

Because the relationship offered by the United States was so limited, the Kyrgyz focused their attention on achieving geopolitical balance, reaching out to China and Russia, rather than putting all their eggs in a U.S. basket.

Selling this policy was relatively easy for Akayev, as the Kyrgyz elite had been divided over how close a relationship was desirable with the United States. Many, especially those with ties to the security establishment, always favored preserving close ties with the Russians, while part of the diplomatic community lobbied quite hard for further improvement in relations with China. Kyrgyzstan's economic reformers predictably favored building close ties with the West, but even they did not believe that these should be at the expense of expanded relationships with Kyrgyzstan's traditional economic partners, the Russians and the Kazakhs. Moreover, unlike elsewhere in the region, there was a lively debate in the Kyrgyz press over what Kyrgyzstan's geopolitical priorities should be. Frequent criticism of U.S. foreign policy and its conduct of the war on terror appeared, even in media outlets that were supported in part through U.S. foreign assistance.[24] From the U.S. point of view, however, there is little to be concerned about from Kyrgyzstan's balancing act, which, for now at least, does virtually nothing to restrict the U.S. exercise of its perceived strategic interests.

Kyrgyzstan's balancing act seems certain to be continued by Askar Akayev's immediate successors. The business dealings between the United States and the Akayev family made it easier for the new Kyrgyz leadership to refute accusations that their revolution was somehow made in Washington. The interim government was able to reestablish relations with Moscow faster than with Washington, as the United States was strongly influenced by the judgment of OSCE observers who were arguing that the situation in Bishkek had yet to stabilize.[25]

Kazakhstan: A Maturing Relationship

Kazakhstan is the Central Asian state of greatest interest to U.S. leaders, despite the circumscribed role the Kazakhs are playing in the war on terror. The bilateral relationship is likely to continue to improve and could mature into one of long-term significance for the United States as well as for Kazakhstan. Moreover, the Kazakhs sense this, and for that reason Kazakhstan did eventually decide to send a small group of twenty-seven troops to Iraq to support the U.S.-led international effort, after initially opposing the war in terms that were only slightly more measured than those of Russia.[26] But the improved U.S.–Kazakh bilateral relationship is not at the expense of improving relations between Kazakhstan and either Russia or China. The subtlety of Kazakhstan's foreign policy suggests a growing professionalism in the country's foreign policy–making elite, both those serving in the diplomatic service and those advising them. It also speaks to the strong diplomatic skills of the country's president and his growing awareness of the potential power of his country as well as of its limitations.

The U.S.–Kazakh relationship has been capable of weathering potentially difficult crises, including as already noted, the ongoing trials and investigation into corruption in Kazakhstan's oil industry in New York. Although these created a shadow over the person of President Nazarbayev, making it impossible for him to be an official guest of the U.S. president, they have not precluded Nazarbayev from meeting with President Bush, and it has not damaged the conduct of U.S.–Kazakh relations more generally.[27] Both sides have proved able to compartmentalize the corruption scandal and to insulate it from damaging the bilateral relationship. There is continuing U.S. pressure on the Kazakhs to democratize their political system, which escalates any time the Kazakhs are perceived as moving backward to further consolidate presidential power and its arbitrary exercise, but there is little sense of threat attached to official U.S. warnings.

Energy issues remain at the core of the U.S.–Kazakh relationship. The war on terror and the prospect of growing instability in the Persian Gulf region only increase the importance of Caspian oil reserves. Even at peak production, Kazakh oil exports will not come close to matching those of Saudi Arabia or Russia, but they will be a valuable and presumably predictable resource in the international oil market.[28] The United States no longer fears that long-term access of Western nations to the Caspian oil might be at risk. The Baku–Tbilisi–Ceyhan (BTC) pipeline seems certain to be a reality. Although the Kazakhs have yet to make a firm commitment to ship oil along this route, they are very likely to make some use of this route once oil production increases during the 2008–2010 period and may even take a small equity interest in the project.[29]

Concerning expansion of military cooperation with the United States, Kazakhstan has been a much more cautious U.S. partner than either Uzbekistan or Kyrgyzstan. It has, however, maintained its strong commitment to help the United States meet the goals of the war on terror. Between October 2001 and May 2002, Kazakhstan's airspace was crossed during over 600 coalition forays as well as during Secretary of Defense Donald Rumsfeld's April 2002 trip to the region.[30] The United States has emergency access rights to three airfields in southern Kazakhstan, and like the Tajiks, the Kazakhs had unfulfilled hopes of full U.S. funding for the refurbishment of these Soviet-era airfields. [31]

Although Secretary Rumsfeld celebrated the security partnership in a return trip to Astana in February 2004, the Kazakhs had been highly critical of U.S. plans to invade Iraq without UN approval.[32] In May 2003, only when the war was already an irrevocable fact, did they agree to send specialized troops to the international peacemaking force. Kazakhs, however, are eager recipients of U.S. military assistance designed to modernize their armed forces, which includes programs for training, improved border security, and the acquisition of military equipment.[33] Caspian Sea security has been a major focus of this assistance in recent years, with the United States providing $5 million of assistance to help the Kazakhs establish a modern coast guard and navy, to protect offshore installations, and to interdict narcotics and other contraband trade.[34] Kazakhstan also continues to receive funding through the Cooperative Threat Reduction (CTR) program, with ten initiatives in Kazakhstan ranging from the elimination of START limited systems and weapons of mass destruction infrastructure to military reductions and reform.[35]

Neither Washington nor Astana sees cooperation as limiting Kazakhstan's flexibility in foreign relations. U.S.–Kazakh relations and Kazakh–Russian relations no longer seem like a zero-sum game. The Kazakhs have managed to improve their relations with Russia, juggle better ties to China, and establish a more visible international presence with deepening security ties to the United States.

Turkmenistan and Tajikistan: On the Margins of U.S. Concern

Turkmenistan and Tajikistan do not figure prominently in U.S. strategic thinking about Central Asia. Given the increasingly more idiosyncratic—perhaps irrational—behavior of Turkmenistan's president, the United States has largely written off the prospect of U.S. firms playing a major role in the development of that country's oil and gas reserves as long as Saparmurat Niyazov remains in power. Nor is there any real likelihood of substantial U.S. foreign investment in the country in the near term, although Turkmenistan remains a market for U.S. farm and oil and gas equipment.[36]

The Turkmen government has tried to show support for the U.S.-led war on terror in Afghanistan, without compromising its stated policy of positive neutrality, but this has led to complications on various occasions. While permitting large volumes of humanitarian assistance bound for Afghanistan to pass through its territory, the Turkmen government was reported at one point to have refused the German Air Force use of Turkmen bases in connection with a counterterrorist operation.[37] The refusal may have come because of the public nature of the request, as off-the-record comments made by U.S. officials suggest that U.S. forces did have some access to Turkmen military facilities, but even off the record this is not a topic that U.S. officials are keen to discuss. Turkmenistan has been a relatively inactive member of NATO's Partnership for Peace Program, even though it was the first Central Asian state to join.[38] Although eligible for CTR assistance since 1997, Turkmenistan receives the least direct U.S. military assistance in the region.[39]

There is, however, increased cooperation between U.S. and Turkmen officials to interdict heroin and opium crossing through the country, because traffic along this route is generally regarded as seriously underreported. In February 2004, for only the second time, the Turkmen agreed to participate in a U.S.-sponsored program to train law enforcement officials in narcotics interdiction.[40]

Ashgabat has preferred to limit security cooperation with the United States, which makes the "sticks" Washington has tried to use in Uzbekistan inappropriate in Turkmenistan. U.S. policy makers are also well aware of how unreliable a partner Turkmenistan can be. A good case in point was Niyazov's policy pronouncements on Iraq, which were just plain confusing, but characteristic of the decision-making environment in Ashgabat. Within a forty-eight-hour span, the Turkmen president first offered his support for the U.S.-led military operation and then turned around and criticized the war.[41]

In Tajikistan, meanwhile, the principal U.S. security concern is improving narcotics interdiction. Tajiksitan's national drug control agency is largely funded through support from the UN Office on Drugs and Crime (UNODC), but the United States is an important source of technical support for it as well.[42] While the United States has provided targeted assistance to deal with drug trafficking in all five Central Asian countries, policy makers in Washington know full well that their policies will only make a small dent in Tajikistan's narco-economy.[43]

Tajikistan's government is eager to cooperate even more closely with the United States, and NATO forces are allowed to use highways bound for Afghanistan as well as have access to bases. The government in Dushanbe is particularly interested in increased military assistance to replace security assistance from Russia. Washington is willing to provide increased U.S. military support, but it is unwilling to do so at a pace that would make the Tajiks capable of maintaining a strong defensive posture in the face of the security threats it might face from Uzbekistan, let alone from Afghanistan. This is particularly true because Dushanbe has little to offer by way of trade for increased U.S. support, as it is moving very slowly to demonstrate that the Tajik government shares many common values with that of the United States.

Russia Works to Redefine Its Presence

Multifaceted Security Cooperation

Somewhat ironically, the increased U.S. security presence in Central Asia worked to Russia's advantage, although Moscow has yet to figure out how to capitalize on it. Where the United States was unwilling to serve as the guarantor of the incumbent regimes in Central Asia, Moscow was unable.

Vladimir Putin has been able to press for an enhanced Russian presence in the name of geopolitical balance, extracting concessions from states in the region that might not otherwise have granted them, such as basing rights for the Russian military in Kant (Kyrgyzstan) or increased coordination of Russia's air defense with Uzbekistan's. These moves did not occasion much of a response from the United States. Many in the Bush administration may have seen blunting Russia's influence in Central Asia as a desirable long-term goal, but their public stance was quite different. Gaining Russian support for the war on terror was clearly the most immediate and important goal, which could not be attained if Russia felt that as part of this effort the United States was determined to eclipse Moscow in its traditional areas of influence.

Much of the enhanced Russian military presence is more show than substance, designed to demonstrate to a domestic audience that Vladimir Putin is successfully reasserting Russian prominence in traditional areas of geopolitical domination, even in the face of U.S. encroachments into their backyard. The evolving security situation in Central Asia has obviously become more palatable to Washington, as U.S. policy makers have become more convinced that for all its territorial bluster, Russia hopes to be taken seriously as part of Europe and the West.

Yet most of Central Asia's leaders have been willing to help Moscow demonstrate Russia's geopolitical resilience, as long as Moscow is seeking to advance its strategic aims by offering attractive incentives for cooperation, instead of trying to get its way through threat or intimidation—a tactic that was too often applied during the Yeltsin years. Despite Russia's own economic problems, it still has the largest economy in the region, with ample capital ready for export in the hands of entrepreneurs who are untroubled by the lack of transparency in the Central Asian states. Geography favors Moscow's desire to play a major economic role in the region, especially in the energy sectors.

When the prospect for improving relations is posed in positive terms, the Central Asian officials are often quite eager to promote better bilateral relations with Russia. Most of Central Asia's ruling elite share more common goals with their Russian counterparts than they do with leaders from most other parts of the world, and all speak the same language. Every Central Asian leader speaks Russian as either a first or a second language.

They also all share a sense of annoyance for having been judged "bad boys" by the United States, and to a lesser degree by the Europeans. All of these states, Russia included, have failed to live up to OSCE norms in public life, in both political and economic institution building. Although there are enormous differences in their relative successes, all of these rulers are tired of being reminded of their failures. The various bilateral relationships between the Central Asian states and Russia have each had their ups and downs, but there is far less role playing in gatherings involving the leaders of these countries than when they meet with heads of Western states.

The ground rules of Russian reengagement being set by the Central Asians are clear. None of the states of the region will trade sovereignty for protection, which leaves most still leery of Russian-dominated multilateral security forces. Because Russia still lacks the resources to reform its own military, its material enticements for enhanced cooperation remain relatively small. As a result efforts to transform the Commonwealth of Independent States (CIS) collective security organization into an effective multilateral force have yielded little fruit.[44] By contrast, there does seem to be substantially improved cooperation between the internal security agencies of the countries in the region, an area in which Russia is seen as having an edge, although this seems to be going on as much outside of the CIS framework as within it.

Putin's efforts with well-publicized annual exercises have made the CIS collective security force more visible in the region. But the force shows few signs of being competent enough to meet the current regional security challenges, which is precisely the task that Moscow would like the organization to be able to fulfill. In fact, several months after the U.S. decision to open bases in the region, senior Russian officials sought to explore the idea of the United Nations recognizing divided security responsibility between the United States and Russia, with the United States being charged with heading the international force that would secure the peace in Afghanistan, and Russia using the structure of the CIS taking on formal responsibility for Central Asia.

In April 2002, Major General Sergei Chernomyrdin, head of the Bishkek headquarters of the CIS collective rapid deployment forces, suggested just such a solution publicly.[45] Nothing ever came from this, largely because the United States had no interest in seeing Russia's military posture in the region gain international recognition.[46] A Russian or enhanced CIS military presence in Central Asia was likely to continue well after the U.S. military departed from Afghanistan. There was also little evidence that the Central Asian states wanted the CIS to be recognized by the United Nations as a Chapter VIII Regional Security Organization.

Putin began pushing for the CIS to play an enhanced role in Central Asia almost immediately after assuming power, but even the three states that remained part of the CIS collective security agreement (Kazakhstan Kyrgyzstan, and Tajikistan) preferred balancing CIS ties with closer cooperation with NATO. As noted earlier, the CIS Anti-Terrorist Center, formed in June 2000, developed an operational force of about 1,500 men by spring

2002 (from Russia, Kazakhstan, Kyrgyzstan, and Tajikistan).[47] This force carried out military exercises in the summers of 2002, 2003, and 2004.[48]

The United States did not support Russia's request for a UN-recognized role in Central Asia, but at the same time it offered no real obstacles to Russia's enhanced military presence in the region. In fact, there were no formal statements that took up the issue of Russia's new air base in Kant, which was opened in October 2003. The air base, which is focused on anti-insurgency as the headquarters operations for the collective security organization, is relatively small, with only ten military aircraft and 500 pilots and maintenance staff permanently based there. Nonetheless, it took a full year to reach readiness.[49] It is intended to support 1,000 servicemen.

Russian media accounts, of which there were many, gave viewers and readers a very different image—that Russia's forward deployment at Kant was making a major contribution to the preservation of security in the region. The base at Kant was even featured in a December 2003 televised, live broadcast in question-and-answer format that linked Putin with clusters of the Russian electorate scattered across 11 time zones. Kant was one of the linked-up sites. Virtually everyone stationed there was lined up on the field, and Russian soldiers talked with pride about the mission that they were fulfilling. One of the unspoken aims of the broadcast was to make ethnic Russians feel secure enough to return to their homes in Kyrgyzstan. This theme was pitched exclusively to Russian voters, because the functions delineated for the base are in no way linked to the protection of the local Russian population, who complain of restrictions on the use of the Russian language in the public life of the Kyrgyz Republic and not about issues of personal security.

The base in Kant allowed Putin to demonstrate to the Russian people that the introduction of the United States in Central Asia was not coming at Moscow's expense. As mentioned in chapter five, the basing agreement seems to have come with a side deal in which Vladimir Putin promised Akayev instructors to help train a new generation of officers for Kyrgyzstan's internal security services, as well as political analysts to work with members of Akayev's staff. But the Russian political analysts either failed to give Akayev good political advice, or the Kyrgyz leader simply ignored what he was told, and even with enhanced training by Russian instructors, Kyrgyzstan's Internal Affairs ministry did not prove loyal to Akayev during the March 2005 national demonstrations. Similarly, while the Russian government subsequently declared that their armed forces stood ready at Kant to evacuate Russian citizens, their capacity to do so was never tested.

In October 2004, Putin demonstrated another tangible success to the Russian population: he opened a permanent base in Tajikistan for some 5,000 troops of the 201st Motorized Rifle Division. The commanders of the division are being based in Dushanbe, allegedly over strong initial Tajik objections, and the troops housed in Kulob and Qurgan-Teppe.[50] The Tajik government also agreed to a forty-nine-year lease for the Russian-manned antimissile warning system at Nurek, for which the Tajiks received a $240 million debt write-off.[51] The agreement followed over three years of tough negotiations; initially the Russians had wanted the Tajiks to contribute to the cost of basing Russian troops.

The request gave the government in Dushanbe an opening to reduce Russia's military presence, as the Tajiks chose not to sign a new accord with Moscow on the joint monitoring of the Tajikistan–Afghanistan border, which led to a staged turnover of control of the border to the Tajiks completed in December 1004. Initially, both the United States and the Russians were unhappy about this situation, but the transfer of responsibility has been a smooth one.

The opening of a U.S. base in Uzbekistan also seems to have facilitated improved relations between Russia and Uzbekistan. Although Uzbekistan would not reenter the CIS collective security organization, from which it withdrew in 1999, there is more of a cooperative spirit in the Uzbek–Russian relationship than existed previously. Some of this is clearly the result of a closer Uzbek–U.S. relationship, which leaves Tashkent free to pursue closer ties with Moscow without the threat of Russian hegemony looming. Also, Karimov has a better personal relationship with Putin than he had with Yeltsin. Putin's background in Soviet state security may hold a certain appeal for Karimov who has a propensity for the threat and use of force. Some of it may also be the result of Putin having bargained for improved military cooperation in exchange for promises of Russian assistance in combating internal security threats.

Putin flew to meet Uzbek President Islam Karimov in Samarkand in August 2003. Karimov reciprocated with a visit to Russia in April 2004 after the bombing campaign in Tashkent, and the communiqués issued spoke of Putin's support for the Uzbek leader, the common threat of terrorism faced by both regimes, and the need for close cooperation in the area of security relations for their mutual self-protection.[52] Karimov ended the meeting with the statement that claimed a "new level of trust is forming between Russia and Uzbekistan."[53] This trust is even reported to include

Russia being given limited basing rights for aircraft at the Uzbek base at Khanabad, which adjoins the U.S. facility Kashi-Khanabad. Russia and Uzbekistan also plan military exercises as part of a vastly improved relationship, particularly in the area of air defense, which was a Russian deficiency in the area.[54]

One sign of the new importance of relations with Russia is that Karimov's daughter Gulnara, who is sometimes cited as a potential successor to her father, lives in Moscow and serves as a counselor in the Uzbek embassy.[55] Gulnara Karimova moved to Moscow after a well-publicized divorce from an American Uzbek named Mansur Maqsudi and she is now a very public advocate of closer ties between the Russian leadership and the Uzbek president.[56]

Partnership with Russia is fine, as long as Moscow does not dictate the terms or demand exclusivity. This said, the Russians remain very eager to define the rules of military engagement (and disengagement) in the Caspian Sea, but they are unable to do this to their complete satisfaction. Fearful that the United States would fully usurp Russia's role in Caspian Sea security, Russian President Vladimir Putin announced in April 2002 that Russia would be beefing up its naval forces in the Caspian Sea and would hold large-scale military exercises there. These exercises, which were held in August 2002, did little to protect Russia from being overshadowed by increasing U.S. military assistance to Caspian littoral states, a situation that leads the Russian government to continually warn off the United States from going too far in trying to marginalize Russia.[57]

Russia remains a major arms merchant in the region, given the virtual dependence of all of Central Asia's military on Russian (or, more accurately, Soviet) equipment, and the ease with which spare parts can be obtained and repairs carried out. The Kyrgyz and Kazakhs cite this as an important reason for continued close military cooperation with Russia.[58] The Uzbeks continue to obtain equipment from the Russians, and Uzbek civil aviation, Uzbek Airways, the region's largest service provider, is involved in a code-sharing and maintenance arrangement with Russia's Aeroflot.[59] Even U.S. officials recognize the cost-effectiveness of providing Central Asian states with Russian equipment. For example, in 2004, U.S. funding was used to allow Tajikistan to purchase all-terrain vehicles from Russia.[60]

Although Western training is becoming increasingly more important for the Central Asian militaries, only a small fraction of their officers have passed through military training schools in the United States or other NATO partner states.[61] Of the latter, Turkey is probably the most important, given the linguistic affinities between the Turks and the Azeris, Kazakhs, Kyrgyz, Turkmen, and Uzbeks. The Uzbeks and Azeris, in particular, seem keen on close military cooperation with their Turkish colleagues. But it will be another generation or maybe even two before Western military training fully supplants that of Russia, as virtually all of the current senior officer corps served in the Soviet Army, and Russia continues to be a major source of military training.

Ties between former Soviet-era professional security officials are even closer than those in the military. The Central Asian states' national security committees have no ready parallel in the West, having been created on the foundation of republic branches of the Soviet era-KGB. Cooperation between Central Asian national security organs and those of Russia has increased under Putin in large part because of the revitalization of Russia's power ministries under the current regime. Although the war on terror has created new and stronger ties between U.S. intelligence and that of partner states such as Uzbekistan, such ties still do not come close to replicating the kind of cooperation that exists between Russia and its four key Central Asian partner states. Even the Turkmen cooperate to some degree with the Russians, although those serving in the Turkmen security forces have been directly subjugated to the whim of their president to an extent unknown in other countries in the region.

In general, the Russian–Turkmen security relationship has suffered in recent years, probably in part because the U.S. military presence in the region was taken by President Niyazov as somehow validating his policy of "positive neutrality." In his mind at least, the assistance Turkmenistan provided served as a balance for ties with Russia. Niyazov's suspicion of the Kremlin deepened in these years, as Russia became a place of temporary refuge for Turkmen political exiles. Niyazov's anger was fueled by his belief that Russia took advantage of Turkmenistan's geographic isolation through the terms offered by Gazprom for long-term purchase of Turkmen gas.

By contrast, the Kazakh–Russian relationship has not been affected by the introduction of U.S. bases in the region. Nazarbayev has consistently maintained that the friendship between Kazakhstan and Russia is special and will continue to be defined by close cooperation in the area of military and security relations. During his visit to Moscow in February 2003, Nazarbayev offered unqualified praise when discussing the state of Astana's relationship with Moscow: "There are no problems between the two nations."[62] After the meeting, Putin felt the need to publicly state that there were areas of the Kazakh–Russian relationship that could in fact be improved, especially in trade cooperation.[63]

Public flattery aside, the Kazakhs realize that a weak Russia is a greater threat to Kazakhstan than a strong one. Russia is still Kazakhstan's dominant trade partner, and an important source of investment in small and medium-sized enterprises in Kazakhstan, which still lack Western investors.[64] The Russian economic recovery makes the regional market stronger and means that Russian-produced goods will be higher priced than currently, making Kazakh products more competitive at home and in Russia. The Kazakhs also feel that a strong Russia is less likely to pursue a chauvinistic ideology and take up the plight of the local ethnic Russians, who remain generally dissatisfied with their de facto second-class status in independent Kazakhstan. To date, the Russian government has generally acquiesced to the situation, although a group of parliamentarians fairly regularly offer statements of concern.[65]

The Kazakh–Russian relationship is not without tension, however, and one of the flash points has been the now Kazakh-owned former Soviet space station at Baikonur.[66] The Russians rent the station for $115 million a year on a lease that was renegotiated in 1994 and then extended to 2050 in 2004. The Kazakhs have complained that they are forced to lease this facility to the Russians at too little benefit, especially since periodic mishaps at the base continue to put the Kazakh population at risk But in the renewal agreement both sides committed to a series of cooperative commercial and military ventures using Baikonur. This is but one small sign of the changing balance in the improved Kazakh–Russian relationship.

Russia's Growing Economic Presence in the Region

In contrast to the area of security relations, Russia's growing role in the economies of the Central Asian states is not at all symbolic and is sometimes not readily apparent by a cursory glance at standard economic indicators. Although all of these countries are increasingly reaching out to a global market, Russia's private and state capital is continuing to capture a piece of these markets—and does so in ways that are not likely to be ephemeral. Russia still is a major trading partner for all the states of the region, and the economies of Kyrgyzstan and Tajikistan, in particular, are still heavily dependent on goods coming in from Russia.[67]

The war on terror and the increased U.S. presence in the region have not slowed Russia's economic expansion. If anything, Russians and their local partners have benefited from the additional loan and technical assistance money coming into the region. But most important, Russia's own economic growth has helped sustain Vladimir Putin's regional strategy.

Russian capital is most visible in Kazakhstan and Kyrgyzstan, two states that have repeatedly pledged to form a common economic space with Russia in 2003, renewing earlier commitments to pursue common trade and other economic policies.[68] It is too soon to predict whether this group of states will evolve in ways analogous to the European Union, developing a common currency and attracting holdout members of the CIS.[69] As Russia and Kazakhstan both move toward World Trade Organization (WTO) membership, economic ties between Kazakhstan, Kyrgyzstan, and Russia are sure to deepen.[70]

The growing U.S. presence in the region has not kept Russia from aggressively pursuing its three major economic priorities in Central Asia: Russia wants a strong voice, if not a veto, on legal questions concerning the development of offshore Caspian oil and gas reserves, dominance in Central Asia's gas industry, and control of Central Asian hydroelectric power. The legal status of the Caspian Sea is still being worked out by the five littoral nations (Azerbaijan, Iran, Kazakhstan, Russia, and Turkmenistan).[71] Although there is talk of steady progress, final agreement has yet to occur, largely because of Iranian, and to a lesser extent Turkmen, objections.[72]

The Kazakhs and Russians have already delineated their national zones, with wide areas of common development, and several joint projects in the Kazakh offshore sector are already being developed by LUKoil, Rosneft, and the Kazakh state oil and gas firm KazMunayGaz, including the valuable Kurmangazy field with reserves of between 700 million and 1 billion tons of crude oil.[73] This field will require a total investment of $10 billion.[74] The Russians may not have acquired their shares under the most competitive of terms, but legislation passed in January 2004 makes them liable for the same increased taxes as other foreign companies, prompting Russian grumbling.[75] The Kazakhs also cooperate quite closely with the Russians in the transport of oil, and some projects have involved members of Kazakhstan's first family.

In its gas sector, however, Kazakhstan has a much less competitive position. The Kazakhs and Russians have still not worked out a satisfactory long-term pricing agreement for the supply of gas from the giant field at Karachaganak to the large Russian refinery system in Orenburg.[76] The

Kazakh and Russian gas industries are working in tandem on these questions of transit of natural gas through Kazakhstan. They created a 50-50 joint venture, KazRosGaz, in 2002, which hopes to become the major source of transit across Kazakhstan. The Russians continue to offer the Kazakhs a relatively low purchase price for gas sold at the Russian border, but unlike with the Turkmen, the Russians have allowed some of their gas to travel all the way to the European market, where gas can be sold at much higher profit than in Russia. Kazakhs have managed to get a small part of Russia's European market.[77] Given Kazakhstan's targeted increase in gas production to 70 billion cubic meters by 2015, Kazakh officials would like to see this preferential treatment expand.[78] The Kazakhs see Russia as a less problematic competitor than Azerbaijan, which offers them the alternative route. The Kazakhs also understood that their access to the Russian pipeline system will push out Turkmen gas, another source of competition.

The Russians would like their relationship with Kazakhstan to serve as a model for development of the gas industry throughout Central Asia. Gazprom has been expanding throughout the region during the last few years, signing a cooperation agreement with Kyrgyzstan and entering into a strategic cooperation agreement with the reorganized Uzbek state gas company Uzbekneftegaz.[79] The Kyrgyz entered into the agreement quite enthusiastically. Partnership with Gazprom provides them better protection from their Uzbek supplier setting arbitrarily high prices, and they hope that partnering with Gazprom will also mean an end to gas shortages incurred when payments are in arrears.[80]

The Uzbeks see Gazprom not only as a gas producer, but also as the operator of the gas transit system through Uzbekistan.[81] This dual role makes them an economic force that must be reckoned with. The Uzbeks have developed a number of joint ventures in both the oil and gas sector with Gazprom subsidiary Zarubezhneftegaz and with LUKoil, which if completed would lead to $2 billion of Russian investment in Uzbekistan's oil and gas sector.[82] These projects are part of a general rapprochement between Moscow and Tashkent and also reflect the growing rivalry between Uzbekistan and Turkmenistan.[83]

Russia's growing partnerships with Central Asia's other gas producers put Turkmenistan in a difficult position, because they increase Russia's ability to isolate Ashgabat, forcing the Turkmen to surrender more control over the marketing and development of its gas industry to Russia.[84] The biggest challenge to Russia will not be gaining access to Central Asia's gas but being able to afford the improvements to the pipeline system to market it. It will cost Russia over $8 billion to market the 90 billion cubic meters of gas that it has contracted to move by 2010, and it may be difficult for Gazprom to raise the money in capital markets for this kind of investment given all their other current projects.[85]

Unified Energy Systems (RAO-UES), Russia's electricity monopoly, has also been moving into Central Asia quite aggressively in the past few years. RAO-UES has been an actor in northern Kazakhstan since the early 1990s, cooperating with U.S.-based Access Industries. Access has been developing the Bogatyr coal pit in Pavlodar since 1996, and in the fall of 1999 received the rights to the Severny pit, which by then was owned by RAO-UES.[86] These steps allow RAO-UES to rationalize supply and demand in central Siberia.

Like Gazprom, RAO-UES would like to use Central Asian energy to serve European markets. Its management has calculated that developing some of the water resources in Kyrgyzstan and Tajikistan would be far more economical than developing hydroelectric power in parts of Siberia, given the presence of the Soviet-era unified electrical grid throughout Central Asia that they have been helping to manage.

More important for its export plans, however, is RAO-UES's bid for control of large hydroelectric stations in both Kyrgyzstan and Tajikistan, which were slated for further investment at the time of the collapse of the Soviet Union.

In August 2004, RAO-UES signed a memorandum of understanding with the Kyrgyz government for building Kambarat hydropower stations 1 and 2 in Kyrgyzstan, a project that requires an additional investment of $1.9 billion, and has commissioned a feasibility study for the project.[87] They have also committed to investing $250 million toward completing the Sangtuda hydroelectric plant in Tajikistan, and the Iranians have committed another $250 million. Russian Aluminum, or RusAl, has also announced a long-term investment in Tajikistan's Rugun hydroelectric complex to facilitate the construction of a large aluminum smelter.[88]

These projects are controversial because they would mean that less water is available to the downstream users (southern Kazakhstan, Uzbekistan, and Turkmenistan) and would also serve to increase seasonal flooding, which has been a serious problem in Uzbekistan and Kazakhstan since the Kyrgyz have increased their production of hydroelectric power. Cotton fields in Uzbekistan and Kazakhstan are dependent on water from outside their republics for around 90 percent of their irrigation needs during the summer and fall. Both are at the mercy of Kyrgyzstan, high in the river-snaked mountains and in control of the immense Soviet-era dam at Toktogul. Kyrgyzstan for its part needs hydroelectric power to generate heat for its citizens in the winter, but if it releases water to power the dam, the surge of water causes massive downstream flooding because the river's carrying capacity is reduced when the northern Syr Darya freezes in the winter.[89]

As Russia's control of hydroelectric power in Central Asia increases, it will gain a critical say in the management of Central Asia's water resources. All five Central Asian states still rely on the Soviet-era reservoir system, which had most of its water storage facilities in Tajikistan and Kyrgyzstan, and water is doled out through negotiated agreements by the five states in an annual quota system that favors the downstream agricultural users.[90] At the same time, each of the states in the region is making unilateral decisions that affect the region's water table, such as the increase in the production of hydroelectric energy by Tajikistan and Kyrgyzstan, or the building of new reservoirs by Uzbekistan and Turkmenistan.[91]

Most observers fear that sooner or later problems of water usage will lead to violent conflict in the region. International efforts to sponsor the creation of a new regional water system have been rebuffed. The states of the region intend to manage this problem themselves, although various international development agencies have small projects there that are designed to increase the efficacy of the current system in incremental fashion.[92]

Russia's leaders are aware of the geopolitical influence that Russia will gain by controlling Central Asia's hydroelectric power and gas pipeline system, but it remains to be seen if Russia has the capital at its disposal to maximize the economic potential of either of these two critical sectors. This is obviously their goal, and one that they are looking for new levers to achieve. In October 2004 Putin got the leaders of four of the states in the region (all but Turkmenistan, which has never been a member) to agree to Russian membership in the Central Asian Cooperation Organization. Moscow's participation can perhaps reinvigorate this almost entirely ineffective organization that since its organization in December 2001, based on the Central Asian Economic Cooperation Organization, has failed to create or direct shared economic initiatives.

If it is able to manipulate the various levers it has been developing, Moscow's influence in the region seems certain to increase and for the next few years at least to keep pace with the growing influence of China.

China: Tomorrow's Superpower

Authorities in China seem to have been more disturbed by the introduction of U.S. troops in Central Asia than were the Russians, because it brings Washington's military presence to within a few hundred miles of the Chinese border. Everyone recognized that the U.S. military presence in Kyrgyzstan and Uzbekistan was an encroachment on Russia's sphere of influence, but China saw it as no less an encroachment on its own sphere of influence. And no one was interested in compensating Beijing, in large part because the Chinese were responding to threats against future influence rather than the current state of play.

Moscow sought to parlay the U.S. launching of the war on terror in Afghanistan to Russia's advantage, but there was little with which China could bargain. Unlike Russia, China was not considered even an indirect party whose sensibilities were affected by the opening of the U.S. bases. Thus, there were few concessions that China could gain from Washington, although one they did get, the designation of the East Turkestan Islamic Movement as an international terrorist organization, was important in Beijing.[93] It had direct consequences in Central Asia, as it led to the outlawing of local Uighur groups.[94]

In the past three years, China has been able to increase its presence in Central Asia, partly because Beijing is able to appeal to the Central Asians in the name of being a counterbalance to both the United States and Russia. If anything, the U.S. military presence in the region has contributed to the strengthening of the Shanghai Cooperation Organization (SCO), rather than to the diminishing of its power, as some thought would be the case when the United States opened its bases in Central Asia.

Even the Uzbeks thought that the SCO's influence would diminish. Tashkent seems to have toyed with idea of dropping out of the organization entirely. Uzbekistan skipped the SCO's first-ever joint military exercises held in the summer of 2003, claiming that its troops were not adequately prepared for the exercises.[95] However, rather quickly President Karimov and the senior Uzbek leadership decided that improved ties with China would not come at the expense of the evolving Uzbek–U.S. relationship. Consequently, Tashkent substituted enthusiasm for its earlier diffidence and became active in the SCO. As their reward, the Uzbeks managed to get the planned SCO Anti-Terrorism Center moved from its first home in Bishkek to Tashkent, where an expanded headquarters was opened in January 2004 and formally inaugurated at the SCO heads of state meeting held there in June 2004.[96] More importantly, China backed Karimov's use of force against protesters in Andijan in May 2005.

Both the Chinese and the Russians view the antiterrorist activities of the SCO as critical to offsetting growing U.S. influence in Central Asia, although the two countries do not fully see eye-to-eye on how best to accomplish this. The Chinese are eager for military cooperation with other SCO states, whereas the Russians would like to see CIS institutions strengthened first, and the CIS states participate as a single collective security bloc in SCO-sponsored activities. China, however, is pressing its cause on a bilateral basis with the various SCO member states. Military cooperation is furthest along with the Kyrgyz, who got $1.2 million worth of military equipment from China, and the Kazakhs, who have purchased equipment worth $3 million, including for communications and for specialized forces.[97] The Kazakhs are more reluctant to engage in joint maneuvers.[98]

The SCO has not yet fully evolved as an organization. It is unclear what its final potential is or even what its final membership will be. Various states have attended SCO meetings as observers. Afghan President Hamid Karzai attended the June 2004 meeting of heads of state in Tashkent in the hopes that Afghanistan, which shares a very small border with China, would eventually be admitted to the organization.[99] Mongolia was invited to attend the summit as well. There has also been talk of inviting both India and Pakistan to join.

Central Asia's leaders are likely to continue to actively participate in the SCO, even if it does not evolve into a more comprehensive security organization or take on functions in the area of regulating economic relations between the member states. The latter is a goal for the organization that has been discussed but not formalized.[100] The SCO serves as a setting in which issues of bilateral and multilateral concern can be thoroughly debated and sometimes even resolved. As one country's top diplomat informally remarked: "With the Chinese in the room, the Russians can't resort to their usual tricks"—a sentiment many other Central Asian leaders may share.

The SCO is but one of the tools China can use to influence developments in Central Asia, and it is probably not its most significant. China's size and economic potential make Beijing at least a silent presence in virtually every setting of importance involving the Central Asian states—and sometimes it is a visible and vocal one. Trade with China is increasingly important to all the Central Asian states.[101] Unlike in the first years of independence, it is legal trade and investment that is now being encouraged by the various

Central Asian governments.[102] China's economic presence is largest in Kyrgyzstan and Kazakhstan. Kyrgyzstan hopes to be a gateway to China because they are both members of the WTO, while China is a major investor in Kazakhstan's oil industry.

China wants increased access to Caspian oil and gas reserves. As discussed in chapter four, the Chinese National Petroleum Company won a tender for a 60-percent stake and control of Aktobemunaigaz in 1997 to develop the Zhanazhol and Kenkiyak fields in the Aktobe region, which later was increased by 25 percent.[103] The project is now moving forward after some early difficulties.[104] So too are plans to build a 2,900-kilometer oil pipeline to link the Kenkiyak field to the Atyrau oil terminal on the Caspian Sea. This $3.5 billion project has been authorized in stages: a $200 million 450-kilometer section going from Atyrau to Kenkiyak was completed in December 2002 and began operating in March 2004. The second stage of the project will run a pipe from Atasu in Kazakhstan's central Karaganda region through the Alashankou rail crossing with China's western province of Xinjiang, a 1,240-kilometer stretch that will allow China to receive Caspian oil.[105] During Nazarbayev's visit to Beijing in May 2004, he and Chinese President Hu Jintao signed an agreement for joint exploration and development of oil and gas resources in the Caspian Sea.[106] The Chinese government, however, was unable to secure a share in Kazakhstan's giant Kashagan oil field for its two principal oil companies.[107]

China is looking to both Kazakhstan and Russia to help reduce Beijing's energy dependency on the Middle East. The prospect of supplying China could create new synergies between the oil industries of both Kazakhstan and Russia. These synergies could also be used by Kazakhstan to parry Chinese pressures in other sectors.

At the same time, China's economic and geopolitical potential make at least two of the Central Asian states that share borders with it quite nervous. The Tajik–Chinese border is relatively small and of limited strategic importance to the Chinese, but the same cannot be said of China's borders with both Kazakhstan and Kyrgyzstan.

The 2002 treaty between Kyrgyzstan and China turned into a major political crisis for President Akayev, and accusations from opposition figures accusing him of treason for signing it clouded the remainder of his tenure. Leaked reports from the negotiating sessions between the Kyrgyz and the Chinese claim that the Kyrgyz side offered the land without undue pressure from the Chinese, but obviously such claims must be viewed with suspicion, because Chinese leaders may well have been subtly signaling that the territory was a priority at other high-level meetings. The transferred land (especially when ceded territories from Kazakhstan and Tajikistan are added as well) creates new possibilities for the Chinese to generate hydroelectric power and moves part of the Chinese–Kyrgyz border from the far side of several mountains, to their top, increasing Chinese legal standing to pressure for further land transfers.

The Kazakhs and the Kyrgyz understand that there is no way that the fate or the future of their countries can be fully separated from that of China, given their long shared borders. Yet there is little indication that they have become more nervous about China in the past few years. In fact, the opposite seems to be true. Both countries seem a bit more comfortable in their ability to manage this relationship, which they see as sometimes requiring concessions on their part, as was the case with the delineations of borders. But the relationship with China is still more problematic to them than the one with Russia, because China's potential power seems almost limitless, and the needs of its growing population could overwhelm those of the Central Asians.[108] For the near term, however, China's posture toward the Central Asian states seems quite predictable and generally supportive of the goals of the leaders of these countries.

Central Asia and the Outside World

The increased U.S. security presence in Central Asia has created no real constraints on the dealings of the Central Asian states with the rest of the world and has left them with a few largely unrealized opportunities.

Using Turkey as a bridge to the region seems less plausible than even a few years ago. The Central Asian states remain very close to Turkey, but the war on terror has done little to stimulate new synergies between Turkey and the Central Asian states. In fact, the increase in direct security ties between the Central Asian states and the United States has made Turkey's role as intermediary less important. Entering Europe is also an increasing preoccupation of Turkey and continues to be a much more important priority than expanding Turkey's influence in Central Asia. Nonetheless, close cultural and economic ties continue to exist between the various Turkic-language states.[109] Turkish investment remains very important in certain sectors of the economy in each of the Central Asian states, for example, in construction, the cotton sector in particular, and light industry more generally.[110] Visits by Turkey's leaders to the states of the region continue to be well publicized, and these men are still treated as honored guests, although there have been fewer summits of leaders of Turkic-language countries in recent years than previously.[111]

Turkey remains much more influential than Iran in the Central Asian region. For a while the Iranians hoped that the war on terror would offer an opportunity for improved cooperation with the United States. Among other things this would have the additional benefit of allowing Iran to become more engaged with the Caspian states in the sale of their oil and gas reserves.

In an effort to take advantage of what he still hoped would be a new opening in April 2002, Iranian President Mohammad Khatami took a trip through the region, reaffirming with all of the region's presidents a shared interest in improving bilateral relations. Kazakh government leaders, once again, stated Kazakhstan's interest in shipping some of its oil to market through Iran. During the Khatami visit, Kairgeldy Kabyldin, general director of the state-owned oil and gas company KazMunayGaz, went on record saying that the Iranian route was the best one for the Kazakhs to ship to the growing Asian markets.[112] While on the same visit, the Iranians signed an agreement on renewed cooperation with the Kyrgyz. Even Islam Karimov, long the most wary of Central Asia's leaders, warmly received the Iranian leader. However, there is unlikely to be any real expansion in Iranian influence in the region as long as Tehran is something of an international pariah.

The continued identification of most of the Central Asian states with the goals of the U.S.-led war on terror has distanced the Central Asian states somewhat from the core Arab states of the Muslim world. For the most part this was a foreign policy stance already adopted by the Central Asian states well before September 11, which was amenable to both sides.

The Central Asian states are all members of the Organization of the Islamic Conference (OIC) and have continued to send representatives to its major meetings.[113] Most also continue to receive loans or grants-in-aid from the Islamic Development Bank.[114] Bilateral relations with OIC member states remain good but are relatively low profile as there have been a very limited number of state visits by their leaders into Central Asia and not much travel to these countries by Central Asia's politicians in recent years as well.

Although all of the leaders of the Central Asian states look for ways to demonstrate pride in the Islamic heritage of their people, this is not their preferred identity or the international image they want to project. Ties with Arab or other Muslim countries are balanced with a desire to maintain good relations with Israel, which continues to be an important partner for all of the Central Asian states except Tajikistan. For Uzbekistan and Turkmenistan, Israel is an important source of investment, and Kazakhstan has played its "Jewish card" as a way to remain on good terms with the United States.

For instance, Aleksandr Mashkevich heads Kazakhstan's private metals conglomerate, the Eurasia Group. He is president of the Federation of Jewish Communities of Kazakhstan, which is an active member of the Federation of Jewish Communities of the CIS and the World Jewish Congress, on whose board he serves.[115] Mashkevich has frequently accompanied Nazarbayev on trips to the United States, and through this connection, Nazarbayev became acquainted with Florida Congressman Robert Wexler, who has been a vocal supporter of Kazakhstan on the floor of the U.S. House of Representatives.[116]

Nazarbayev has actively pursued a policy of religious toleration as part of his foreign policy strategy more generally. In September 2003 he presided over the Congress of World and Traditional National Religions, which was attended by representatives of the United Nations, the OSCE, the UN Educational, Scientific, and Cultural Organization, and the UN Children's Fund (UNICEF).[117] In September 2001 Kazakhstan became the only country in Central Asia to have hosted a papal visit.[118] This policy of religious toleration has only had a marginal impact on Kazakhstan's international reputation.

Potentially more important is Kazakhstan's Asian strategy. Of all Central Asia's nations, Kazakhstan has the chance to develop a significant diplomatic presence in the region.[119] Nazarbayev was first to propose the idea of establishing a regional forum aimed at increasing security and cooperation in Asia in 1992 at the UN General Assembly. The first summit for this initiative— given the unwieldy name Conference on Interaction and Confidence-Building Measures in Asia, or CICA—was held in Almaty in June 2002, attended by the Chinese and Russian presidents and the Indian prime minister, as well as representatives from thirteen other states, and a follow-up meeting was held in January 2003 in Almaty.[120] Nazarbayev has expressed some hope that this could eventually lead to the creation of an organization similar to the SCO or possibly the expansion of the latter group. Periodic meetings of Asian leaders in Almaty may remain little more than a forum for the discussion of issues of mutual interest, but they have been a good source of publicity for enhancing Nazarbayev's reputation in the Asian press. It has also helped serve India's interests in the region, allowing Delhi a periodic and high-level window into Central Asia. The first Asian summit was even preceded by a celebration of Indian–Kazakh friendship during a meeting in New Delhi.[121]

India remains interested in playing an increasing role in Central Asia, but it has yet to make increased engagement with these states an economic or security priority. The Indians are biding their time, waiting to see how the region develops before they waste too much diplomatic capital, not to mention investment capital in the region. Potential Indian investors are keeping close watch on the efforts to create a new transportation corridor across the region, the Traceca project (Transport Corridor Europe–Caucasus–Asia). Delhi also closely monitors the security situation and is reported to have a small military presence in Tajikistan, at a twenty-five-bed hospital in Farkhor that was used to treat fighters from the Northern Alliance in Afghanistan. Allegedly staffed by "advisers," the facility included helicopter repair facilities for Mi-17 and Mi-35 attack helicopters and is reported to have provided aerial reconnaissance and electronic intelligence.[122]

The Pakistanis, too, are interested in increasing their influence in the region, but they are stretched so thin economically and diplomatically that it is hard to imagine them playing too active a role in the region. However, their role will increase somewhat if reconstruction in Afghanistan succeeds in creating a functioning state. Should this occur, Afghanistan as well will be an increasing presence in the Central Asian region, particularly in Tajikistan, where the government is particularly eager to support joint initiatives with the Afghans.

The Central Asian states were very interested in increased engagement with major Asian states, especially if there was a chance that it would be combined with increased investment. But they did not want their Asian side to develop at the expense of increased engagement with the major countries of Europe, especially the strong European industrial democracies.

Kazakhstan, Kyrgyzstan, and Uzbekistan all wanted to be invited to participate with European institutions, although none thought of themselves as likely European Union or NATO members. Kazakhstan has the greatest chance to develop a presence in Europe, depending on whether or not it manages to meet the standards necessary for the OSCE chairmanship in 2009. In general, however, the Central Asian states have moved further away from Europe since late 2001. There is little chance that three of the states—Tajikistan, Turkmenistan, and Uzbekistan—will meet European political or economic norms anytime soon. Even if Kyrgyzstan does, it will have a marginal contribution to make, at best, given its distance from Europe and the small size of its polity and economy.

The Uzbeks have been stung by what they see as Europe's changing priorities in the region, and the formal rebuke they received from European Union foreign ministers in the aftermath of the May 2005 unrest in Andijan. The EU statements were a predictable follow-through of the changing attitude of the European Bank for Reconstruction and Development (EBRD) toward Tashkent. By the time that the EBRD board of governors assembled there for their 2003 annual meeting, the 1999 managers who had granted Tashkent the privilege of hosting had largely turned over and the new management used the annual meeting to criticize the Karimov government for its failure to enact economic or political reform.[123] This tactic also served to deflect criticism away from the EBRD's own policies in the Central Asian region, which had previously never linked assistance to performance benchmarks in any serious way. The Uzbeks, who spent millions of dollars building new hotel rooms for this event, were somewhat startled by the critique, so much so that at one point they disconnected live TV coverage so that the Uzbek viewers wouldn't see their leaders getting chastised by foreign officials. It came as no surprise to Tashkent when EBRD assistance was cut off a year later after Uzbekistan failed to meet the performance benchmarks set at the Tashkent meeting.[124]

In general, Europeans seem to be wearying of Central Asia's concerns, as they are, too, in Afghanistan. They certainly hoped, and may even have believed, that the reconstruction of Afghanistan would be simpler than it turned out to be. Instead, they find themselves concerned that their capitals will become targets of international terrorist groups who still use the Pakistan–Afghanistan nexis as a training ground. Although the UN Development Program continues to push for a regional strategy for rebuilding Afghanistan, and even held a meeting to gather support for this in Bishkek in May 2004, with each passing year it is becoming harder for the United Nations to raise reconstruction money pledged for Afghanistan, let alone get extra funds for projects involving the Central Asian states. This is even true of funds earmarked for the eradication of the drug trade that originates in Afghanistan and travels to Europe through Central Asia, which originates in Afghanistan. The United Kingdom was assigned to take the lead in this effort, but until 2004, relatively small amounts of money were allocated for projects in this sector, and even with increased funding, the Europeans are spending only 100 million euros.[125]

The events of 9/11 may have reawakened the world to the strategic potential of Afghanistan and the Central Asia region. But for many of the great powers, the epiphany was short-lived, as this new awareness seems to have been transcended by more pressing or traditional concerns. Weaker states like Iran, Turkey, and Pakistan continue to dream of affecting outcomes in this region, but without much prospect for success.

The U.S. presence in the region has nominally increased, but outside the energy sector, Washington's renewed commitment appears transient. For the U.S., Central Asia is unlikely to attain the strategic importance of the Middle East, and the same goes for the United States' European allies. Meanwhile, states in Asia may be driven to closer ties with Kazakhstan, depending on how Astana markets its oil.

States like Russian and China that view Central Asia as inexorably tied to their own national security interests are no less determined now to stay the course in the region than they were in the beginning of the century. Russia's and China's chances for future success continue to depend far more on their respective internal strengths and weaknesses than on any plans made in Washington.

7

What to Expect from the Future: Dealing with Common Problems

The terrorist attacks of September 11 on New York and Washington were a defining moment in international affairs. They led to a major reorientation of U.S. foreign policy, with Washington deciding to counterattack at the sources of terror, and to an energized effort by the global community to curtail support for terrorist groups.

It is still much too early to say whether the U.S. will achieve its new foreign policy objectives. The security situation in Afghanistan is stabilizing, and a popularly elected government is in place. Now it remains to be seen whether President Hamid Karzai can get the international and domestic support necessary to rebuild his country's economy and create a modern political system.

The situation in Iraq, however, is far from stabilized. Saddam Hussein has been ousted, elections have been held, but even with the presence of a large U.S.-dominated international military contingent, civil order has not been restored. Instead of being defeated, international terrorist groups seem emboldened by the way that the war on terror has progressed. Osama bin Laden remains at large, and new terrorist cells are being created, leading to new risks for fragile states. Yet, meanwhile, pro-democracy groups are also gaining greater stature in the Middle East and elsewhere.

U.S. attention to nation building has generally focused on Iraq and Afghanistan, where the funds required for two military campaigns far exceeded Washington's initial expectations. What money or imagination is left over is being applied to the Middle East rather than Central Asia.

The challenges facing the Central Asian states are growing, but governments there have received few new tools to address them, either in the form of advice, technological assistance, or security guarantees. Nor have their economic prospects changed appreciably, save in the case of Kazakhstan, whose economy has been bolstered by high energy prices rather than any sustained reform. The political systems have been slow in opening themselves to wider public participation. Chances are slim that we will see the another Central Asian regime toppled by a challenge by organized elites, as we have seen in Georgia, Ukraine, and Kyrgyzstan. Instead, there's much greater likelihood that popular upheaval will come in the form of groundswells organized by radical religious groups, rather than by disenfranchized secular elites.

This chapter discusses the common problems that remain and the difficulty in resolving them at the international, regional, and national levels. These challenges include (i) a lingering tension surrounding management of common water supplies; (ii) borders and the treatment of minority populations; (iii) the difficulty of trade within the region; (iv) the threat posed by narco-traffic and organized crime; and (v) the export and spread of extremist ideologies. State failure in one or more countries in the region is the most grave potential problem, and the risk will increase as the transfer of power to a post-Soviet generation of leaders occurs.

Finally, the chapter concludes by considering whether the international community could have been more effective in helping these states address problems of political and economic institution building and thus minimize the security risks created by failed effort. Must there be revolutionary change within the Central Asian states themselves before market economies and participatory political systems can develop? Could the outlook for the Central Asian states have been changed by more money and a substantial reconsideration of how foreign assistance needs are assessed? Is it still possible to influence developments in this region?

Is Central Asia Still a Coherent Region?

There is much debate over whether the problems of Central Asia can be efficiently addressed collectively, with all the states lumped together and viewed as part of a coherent whole. They are sovereign, independent states but whether they like it or not, their fates are more closely intertwined than any other cluster of neighbors, with the possible exception of the three countries of the south Caucasus.

Policy makers in Moscow believed a regional approach furthered the dependence of the Central Asian states on Russia. Many U.S. policy makers, therefore, believed that establishing U.S. military bases in several Central Asian states would directly and indirectly reduce their dependence on Russia, both by introducing close bilateral relations with the United States and by accelerating the breakdown of Central Asia as a distinct geopolitical subregion. The increased U.S. presence has led to a greater differentiation in the foreign policies of the Central Asian states and less of a sense of regional unity.

At the same time, however, the war on terror has inadvertently had the opposite effect. Both Russia and China have used the enhanced U.S. military presence to press for their own increased security roles. Both have preferred regional approaches to bilateral ones as the way to maximize their respective presences in what for each is a critical border region.

From the vantage point of U.S. policy makers, there is little to be gained by a strong sense of unity among the Central Asian states. Washington's strategic goals in the region—energy security and military cooperation—are best advanced on a bilateral basis. Although the U.S. sees a certain degree of regional cooperation between these states as desirable—that is, they should not create new problems for one another—it does not believe that regional cooperation would do much to foster economic development or political reform. Furthermore, some economic observers argue that too much regional cooperation could be a bad thing. They point to the need for each of these states to orient itself toward a global market, especially with regard to the development of its natural resources. But this argument minimizes both the importance of the local regional market for creating employment and economic diversification, and the importance of incentives for improved transit links within the region that are necessary for access to world markets.

There is also concern that too much good will between Central Asia's leaders could be bad for political reform and stability, particularly if combined with advice from Russia. Moscow is offering the Central Asian states technical assistance to introduce their concept of "guided democracy," one led by a strong president, in an effort to thwart grass-roots oriented democratic institution-building projects supported by Washington. But as Kyrgyzstan demonstrated, "guided democracy" can become a recipe for political instability: for his country and the region, the ouster of Askar Akayev created greater uncertainty than would have been the case had he been willing to allow an unfettered electoral process to choose a new legislature and then a new president.

The United States is also concerned about backdoor arrangements between Central Asian leaders and Russian oil and gas companies. These arrangements tend to work against the development of economic transparency and undermine the status of Western investors in these countries, while diminishing the U.S. role in the development of Caspian energy resources and impeding military cooperation.

In the aftermath of September 11, there was talk in the Washington foreign policy community of the need for a focused and coherent U.S. "Central Asian" policy, but the Bush administration has not pursued any such regional strategy. As was true under the Clinton administration, Washington continues to focus on bilateral initiatives as a way to enhance the independence of these states.

At the State Department, Russia and Central Asia are the responsibility of the assistant secretary for European affairs, but there is a separate deputy assistant secretary who supervises the Central Asian and Caucasian states.[1] Foreign assistance is approved on a bilateral basis, and with increased assistance, more responsibility has shifted from the regional U.S. Agency for International Development (USAID) office in Almaty to various national offices.[2]

This structure, plus the preference of the recipient countries to be dealt with on a strictly bilateral basis, has made it very difficult for the United States to pursue priority regional projects, such as facilitating trade within Central Asia, which is of particular concern in the USAID missions in Kyrgyzstan, Tajikistan, and Uzbekistan. Trade barriers are recognized as an impediment to economic reform. After over a decade of reinforcing the state-to-state approach of assistance projects, it is now harder for the United States to find ways to effectively lobby governments in the region to be more mindful of the negative consequences their decisions have on neighboring states. The bilateral approach to achieving the goals of the war on terror has further diminished the importance of preexisting U.S. regional projects.

One positive example is NATO's Partnership for Peace Program. It remains an important structure in the delivery of military assistance, yet the calculations of what U.S. assistance to offer in Central Asia are being made with a whole new set of priorities since the start of the war on terror. These priorities supersede earlier NATO efforts at reforming these militaries solely with the intent to address shared regional security problems.

European institutions have placed more priority on regional goals, spearheading the Traceca program to build a transport route from Europe to Asia through the Caucasus and Central Asia. The Asian Development Bank also contributed heavily to this project. But most European nations, and particularly those with stakes in multibillion-dollar energy projects in the region have placed their priority on bilateral rather than multilateral exchanges, with an eye toward advancing their countries' commercial interests. Korea and Germany are giving particular preference to countries where there are large communities of ethnic co-nationals. These approaches may well make sense in the short term, but they do little to provide long-term guarantees that regional security threats will not undermine the value of commercial investments.

In sharp contrast, both Russia and China are pursuing an aggressive regional strategy to complement the strong bilateral relationships their leaders are working hard to cultivate. Both countries believe geopolitical influence is accrued through regional organizations which unite the Central Asian states and which they dominate. The Russians see such regional initiatives as a necessary complement to bilateral relationships in maintaining Russia's global image as a powerful nation. The Chinese similarly see a regional approach, mainly through the Shanghai Cooperation Organization, as minimizing potential security threats that might emanate from Central Asia. It could be that in the end the regional strategies pursued by Russia and China will do more to hold these states together than U.S. and European policies that are content to see them drift apart—which would certainly be the case if the United States withdrew from Central Asia.

Any sign that U.S. commitment in Central Asia is weakening stimulates a Russian effort to fill the potential void. Simply observe how quickly Putin increased his outreach efforts after the difficulties Tashkent had achieving certification to receive FY2004 U.S. assistance. Although senior officials from the Pentagon continue to sweeten what is on offer to Tashkent in the area of military assistance, the opportunities for increased military cooperation between Russia and Uzbekistan are likely to increase even faster than those between the United States and Uzbekistan. Putin used the United States' finger-wagging to gain an entry long denied him, and he is certain to continue to use the lever of U.S. domestic policy to further distance Washington from its least important foreign friends.

Putin's pragmatic approach in dealing with the Central Asians creates new opportunities to expand Moscow's influence in the region, both in the area of economics and in security cooperation, because Russia will not link support to either political or economic reforms. Although Moscow does not want to see the Central Asian states develop into a security threat that reaches into Russia proper, the Kremlin sees little gain from maximization of these states' individual economic and political potential. Putin and most policy makers in Moscow would like to see a common economic space that favors the interests of Russian capital, rather than any common good, and this is best served by a continuation of cronyism and less-than-democratic regimes. To most Russians, and to more than a few Central Asians, this approach is seen as the "natural order of things," and preferable to Western attempts to transform their region into "something that they were never meant to be."

The Russian state is weak and thus its capacity to maximize its national interests in Central Asia is in doubt. Therefore, Russia's membership in the Central Asian Cooperation Organization (CACO) is unlikely to reinvigorate that organization.[3] Moscow has little interest in having multilateral economic relations disrupt bilateral economic relations with various CACO member states. And while Russia's presence may lead to new pressure on Ashgabat to join, it will do little to mute the competition between the leaders of the member states.

The Central Asian leaders have not been eager to reinforce the regional identities of their countries. The five presidents have competed among themselves for international preeminence, with the rivalry being especially keen among Islam Karimov of Uzbekistan, Nursultan Nazarbayev of Kazakhstan, and Saparmurat Niyazov of Turkmenistan, all of whom served together in Mikhail Gorbachev's last Politburo. The difficulty of cooperation is further impeded by Turkmenistan's policy of "positive neutrality," which Niyazov has interpreted as preventing membership in regional associations.[4] The prospects of regional cooperation will also be inhibited, at least temporarily, by the change of regime in Kyrgyzstan, as the interim Bakiyev government will be viewed as political usurpers by Akayev's former colleagues.

In a fashion reminiscent of Soviet practice, Central Asia's leaders have substituted virtual cooperation for real economic cooperation; the CACO lacks authority and institutional capacity to manage economic relations among the member states. Annual summit meetings are also held, more as a forum for communication than decision making, and they are likely to become less frequent when the current group of presidents is replaced by a cohort with little experience with Communist Party practices.

Few mechanisms for improved communication among these leaders have been developed, but that does not diminish the common problems that these states need to address. And many of these problems are best handled on a regional basis. Each Central Asian leader believes he knows better than his neighbors how to handle these common problems, so most solutions are being developed in isolation at the national level with only limited regional or international engagement.

Shared Security Problems

Stopping Drug Trafficking through Central Asia

The question of how best—even whether—countries captive to opium cultivation and narcotics trafficking can be successfully transformed is very controversial.[5] But for international policy makers, the pernicious impact of the drug trade in Central Asia has always taken a backseat to the problem of reconstruction of Afghanistan.

Prior to the general elections in Afghanistan on October 9, 2004, U.S. policy makers were persuaded by the argument that drug cultivation was a "traditional" Afghan economic pursuit that should not be disrupted during a difficult political transition. But once Hamid Karzai was elected president, U.S. priorities began to change, as did those of the Afghan government.

In 2004, opium cultivation increased by 64 percent over the previous year.[6] But dramatic increases in production had been accompanied by only slight improvements in interdiction.[7] More disturbing still, opium cultivation had moved into parts of Afghanistan that had previously never grown this crop. These factors increased pressure within the U.S. and Afghan governments for a change in strategy.[8]

A declaration on counternarcotics signed at the Berlin Donors' Conference in April 2004 called for increased measures to combat illegal cultivation, production, and trafficking of opium and other related substances.[9] This approach was designed to build on earlier efforts that had combined toleration, targeted financial enticements for farmers to abandon cultivation, and limited application of criminal sanctions against large producers and traders.[10]

But the United States no longer had confidence in the ability of its European partners to make use of the international coalition to raise funds for these projects or to effectively administer them.[11] In March 2004 Secretary of State Colin Powell announced $1 billion in aid in addition to the $1.2 billion the United States pledged for 2004 with the support of the Afghan government, which was now prepared to take over increased responsibility for policing its borders and to make aggressive efforts to achieve crop substitution and economic diversification.[12]

The international community's go-slow approach to halting the expansion of opium production in Afghanistan from 2000-2004 had substantial costs to the Central Asians, in the form of the increased criminalization of the economies of two or three states. This was seen as "peripheral damage" in a much greater war, which could be partially mitigated by increasing the capacity of the border controls and police forces of the Central Asian states. Had there been increased and better targeted international assistance toward drug eradication programs in the Central Asian states, the pace of the criminalization of some of these economies could have been slowed. This money should have been spent through the UN Office on Drugs and Crime (UNODC), and by making Central Asia more of a priority for the U.S. war on drugs established through the U.S. Office of National Drug Control Policy (ONDCP).[13]

The challenge of fighting drug trafficking in Central Asia has been exacerbated by the complete absence of modern technology along Central Asia's borders in the early 1990s—both among the former Soviet republics and with neighboring China, Iran, and Afghanistan. This is slowly being rectified, but large portions of the border regions, especially those that Tajikistan shares with Kyrgyzstan and Afghanistan, still lack all but the most cursory supervision, making effective narcotics interdiction impossible. Even though improved training for police and border authorities would not have solved Central Asia's drug problem, it would have created a much more supportive environment for combating it.

Soviet-era security officials were trained differently than their Western counterparts, but most shared a mentality of being professional law enforcement officials, willing to enforce the legal norms that their governments demanded of them. Central Asia's security forces were able to profit from retraining and from learning to use new kinds of technology for spotting criminals and illegal cargo.[14]

Such efforts would not have led to the disappearance of corrupt officials in Central Asia, but they would have made it harder for them to recruit new associates, especially if the reforms had been linked to higher salaries for security officials and harsher penalties for government employees implicated in the narcotics trade. Similarly, the effectiveness of such efforts would have been enhanced had they been directly linked to other projects involved with judicial reform. Even if only Kyrgyzstan and Tajikistan had been targeted—and both countries had been very receptive to speeding up the pace of reform of their criminal justice systems—trade routes to Afghanistan would have been disrupted, and the impact of drug trafficking on these two fragile states would have been lessened.

Although it is not too late to introduce reforms, it would have been more effective to have done so in 2002, before the dramatic increase in opium production and heroin trafficking from Afghanistan. It would also have been better to engage in large-scale judicial reform before improved cooperation between Russian and Central Asian security forces was introduced. Russian understanding of judicial transparency is quite different from the West's, so reforming the interconnected security services is a greater challenge than reforming each national security service. Increased cooperation with Russia also has fueled closer collaboration between corrupt elements in the security forces, which continue to be manned by officers who studied and served together during the Soviet period.

Yet even the existing level of funding has led to increased seizures of heroin at various transit points throughout Central Asia, especially at the Tajik–Afghan border, where 6 tons of heroin were seized in 2003, a thousand-fold increase since 1996.[15] Drug seizures increased in 2004 as well.[16] More ominously, the proportion of heroin in the intercepted narcotics was up considerably, meaning that the cut going to traffickers is up as well, given heroin's greater commercial value over opium.[17] Afghan antinarcotics officials estimate that a kilogram of heroin is worth from $5,000 to $20,000 in Afghanistan, but that rockets to anywhere from $70,000 to $300,000 on the international black market, depending on quality.[18]

Creating inroads against Central Asia's drug trade today will be far more costly and more complex than it would have been a few years ago, simply due to the growing magnitude of the problem given the string of recent bumper crops.

Although good statistics are very hard to come by, organized crime is at least as serious a problem in Central Asia as it was several years ago. Some of the Central Asian crime groups are linked to those in Afghanistan, and these entrenched criminal groups, swollen with the profits of the past few years, will work hard to undermine international efforts to eradicate Afghanistan's poppy crop.

There is also the risk that remote regions of Central Asia will become areas of cultivation to replace crops from Afghanistan. Historically, opium has been produced in parts of all five of the Central Asian countries.[19] Criminal groups are looking for ways to perpetuate their activities. One of the ways that they are doing this is by discounting drugs to people in the distribution chain, which has made drug addiction a growing problem in the region. Increased addiction has also led to increased trafficking in women (a way that addicts raise money) and the rapid spread of HIV/AIDS. Increases in drug addiction have reached epidemic proportions in parts of Kazakhstan, Kyrgyzstan, and Uzbekistan and increases in HIV/AIDS place major stress on the region's decaying health-care delivery systems. Because many of the Central Asian governments shy away from a frank discussion of these problems, the international community has been hampered in trying to effectively target assistance in these areas.[20] But the amount of international assistance available even to the most cooperative of states in the region, Kazakhstan, falls far short of that country's needs in combating HIV/AIDS. If the West led by example and devoted sufficient international resources to the development and execution of a successful HIV/AIDS prevention and remediation program, then it would become easier to prod the governments to begin addressing these diseases as well.

Combating Islamic Extremism and Terrorism: A War of Minds

Central Asian leaders continue to see the sale of illicit substances as a key means for Islamic extremist groups to fund their activities, although conclusive linkages are difficult to establish. Unquestionably, extremist groups have relied on narco-trafficking to bankroll their activities, but most traffic seems to be run by organized crime groups who enjoy protection from within the regime—not those opposed to it. Eliminating drug trafficking will not defeat Islamic extremism, and likewise getting rid of Islamic extremism will not put a dent in drug trafficking. Yet better monitoring of money laundering and other forms of illegal funds transfers would make it harder for extremist Islamic groups to operate.

The United States has been pressing for international measures to track money transfers and has been trying to enlist the Central Asian states in these efforts. Assistance in this realm is designed to help these states protect themselves against the security threats posed by international terrorist groups. But the bilateral assistance on offer will only improve capacity in a slow and piecemeal fashion. Much more could be done in this area.

U.S. assistance is not always compatible with what Russia and China are offering individually and through the CIS and the SCO. This multiplicity of patrons is exposing the Central Asians to very different kinds of legal standards, incompatible notions of due process, and very different models of what kind of intelligence should be gathered—and how. The British ambassador to Uzbekistan was relieved of his post in October 2004, in part because he argued that the British should not receive or share intelligence with a state that uses torture on prisoners. [21] It is hard to imagine an SCO member nation making the same objections. The different technical standards of competing patrons may eventually force the Central Asian states to choose among them and reduce or even eliminate participation in one or more of the multilateral settings.[22]

U.S., Russian and Chinese officials all talk about cooperation in the war on terror, but little has been done to coordinate their activities. The United States has been reluctant to share its global leadership on these questions with any but its closest allies, while Russia is still searching for functions that will validate the CIS, and both Russia and China seek to invigorate the SCO.

Even if the Central Asian states improve their technical capacity to detect and disarm extremist groups, they have the problem of reducing their appeal. As we discussed in chapters four and five, the behavior of some presidents has substantiated the rhetoric of religious extremists. The prevalence of bribe taking by officials serves as a testament of their godlessness in the eyes of believers; so too does the beating and torture of prisoners detained for their religious activities. These kinds of actions reinforce the arguments of Islamist groups that the government rules in its own interests, not those of the population. Such policies have also been a source of regional discord. Policy makers in neighboring countries will argue privately that Uzbek behavior is fueling rather than diminishing the appeal of extremist groups, although they generally share with the Uzbeks the definition of what constitutes radical or extremist groups and the view that both should be banned.[23]

Regardless of what governments do, radical Islamic groups are going to continue to spread their ideology in Uzbekistan and elsewhere. Officials in the Central Asian states as well as their Western partners are eager to identify and encourage indigenous sources of moderation in Islam.

The actions of U.S. policy makers, who are grappling with state building and the promotion of democratic values throughout the Muslim world, are shaped by an understanding of secularism that is firmly rooted in the Christian heritage. They see Sunday as a secular day of rest, while taking Friday off is an assertion of potentially radical religious sentiment. This view has much in common with the biases of Central Asian elites. Rooted in their Soviet experience, they view secularism as synonymous with atheism. Meanwhile, Western authorities regularly chide the various Central Asian regimes for discriminating against evangelical Christian groups, which, unlike Russian Orthodox or Roman Catholics, can find their activities sharply restricted by local authorities.[24]

These concerns not withstanding, U.S. leaders believe that the Soviet-style secularism of many Central Asian leaders makes them suitable participants for U.S. programs designed to spread religious tolerance. Many of these programs are designed around short-term visits to the United States and account for several million dollars in U.S. assistance to the region per year. The effectiveness of these kinds of projects has not been well studied, but the long-term impact of spending analogous sums of money on improving the quality of secular education in the region is much more certain. Arguably, the causes of secularism and religious moderation would be better served if this money were spent on projects for upgrading secular education systems. Questions of curriculum reform can be controversial, but projects that improve school infrastructure—such as restoring heat and potable water— enjoy everyone's support and bring children back to state schools. These efforts make them more likely to graduate and less likely to be attracted to alternative education programs run by unsupervised religious groups.

Securing Borders and Protecting Minority Populations

The risk of infiltrating Islamic terrorists has increased fear about the need to secure and protect national boundaries. The most extreme of these policies was the mining of borders, mostly by Uzbekistan, leading to dozens of deaths of Tajik and Kyrgyz civilians.[25] Even though the Uzbek government announced plans to begin the gradual de-mining of these borders in August 2004, many find it very difficult to visit relatives just across the border in neighboring republics or to trade with neighboring states.[26]

While progress has been made in delineating the Kyrgyz–Uzbek border, communities remain permanently split and minority communities continue to feel at risk, especially the Kyrgyz minority community in Uzbekistan.[27] Kyrgyz residents in much of the southern part of the country are still dependent on transit across Uzbek territory and are consequently subject to changing Uzbek evaluations of their security risks. For example, after the bombings in spring 2004, the Uzbeks introduced a $300 border-crossing charge on every vehicle entering the country. This led to the immediate doubling of most bus fares in southern Kyrgyzstan. And the final status of small ethnic enclaves of Uzbekistan and Tajikistan contained within Kyrgyzstan, which were established in Soviet times, is still not fully resolved.[28]

All of this makes the treatment of minority populations throughout Central Asia a matter of concern. No Central Asian state grants dual citizenship. So with the exception of those living in certain enclaves, local minorities are citizens of the country in which they are living, but many still feel greater loyalty to the neighboring state to which they are ethnically tied. This sense of dual loyalty is diminishing in Kazakhstan and Kyrgyzstan, where minorities are well treated and the economic situation is improving for many, but it remains a constant factor elsewhere in the region. In general, treatment of minorities is an area in which the international community has little clout, although the OSCE High Commissioner on National Minorities is closely monitoring the situation of ethnic minorities in Turkmenistan. And Central Asians themselves often have only minimal diplomatic representation to which aggrieved ethnic kin can appeal. For example, the Turkmen still lack diplomatic representation Kyrgyzstan.

The Uzbek government also maintains a watchful eye on developments in southern Kyrgyzstan. But at the time of Akayev's ouster in March 2005, Tashkent did nothing more than close its borders with Kyrgyzstan, as did Beijing, Astana, and Dushanbe. More troubling is the prospect of mass refugee flows to Kyrgyzstan in case of further unrest in Uzbekistan.

Greater economic cooperation with Russia could help solve some of the labor issues and, if properly handled, could provide legal protection for the large migrant labor forces that are spread throughout Central Asia and Russia. The trend of labor moving from less prosperous regions at home to more prosperous regions across the border is likely to continue as long as borders are relatively porous and economic opportunity is in short supply at home. This is as troubling for the Kazakhs and Kyrgyz as it is for the Russians, for much the same reasons. Migrants are seen as potential security threats because they include small numbers of individuals who want to spread extremist ideas.

Bilateral and multilateral working groups charged with regulating interstate relations remain active in the region, and there continues to be progress on delineating the national borders that separate the Central Asian states from each other.[29]

The delineation of the Kazakh–Uzbek border was completed after the Kazakhs agreed to return some territory and settlements that were reassigned from Uzbekistan to Kazakhstan in 1956.[30] This created substantial displeasure among local Kazakh residents, where the villages of Baghys and Turkestanets declared their sovereignty in December 2001 as a protest over the border dispute. They named their short-lived country the Kazakh Republic of Bagystan. In return for the ceded territory, the Kazakhs received Baghys (with 1,059 ethnic Kazakhs) and a section of the Arnasai reservoir, including the dam and five settlements.

Nevertheless, the Kazakh–Uzbek border remains a source of low-level tension between the two states, given its 2,330-km length and permeability. The Uzbek government has found it much easier to regulate trade than the flow of people across the border. Some of those responsible for the bombings in spring 2004 are generally assumed to have found sanctuary in Kazakhstan, and individuals linked to the July 2004 bombings were tied to an Islamic Movement of Uzbekistan (IMU) cell based in the Shymkent region, just across the Kazakh border from Tashkent.[31]

Russia and Kazakhstan have allowed some transfer of territory to allow divided communities to be assigned to a single state. These decisions were largely designed to assign Russian communities to Russia and Kazakh communities to Kazakhstan, and were not particularly controversial.

Uzbekistan's borders with both Tajikistan and Turkmenistan are also not fully delineated: The former seem certain to prove problematic in the future; the latter were the subject of a November 2004 meeting between Presidents Niyazov and Karimov in Bukhara devoted to border issues. Topics discussed included management of the Amu Darya, measures to facilitate cross-border trade, and improving access of citizens living in border areas to the neighboring state. Although three separate agreements were signed, their implementation depends exclusively on the good will of the two men who signed them. How long the two will remain on good terms is difficult to predict. The November 2004 meeting was filled with effusive demonstrations of friendship. Traditional terms of respect were used, and Karimov gave a car to Niyazov, who collects automobiles. The choice of car, however, an inexpensive Uzbek-produced Daewoo, says much about the quality of the relationship between these two rivals.[32]

Allocation of water resources is potentially the most problematic of all the security issues facing the Central Asian states. Chapter six examined how Russia's growing role in the hydroelectric sector could have a positive influence in the area of management of shared water resources and may alleviate tensions that have arisen from unpaid energy bills within the region, money owed mostly to Uzbekistan. Yet there is no long-term management plan and the roles granted to the international community by these states are insufficient. Actors like the UN Development Program that have been given some scope to address the problem have proven ineffective. For example, in 2004, the UNDP made water issues a particular focus for their human development survey of Central Asia, but only two countries, Kazakhstan and Kyrgyzstan, prepared reports in a timely fashion. These reports contained detailed analysis on plans for conservation and water purification and the consequences for society of failure to improve water quality, but regional water usage issues were beyond their purview, as were suggestions as to realistic plans or policies to better manage them.[33]

Lurking Economic Problems

Each Central Asian government can conjure economic statistics to defend its performance. The leaders of Kazakhstan and Kyrgyzstan can claim that their economies have climbed out of the economic morass created by the collapse of the Soviet Union. The presidents of Uzbekistan and Turkmenistan can take pride in their ability to sustain many Soviet-era social benefits, and the Tajik government can point to its postwar economic recovery. However, none of the Central Asian countries have fully recovered from the economic collapse occasioned by the dissolution of the Soviet Union. The economic performance of some states has been better than that of others, but none has maximized the opportunities for economic development that independence brought with it. This was true of the first decade of independence, and it has continued to be the case in the years following increased U.S. engagement in the region.

Bad Leadership Is Part of the Problem

The tasks of economic reconstruction that confronted Central Asia's leaders were formidable. Leaders often questioned the motives behind those who offered them advice, preferring to trust their own instincts. Each had a deeply ingrained suspicion of Westerners based on their long years of service to the Soviet state. These men feared that market reforms would become an instrument for allowing multinational firms to control their resources and dictate the terms of their development. Presidents Akayev and Nazarbayev were the first to understand that structural reforms would make their economies more competitive and resilient, but as we have seen, Nazarbayev continues to believe that Kazakhstan must protect its national interests by restricting foreign ownership of its oil and gas assets, which annoys Western investors, who feel they are entitled to high returns in high risk environments.

Central Asia's leaders were also deeply distrustful of Russia's motives, which were familiar to them. Thus they felt better able to predict and counter Russia's actions than those of Western governments, multilateral institutions, or investors. Presidents Nazarbayev and Karimov feel most confident in their ability to handle Moscow because they both spent part of their careers working in senior positions in the Soviet economic system. Of all the foreign actors, the Central Asians were most intrigued by the Chinese, but they saw limited applicability of the Chinese experience to their own region, given the circumstances surrounding the collapse of the Soviet Union.

Even those leaders who opted to introduce market economies handicapped the process of reform by the top-down management styles they employed. People with Western training were often pushed out of inner circles even in the more reform-minded states and were replaced by those more interested in pleasing the president and less concerned about questions of transparency.

The introduction of market economies has been distorted by the endemic nature of corruption in these economies, which became more prevalent after independence because of the newly acquired ability to regulate investment as well as legal and illegal trade.

The economies of Kyrgyzstan and Kazakhstan may be able to withstand some of the negative effects of corruption. Both have experienced high growth rates in recent years, and both have strong private sectors that will continue to press for further transparency. But popular expectations in both countries are changing, to such a point that allegations of corruption were already instrumental in bringing down Kyrgyzstan's president. And it is not clear that the new government in Kyrgyzstan will be able to meet heightened public expectations of a rapidly improving standard of living. If the new leaders think voters will give them only a short tenure, official corruption may actually increase, as those hailed as democrats rush to line their pockets before their time runs out.

In both Turkmenistan and Uzbekistan the private sectors are so small, and corruption in these countries is so endemic, that it may be impossible to transform either of these economies through incremental change. Uzbekistan squandered the opportunity to do this in 2002, and Turkmenistan has never shown any willingness to modify its current economic system. Unless there is a precipitous drop in opium cultivation in Afghanistan, economic reform in Tajikistan will take second place to the drug trade.

Bad Advice and Tight Budgets

The pervasiveness of corruption is used as an excuse by the international community to justify its failure to bring about economic reform. Had the multilateral financial institutions set different rules for engagement in the region, and had the United States and other Western aid donors been willing to spend more money, and expand projects that were simply for PR effect, there might have been more economic success stories in the region. Corruption has served to thwart economic reforms, but limited support by the United States and the international financial institutions served to further stimulate corruption, both directly and indirectly. There were frequent rumors that some of the early assistance money, especially lines of credit, was given to favorites of those in office—both family members and those who paid bribes for access.[34] Some of this behavior could have been controlled by better supervision.[35]

And when those in charge in the countries with small economies, such as Kyrgyzstan and Tajikistan, realized that the international community was helping fund a project of reform that was not going to lead to a vibrant market economy anytime soon, they lost the incentive to swap rent seeking for turning a profit in a market economy. The IFIs had fewer means of control available to them in the larger economies, such as in Kazakhstan or Turkmenistan, where economic restructuring could largely be funded by the state itself. In these cases pressure for reform had to come from within the countries themselves. For example, as we saw in chapter four, the pressure for reform in Kazakhstan is considerable.

The causes of corruption have varied, but the fight against it always creates a circular problem. Unsuccessful economic reforms made corruption more pervasive, but the presence of rent seeking poisoned the atmosphere necessary for reform. The cycle was hardest to break in the poorest countries, where the private sector provides limited opportunities and regimes reward regional elites for loyalty by allowing them to pocket some of the profits in a state-dominated sector, or to tap into illegal rents such as those in the drug trade. The presence of an active private sector changes the dynamics of corruption, as state officials then leech profits from private businesses, and can prevent them from expanding to the natural limits imposed by the market, as has been too often the case in Kyrgyzstan and Kazakhstan. This, much more than the theft of assistance money, is the kind of corruption prevalent in Central Asia.

In fact, increased assistance might have served as a valuable "good" that local elites could have helped distribute, speeding the privatization process, assuming that the priority was the speed of the process and not its equity or the long-term financial health of the financial institutions that distributed the assistance.

But only Kazakhstan and Kyrgyzstan set the goal of developing the Western-style banking systems that would facilitate high loan traffic, and only the Kazakhs realized this goal. Lending in Turkmenistan and Uzbekistan was hampered by the inability of local borrowers to get access to hard currency, which was a precondition of most IFIs to set up loan programs.

Small and micro loans are considered attractive assistance projects by most IFIs because they do not require much banking infrastructure and target a broader audience. Yet the amount of money available in the region never came close to meeting the potential demand. Because borrowers lacked assets to guarantee loans they were forced to pay high interest rates that cut into the profitability of their businesses, which were often liable for high taxes as well. Small businesses that did survive had a lot of trouble getting the financing necessary to expand and diversify their holdings, and if they did, the larger operations often fell prey to corrupt competitors.

In general, economic recovery of the region would have been served by structuring assistance differently, by changing the balance between loans and grants. With both longer and better terms of repayment, Uzbekistan might have gone through with structural reforms, including privatization, rather than abandoning its IMF stabilization program in 1996. Admittedly, this would have been a hard sell, given Uzbekistan's paranoia about how unrest in Afghanistan and disorder in Tajikistan would contaminate its economy, but there was a chance that Uzbekistan might have agreed had "shock therapy" been defined in a way that was not inconsistent with a gradual shift away from Soviet-era social welfare benefits. A changed structure of foreign assistance might have been used as a lever to pressure Uzbekistan to open its borders to trade with neighboring countries, which would have stimulated the growth of an Uzbek private sector and economic recovery in Kyrgyzstan and Tajikistan as well.

The international community had another opportunity to affect economic outcomes in Uzbekistan in 2002 by offering enough money to help the Uzbeks meet their projected budget deficits, roughly an additional $500 million per year. And it could have been done without restructuring the assistance process. Even more flexible use of conditionality by the IMF might have been sufficient, something not supported by current rules. Some IMF economists have suggested that the IMF should consider changing these rules, though this is quite unlikely. A September 2001 IMF working paper argued for floating tranche conditionality to replace the current strict timetables for staged project completion.[36] They also argued for what they termed "outcomes-based" conditionality, which would allow the IMF and recipient governments to negotiate a series of shared policy objectives, with a flexible timetable for meeting them, rather than continued funding being predicated on performance of goals according to strict timetables. The latter in particular is something that the IMF is reluctant to pursue because it would lead to front-loading of funds.

The United States and the international community have been reluctant to reexamine how they define their responsibility for providing foreign assistance, both in 1991 at the end of the Cold War and in 2001 with the start of the war on terror. The EBRD was created in 1991 to provide an additional financial instrument to help fund the reconstruction of the countries created or redefined by the collapse of communism.[37]

The balance of spending between defense and foreign assistance has not changed appreciably since the war on terror began. Technology-based solutions still absorb virtually all money available for preventive security measures. The Bush administration continues to advocate a National Missile Defense Program, which could cost up to $60 billion. With the exception of offering massive foreign assistance for Iraq, foreign assistance for potential battlegrounds in the war on terror has increased very slowly.

The one major innovation that the United States made in the delivery of foreign assistance was the creation of Millennium Challenge Accounts (MCA), announced in 2002 and funded in 2004. This program is designed to spur the development of strong private sectors in some of the world's poorest countries, but so far none of the Central Asian states have been judged eligible to receive MCA grant money because they have made insufficient progress toward the development of transparent economic and political systems.[38]

As a result, many of the complaints made about the way that IFIs operate—and how traditional U.S. foreign assistance is delivered in other parts of the world—apply to the situation in Central Asia. For example, critical comments made by Nicolas Van de Walle and Timothy Johnston in their 1996 study of assistance to Africa are applicable to the experience in Central Asia.[39] They complained that there was too much duplication among aid agencies and at the same time that there were too many stand-alone projects.

This was less of a problem in Central Asia than in Africa, but the Central Asian policy makers confronted a somewhat analogous problem, in that different donors had different criteria in deciding whether to provide loans and technical assistance in a particular project area. This sent mixed messages to the Central Asians. For example, the Asian Development Bank was eager to fund education projects in Uzbekistan, and did not demand the same demonstration of willingness to reform the educational system or school curricula that European and U.S. donors sought.

The Central Asians were also plagued by another problem noted by Van de Walle and Johnston. They argued that host governments had real difficulty covering recurrent costs and were frustrated by an assistance culture in which donors were not interested in turning projects over to host governments, which further undermined the development of local capacity. Walle and Johnston also complained that many projects are designed to satisfy constituencies in the donor country rather than address pressing problems in the recipient country.

This is certainly true of many of the projects in Central Asia that relate to gender issues and trafficking in persons. The former is such a major priority of USAID in the region that businesses seeking small and medium enterprise loans use a female "front," and women interested in organizing nongovernmental organizations (NGOs) to deal with general health or education issues adopt a gender focus to secure support and conceal their broader aims. Similarly, local law enforcement officials complain that projects designed to combat trafficking in persons ignore the root conditions—the sale of women by drug-addicted family members.[40] Similarly, those brought in to run gender awareness programs in the region often have little awareness of the cultural context in which they are operating, and no sense of responsibility for the fates of women whose consciousness is raised and who are subsequently rejected by their families as a result.

Some of the international aid workers fell prey to the same enthusiasms that the Central Asians did, seriously underestimating what it would take to sustain economic growth in the poorer countries such as Kyrgyzstan and Tajikistan. In both countries, economic planners were unjustly optimistic and failed to consider the isolation of the region and the potentially crippling interdependence of these states with the regional market.

This said, there were plenty of smart people working for the IFIs in the region and for USAID, and employees with relevant language and cultural exposure prior to coming to the region are increasing in number. Any interested reader can look at the website of any of the multilateral financial institutions and find well-written explanations of the causes of disappointing economic performance in any of these countries, and good suggestions as to how it might be improved. But one of the problems with Central Asia is that things have never gotten bad enough to provide a forum for these critics to lobby for broader international engagement or even for rethinking the developmental paradigms that have been applied.

Failures of Regional Trade

International assistance toward the development of a strong regional market, reaching from Central Asia into western Siberia, down into Afghanistan, and even eastern Iran would have benefited all five Central Asian states, but was never considered. The U.S. priority was to get these countries to think in global terms, and to decrease the Soviet-era dependencies or interdependencies that would be recreated—only now dependent upon market forces—through the reconstitution of a regional market.

Uzbekistan, in particular, had the capacity to become an important regional producer of processed foods, clothing, and textiles. Its problem is one of lost opportunity because with a domestic market of 26 million, trade barriers have damaged but not destroyed Uzbek industry. The failure to develop a regional market has proved particularly costly to the weaker economies of the region, Kyrgyzstan and Tajikistan, where light industry is all but impossible to sustain without access to some foreign markets.

Except for the ADB, the IFIs advising these countries did not sufficiently anticipate the costs of the failure to develop regional trade linkages on a country-specific basis, and economists from the ADB were not able to influence the thinking in other IFIs. Ironically, this was partly the product of a desire by the World Bank and the IMF to be more sensitive to the wishes of recipient governments than had been the case in the 1970s and 1980s, when they were criticized for ignoring local preferences in the design of the projects.[41] Then, as now, of course, recipient government approval was required for projects of the World Bank, IMF, and UNDP. But international influence could have been used to stress the importance of recreating Soviet-era economic cross-border synergies on a market basis.

Several of Central Asia's leaders had little interest in cooperating with each other, and financial incentives to change their minds were limited. Virtually every state was in violation of trade and border agreements that their leaders had at some point signed, most through CACO, where Turkmenistan opted out. Had the IFIs wanted to get tough with the Central Asian states, country-specific projects could have been made conditional on the observance of regional and bilateral agreements.

IFIs must strive to attain a difficult balance between being sensitive to clients' desires and having a deeper, more refined vision of development than local economists, and to anticipate failures in development planning. Most projects in the region are country driven and prioritize trade with the donor country or its allies, usually making the donor country the mandatory supplier of vital technology or equipment, as opposed to trying to match the goods of the Central Asian countries to local markets.

The region's major commodities—its oil, gas, gold, and cotton—must find their way to a global marketplace to realize maximum profit. But the Central Asian states also need projects that are focused on increasing employment because the region's population is young. Regional rather than simply national initiatives are most likely to stimulate new job creation.

Central Asia itself has placed little priority on building regional markets, save for some well-placed rhetoric. The CACO never developed mechanisms to orchestrate concerted action. Although adherence to an international trade regime is the most effective way of facilitating trade between the various states, the dramatic difference in the pace of structural reform across the region means that even today only a regionally instituted trade regime could boost trade.

Even if CACO should prove more effective in the coming years, it cannot compensate for the lost opportunities for creating economic synergies that improved terms of trade would have provided the region in recent years. There is, however, still significant regional trade on which to build. Tajikistan, Kyrgyzstan, and Uzbekistan remain important partners for one another, accounting for a significant share of each other's exports.[42]

The regional market amounts to over 75 million people when neighboring parts of Russia are included. It can be reached without great transportation costs, if terms of cross-border transit are improved. Transportation costs to more distant markets in the United States, Asia, and Europe are quite high, much higher than in China or Pakistan, both of which are competing producers in these distant markets with lower labor and transit costs. But many locally produced foodstuffs, pharmaceuticals, and even certain textile items would be cheaper than imported goods from China. If local industries are not revitalized and expanded now and part of the market share captured, it will become much more difficult to do this after Russia and Kazakhstan join Kyrgyzstan as World Trade Organization (WTO) members.

The failure to appreciate the importance of the regional market diminished the potential success of the developmental paradigm that was being imposed, particularly on Tajikistan and Kyrgyzstan, making the economic targets necessary to minimize long-term debt virtually unattainable. Moreover, the size of the current debt and the amount of it going to foreign consultants and the purchase of foreign equipment created an atmosphere of distrust toward Western institutions, which will continue to influence domestic politics throughout the region.

While many of these countries may have unrealistic ideas about import substitution, and their own capacity to build equipment necessary to complete technologically complex projects, a lot of political good will could be created by the IFIs and international donors if more effort was made to source equipment locally, or at least within the regional market. Similarly, USAID and the IFIs could modify the structure of loans so that the differential salary structure between foreign experts and local experts would not be built into the loan, but would be borne by a special fund created by the donor. Fifteen years into independence, many of these "foreign" experts have backgrounds that are not dissimilar to the local experts that they work beside. Many are Soviet-era émigrés. More creative thinking would break down at least some barriers.

Failures of Political Institution Building

More than fifteen years after independence, the Central Asian states have failed to develop political institutions that are either democratic or provide for the transfer of power in ways recognized by society as legitimate. Each of these states must still go through the challenge of transferring power from the Soviet-era generation that still dominates political life.

If anything, these regimes have become less rather than more democratic since the United States began its military presence in the region. Nation building has not been a priority for Washington. U.S. policy makers and most of their Western counterparts have largely discounted the prospects of reforming the current elite. The populations of most of these countries are so ill-prepared for democratic transitions that only the most gradual approach to political institution building is likely to have the desired outcome. As a result, most policy makers concerned with the region see little reason to increase the sums allocated for political assistance to these states or to challenge the developmental paradigms that are at the core of how assistance is being delivered.

Central Asia's leaders have both exaggerated the risk of extremist groups and overestimated popular patience. The perception of psychological empowerment that independence brought to these populations is diminishing with time. We saw clear evidence of how it can boil over in Kyrgyzstan in March 2005, and then again in Uzbekistan in May.

Those who live in a country should feel some stake in its future, or failing that, feel some hope for their own future or that of their children. But the rulers and the ruled seem to tell time in different ways. Most people need the hope that things will improve either in their lifetime or that of their children. Those born in the Soviet Union were raised on a diet of "deferred gratification"; all independence seems to have brought is a new version of the old dietary staple. Those born later are likely to have less patience. Most of them, unlike many of their parents, have direct contact with the global information age and their expectation of the future is partly shaped by their knowledge of what is going on elsewhere.

The population in the region will take to the streets when they feel pressed, but just as in most of the rest of the postcommunist world, their preference is to find peaceful means to make their dissatisfaction known. The history of public protest in recent years provides limited evidence of any great risks posed by the threat of mob rule, but it does make clear that absent public approval, the durability of the current leadership will prove short-lived.

Outside Kyrgyzstan there have been a few large public protests over the past decade that the respective governments have not been able to defuse, but as the events in Andijan showed, the costs associated with defusing them are growing.

The Kazakhs have less of a history of public protest than do the Kyrgyz. In the late 1990s unresolved labor disputes sparked mass protests in southern Kazakhstan, but the increased restrictions on public demonstrations combined with the country's economic upturn that enabled the repayment of public debt defused much of the tension.[43] In recent years, public protest has become more of an elite activity in Kazakhstan, posing little direct threat to the Nazarbayev regime. Opposition efforts to get the public to protest the seriously flawed parliamentary elections of 2004 almost immediately fizzled out, but despite the new ban on public demonstrations during election periods, organized opposition to Nazarbayev will continue to target the presidential elections of January 2006 as their deadline for regime change.

Tensions are increasing in both Turkmenistan and Uzbekistan. Small demonstrations in Turkmenistan have been organized by the disenfranchised members of society, relatives of political prisoners, and local Russians affected by changes in the dual citizenship law.[44] These were not easily put down. Protests in Uzbekistan are potentially very destabilizing. Some have been spontaneous, like road blockages by women outside Tashkent in July 2004 to protest the absence of potable water during the summer heat, while others appear to be organized, such as the November 2004 protests by thousands of merchants in bazaars across several cities.[45] The May 2005 demonstrations in Andijan were very well organized and are likely to trigger future protests, even if the Uzbek government answers these with the use of force.

Yet all this does suggest that Soviet-style social engineering techniques that have been used by Central Asia's leaders to create new political loyalties—part nationalist and part personal—are not having their desired effect. The region's leaders have not succeeded in creating for themselves the status of founding fathers, men who can dictate the terms of their own succession because of the strength of their performance in office. However, the attempts at social engineering could be creating potentially dangerous situations, because they are leading to a growing sense of ethnic empowerment by the titular nationality, as well as by religious opposition groups who claim that the corruption of the ruling elite is proof of the tainted nature of their ideology.

Efforts to reinstate some sort of modern-day monarchic system in any part of Central Asia would be very dangerous, and yet this may be the plan of several of Central Asia's leaders. The societies that they rule are complex, filled with populations reluctant to accept a loss of the benefits they are accustomed to enjoying and replete with former political and economic stakeholders accustomed to being accommodated. When the opposition came together in Kyrgyzstan this was enough to bring down the president, for included in their number were enough representatives of the country's security forces to make the use of force a virtual guarantee of civil war.

Although some might use the electoral process as their means of executing a succession, all of the region's presidents seem determined to skew the playing field to their own personal advantage. Free and fair presidential elections therefore may become a fact in style, not substance. The key political decisions in all five countries as to who can and cannot contend for high office are likely to continue to be made behind closed doors, and this is true even of the presidential elections scheduled for July 2005, to choose Askar Akayev's elected successor.

Yet generational change must inevitably occur throughout the region. Some leaders in Central Asia may in the short run be able to insulate themselves from outcomes like those of Georgia, Ukraine, and Kyrgyzstan, by making it harder for independent political groups to function in their countries, but they will find it harder to minimize the role of regional influences within Central Asia. The transfer of power in one country will lead to a substantial politicization of the region in ways that will maximize the uncertainty of political outcomes. The events of March 2005 in Kyrgyzstan and May 2005 in Uzbekistan create politically destabilizing conditions for the region more generally, although their full effect may not be apparent for several years.

The relative absence of sharp inter-elite struggles in most of the region has been in large part a product of the uneven playing field in these countries. But the departure of a sitting president changes the situation immediately, which is especially true if he dies or is forced from office before the end of his term. There is a push-and-pull quality to the interchange going on between the region's presidents and the top layers of the political elite whose support helps facilitate their rule. This tension has now been exacerbated throughout the region, making the population in each country aware that a political transition is approaching. While presidents Niyazov, Karimov, and Nazarbayev have all enhanced the power that they inherited with independence,

they have not really legitimized it. That the post of president was constructed on the remnants of the republic Communist Party structure gave
these presidents a critical tool to use in their accumulation of power. The
incumbents strengthened the institution of the presidency and then advanced
their own personal rule, moving away from the notion of collegial leadership
that had dominated throughout the post-Stalin era in the Soviet Union.

Even those who have enough authority to hand over power will not create a risk-free environment for their successors to secure their own power.
And in cases like Kyrgyzstan, where the incumbent is ousted, the process of
securing the legitimacy of his successor will be even more problematic.

Further challenges will come after the political transitions are completed.
Disgruntled members of the elite, some longtime opponents and others
who were previously silent, are likely to take advantage of the inherent
weakness of a new president.

Those who seek political power are going to use all the potential tools at
their disposal to advance their cause. Many will see these contests as their
final chance to take power, which could make substate identities and ethnic loyalties of greater importance than they have been in the past few years.
But ethnic identities and loyalties are unlikely to play the same role that they
did in the period just after independence, when ethnic, subethnic, and
regional identities became increasingly important throughout the region. In
general, in today's Central Asia, subethnic identities create a sense of mutual
obligation. They may get you in someone's door, but for most of the region
they are but one factor in what are becoming increasingly more complex
political environments.

The existence of these loyalties introduces an element of greater volatility
into the situation. With the exception of Tajikistan, however, the elite in Central Asia has been quite sensitive to the incendiary capacity of attempting to
mobilize populations along ethnic or subethnic lines, but while today's political elders and the next generation may not seek to advance their claims in
such a dangerous fashion, ethnic polarization can still occur spontaneously.

Ethnic identities are only one source of potential danger: Throughout
Central Asia, there are various "have-not" groups that have been waiting to
make their presence felt. These groups include those from the presidential
entourages who will feel slighted and damaged by the choice of a successor,
as well as excluded members of the old-Soviet elite and their children, many
of whom have accumulated economic levers to use in advancing their cause.
Added to this are the remnants of the alternative elite, who had counted on

independence providing them with new economic and political opportunities, but who were thwarted in their plans. The alternative elite include both those with secular and religious orientation. The mix of forces varies quite substantially from country to country, as do the tools available to use in their struggle for power. But most have added new economic and cultural tools of "global outreach" to their traditional arsenal, which includes manipulation of political position or ethnic status.

Moreover, the next group of leaders who come to power may have far less in common than the current political incumbents and may prove to have far less political staying power. The next group of presidents is likely to lack even the minimal loyalty that the current set feels toward one another. In fact they may feel outright hostility if it seems to one sitting president that the way a leader came to power in a neighboring country is a direct threat to his own political longevity.

Because of this, some of the region's leaders may become much more aggressively involved in the internal politics in neighboring states, not just to prevent unrest from spilling over, but to assert national advantage. All of the states are likely to strongly resist Islamic groups coming to power just across their borders, even in power-sharing relationships. The Uzbeks and Kazakhs are likely to watch closely the continuing transfer of power in Kyrgyzstan and try to maximize the likelihood that the new president favors their respective economic and demographic interests and all will watch developments in Uzbekistan with great nervousness.

In places where political institutions to regulate the transfer of power are weak or nonexistent, ambitious elites will seek to use extralegal ways to advance their cause. We have already seen an attempt at this in Turkmenistan during Shikhmuradov's failed November 2002 coup. Throughout Central Asia, members of the elite from disfavored clans and families have been sitting by, waiting for the opportunity to grasp more economic and political power. As institutions to ensure a peaceful transfer of power do not exist, there is no foundation on which they can rest their hopes.

As the leaders in Central Asia leave office, the populations of the region will begin embarking on a difficult transition. Some are looking forward to it enthusiastically as the decisive end of the Soviet system, restarting the stalled democratic revolutions of 1989–1991, while others see it as a journey into a great unknown.

The first test will come in Kyrgyzstan, where the interim government that encouraged the ouster of Akayev must legitimate its hold on power.

Kurmanbek Bakiyev, the interim president who has thrown his hat into the presidential race and who was affirmed by a parliament whose election was so corrupt that it brought down the sitting president, has inherited the responsibility of conducting democratic presidential elections.

And after these elections parliament must decide whether or not to engage in fundamental political reform, to put in place constitutional guarantees against the abuse of power. This parliament also must consider whether or not it has a legitimate enough mandate to complete its term of office, or dissolve itself—a rather unlikely scenario.

It is hard to imagine that Kyrgyzstan's elite is up to this task, and if they are not, there is good reason to fear that the Kyrgyz population will not grant them a long grace period. The grace period in Uzbekistan may be shorter still, especially if the Uzbek government fails to introduce economic reforms, such as freeing the purchase price on cotton and grain and reducing taxes on small businesses. In both countries, economic conditions have been exacerbated by political favoritism and the corruption of the ruling elite. But it is also the result of the very nature of the economic transition that was triggered by the collapse of the Soviet Union.

After fifteen years of learning to distrust one's leaders—and there was little political trust inherited from the Soviet period—it will take a long time for Central Asia's population to trust its leadership. But choosing these leaders democratically would be a good start to the process.

Blame Lies with the Region's Leaders

The kind of instability looming in Central Asia was not preordained. Although caused by the local elite, it could have been more effectively headed off by better-considered interventions by the international community, either immediately preceding independence in 1991 or again after September 11, 2001. Instead, the international community decided that in the face of more immediate threats it was better to work with the forces that were in power in the region, and not press them too hard to change their policies. Partly, they believed that the existing rulers were less likely to be a source of instability than the populations that they ruled. Now that the Soviet-era rulers of post-Soviet states have begun to be ousted, the U.S. and other western countries have less leverage to apply.

Nobody argued more strongly than Central Asia's presidents and senior officials that the population in the region was too inexperienced to accept the burdens of living in a democratic society. The precolonial history of Central Asia seems made to order for elites reluctant to share power. With one breath, they spoke of lessons of statehood learned from earlier rulers like Timur (Tamerlane), who ruled from Samarkand, Karimov's birthplace, or like Tole Bi from the eighteenth century, who like Nazarbayev came from the Great Horde, or in the Kyrgyz case, from the 2,200 years of statehood that they celebrated in 2004. [46] And with the next breath, they stressed the newness of their nations and how their modern history was one in which democratic institutions played no part.

It is true that there is no history of modern statehood in the region, but the preconditions for developing democratic institutions were not dramatically different here than elsewhere in the former Soviet Union. Much has been written about the pervasiveness of the clan structure in Central Asia. Partly kin-based patronage groups exist in each of the countries in the region, but patronage networks are found in all the post-Soviet states (and exist even in developed democracies). In Central Asia as elsewhere, these groups evolve and are modified by changing political circumstances. However, the populations in Central Asia were not given any opportunity for political participation until the late 1980s.

At that time some highly structured and well-supervised venues of competition were organized, which continued to enjoy official sponsorship until the early or mid-1990s. There was also strong popular support for the introduction of competitive elections in Central Asia in the late 1980s and early 1990s, with independent candidates for legislature and president finding it easy to get petitions signed. The Central Asians did not seem to see this as inconsistent with their deeply rooted tradition of respect for elders and authorities. [47] But when elections throughout the region became more controlled than competitive, in most countries the population quietly acquiesced. Their acquiescence facilitated the spread of corruption that made future democratic elections harder to organize, and this in turn created the sociopolitical pressure cooker that resulted in the Georgian, Ukrainian, and Kyrgyz revolutions.

Demographically the Central Asians are not too different from citizens in much of the Soviet Union, with the exception of their slightly lower levels of education. Although the majority of the Central Asians lived in rural areas, the gap between rural and urban was often easily breached, through military service, access to merit-based higher education, or simply through hospitality provided by urban-dwelling kin.

Although political conditions have sharply limited the kind of polling that can be done in Central Asia, existing survey data suggest that a significant portion of the population in Kyrgyzstan and Kazakhstan favor a rapid development of democratic institutions. Surveys conducted by the International Foundation of Electoral Studies (IFES) in 2002 showed that substantial portions of the population supported direct election of all legislators (in Kazakhstan) or further empowerment of parliament (in Kyrgyzstan).[48] They also showed that people in both countries identified the need for a system of checks and balances, especially the strengthening of the independence of a judiciary to combat corruption.[49] The demonstrations of March 2005 that resulted in Askar Akayev's ouster are strong confirmation of the Kyrgyz survey data. IFES studies from Tajikistan also showed popular support for further development of democratic institutions, but unlike in Kazakhstan and Kyrgyzstan, those conducting the surveys expressed concern that the rural population lacked an understanding of what this would entail. The same seems certain to be true in both Uzbekistan and Turkmenistan, which were not surveyed. But the high education levels and penetration of media in all five countries suggest that there has been a much greater capacity for working with the population to create an understanding of democratic institution building than their leaders have been willing to grant.

Central Asia's leaders also claim that political liberalization would expose the country to the risk of mob rule, but here too the leaders are spinning self-serving myths. There has been very little violence in Central Asia, in comparison with the Caucasus, Moldova, and parts of Russia. There was interethnic fighting, involving small groups of minority populations in the Ferghana region of Uzbekistan and in Novy Uzen (Kazakhstan) in 1989, and much larger clashes between Uzbeks and Kyrgyz in Osh in 1990. But unlike in the Caucasus where local clashes turned into regional wars, tempers cooled down after independence in Ferghana, Novy Uzen, and Osh.

The Tajik civil war in the early 1990s was a very bloody affair, but its roots were in a contestation for power by competing regional elites, rather than a democratization movement run amok.[50] Even in Uzbekistan, where the regime has shown signs of fraying, no militant Islamic group has demonstrated a capacity for mass mobilization, including both the controversial and outlawed Hizb ut-Tahrir, and the IMU, which espoused the achievement of militant goals through terrorist methods.

The real stumbling block preventing the introduction of democratic political institutions in Central Asia is not the background of the population, but the opposition of significant portions of the ruling elite. Central Asia's presidents are also critical of reform because the biggest proponents of it come from competing members of the elite. Given how the ruling elites in all the countries of the region have managed to enrich themselves since independence, it is not too hard to understand their resistance to political reform, at both the national and the local levels.

The persistence of rent-seeking behavior of local elites (meaning fewer spoils for federal elites) has created enormous disincentives for governments in Central Asia to introduce local elections for provincial leaders. The Kyrgyz and Kazakhs have begun the slow transition to an election of district leaders, with the election of governors said to follow gradually.[51]

Some of Central Asia's leaders would be returned to office in free and fair elections, but other powerful political incumbents at the national and regional levels would be defeated. Public accountability would transform the nature of political power at all levels of government. It would threaten the perquisites of office that are linked to current patterns of patronage and inevitably transform the relationship between politics and economics. A democratic political reform brings with it great political uncertainties and creates a political world that is almost antithetical to that of the top-down style of decision making with which the Soviet-trained political elite is familiar. But in most developed democracies, this unpredictability is mitigated by the fact that the masses chose from a range of choices brought to them by the elites, as they decide between empowering representatives of the governing parties and those of the "loyal" opposition.

The political ferment of the late Gorbachev years created some of the beginnings of just such a loyal opposition in much of Central Asia, as competing groups within the ruling elite were able to use the political and economic debate and the new freedom to use public opinion to advance their claims to power. A number of rising political pretenders reached out to the population and at least paid lip service to the cause of democratic institution building. Many of these came from the nationally respected Soviet artistic establishment, and all became organizers or active members in the various "pro-democracy" political groups that were mentioned in chapter and outlawed Hizb ut-Tahrir, and the IMU, which espoused the achievement of militant goals through terrorist methods.

The real stumbling block preventing the introduction of democratic political institutions in Central Asia is not the background of the population, but the opposition of significant portions of the ruling elite. Central Asia's presidents are also critical of reform because the biggest proponents of it come from competing members of the elite. Given how the ruling elites in all the countries of the region have managed to enrich themselves since independence, it is not too hard to understand their resistance to political reform, at both the national and the local levels.

The persistence of rent-seeking behavior of local elites (meaning fewer spoils for federal elites) has created enormous disincentives for governments in Central Asia to introduce local elections for provincial leaders. The Kyrgyz and Kazakhs have begun the slow transition to an election of district leaders, with the election of governors said to follow gradually.[51]

Some of Central Asia's leaders would be returned to office in free and fair elections, but other powerful political incumbents at the national and regional levels would be defeated. Public accountability would transform the nature of political power at all levels of government. It would threaten the perquisites of office that are linked to current patterns of patronage and inevitably transform the relationship between politics and economics. A democratic political reform brings with it great political uncertainties and creates a political world that is almost antithetical to that of the top-down style of decision making with which the Soviet-trained political elite is familiar. But in most developed democracies, this unpredictability is mitigated by the fact that the masses chose from a range of choices brought to them by the elites, as they decide between empowering representatives of the governing parties and those of the "loyal" opposition.

The political ferment of the late Gorbachev years created some of the beginnings of just such a loyal opposition in much of Central Asia, as competing groups within the ruling elite were able to use the political and economic debate and the new freedom to use public opinion to advance their claims to power. A number of rising political pretenders reached out to the population and at least paid lip service to the cause of democratic institution building. Many of these came from the nationally respected Soviet artistic establishment, and all became organizers or active members in the various "pro-democracy" political groups that were mentioned in chapter two.[52] But one way or another, the prominent and self-proclaimed pro-democracy reformers who were part of the ruling elite were pushed out of the political system.

Instead, throughout the region, the presidents and their cronies have tried to establish their own top-down party system, to replace the pre-independence and various postindependence efforts to develop opposition parties.[53] And even officially sponsored political parties can be subject to vote fraud if they outperform more favored pro-regime groups.

The actions of the leaders in much of Central Asia have in fact rendered their populations less competent to protect their own interests in democratic societies than they were a decade ago. The deterioration in the state of secular opposition throughout much of the region underscores the dangers associated with even relative Western disengagement, because the playing field in most parts of Central Asia is rather quickly altered. And where they have been all but eliminated, pro-Western secular forces will find it very difficult to become dominant political forces.

However, it would be unfair to tar all of Central Asia's leaders with the same brush. Although there is a great deal to criticize in the human rights records of all five regimes, some of these countries allow far less political autonomy to their citizens than others. In all of these states, members of the political opposition have had little opportunity to achieve political maturity, because they are almost always barred from serious engagement in political decision making. This may make the region's leaders feel more secure in the short run, but over time the reluctance of Central Asia's elites to pursue political reforms may prove far more destabilizing politically than the supposed immaturity of the populations.

Assumptions of the Aid Givers

The international community has given no priority to influencing the development of democratic institutions in Central Asia, either at the time of independence or subsequent to the United States launching a war on terror. The same model of political institution building, the "democracy template" as Thomas Carothers has called it, was applied throughout post-Soviet space.[54] The focus of U.S. democracy assistance has been on electoral aid and political party building, constitution drafting, local government development, and civil–military relations. European assistance programs, such as those run by the German political parties of the European Parliament, have employed a similar approach, even though from the very beginning Western democracy builders were very pessimistic as to its applicability in the context of Central Asia.

Many Western observers looking at the current situation in Central Asia accepted the pessimistic evaluations of the leaders of these countries—that the populations are ill-prepared for democracy—and therefore decided that they needed to focus on capacity-building projects with long-range rather than short-range goals. By the mid-1990s, most scholars and activists focused on political development had come to believe that without regime change none of these states would develop into genuine participatory democracy. They held out hope that the leaders of both Kyrgyzstan and Kazakhstan might be cajoled into expanding political participation, and this hope kept many actively working in the region.

The fact that the Kyrgyz were able to organize a popularly supported protest that led to the largely peaceful ouster of their president is testament to the success of long-term political capacity building. Kyrgyzstan had the best organized NGO sector in the region, and they clearly played a role in raising public expectations as to government accountability, both during elections and more generally.

Rather than destabilizing the government these organizations helped channel popular dissatisfaction in a peaceful fashion, and the civic awareness that they helped sponsor went a long way toward the rapidity with which order was restored both in Osh and in Bishkek after crowds stormed government buildings.

The challenge for U.S. policy makers is how to treat those governments that are hostile to the development of independent nongovernmental organizations. For a certain group of policy makers, those concerned with monitoring the democratic progress of these governments, the leaders in charge of these states have effectively become the enemy, men whose departure from political life was viewed as a good thing for their populations. At the same time, however, other branches of the U.S. government are busy trying to enlist these same men to grant the United States basing rights and to commit resources and manpower to fight alongside U.S. troops in the war on terror.

The U.S. foreign assistance strategy has led to much ill will on all sides, without substantially enhancing the capacity of either government or opposition to govern in a democratic fashion. This was true even before the ouster of Eduard Shevardnadze in Georgia, and has become an ever growing tension since.

U.S. NGOs and their local counterparts operating in Central Asia have grown more and more frustrated since the beginning of the war on terror. They have been content to continue to receive U.S. funding, but they are also angry that sufficient resources have not been forthcoming to allow them to shift the local balance of power in their favor. They have also objected to what they saw as the hypocrisy of the United States siding with a tyrant in Uzbekistan as part of its efforts to oust a tyrant in Iraq.

For their part, the United States' Central Asian partners in the war on terror strongly resented being listed among the most repressive regimes in the world. They thought that their support of the United States in the early days of the war, as well as later, should have meant more respect and greater material benefit to them. At the beginning of the war, when their expectations of foreign assistance were larger than proved true, they were willing to support incremental political changes. But they became upset with the idea of even a gradual democratic transition, when so much assistance money for political institution building went to people these rulers understood to be their enemies.

Central Asia's leaders find it difficult to accept the commitment to an ongoing rotation of elites that is a core value in Western-style participatory democracies. They reached political maturity in the winner-take-all rules of the Soviet system, and most have moved their political systems even further in that direction since independence. They fear that losing power would mean a loss not just of privilege, but of the wealth they had accumulated. They expected little respect or understanding from the political opposition. And they found it difficult to understand why the West found the political opposition preferable to the current regime. Should the opposition take power, they would behave little differently than the ruling elite, given the way that their political parties have operated.

Members of Central Asia's opposition have not always behaved faultlessly. Recipients of Western political assistance have sometimes been guilty of the same kinds of corrupt behavior of the leaders they seek to replace. Some receive money from businessmen with questionable incomes; others indulge in nepotism. More common, and even more serious, many of these groups are very small and sometimes consist of a single individual. Most have no capacity to become self-sufficient if Western assistance money dried up.[55] Opposition leaders often exhibit the same authoritarian-style personalities as the current incumbents and so it is difficult to find common ground with other regime critics. In this regard, all eyes will be on Kyrgyzstan as its new elite emerges.

Certainly, this is not meant to imply that all democracy assistance is wasted. Many projects become self-sustaining, many neutral figures received foreign assistance as well, and a host of community-based initiatives exist that could never have developed without foreign assistance. But democracy assistance requires the tacit approval of the existing regimes, either because of the nature of the foreign assistance allocations that funded them, or because of rules put in place by the Central Asian governments to regulate elections, the functioning of the media, and the organization of political parties, NGOs, and so on. This creates real incentives for the Central Asian regimes to form their own informal NGOs and political parties to ensure that loyalists absorb some of this assistance money as well, and to imitate democratic forms without actually introducing them.

All are in fact obliged to advance democratic norms as part of their membership in OSCE norms. Although the OSCE has been rigorous in monitoring elections and in its criticism of civil and human rights abuses in the region, there are few consequences dealt for poor performance. Instead, their poor performance is fueling a debate within the OSCE as to whether there should be a shift in emphasis in Central Asia away from strategies of political institution building that some member states believe are doomed to fail toward strategies that bolster state capacity to cope with transnational security threats.

It is easy to be critical of the OSCE for backing away from a challenge, but in reality there is little that the OSCE could do. Only about 6 percent of OSCE funding goes to projects in this region, giving its national missions limited informal powers of persuasion, and the OSCE charter does not include formal disciplinary mechanisms.[56]

Many of the same complaints can be made of U.S. assistance in the area of political institution building. The sums involved are largely designed for image purposes, and there has generally been little negative consequence for poor performance on the part of Central Asia's ruling elite, except that such sums might be withheld.

There is still a great deal of uncertainty about how to introduce democracy in post-Soviet states. Each success like that of Georgia or Ukraine, and maybe even Kyrgyzstan, seems to reinforce a particular model—that is, using parallel vote counts to mobilize a population against electoral irregularities. Similarly, each setback for democracy, like the passing of power from father to son in Azerbaijan or Putin's restrictions on independent media and the recentralization of state power, serves to convince Western strategists of the impossibility of the task in places like the countries of Central Asia.

So in the end, negative and positive developments fail to spur fundamental rethinking about how to better influence political institution building in this region. Over the next several years, freer and fairer elections may well become commonplace in Kyrgyzstan and Kazakhstan, but in both places a relatively small ruling elite is likely to decide the parameters of acceptable political change. In both these countries, the move toward expanding the role for the political electorate comes more from local initiative than from Western pressure. It depends as much on the support of pro-regime reformers (many from the younger generation) as it does on pressure exerted from those active in anti-regime nongovernmental groups. And it is the latter more than the former who are the beneficiaries of the U.S. and other Western assistance. Similarly, if Uzbekistan moves more toward opening the political system in the next decade, something that is far less obvious, it will also be because of pro-regime reformers, largely those in the 15- to 45-year-old age cohort, not due to pressure from seeds planted with U.S. assistance.

This does not mean that the United States does not play an important role. The pro-regime and pro-reform elites in all three countries are eager to make their nation seem credible to the United States and Western Europe. They recognize that to do this their countries must, at least, move more self-consciously to embrace western European political norms. Few among them would see the transition as rapid, and most do not even believe that it will be completed in their lifetimes, but many throughout Central Asia do believe that it is critical for their political systems to open up, including large numbers of talented people in the ruling elites in Kazakhstan, Kyrgyzstan, and Uzbekistan. In Kazakhstan and Kyrgyzstan, these people support expanded parliamentary responsibility and election of local government officials, as well as greatly expanded freedoms of the press, association, and assembly. In Uzbekistan and Tajikistan, their goals are more modest and their timetables more extended.

U.S. foreign assistance, as it is currently constructed, is not terribly effective in relating to supporters of reform who still hold posts that make them members of the ruling elite. In part this is the result of the type and relatively small scale of U.S. assistance, but it is also because pro-reform elements of the regime are regarded as too tainted for U.S. proponents of democracy assistance to work with.

If the United States wants to promote the development of democratic institutions in Central Asia over the long term, it has to learn to work more effectively with pro-regime groups and the anti-regime opposition, and with politically unaffiliated elements as well. The United States is hampered by how little money it actually spends in the region on democracy-building activities. Most of the funding in this area—less than $1 per Central Asian per year—actually goes to pay salaries and other administrative costs of the U.S. contractors engaged in the democracy-building activity. In absolute terms, most of the money goes for salaries of U.S. or other Western nationals, although the number of locals employed by partner NGOs may far exceed that of the expatriate employees.

There is a similar bias in spending on public diplomacy, where the emphasis is on bringing large numbers of people to the United States for short stays, rather than a small number for lengthy training or residence. Again this works to the clear benefit of the U.S. host organizations (as well as motels and Wal-Marts in distant state capitals and college towns). Even long-term spending is of greater benefit to the U.S. educational institutions, which receive far more than tuition for the visiting students (and which often depend on the funds to keep divisions of their universities in the black) than the cause of educational reform in the Central Asian countries themselves.

All these may be satisfactory ways to spend U.S. foreign assistance. (It certainly makes congressmen whose districts benefit more popular.) Yet it does not maximize the likelihood that U.S. taxpayer funding will serve to stimulate the growth of democratic institutions in Central Asia anytime soon.

Educational reform is an area where the United States could have done a great deal more with the same money, had the allocations been spent almost entirely *in* country and on *local* salaries and expenses. Although each government would have put some restrictions on the kinds of projects the foreign assistance money could have funded, in every country but Turkmenistan the range of acceptable activities would have been extensive.

Similarly, all the states of the region had the capacity to absorb a great deal more assistance money in projects designed to overhaul the judicial and criminal justice systems. It would take decades to fully overhaul the Soviet-era legal system, but a higher level of engagement between officials in Central Asia with those from other more progressive post-Soviet states would expedite the process. The trainers need not come from countries such as Georgia, Serbia, or Ukraine but could come from any place where they will not be suspected of having a broader agenda.

Appendixes

Appendix 1. Basic Information by Country

Kazakhstan

Official Name	Republic of Kazakhstan (Qazaqstan Respublikasy)
Derivation	Kazakh is a Turkic word meaning "someone independent and free." The name was later used by Russian people, eventually known as the Cossacks.
Capital City	Astana (pop. 288,000)
Land Area	2,717,300 sq km (1,049,150 sq miles)—about four times the size of Texas—making it the 9th largest nation in the world
Borders	Russia (6,846 km) Uzbekistan (2,203 km) China (1,533 km) Kyrgyzstan (1,051 km) Turkmenistan (379 km)
Natural Resources	Petroleum, natural gas, coal, iron ore
Population	15.2 million (2005 estimate)
Pop. Growth Rate	0.26%
Ethnic Groups	Kazakh 53 %, Russian 30%, Ukrainian 4 %, Uzbek 3 %, German 2.4 %, Uighur 1.4 %, other 7 %
Religion	Muslim 47%, Russian Orthodox 44%, Protestant 2%, other 7%
Executive Branch	Chief of State: President Nursultan Nazarbayev—7-year terms Next Elections: 2006

Legislative Branch	Bicameral Parliament
	    Senate (39 seats, 6-year terms)
	    Majilis (77 seats)

Judicial Branch	Supreme Court (44 members); Constitutional Council (7 members)
National Currency	Tenge (KZT)
GDP*	$118.4 billion
GDP per Capita*	$7,800
GDP Composition by Sector	Agriculture: 7.4% Industry: 37.8% Services: 54.8%
Exports	In 2003, exports totaled $13.2 billion. The main exports were oil, natural gas, coal, wood products, metals, chemicals, grain, wool, and meat. Top customers were Russia, Ukraine, Uzbekistan, the Netherlands, and China.
Imports	Kazakhstan's imports in 2001 were $9.1 billion. The main imports were coal and electricity. The largest imports were from Russia, Germany, and China.
Miscellaneous	Kazakhstan is believed to possess about 1% of the world's total natural gas and petroleum reserves. In the post-Soviet era, Kazakhstan has received about 80% of foreign investment in Central Asia.

*(2004 estimate, purchasing power parity)
Sources: *CIA World Factbook*, Library of Congress Country Profiles.

Kyrgyzstan

Official Name	Kyrgyz Republic (Kyrgyz Respublikasy)
Derivation	In the old Turkic language, kyrg means "40" and yz means "tribes," so the word itself means "40 tribes." The Kyrgyz originated in Mongolia.
Capital City	Bishkek (pop. 824,000)
Land Area	191,300 sq km (76,640 sq miles)—slightly smaller than South Dakota
Borders	Uzbekistan (1,099 km) Kazakhstan (1,051 km) Tajikistan (870 km) China (858 km)
Natural Resources	Abundant hydropower; significant deposits of gold and rare earth metals; locally exploitable coal, oil, and natural gas.
Population	5.2 million (2005 estimate)
Pop. Growth Rate	1.25%
Ethnic Groups	Kyrgyz 67%, Uzbek 14%, Russian 11%, Dungan (ethnic Chinese Muslim) 1%, Tatar 1%, Uighur 1%, other 6% (2003 U.S. State Dept. estimate)
Religion	Sunni Muslim (75%), Russian Orthodox (20%), other (5%)
Executive Branch	Chief of State: Kurmanbek Bakiyev (interim)—5-year terms Next Elections: July 2005
Legislative Branch	Bicameral Supreme Council, or Zhogorku Kenesh Assembly of People's Representatives (70 seats; 5-year terms) Legislative Assembly (35 seats; 5-year terms); NOTE: After a 2003 referendum, Parliament is slated to become unicameral with 75 deputies after the 2005 elections.
Judicial Branch	Supreme Court (judges appointed for 10-year terms); Constitutional Court; Higher Court of Arbitration
National Currency	Som (KGS)
GDP*	$8.495 billion
GDP per Capita*	$1,700
GDP Composition by Sector	Agriculture 28.5 % Industry 22.8 % Services 38.7 %.
Exports	2003 estimated value: $581 million. The main exports were cotton, wool, meat, and electricity. Principal customers are Kazakhstan, Russia, China, the United States, Uzbekistan, and Germany.
Imports	2003 estimated value: $717 million. The main imports were fossil fuels, machinery, chemicals, textiles, and food products. The imports are predominantly from Russia, Uzbekistan, Kazakhstan, Germany, and China.
Miscellaneous	Kyrgyzstan has the world's largest natural growth walnut forest.

*(2004 estimate, purchasing power parity)
Sources: *CIA World Factbook*, Library of Congress Country Profiles.

Tajikistan

Official Name	Republic of Tajikistan (Jumhurii Tojikiston)
Derivation	In Persian, taj means "crown" and ik means "head," so tajik means "a person wearing a crown on his head." Tajiks were originally Persians.
Capital City	Dushanbe (590,000)
Land Area	143,100 sq km (55,251 sq miles)—slightly smaller than Wisconsin
Borders	Afghanistan (1,206 km) Uzbekistan (1,161 km) Kyrgyzstan (870 km) China (414 km)
Natural Resources	Hydropower, some petroleum, uranium, mercury, brown coal, lead, zinc, antimony, tungsten, silver, gold
Population	7.2 million (2005 estimate)
Pop. Growth Rate	2%
Ethnic Groups	Tajik 65%, Uzbek 25%, Russian 4%
Religion	Sunni Muslim 85%, Shiite Muslim 5%, other 20%
Executive Branch	Chief of State: President Imamali Rakhmonov. 7-year terms. Next Elections: 2006
Legislative Branch	Bicameral Supreme Assembly or Majlisi Oli Majlisi Namoyandagon with 63 seats; 5-year terms. Majlisi Milliy with 33 seats, indirectly elected, 5-year terms.
Judicial Branch	Supreme Court (judges appointed by the president)
National Currency	Somoni (TJS)
GDP*	$7.95 billion
GDP per Capita*	$1,100
GDP Composition by Sector	Agriculture 23.7 % Industry 24.3% Services 52%
Exports	In 2003, exports were worth $750 million. Main exports were aluminum (accounting for over half of export value), electricity, cotton, fruits, vegetable oil, and textiles. Most went to the Netherlands, Turkey, Latvia, Switzerland, Uzbekistan, Russia, and Iran.
Imports	In 2003, imports were worth $890 million. The main imports were electricity, fossil fuels, alumina (for processing), grain, and flour. Most came from Russia, Uzbekistan, Kazakhstan, Azerbaijan, Ukraine, and Romania.
Miscellaneous	About 15–20% of the working population is estimated to be in Russia. In 2003, the average wage of a public-sector employee was $10/month, well below the poverty line.

*(2004 estimate, purchasing power parity)
Sources: *CIA World Factbook*, Library of Congress Country Profiles.

Turkmenistan

Official Name	Republic of Turkmenistan
Derivation	In the Turkic language, turk refers to the ancient Turks of Asia. The word men means "I" or "me." Turkmen then means "I am a Turk." The Turkmen, originally known as the Oghuz, came from what we now call Mongolia.
Capital City	Ashgabat (727,000)
Land Area	488,100 sq km (188,455 sq miles) – slightly larger than California
Borders	Uzbekistan (1,621 km) Iran (992 km) Afghanistan (744 km) Kazakhstan (379 km)
Natural Resources	Petroleum, natural gas, coal, sulfur, salt
Population	4.95 million (2005 estimate)
Pop. Growth Rate	1.81%
Ethnic Groups	Turkmen 85%, Uzbek 5%, Russian 4%
Religion	Sunni Muslim (89%), Eastern Orthodox (9%), unknown (2%)
Executive Branch	Chief of State: President Saparmurat Niyazov, whose term was extended indefinitely in 1999
Legislative Branch	There are two separate parliamentary bodies: The People's Council or Halk Maslahaty, with up to 2,500 delegates The Majilis (50 seats; 5-year terms)
Judicial Branch	Supreme Court (judges appointed by the president)
National Currency	Manat (TMM)
GDP*	$27.6 billion
GDP per Capita*	$5,700
GDP Composition by Sector	Agriculture 28.5% Industry 42.7% Services 28.8%
Exports	In 2003 exports totaled $3.6 billion. Main exports were gas, crude oil, petrochemicals, cotton fiber, textiles. Top buyers are Ukraine, Italy, Iran, Azerbaijan, Turkey.
Imports	Estimated value 2003: $2.5 billion. Main imports were machinery and transport equipment, chemicals, food. Top suppliers are Germany, Ukraine, UAE, Russia, and Turkey.
Miscellaneous	The Kara-Kum desert occupies over 80% of the nation's territory. Foreign firms have been active in the construction industry, with French, Turkish, and Ukrainian firms helping build government buildings and infrastructure projects. French and German firms have been involved in upgrading the national telecommunications system.

*(2004 estimate, purchasing power parity)
Sources: *CIA World Factbook*, Library of Congress Country Profiles.

Uzbekistan

Official Name	Republic of Uzbekistan (Ozbekiston Respublikasi)
Derivation	Uzbek is considered to come from two turkish words: uz, which means "genuine," and bek, which means "genuine man." The Uzbeks are a mixture of nomadic Turkic tribes and ancient Iranian peoples.
Capital City	Tashkent (2.15 million)
Land Area	447,400 sq km (172,741 sq. miles)—slightly larger than California
Borders	Kazakhstan (2,203 km) Turkmenistan (1,621 km) Tajikistan (1,161 km) Kyrgyzstan (1,099 km) Afghanistan (137 km)
Natural Resources	Natural gas, petroleum, coal, gold, uranium, silver, copper, lead and zinc, tungsten, molybdenum
Population	26.9 million (2005 estimate)
Pop. Growth Rate	1.67%
Ethnic Groups	Uzbek 80%, Russian 5.5%, Tajik 5%, Kazakh 3%, Karakalpak 2.5%, Tatar 1.5%, other 2.5% (1996 est.)
Religion	Muslim 88% (mostly Sunnis), Eastern Orthodox 9%, other 3%
Executive Branch	Chief of State: President Islam Karimov Seven-year terms Next Elections: December 2007
Legislative Branch	Unicameral Supreme Assembly or Oliy Majlis: 250 seats; elected by popular vote to 5-year terms.
Judicial Branch	Supreme Court
National Currency	Som (UZS)
GDP*	$47.59 billion
GDP per Capita*	$1,800
GDP Composition by Sector	Agriculture 28% Industry 26.3% Services 35.7%
Exports	In 2003 exports totaled $2.8 billion. Main exports are cotton, gold, natural gas, and fertilizers. Main customers are Russia, Ukraine, Italy, South Korea, and Tajikistan.
Imports	In 2003, imports totaled $2.3 billion. The main imports were machinery, chemicals and plastics, foods and metals. Main source countries are Russia, South Korea, Germany, the United States, Turkey, and Kazakhstan.
Miscellaneous	Along with Lichtenstein, one of two doubly-landlocked countries in the world, meaning they are completely surrounded by other landlocked countries. Minimum wage is $6.40/month.

*(2004 estimate, purchasing power parity)

Sources: *CIA World Factbook*, Library of Congress Country Profiles.

Appendix 2. Key Economic Indicators

	Kazakhstan	Kyrgyzstan	Tajikistan	Turkmenistan	Uzbekistan
Gross domestic product $ Billions	118.4	8.495	7.95	27.6	47.59
GDP per capita	7,800	1,700	1,100	5,700	1,800
GDP real growth rate (2004 estimate)	9.1%	6%	10.5%	7.5%[a]	4.4%
Private sector share of GDP	60	60	45	25	45
Percent living in urban areas	56	34	25	45	37
Percent living on less than $2 a day (Based on expenditures)	8.5	27.2	50.8	44	77.5
Arable land (% of total)	8	7.3	6.6	3.7	10.8
Permanent cropland	0.1	0.3	0.9	0.1	0.8
Irrigated land (as % of cropland, 1999-2001)	10.8	74.2	68.3	100.1	88.6
Food production index 2000-2002 (if 1989–91=100)	73.5	132.5	60.5	131.6	122.3
Labor force (millions)	7.95	2.7	3.19	2.32	14.64
Gini Index (the higher the number, the greater the inequality)	31.5	29	34.7	40.8	44.7
Unemployment Rate (2004)	8	18	40	60	20[b]
Foreign exchange and gold reserves (2004)	$14.35 billion	$498.7 million	$145.3 million	$3.034 billion	$1.6 billion
External debt (2004)	$26.03 billion	$1.97 billion	$888 million	$2.4 to $5 billion	$1.35 billion

Sources: European Bank for Reconstruction and Development, *Transition Report 2004*; International Monetary Fund, *International Financial Statistics 2004*; World Bank, *World Development Indicators, 2004*; and Central Intelligence Agency, *CIA World Factbook*, updated April 2005.
a. This is an IMF estimate. Official government statistics show 21.4 percent growth, but these are notoriously unreliable (2004 estimate).
b. This represents underemployment. Officially, Uzbek unemployment is 0.6 percent.

Appendix 3. Key Social Indicators

	Kazakhstan	Kyrgyzstan	Tajikistan	Turkmenistan	Uzbekistan
Population (million)	15.1	5	6.3	4.8	25.3
Population density (people per sq. km.)	6	26	45	10	62
Average annual population growth rate since 1980	0	1.5	2.1	2.3	2.1
Net migration (per 1,000 people)	-3.4	-2.5	-2.9	-0.9	-1.7
Crude birth rate (per 1,000 people)	15	20	23	22	20
Crude death rate (per 1,000 people)	12	7	7	8	6
Fertility rate (births per woman)	1.8	2.4	2.9	2.7	2.3
Infant mortality rate	7.6	5.2	9	7	5.5
Male survival to age 65 (% of cohort)	47	56	62	57	63
Female survival to age 65 (% of cohort)	71	75	75	72	77
Age structure					
0-14	24	32	39	36	34
15-64	68	62	56	60	61
65+	8	6	5	4	5
Median age	28	23	20	21	22
Male life expectancy	60.7	64.2	61.7	58	60.8
Female life expectancy	71.7	72.4	67.6	65	67.7
Literacy rate	98.4	97	99.4	98	99.3
People living with HIV/AIDS (2003)	16,500	3,900	<200	<200	11,000

Sources: World Bank, *World Development Indicators 2004*. Also, *CIA World Factbook*, updated April 2005.
Note: Most data are for 2002.

Appendix 4. Multilateral Assistance

Table A4-1. Total Assistance, 1994–2004
(in millions of U.S. dollars)

	World Bank	IMF	ADB	USAID
Kazakhstan	1,248.8	0.4	822.0	448.3
Kyrgyzstan	443.6	206.7	168.0	318.1
Tajikistan	193.3	134.1	272.9	226.3
Turkmenistan	32.1	—	—	65.7
Uzbekistan	301.8	165.2	971.6	310.0

Sources: World Bank website, www.worldbank.org; International Monetary Fund website, www.imf.org, Asian Development Bank website, www.adb.org, U.S. Agency for International Development website, www.usaid.gov.

Table A4-2. Average Multilateral Aid per Capita, 1994–2004
(in U.S. dollars)

	World Bank	IMF	ADB	USAID
Kazakhstan	86.72	0.03	57.08	31.13
Kyrgyzstan	92.42	43.06	35.00	66.27
Tajikistan	29.74	20.63	41.98	34.82
Turkmenistan	5.35	—	—	10.95
Uzbekistan	11.61	6.35	37.37	11.92

Source: European Bank for Reconstruction and Development, *Transition Report 2004* (London: November 2004). Based on 2004 population estimates.

Appendix 5. U.S. Government Assistance Before and After 9/11

Table A5-1. U.S. Government Aid Allocations, FY1995–FY2005
(in millions of U.S. dollars)

Country	FY1995	FY1996	FY1997	FY1998	FY1999	FY2000	FY2001	FY2002	FY2003 (budgeted)	FY2004 (estimate)	FY2005 (request)
Kazakhstan	47.2	33.0	35.4	40.3	50.5	44.8	71.5	81.6	100.4	41.6	40.2
Kyrgyzstan	22.7	19.0	20.8	24.3	32.0	30.1	40.6	49.0	54.7	43.2	39.5
Tajikistan	9.2	4.0	5.0	12.0	13.1	9.9	56.4	85.3	49.4	32.5	36.4
Turkmenistan	5.4	4.0	5.0	5.3	11.3	6.2	12.2	16.4	11.0	8.6	9.3
Uzbekistan	11.8	19.0	21.6	20.5	27.3	20.0	55.9	161.8	83.5	48.4	53.2

Source: Congressional Research Service.

Figure A5-1. Average of U.S. Government Aid Allocations before and after 9/11

(in millions of U.S. dollars)

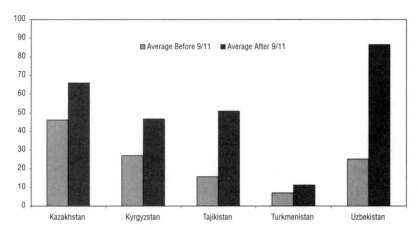

Source: Congressional Research Service.
Note: Average before 9/11 is FY 1995–2001; average after 9/11 is FY 2002–2005.

Table A5-2. USAID Assistance, 1992–2005

(in millions of U.S. dollars)

	Combined Total FY1992-2000	Total FY2001	Total FY2002	Total FY2003	Total FY2004	Total FY2005 Request
Kazakhstan	273.0	48.8	49.7	43.4	33.3	28.0
Kyrgyzstan	141.5	32.6	71.2	36.9	35.9	33.0
Tajikistan	47.2	29.4	82.2	35.9	31.7	35.0
Turkmenistan	33.9	6.1	12.1	7.8	5.8	6.0
Uzbekistan	83.9	26.0	124.9	39.4	35.7	36.0

Source: Eurasia Program Summary, available at www.usaid.gov.
Note: The higher 2002 figures reflect one-off supplemental disbursement of additional Freedom Support Act funds for each country.

Figure A5-2. Average of USAID Assistance before and after 9/11

(in millions of U.S. dollars)

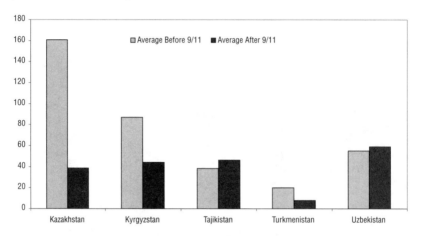

Source: Eurasia Program Summary, available at www.usaid.gov.
Note: Average before 9/11 is FY 1992–2001; average after 9/11 is FY 2002–2005.

Table A5-3. Breakdown of Recent U.S. Assistance to Central Asia, FY2003

(in millions of U.S. dollars)

	Kazakhstan	Kyrgyzstan	Tajikistan	Turkmenistan	Uzbekistan
Democratic Reform	15.3	14.3	7.6	5.2	16.0
Economic and Social Reform	27.8	19.9	14.3	2.5	18.5
Security and Law Enforcement	54.4	11.4	1.6	1.2	32.2
Humanitarian Aid	1.0	5.3	21.4	0.5	13.1
Cross-Sectoral Initiatives	4.7	3.9	4.5	2.2	4.4
TOTAL	103.2	54.8	49.4	11.5	84.2

Table A5-4. Breakdown of Recent U.S. Assistance to Central Asia, FY2004

(in millions of U.S. dollars)

	Kazakhstan	Kyrgyzstan	Tajikistan	Turkmenistan	Uzbekistan
Democratic Reform	10.6	12.2	10.2	4.2	15.7
Economic and Social Reform	21.5	21.8	12.6	4.5	21.2
Security and Law Enforcement	39.4	11.6	6.9	1.1	10.7
Humanitarian Aid	0.3	4	20.5	0.2	2
Cross-Sectoral Initiatives	2.4	1.2	0.5	0.4	1
TOTAL	74.2	50.8	50.7	10.4	50.6

Table A5-5. Types of U.S. Military Assistance

Category	Types of Assistance	Description
Sales	Foreign Military Sales	Sales from U.S. government to foreign governments
	Direct Commercial Sales	Sales from U.S. companies to foreign governments
Financing	Foreign Military Financing	Congressionally appropriated grants and loans given to foreign governments to help finance sales (above)
Equipment Grants	Excess Defense Articles	Older surplus equipment that the Pentagon gives away at little or no cost
	Drawdowns	Grants of current (often nonlethal) defense stock given by the U.S. government in emergency situations
Training	International Military Education and Training	U.S. training of foreign military personnel

Table A5-6. Military Aid to Central Asia, FY 2002–FY 2004

(in millions of U.S. dollars)

	Training	Financing
Kazakhstan	2.9	10.7
Kyrgyzstan	2.9	20.9
Tajikistan	1.0	4.4
Turkmenistan	1.1	1.4
Uzbekistan	3.7	54.8
TOTAL	11.6	92.2

Source: U.S. Department of State, January 2004.
Note: These data reflect defense assistance in publicly disclosed categories.

Table A5-7. Central Asian Security Program Spending, FY1992–FY2001

(in millions of U.S. dollars)

Dept.	Program	Freedom Support Act and Other Funds
Defense	Comprehensive Threat Reduction	180.1
Energy	Arms Control Support	33.1
Energy	Materials Protection, Control and Accounting	32.0
State	Warsaw Initiative	29.0
State	Science Centers	18.2
State	Export Control and Border Security	15.4
State	International Military Exchanges and Training	9.8
NSF	Civilian R&D Foundation	6.6
State	Anti-Terrorism Assistance	5.6
USDA	Collaborative Research Program	4.6
Energy	Initiatives for Proliferation Prevention	4.3
Energy	Nuclear Export Control Program	3.6
Defense	Counterproliferation (w/ FBI)	3.2
State	Nonproliferation and Disarmament Fund	3.0
State	NADR Counterproliferation	3.0
Health	Health and Human Services	2.4
Defense	Customs Border Security and Counterproliferation	2.3
Total Security Programs		356.1

Source: Congressional Research Service.

Table A5-8. U.S. Assistance to Central Asia, as Share of Total Foreign Operations Appropriations

(Discretionary funds, in millions of U.S. dollars)

	FY2003	FY2004 Estimate	FY2005 Request
Total Foreign Operations	23,677	38,003	21,331
Total Aid to Central Asia	307	209	179
Percent of Total	1.30	0.55	0.84

Source: Congressional Research Service.

Appendix 6. Freedom Support Act Funding 1992–2003

Table A6-1. Selected FSA Expenditures, FY1992–FY2000

(in millions of U.S. dollars)

	Kazakhstan	Kyrgyzstan	Tajikistan	Turkmenistan	Uzbekistan	Total 1992–2000	Average per Year
USAID	272.98	141.46	9.09	18.82	45.83	488.18	54.24
Economic Reform	52.63	34.83	1.96	5.16	20.5	115.08	12.79
Private-Sector Initiatives	77.74	43.75	0.23	0.10	6.20	128.02	14.22
Democratic Reform	28.64	14.81	4.89	2.74	7.82	58.90	6.54
State Dept.	34.03	18.11	6.14	7.14	17.25	82.67	9.19
Humanitarian Asstce. (via State)	183.79	132.86	43.77	43.83	123.26	527.51	58.61
Commerce Dept.	3.15	0.72	0.44	0.47	1.69	6.47	0.72
NSF - Civilian R&D	0.30	0.29	—	—	0.69	1.28	0.14
Trade & Devp. Agency	6.34	0.18	—	4.14	3.81	14.47	1.61
Peace Corps	6.82	4.39	—	4.35	4.60	20.16	2.24
Agriculture Dept.	1.54	1.05	0.55	0.65	1.02	4.81	0.53
Treasury Dept.	2.04	1.14	0.11	—	—	3.29	0.37
Justice Dept.	0.20	—	—	—	0.46	0.66	0.07
TOTAL	511.19	300.2	60.1	79.4	198.61	1,149.50	127.72

Note: This is only a representative snapshot of funding trends. It does not reflect every category of budget spending.

Table A6-2. Selected FSA Expenditures, FY2001

(in millions of U.S. dollars)

	Kazakhstan	Kyrgyzstan	Tajikistan	Turkmenistan	Uzbekistan	Total FY2001
USAID	10.86	6.49	9.56	4.59	7.26	38.76
Economic Reform	4.24	2.68	—	0.02	0.37	7.31
Private-Sector Initiatives	8.41	8.20	1.24	0.52	0.93	19.30
Democratic Reform	5.82	5.64	2.02	0.06	3.04	16.58
State Dept.	2.39	0.37	0.15	2.25	1.83	6.99
Humanitarian Asstce. (via State)	20.77	9.96	6.85	3.93	26.71	68.22
NSF - Civilian R&D	0.10	0.18	—	0.02	0.32	0.62
Commerce Dept.	0.47	0.09	0.10	0.03	0.22	0.91
Agriculture Dept.	1.64	0.04	0.01	0.03	0.08	1.80
Treasury Dept.	0.01	0.13	—	—	—	0.14
Justice Dept.	—	—	—	—	0.21	0.21
TOTAL	36.24	17.26	16.67	10.85	36.63	117.65

Note: This is only a representative snapshot of funding trends. It does not reflect every category of budget spending.

Table A6-3. Selected FSA Expenditures, FY2002
(in millions of U.S. dollars)

	Kazakhstan	Kyrgyzstan	Tajikistan	Turkmenistan	Uzbekistan	Total FY2002
USAID	18.11	10.8	7.09	1.45	11.13	48.58
Economic Reform	8.10	—	—	—	—	8.10
Private-Sector Initiatives	11.77	21.79	2.09	0.75	9.03	45.43
Democratic Reform	6.35	5.13	2.97	6.71	2.05	23.21
State Dept.	2.73	0.56	0.18	0.50	2.55	6.52
NSF - Civilian R&D	0.64	0.11	0.03	—	0.77	1.55
Commerce Dept.	0.54	0.13	0.16	0.03	0.32	1.18
Agriculture Dept.	1.46	0.14	0.10	0.09	0.28	2.07
Treasury Dept.	—	0.80	—	—	0.01	0.81
Justice Dept.	—	—	—	—	0.02	0.02
TOTAL	23.48	12.54	7.56	2.07	15.08	60.73

Note: This is only a representative snapshot of funding trends. It does not reflect every category of budget spending.

Table A6-4. Selected FSA Expenditures, FY2003

(in millions of U.S. dollars)

	Kazakhstan	Kyrgyzstan	Tajikistan	Turkmenistan	Uzbekistan	Total FY2003
USAID	31.82	32.67	23.51	4.39	39.66	132.05
Economic Reform	1.49	1.13	—	—	—	2.62
Private-Sector Initiatives	13.74	15.24	6.51	1.23	6.05	42.77
Democratic Reform	5.08	5.96	3.55	0.83	5.01	20.43
State Dept.	5.55	7.85	8.44	3.06	9.32	34.22
NSF - Civilian R&D	0.17	0.11	0.01	—	0.56	0.85
Commerce Dept.	0.59	0.12	0.04	0.04	0.2	0.99
Agriculture Dept.	1.19	0.28	0.07	0.09	0.42	2.05
Treasury Dept.	2.80	2.37	0.25	—	1.10	6.52
TOTAL	42.12	43.40	32.32	7.58	51.26	176.68

Note: This is only a representative snapshot of funding trends. It does not reflect every category of budget spending.

**Table A6-5. Average Annual State Department and USAID Aid Before
and After 9/11**

	Average 1992-2001	Average 2002-2003
USAID	52.7	90.3
Economic Reform	12.2	5.4
Private-Sector Initiatives	14.7	44.1
Democratic Reform	7.5	21.8
State Dept.	9.0	20.4

Notes:

Budget categories vary from year to year.

The only available FY2004 numbers can be found in Table A5-4

As this book went to press, FY 2005 numbers were not yet available. They are expected in July 2005.

Sources: www.state.gov and www.usaid.gov.

Appendix 7. Economic Growth, 1990–2002

Figure A7-1. Gross Domestic Product, 1990–2002

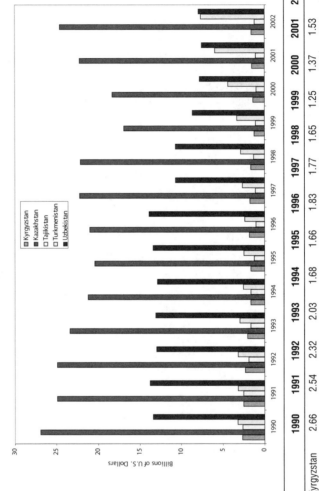

	1990	1991	1992	1993	1994	1995	1996	1997	1998	1999	2000	2001	2002
Kyrgyzstan	2.66	2.54	2.32	2.03	1.68	1.66	1.83	1.77	1.65	1.25	1.37	1.53	1.6
Kazakhstan	26.9	24.9	24.9	23.4	21.2	20.4	21	22.2	22.1	16.9	18.3	22.2	24.6
Tajikistan	2.63	2.54	1.9	1.65	1.65	1.23	1.05	1.12	1.32	1.09	0.99	1.06	1.21
Turkmenistan	3.23	3.2	3.2	2.98	2.56	2.48	2.38	2.68	2.86	3.31	4.4	5.96	7.67
Uzbekistan	13.4	13.8	13	13.1	12.9	13.4	13.9	10.7	10.7	8.67	7.81	7.55	7.93

Appendix 8. Major Joint Venture Projects

Kazakhstan

Project	Partners	Key Information
Tengiz oil field	TengizChevroil (TCO) 50% ChevronTexaco (US) 25% Kazakhoil 25% ExxonMobil (US) 5% LUKoil (Russia)	• Launched in 1993 as a joint Kazakh–U.S. 40-year venture • Estimated cost: $20 billion • Main fields: Tengiz and Korolev—6-9 billion barrels of reserves
Kashagan offshore oil field	Agip KCO (formerly known as OKIOC) 18.52% ENI (Italy) 18.52% ExxonMobil (US) 18.52% Royal Dutch/Shell (UK-Netherlands) 18.52% TotalFinaElf (France) 9.26% ConocoPhillips (US) 8.33% Inpex (Japan) 8.33% KazMunayGaz	• Kashagan is thought to hold between 9 and 13 billion barrels of recoverable reserves, making it roughly the world's 5th largest. • Assuming proven crude oil reserves in the neighborhood of 8 billion barrels, the Kashagan field alone would hold roughly the same amount of oil as Brazil, South America's second largest oil producer. • ENI (formerly Agip) operates the site. • First oil was due in 2005; now that has been pushed back to 2007 or 2008 due to disagreements between the Kazakh government and the foreign operators. • The initial development phase at Kashagan may cost the consortium $9 billion, making it the largest undertaking in the world's oil business today. • The field is projected to pump 3 million barrels per day by 2015. • Eni, Conoco, Inpex, and Total also own stakes in the Baku-Tbilisi-Ceyhan pipeline project.
Karachaganak oil and gas field	Karachaganak (KIO) 32.5% British Gas 32.5% ENI 20% ChevronTexaco 15% LUKoil	• Launched November 1997 • Oil reserves: 2 billion barrels • Gas reserves: 28 trillion cubic feet
Pipeline from Tengiz to Novorossiisk	Caspian Pipeline Consortium (CPC) 24% Russia 19% Kazakhstan 15% Chevron-Texaco 12.5 % LUKArco 7.5% ExxonMobil 7% Oman	• Launched in 1999 • Estimated cost of first phase: $2.6 billion • Project includes a 1510-km pipeline that became operational in 2001. • At peak, 1.2 million barrels per day will be pumped from Tengiz to Novorossiisk on the Black Sea.

Kyrgyzstan

Project	Partners	Key Information
Kumtor gold mine	Centerra Gold Inc. 54% Cameco (Canada) 16% Kyrgyz government * Remainder is traded on the open market; Centerra listed on the Toronto stock exchange in June 2004.	• Kyrgyz government reduced its stake from 27% to 16% by selling 7.5 million shares of stock, reaping $116 million. • Mine located southeast of Bishkek in the Tien Shan mountains, 60 km from Chinese border. • Estimated deposits of about 700 metric tons. • Image tainted by incident in May 1998, when a truck accident caused an estimated 2 tons of cyanide to spill into the Barskoon River, hospitalizing some 1,000 local people. • Kumtor revenues constituted 7% of GDP in 2003, but is expected to close by 2010.

Tajikistan

Project	Partners	Key Information
Sangtuda hydropower station	RAO-UES (Russia), Iran, Tajik government	• Under protocol signed January 2005, Russia and Tajikistan will build the Sangtuda-1 facility and Iran and Tajikistan will build Sangtuda-2. • Construction of Sangtuda was launched in 1989 but interrupted by civil war in 1992. • Projected cost to complete: $500 million over four years. • Located on the Vaksh River 125 miles south of Dushanbe. • Project will allow Tajikistan to fully meet its own electricity needs and sell to neighbors Afghanistan and Pakistan.
Rugun hydropower station	Russian Aluminum	• RusAl agreed in October 2004 to invest $560 million of the total $600 million needed to construct the Rugun facility, which will provide cost-effective power for RusAl's planned aluminum processing plants throughout the country. • Tajik Economy Minister Halim Soliev told Russian newspaper *Vedomosti* at the time that RusAl's total investment in Tajikistan over the next seven years will total $1.6 billion.

Turkmenistan

Project	Partners	Key Information
Cheleken	Dragon Oil (Ireland-UAE)	• Proven reserves: 600 million barrels • 2004 production: 10,000 barrels per day • 25-year production sharing agreement with Turkmen government from 1993 covers two offshore deposits: Jeikhun and Jigalybek
Nebit Dag	Burren Energy (UK)	• Proven reserves: 100 million barrels • 2004 production: 10,000 barrels per day

Uzbekistan

Project	Partners	Key Information
Central Ustyurt & Southwest Gissar oil and gas fields	UzPEC Ltd. Subsidiary of Trinity Energy (UK)	• Projected by 2006: 2,600 barrels per day of oil and 71 billion cubic feet (2 billion cubic meters) of gas. • Projected direct investment: $400 million. • In 2001, Trinity signed a 40-year production sharing agreement with national holding company Uzbekneftegaz—the country's first PSA—for the oil and gas deposits at Usyurt and Gissar (also called Pamiro-Alai).
Muruntau goldmine	Zarafshan-Newmont JV 50 % Newmont Mining (U.S.) 50 % Uzbekistan–Navoi Mining (private) and Goskomgeologia (state)	• Estimated cost of JV: $250 million • Muruntau, meaning "hilly place," and the nearby town of Zarafshan are located 250 miles west of Tashkent in the Kyzylkum desert. • The open-pit mine has been in operation since 1969. • JV produced its first gold in 1995, scheduled to operate through 2011. • Colorodo-based Newmont estimates that the JV has pumped $500 million into the Uzbek economy (www.newmont.com).

Sources: U.S. Department of Energy, news agencies, company websites, BISNIS (Business Information Service for the Newly Independent States, www.bisnis.doc.gov).

Appendix 9. Energy Production

Gas Production

(in millions of cubic meters)

	1990	1996	2003
Kazakhstan	7,100	6,500	7,200
Turkmenistan	87,800	35,400	53,400
Uzbekistan	41,000	49,000	58,000

Oil Production

(in thousands of metric tons)

	1990	1996	2003
Kazakhstan	21,700	21,100	44,500
Turkmenistan	5,000	4,400	8,400
Uzbekistan	1,300	3,000	7,100

Electricity Production

(in million kilowatt hours)

	1990	1996	2003
Kazakhstan	87,400	59,000	63,700
Kyrgyzstan	13,370	13,800	14,000
Tajikistan	18,200	15,000	15,200
Turkmenistan	14.6	10.1	10.8
Uzbekistan	56,300	45,400	49,400

Coal Production

(in thousands of metric tons)

	1990	1996	2003
Kazakhstan	128,000	76,800	84,700
Kyrgyzstan	na	410	411
Uzbekistan	6,500	2,840	1,910

Source: Asian Development Bank, www.adb.org.

Appendix 10. Freedom House Democracy Indicators

Kazakhstan

	1997	1998	1999	2001	2002	2003	2004
Electoral Process	5.50	5.50	6.00	6.25	6.25	6.50	6.50
Civil Society	5.25	5.00	5.00	5.00	5.50	5.50	5.50
Independent Media	5.25	5.50	5.50	6.00	6.00	6.25	6.50
Governance	5.50	5.50	5.00	5.00	5.75	6.25	6.25
Constitutional, Legislative, and Judicial Framework	5.00	5.25	5.50	5.75	6.00	6.25	6.25
Corruption	n/a	n/a	6.00	6.25	6.25	6.25	6.50

Kyrgyzstan

	1997	1998	1999	2001	2002	2003	2004
Electoral Process	5.00	5.00	5.00	5.75	5.75	6.00	6.00
Civil Society	4.50	4.50	4.50	4.50	4.50	4.50	4.50
Independent Media	5.00	5.00	5.00	5.00	5.75	6.00	6.00
Governance	4.25	4.50	5.00	5.25	5.50	6.00	6.00
Constitutional, Legislative, and Judicial Framework	4.50	4.50	5.00	5.25	5.25	5.25	5.50
Corruption	n/a	n/a	6.00	6.00	6.00	6.00	6.00

Tajikistan

	1997	1998	1999	2001	2002	2003	2004
Electoral Process	6.00	5.75	5.50	5.25	5.25	5.25	5.75
Civil Society	5.50	5.25	5.25	5.00	5.00	5.00	5.00
Independent Media	6.25	6.00	5.75	5.50	5.75	5.75	5.75
Governance	7.00	6.75	6.25	6.00	6.00	6.00	5.75
Constitutional, Legislative, and Judicial Framework	6.25	6.00	5.75	5.75	5.75	5.75	5.75
Corruption	n/a	n/a	6.00	6.00	6.00	6.00	6.25

Turkmenistan

	1997	1998	1999	2001	2002	2003	2004
Electoral Process	7.00	7.00	7.00	7.00	7.00	7.00	7.00
Civil Society	7.00	7.00	7.00	7.00	7.00	7.00	7.00
Independent Media	7.00	7.00	7.00	7.00	7.00	7.00	7.00
Governance	6.75	6.75	6.75	6.75	6.75	6.75	7.00
Constitutional, Legislative, and Judicial Framework	6.75	6.75	6.75	7.00	7.00	7.00	7.00
Corruption	n/a	n/a	6.00	6.25	6.25	6.25	6.25

Uzbekistan

	1997	1998	1999	2001	2002	2003	2004
Electoral Process	6.25	6.50	6.50	6.75	6.75	6.75	6.75
Civil Society	6.50	6.50	6.50	6.50	6.75	6.50	6.50
Independent Media	6.50	6.50	6.50	6.75	6.75	6.75	6.75
Governance	6.00	6.25	6.25	6.00	6.00	6.25	6.25
Constitutional, Legislative, and Judicial Framework	6.50	6.50	6.50	6.50	6.50	6.50	6.50
Corruption	n/a	n/a	6.00	6.00	6.00	6.00	6.00

Note: Democratic progress ratings are based on a scale of 1 to 7, with 1 representing the highest and 7 the lowest.

Source: Alexander Motyl and Amanda Schetzer, *Nations in Transit, 2004: Democratization in East Central Europe and Eurasia* (New York: Freedom House, 2004).

Appendix 11. Combating the Flow of Drugs

Table A11-1. U.S. Expenditures on Narcotics and Law Enforcement

	FY 1992 –2000	FY 2001	FY 2002	FY 2003	Average Annual Spent Prior to 9/11	Average Annual Spent After 9/11
Kazakhstan	2,180,000	750,000	1,050,000	510,000	293,000	146,500
Kyrgyzstan	1,340,000	90,000	50,000	1,800,000	143,000	71,500
Tajikistan	110,000	40,000	90,000	2,820,000	15,000	7,500
Turkmenistan	360,000	20,000	110,000	770,000	56,000	28,000
Uzbekistan	1,500,000	32,000	1,070,000	1,560,000	182,000	91,000
Total	5,490,000	1,400,000	2,370,000	7,460,000	689,000	344,500

Source: U.S. Department of State.

Table A11-2. Kilograms of Opium Seized, 1997–2002

	1997	1998	1999	2000	2001	2002
Kazakhstan	1,000	297	170	136	36	14
Kyrgyzstan	1,639	172	151	1,405	469	109
Tajikistan	3,456	1,190	1,269	4,778	3,664	1,624
Turkmenistan	1,410	1,412	4,600	2,300	No Report	1,200
Uzbekistan	2,364	1,935	3,292	2,008	242	76

Source: U.N. Office on Drugs and Crime, 2004 World Drug Report.

Appendix 12. Key Political Parties

Kazakhstan

Otan (Fatherland)
Pro-presidential
In the October 1999 parliamentary elections, Otan fielded the largest number of candidates (some sixty in all) and won the largest number of seats, twenty in constituency contests and four in the national list section. Shortly after its formation, Otan stated its goal was the reelection of Nazarbayev in the 2006 presidential elections. In the September 2004 parliamentary elections, Otan received nearly 43 percent of the votes.

Asar
Pro-presidential
Led by President Nazarbayev's daughter Dariga, Asar publicly supports Nazarbayev's policies. Dariga Nazarbayeva stated that Asar hoped to take 50 percent of the seats in the October 2004 parliamentary elections. In the September 2004 parliamentary elections, Asar took about 19.1 percent of the votes.

Ak Zhol (Bright Path)
Opposition
Offshoot of the Democratic Choice of Kazakhstan in 2002. Won 22.9 percent of the parliamentary vote in September 2004. The party split in February 2005, with former co-chairmen Bulat Abilov, Uraz Zhandosov, and Altynbek Sarsenbayev creating a new party "Naghyz Ak Zhol," or True Bright Path, ahead of the 2006 presidential elections.

Democratic Choice of Kazakhstan (DMK)
Pro-business opposition
Movement founded in fall 2001 by members of the government and business elite, many of whom had benefited from the privatization of state property in the 1990s and were so-called "New Kazakhs." Main figures in the movement included Mukhtar Ablyazov, energy minister and head of the Astana-Holding investment group, Deputy Prime Minister Uraz Zhandosov, Governor of the northern Pavlodar region Ghalymzhan Zhakqiyanov and the parliamentary deputy Tolen Tokhtasinov.

Republican People's Party of Kazakhstan (RPPK)
Opposition
Akezhan Kazhegeldin, a former prime minister, joined the opposition in mid-1998, and his rhetoric calling for the enactment of democratic ideals in the country quickly gained him a relatively broad following. RPPK, founded in 1999, but Kazhegeldin was barred from running for president. Opposition members formed the new Forum of Democratic Forces of Kazakhstan (FDPK) in October 1999, presided over by Kazhegeldin, with the goal of intensifying the struggle against Nazarbayev's growing power. However, governmental obstruction and the group's own organizational shortcomings stymied its rise, and the opposition lay dormant for almost two years.

Azamat
Pro-democracy
In April 1996, ex-Ministers Peter Svoik and Galim Abilsiitov created the new Azamat movement, along with Kazakhstan's former envoy to China, Murat Auezov. However, while prominent, this group lacked the funding and connections to pose a serious political threat to the regime

Sources: RFE/RL, EurasiaNet.org.

Kyrgyzstan

BLOC: National Movement of Kyrgyzstan (NMK)
Kurmanbek Bakiyev
The People's Movement of Kyrgyzstan election bloc was formed in September 2004 from nine parties and movements, including the Party of Communists, the Communist Party, the Republican Party, Asaba, the Democratic Movement of Kyrgyzstan, Kairan El, New Kyrgyzstan, Erkin Kyrgyzstan, and Erkindik.

BLOC: For Fair Elections
Misir Ashirkulov
The "For Fair Elections" election bloc was formed in May 2004 and combines the Ar-Namys, El, Ata Meken, and Social Democratic parties.

Ata-Jurt (Fatherland)
Roza Otunbayeva
Otunbayeva, a former foreign minister and UN envoy to Georgia, has a power base in the north and among the political establishment. Her alliance with Bakiyev, a southerner, gives her broader appeal.

Asaba
Azimbek Beknazarov
The nationalist party came out publicly against allowing the U.S.-led coalition fighting in Afghanistan to use a base in Kyrgyzstan. Asaba similarly has been against the Russian-led CIS Collective Security Treaty Organization's base at Kant and against an agreement that ceded land to China. Party members are mainly entrepreneurs and peasants.

Ata-Meken (Fatherland)
Omurbek Tekebayev
Nationalist-socialist in orientation. Many supporters also come from rural areas in the South. The party's main goal is to gain southerners a more prominent role in the political and economic life of the country.

Ar-Namys (Dignity)
Feliks Kulov
Created in 1999 and gained a solid reputation among students, unemployed youth, and the rural population. Kulov, a rival to Bakiyev in the July 2005 presidential elections, prioritizes stabilization of the current political situation, providing security, and preventing an exodus of the country's diminishing Russian-speaking minority.

Alga, Kyrgyzstan (Forward, Kyrgyzstan)
Bermet Akayeva
Pro-Akayev party through which supporters of the deposed president remain politically active.

Erkindik (Freedom)
Topchubek Turgunaliyev
Turgunaliyev, a Kyrgyz nationalist, has been an outspoken critic of the Akayev regime. He was sentenced to sixteen years in jail in 1999 for masterminding a plot to assassinate the president, a conviction widely regarded

as an attempt to silence his outspoken criticisms of Akayev, and released two years later.

Zhani-Bagyt
Muratbek Imanaliyev
Previously, former foreign minister Imanaliyev was head of the centrist Party for Justice and Progress.

People's Patriotic Movement
Tursunbek Akunov
Akunov, a human rights activist and prospective presidential candidate, heads this nationalist movement.

Sources: RFE/RL, EurasiaNet.org, Reuters, Institute for War and Peace Reporting.

Tajikistan

People's Democratic Party (PDPT)
Government
President Rakhmonov formally joined the party in March 1998 and was elected as head of the party the following month. From 2000–2005, the party had a 65 percent majority in parliament. In January 2005, it boosted its majority to 80 percent.

Communist Party
Government
Leader is Shodi Shabdolov. Allied with PDPT in parliament.

Islamic Renaissance Party
Opposition
Members are represented in the various government institutions through a power-sharing agreement negotiated to end the country's 1992–97 civil war. (The IRP dominated the United Tajik Opposition—the umbrella group for rebels.) However, this arrangement, under which opposition forces are entitled to a 30 percent share of government posts, has looked increasingly precarious of late. Party leader is Said Abdullo Nuri.

Democratic Party of Tajikistan
Opposition
Two factions lay claim to the Democratic Party of Tajikistan: the Almaty platform, which is registered in Tajikistan, and the Tehran platform. The Almaty platform is led by Mahmadruzi Iskandarov, who has been arrested on criminal charges from Moscow. The Tehran platform is led by Azam Afzali and has recently transformed itself into the Taraqqiyot Party. The Democratic Party split into two factions over a disagreement over whether to remain with the United Tajik Opposition and fight, or open negotiations with the Tajik government. The Almaty platform opted for fighting and was rewarded after the peace deal between the UTO and the Tajik government.

Socialist Party
Split
The Socialist party is divided into two factions: the pro-government faction led by Abduhalim Ghaffarov is still registered with Tajikistan's Justice Ministry, and the faction led by Mirhusein Narziyev is not recognized. The party's founder, Safarali Kenjayev, was assassinated in Dushanbe in late March 1999. The party has not been able to regroup since Kenjayev's death. It received less than two percent of the votes cast in the 2000 parliamentary elections.

Social Democratic Party
Secular opposition
Based on the Justice and Development party, banned in 2000. Failed to cross the 5 percent threshold to win seats in the January 2005 parliamentary elections. Leader Rahmatullo Zoirov claimed authorities and state media are attempting to link the current opposition parties with the Islamist political opposition during Tajikistan's five-year civil war.

Sources: RFE/RL, EurasiaNet.org.

Turkmenistan

Democratic Party of Turkmenistan (DPT)
Pro-president
Founded and chaired by President Saparmurat Niyazov. The only legal party.
In February 2001, Niyazov said that the next presidential elections would
be held in 2010 and confirmed that no other parties would be legalized until
then. It was the only party that participated in the December 2004 parliamentary elections, which was represented by 131 candidates contesting
fifty seats in the parliament

United Democratic Opposition of Turkmenistan
Opposition in exile (first wave)
Originally organized in Moscow as the Turkmenistan Foundation by Avdi
Kuliev, Turkmenistan's first foreign minister, who left the government in
protest of Niyazov's policies in 1992. In April 1998, during Niyazov's official visit to Washington, Kuliev himself attempted a return to Ashgabat,
but was detained at the airport upon arrival and ultimately deported. Opposition activity was limited from 1998-2001, with the reinstatement of exit
visas, which made it difficult for Niyazov critics in exile to maintain ties with
opponents inside the country. The movement depends on NGO grants for
funding.

Union of Democratic Forces of Turkmenistan
Opposition in exile (second wave)
Led by Kuliev's successor as foreign minister, Boris Shikhmuradov, who
broke with Niyazov in 2001 and was jailed in December 2002 for involvement in an attempted coup. Organization was formed after meetings in
Vienna and Prague in 2003 by leaders of political parties Vatan, the Republican Party of Turkmenistan, and Renaissance. Like Kuliev, Shikhmuradov
advocates democratic principles; however, in the event of a regime change
Shikhmuradov's group would declare an eighteen-month "transitional
period" in which no elections would be held. (Kuliev has said he would call
for immediate elections.) This would be a period of intensive economic
reform, involving the privatization of a number of state-owned industries.
Despite accusations that he used his governmental positions for personal
enrichment, Shikhmuradov's platform is popular with pro-Western intellectuals and educated youth in Ashgabat. He also claims to have the support

of many officials remaining in Niyazov's government who are allegedly fed up with Niyazov's extremes.

Sources: RFE/RL, EurasiaNet.org.

Uzbekistan

Khalk Demokratic Partijasi—People's Democratic Party (PDP)
Pro-presidential
Formerly the Communist Party of Uzbekistan, restructured in September 1991. Islam Karimov led PDP until 1996. PDP won forty-eight seats in the December 1999 parliamentary elections.

Vatan Tarakkiyoti—Progress of the Fatherland Party
Pro-presidential
It has been supportive of the dominant PDP. In the December 1999 parliamentary elections, it won twenty seats.

Adolat Social-Democratic Party
Pro-presidential
It won eleven seats in December 1999 parliamentary elections and two seats in December 2004 parliamentary elections.

Birlik (Unity)
Opposition
Party leader is Abdurahim Pulot, who lives in exile in the United States. Though banned since 1992, Birlik managed in April 2002 to hold a number of meetings—including seven regional congresses—without interference from the authorities. The party is working toward a national congress and official registration in 2003, backed by the public support of the US government.

Erk Democratic Party (Freedom)
Opposition
Party leader Muhammad Salih ran against Karimov for president in 1991, winning 12 percent of the vote. A brief cooperation with the government following independence quickly soured and the party was banned in 1992.

Salih fled Uzbekistan in 1993, and gained asylum in Norway. He has been accused of involvement in the 1999 Tashkent explosions, though human rights leaders say the charges are politically motivated.

Sources: RFE/RL, EurasiaNet.org.

Appendix 13. Islamic Organizations

Official

Board of Muslims of Central Asia and Kazakhstan (SADUM)
During World War II, the Soviet government reconciled with Central Asian clerics and established the Muslim Board of Central Asia and Kazakhstan, the central regional organ located in Tashkent during the Soviet years. The Muslim Board was the core of official Islam during the postwar Soviet period. With the *Mufti* at its head, it was charged with regulating the registration of mosques, appointing *imams* to lead local congregations, and even dictating the content of sermons and the nature of "proper" Islamic practice. The official Muslim clergy was co-opted and played by the rules of the Communist Party leadership. Some people in Central Asia managed, however, to practice a private form of Islam in secret and beyond official Islam. By 1992, the Muslim Board of Central Asia and Kazakhstan was decentralized, with the establishment in each Central Asian state of a Muslim regulatory board. The state-appointed *muftis* of Central Asian countries control religious activities just like during the Soviet years. Allowing Islam a greater space to operate, the state retains the old communist distrust of religion and religious fanatics and keeps a tight control over Islamic religious activities through the *muftis*. *Muftis* for the Central Asia region included the following:

- **Uzbekistan:** Ishan Babakhan bin Abdul Majid khan (1943–1957), his son, Ziyaddin khan Ishan Babakhan (1957–1982), and, in turn, his son Shamsuddin khan Babakhan (1982–1989). Shamsuddin was ousted, largely by pressure from within Uzbekistan's Islamic elite, and replaced by Muhammad-Sadyk Muhammad-Yusuf (1989–1993); Mukhtarjan Abdullo Al-Bukhari (1993–1995), Abdurashid Bakhromov (1995–).
- **Kazakhstan:** Ratbek-kazi Nysanbaiuly (February 1990–2000), Absattar Derbisaliyev (2000–).
- **Kyrgyzstan:** Sadykjan Kamalov (1990–1995), Kimsanbai-hadji Abdrakhmanov (1995–2002), Murataly-hadji Djuman-uulu (August 2002).
- **Turkmenistan:** Nasrullah ibn Ibadullah (sentenced to twenty-two years in jail in January 2002), Kakageldy Vepayev (January 2002–dismissed in August 2004), Rovshen Allaberdyyev (August 2004–).
- **Tajikistan:** Haji Akbar Turjanzoda, Fachulo Sharifsoda (December 1992–murdered in January 1996), Amonulloh Nematzoda (June 1996–).

Unofficial

Islamic Renaissance Party (IRP)
The IRP was founded in June 1990 in Astrakhan, Russia, mainly by Tartar intellectuals who sought to organize Muslims within the Soviet Union to campaign for the introduction of *sharia* in Russia. Then IRP opened independent branches in the Central Asian republics; however, it found it hard to establish a major presence following the collapse of the USSR. Banned in other Central Asian countries, the IRP is a legal party only in Tajikistan. Reportedly, the IRP in Tajikistan has been co-opted into the regime, which significantly weakened its base.

Adolat
This Islamic militia group, led by Tahir Yuldash, was founded in 1991 in the Uzbek town of Namangan as an alternative to IRP. Adolat saw IRP as the Uzbek government's pawn and as unwilling to demand an Islamic revolution. Adolat sponsored and ran many mosques and medressehs across the Ferghana Valley. After it gained significant power in Namangan, thus alarming the Uzbek authorities, the organization disintegrated in 1992 following a government crackdown on its members, which resulted in the flight of some of its leadership to Tajikistan, Iran, and Afghanistan and the jailing of others.

Islamic Movement of Uzbekistan (IMU)
The IMU was founded by a former leader of Adolat, Tahir Yuldash, and Juma Namangani following the suppression of Adolat and the jailing of its members. Uzbek Islamists who fled to Tajikistan fought alongside the United Tajik Opposition. Juma Namangani, a military leader of the IMU, was even an aide to the most influential Tajik field commander, Mirzo Zioev. In 1993, the Uzbek Islamists followed fleeing Tajik opposition elements into Afghanistan, where the IMU was officially formed. The IMU established bases in northern Afghanistan (namely, in Kunduz), Uzbekistan (in the Ferghana Valley), Tajikistan (Tavildar, a mountainous area in the Karategin Valley), and the southern part of Kyrgyzstan. The IMU launched an armed attack from Karategin in an attempt to break into Uzbekistan through the territory of Kyrgyzstan in the summer of 1999. IMU's goal was to overthrow the secular Uzbek government, "liberate" the Ferghana Valley and establish an Islamic state. After long and heavy fighting with the armed forces of

Uzbekistan and Kyrgyzstan, the militants withdrew to the mountainous areas of Tajikistan. In 2000, the militants returned, invading both Kyrgyzstan and the Surkhan Darya administrative region of Uzbekistan. Reportedly, in the fall of 2000, most IMU fighters moved from Tajikistan to Afghanistan, where IMU set up bases in Taliban-controlled parts of the country. The IMU was significantly weakened after the United States crushed the Taliban regime in Afghanistan; its remaining forces are reportedly being scattered in Iran, Tajikistan, and the tribal areas of Pakistan. Tahir Yuldash is reportedly trying to revive even the small remaining forces and is hiding somewhere in tribal regions of Pakistan. There are speculations among Western diplomats in Dushanbe, Tajikistan's capital, that with the reemergence of the battered IMU that Yuldash seems to be reforming, the group may engage in real terrorist activities such as urban terrorism, abductions, extortions, and even an incursion through Turkmenistan.

Hizb ut-Tahrir
Established in the 1950s in Palestine, Hizb ut-Tahrir al-Islami (Islamic Party of Liberation) took root in Central Asia around ten years ago. Unlike the IMU, Hizb ut-Tahrir, which also declared *jihad* in Central Asia, seeks to reunite the Central Asian republics and eventually replace governments of the Muslim world with an Islamic state in the form of a caliphate through nonviolent means. Although the group promulgates only peaceful means to achieve its goals, Central Asian governments have mostly taken harsh measures against it. Uzbek authorities suspect it may be behind the March and July 2004 terrorist attacks that killed several people there. About 5,000 alleged members of the Hizb ut-Tahrir are reportedly lingering in Uzbek prisons. Other Central Asian governments also perceive Hizb ut-Tahrir as a threat to their secular constitutions and state security. Analysts warn that repression of Hizb ut-Tahrir members has radicalized the movement and threatened to sow the seeds of greater Islamist extremism.

Jamaat of Central Asian Mujahideen
Spinter group of the IMU, created after the destruction of the IMU camps in Afghanistan following September 11, 2001. Tahir Yuldash and others joined with international Al Qaida brigades, but this group remains focused on terror acts in Central Asia.

Note: This Jamaat is separate and distinct from the Jamaat Tabligh, an international Islamic missionary organization that the Karimov government in Uzbekistan has tried to suppress.

Baiat

The underground Islamic extremist group Baiat ("covenant" in Arabic) is active in northern Tajikistan. In April 2005, two members were convicted and another ten put on trial as part of the country's crackdown on extremism.

According to the Tajik Interior Ministry, Baiat began instructing young people in the mosques under its control in the village of Chorkukh in 1991. It also organized Sharia courts. Members fought on the side of the Islamic opposition during the 1992–1997 civil war. Later, they were partisans of the Taliban in Afghanistan, where three were arrested by U.S. servicemen and held at Guantanamo.

Baiat's doctrine vilifies non-Muslim groups as well as Muslim groups that it considers too moderate. In 2003, several mosques were defaced or burnt down just in the Isfara district of the Sughd oblast, because their attendants were too close to the secular government, ITAR-Tass reported.

One member, Sadullo Madyerov, was recently sentenced to twenty-four years in jail for the 2003 murder of the head of a local Baptist congregation, Sergei Bessarabi. The Tajik special services believe Baiat is funded by the Libyan movement "Al-Baiat" and also by groups in Uzbekistan.

Appendix 14. Major Cities—Old and New Names

Current Name	Former Name
Kazakhstan	
Astana	Aqmola
Aktau	Shevchenko
Almaty	Alma-Ata
Aqtobe	Aktyubinsk
Atyrau	Guryev
Karaganda	
Oskemen	Ust-Kamenogorsk
Pavlodar	
Semey	Semipalatinsk
Shymkent	Chimkent
Taraz	Zhambul
Kyrgyzstan	
Bishkek	Frunze
Jalalabad	
Kara-Balta	
Karakol	Przhevalsk
Osh	
Tokmok	
Tajikistan	
Dushanbe	Stalinabad
Istravshan	
Gharm	
Horog	Khorog
Khujand	Leninabad
Kulob	
Qurgan-Teppe	Kurgan-Tiube
Turkmenistan	
Ashgabat	
Balkanabat	Nebit-Dag
Dashoguz	Dashhowuz
Mary	

Turkmenabat   Charjew
Turkmenbashi   Krasnovodsk

Uzbekistan*
Tashkent
Namangan
Samarkand
Andijan
Bukhara
Nukus

Source: Library of Congress country profiles, updated October 2004.
*In Uzbekistan, some spellings have changed, for example, to Samarqand or Andijan, but the names have not.

Notes

Chapter One

1. President George W. Bush, "State of the Union Address," February 2, 2005, available at www.whitehouse.gov/news/releases/2005/02/print/20050202-11.html.

2. Akayev replaced Absamat Masaliyev.

3. Kazakhstan did not confirm its participation in the antiterrorism coalition until Secretary of Defense Donald Rumsfeld's visit on April 28, 2002. See RFE/RL NewsLine, April 29, 2002, available at www.rferl.org.

4. Alone among the Central Asians, the Turkmenistan government lobbied hard for international recognition of the Taliban regime until 1999, in the hopes that this would help facilitate the construction of a pipeline to ship Turkmen gas across Afghanistan to markets in Pakistan and India.

5. Russia's military presence in Tajikistan consists of the formerly Soviet and now Russian 201st Motorized Rifle Division that has been stationed there since 1945 (and includes many Tajiks) and the Russian Federal Border Service created in September 1992.

6. There were six explosions, including several car bombs in Tashkent. Some fifteen people were killed (including two attackers), and 150 others were wounded. See Intercon Daily Report on Russia, Washington, D.C., February 23, 1999.

7. For details, see "Secretary Rumsfeld Interview with Reuters TV and Wire," U.S. Department of Defense news transcript, March 4, 2004, available at www.defenselink.mil/transcripts/2004/tr20040325-secdef0564.html, and the June 26, 1996, memorandum for correspondents on a meeting between Islam Karimov and William Perry, available at www.defenselink.mil/news/Jun1996/m062696_m144-96.html.

8. For a discussion of some of these rivalries during the Soviet period, see Bahdan Nahaylo and Victor Swoboda, *Soviet Disunion: A History of the Nationalities Problem in the USSR* (London: Hamish Hamilton, 1990).

9. Initially the Uzbek government accepted a macrostabilization program backed by the International Monetary Fund (IMF) that included convertibility but then retreated to pursue an inwardly focused national development strategy in 1996.

10. Current account convertibility means that commercial account holders can convert the national currency (som) to dollars, which allows them to make and receive trade-related payments. Technically, Uzbek account holders have been permitted to do this freely since October 2003, but in reality there is still a "line" to get money from the national bank, and individual citizens also commonly encounter shortages when they try to use som to purchase dollars at the official change points.

11. Kazakhstan declared independence on December 16, 1991; Kyrgyz Republic on December 12, 1991; Tajikistan on September 9, 1991; Turkmenistan on October 27, 1991; and Uzbekistan on August 31, 1991.

12. Martha Brill Olcott, "Central Asia's Catapult to Independence," *Foreign Affairs*, vol. 71, no. 3 (Summer 1992), pp. 118–28.

13. The five-year civil war in Tajikistan ended in June 1997 with the peace accords signed by the two Tajik parties in Moscow. The agreement, implementation of which was delayed, stipulated that the government would lift the ban on all parties of the United Tajik Opposition prior to parliamentary elections in 2000.

14. To enhance security in the southern regions following the events in Osh oblast, the Kyrgyz government reduced the size of the oblast by moving three districts (Batken, Leilek, and Kadamjaito) into a newly created Batken oblast. RFE/RL Kyrgyz Report, October 12, 1999, available at www.rferl.org.

Kyrgyzstan's security problems were discussed at meetings of the member states of the Commonwealth of Independent States (CIS) collective defense agreement (Armenia, Belarus, Kazakhstan, Kyrgyzstan, Russia, and Tajikistan) on November 5, 1999. The discussion led to the signing of the Bishkek Memorandum to combat international terrorism on December 3, 1999, by the heads of interior and security services of China, Kazakhstan, Kyrgyzstan, Russia, and Tajikistan. RFE/RL Kyrgyz Report, November 5, 1999, and December 3, 1999, available at www.rferl.org.

15. The length of Afghanistan's border with Tajikistan is 1,206 kilometers; wth Turkmenistan it is 744 kilometers; with Uzbekistan and Afghanistan it is 137 kilometers. See Central Intelligence Agency, *CIA World Factbook*, accessible online.

16. Off-the-record interviews with author, conducted in Kyrgyzstan and Uzbekistan in 2004 and 2005 respectively.

17. For some examples see Fiona Hill, "Central Asia: Terrorism, Religious Extremism, and Regional Stability," Testimony before the House Committee on International Relations, Subcommittee on the Middle East and Central Asia, October 29, 2003, available at wwwc.house.gov/international_relations/108/90361.pdf; Stephen Blank, "Radical Islamic Challenges in Central Asia," Testimony before the House Committee on International Relations, October 2003, available at wwwc.house.gov/international_relations/108/90361.pdf; Martha Brill Olcott, "Central Asia: Terrorism, Religious Extremism, and Regional Stability," Testimony before the U.S. House of Representatives, Committee on International Relations, Subcommit-

tee on the Middle East and Central Asia, October 29, 2003, available at www.house.gov/international_relations/108/90361.pdf.

Chapter Two

1. For a characteristically optimistic account of Central Asia's prospects written in the first decade of independence see S. Frederick Starr, "Making Eurasia Stable," in *Foreign Affairs*, January/February 1996, vol. 75, available at www.foreignaffairs.org/19960101faessay4173/s-frederick-starr/making-eurasia-stable.html. For a characteristically negative account see *Central Asia a Gathering Storm,* Boris Rumer, ed. (Armonk: M. E. Sharpe, 2002).

2. See appendix eight on natural resource wealth of Central Asian countries.

3. See various writings and testimonies by Martha Brill Olcott: "Politics of Economic Distribution in the Caspian Sea States," Testimony before the U.S. Senate Foreign Relations Committee, Subcommittee on International Economic Policy, Export, and Trade Promotion, Washington, D.C., April 12, 2000, available at www.ceip.org/files/Publications/senatetestimony.asp; "Democracy in the Central Asian Republics," Testimony before the House International Relations Subcommittee on Asia and the Pacific on Democracy in the Central Asian Republics, April 12, 2000, available at www.ceip.org/files/Publications/housetestimony.asp; Testimony before the U.S. Congress's Commission on Security and Cooperation in Europe on the Challenge of Building Democracy in Kazakhstan, May 6, 1999, available at www.eurasianet.org/resource/kazakhstan/links/olcott.html; "Caspian Sea Oil Exports," Testimony before the Subcommitte on International Economic Policy, Export and Trade Promotion, Senate Foreign Relations Committee, July 8, 1998, available at www.ceip.org/people/olccaspw.htm; and "Facing the Future: Twelve Myths about Central Asia," paper presented at the Central Asian Conference on Regional Cooperation, Bishkek, Kyrgyzstan, 1995.

4. See appendix eight for information about major mineral resource extraction projects in Central Asia.

5. For an overview of each country's approach to economic and political reform, see appendix twelve.

6. The first Arab incursions into Central Asia began around 667 A.D. Islamization of the indigenous people was gradual and not coercive. See H. A. R. Gibb, *The Arab Conquests in Central Asia* (New York: AMS Print, 1970).

7. Chingis Khan (c. 1155–1227) founded the Mongol Empire after unifying various Mongol tribes under his banner by 1206. The Goldon Horde held Eurasia under its domain until the 15th century.

8. The Kazakh tribesmen were known then as Kirghiz, and the Kyrgyz were referred to as Karakirghiz, or black Kyrgyz.

9. The Russians annexed Kazakhstan in 1863 as its Steppe District and ruled much of the region by military governor generals. The Khanate of Khiva and the Emirate of Bukhara became Russian protectorates and were reduced in size.

10. For a detailed discussion of Stalin's nationality policy, see Stephen Blank, *The Sorcerer as Apprentice: Stalin as Commissar of Nationalities, 1917–1924* (Westport, CT: Greenwood Press, 1994).

11. The Governor-Generalship of Turkestan was divided among southern Kazakhstan, eastern Turkmenistan, Kyrgyzstan, Uzbekistan, and Tajikistan. Western Turkmenistan became part of the Trans-Caspian military and northern Kazakhstan was administered by the Steppe Governor-Generalship.

12. Samani (849–907) was the founder of the Persian-speaking Samanid dynasty. A picture of the monument to him is on the cover of this book.

13. For details, see Muriel Atkin, "The Subtlest Battle: Islam in Soviet Tajikistan" (Philadelphia, PA: Foreign Policy Research Institute, 1989).

14. The interethnic clashes between Kyrgyz and Uzbeks that initially started over a minor land dispute escalated into riots with high fatality rates in the Osh region of Kyrgyzstan in the summer of 1990. See A. Elebayeva, "The Osh Incident: Problems for Research," *Post-Soviet Geography*, vol. 33, no. 2 (1992), pp. 70–8; and Anatoly Khazanov, "After the USSR: Ethnicity, Nationalism, and Politics in the Commonwealth of Independent States" (Madison: University of Wisconsin Press, 1995). A clash between local Tajik and Kyrgyz populations of the Isfara district in Tajikistan, located between Uzbekistan and Kyrgyzstan in the Ferghana Valley, resulted in violence and one death. See "Nationalities," *Current Digest of the Soviet Press*, August 9, 1989.

15. The Aral Sea basin's surface water resources are distributed among the Central Asian countries in the following way: Tajikistan (54.4 percent), Kyrgyzstan (25.3 percent), Uzbekistan (8.2 percent), Afghanistan (6.8 percent), Kazakhstan (2.6 percent), Iran (2 percent), and Turkmenistan (0.7 percent). See Necati Polat, *Boundary Issues in Central Asia* (New York: Transnational Publishers, 2002). Water usage patterns, however, are just the opposite.

16. Phillip Micklin, *Managing Water in Central Asia* (London: Royal Institute of International Affairs, 2000).

17. For instance, the industrial output that year in Kazakhstan constituted 68.3 percent of its 1991 production level, in Kyrgyz Republic (58.1 percent), in Tajikistan (31.2 percent), in Turkmenistan (61.6 percent), and in Uzbekistan (83.8 percent). Jeromin Zettelmeyer, "The Uzbek Growth Puzzle," *IMF Staff Papers*, vol. 46, no. 3 (September/December 1999), p. 275.

18. International Crisis Group, *Central Asia: Water and Conflict* (Osh/Brussels: May 30, 2002), p. 3.

19. For details see appendix thirteen.

20. For detailed profile of the movement, see the GlobalSecurity.org website: www.globalsecurity.org/military/world/para/hizb-ut-tahrir.htm. For a comprehensive account of Hizb ut-Tahrir in Central Asia, see International Crisis Group, "Radical Islam in Central Asia: Responding to Hizb ut-Tahrir," Asia Report no. 58 (Brussels: June 30, 2003), available through www.icg.org.

21. As of July 1998, Kazakhstan had an estimated population of 16.8 million. Its ethnic mix includes 46% Kazakh, 34% Russian, 4.9% Ukrainian, 3.1% German, 2.3% Uzbek, 1.9% Tatar, and 7.1% other.

22. The first wave of Russian resettlement *en masse* began in the late eighteenth and early nineteenth centuries, especially promoted by the Russian government under Stolypin. The next large-scale influx of Russians took place as a part of the Virgin Land Project initiated by Brezhnev in the 1960s. See Martha Brill Olcott, *The Kazakhs*, 2nd ed. (Stanford, CA: Hoover University Press, 1995), pp. 83–99, 225–40.

23. Marlene Laruelle and Sebastien Peyrouse, *Les Russes du Kazakhstan: Identités nationals et nouveaux États dans l'espace post-soviétique* (Paris: Maisonneuve & Larose, 2003), p. 336.

24. Total external debt more than doubled from $1,848 million in 1993 to $4,587 million in 1997. International Monetary Fund, "Republic of Kazakstan: Recent Economic Developments," IMF Staff Country Report no.98/84 (Washington, DC: August 1998), p. 64.

25. Cattle numbers decreased from 9,400,000 head in 1993 to 4,299,000 head in 1997.

26. Kazakhstan's leading banks include the Kazakh National Bank, TuranAlemBank, Halyq Bank, and the widely respected KazKommertzBank, which enjoys a strong international rating.

27. In fact, it has been so difficult that in 2005 the government of Kazakhstan announced that it is going to require all international flights coming to Kazakhstan to land first in Astana.

28. See Energy Information Administration, *Kazakhstan Country Analysis Brief* (Washington, DC: U.S. Department of Energy, November 2004), available at www.eia.doe.gov/emeu/cabs/kazak.html.

29. Chevron was initially invited to develop this field by Soviet President Mikhail Gorbachev. After the breakup of the Soviet Union, the U.S. firm negotiated a new contract with the Kazakh government, in which it promised to invest $20 billion in the project.

30. The CPC project began construction in 1993, but the first oil did not ship until March 2001, and the pipeline did not become fully functional until October 2001.

31. The Karachaganak consortium includes British Gas (United Kingdom) with 32.5 percent of holdings; Agip (Italy) with 32.5 percent; Chevron-Texaco (United States) with 20 percent; and LUKoil (Russia) with 15 percent. The project is managed by KazMunayGaz.

32. See U.S. District Court, Southern District of New York, *United States v. James H. Giffen*, Indictment S1 03 Cr. 404 (WHP), April 12, 2004.

33. In early March 1995, the constitutional court of Kazakhstan ruled in favor of Tatyana Kvyatkovskaya, a journalist from the Abylaykhan electoral district of Almaty. Kvyatkovskaya charged that the electoral districts for the 1994 election had been drawn disproportionately. The constitutional court ruled that the entire 1994 parliamentary elections had been unconstitutional.

34. Of the forty-seven members of the Senate (upper house), forty are elected by regional assemblies (special electoral colleges composed of members of local councils), and seven are appointed by the president. Sixty-seven members of the Majilis (lower house) are directly elected, and ten are elected on the basis of party lists according to the proportional representation system and on the territory of the entire nationwide constituency.

35. For more on Turkmenistan's oil reserves, see Energy Information Administration, *International Energy Outlook* (Washington, DC: U.S. Department of Energy, April 2004); for more on its undeveloped and potential reserves, see International Monetary Fund, *Turkmenistan: Recent Economic Developments*, IMF Country Staff Report no. 99/140 (Washington, DC: 1999), p. 9.

36. David B. Ottaway and Dan Morgan, "Gas Pipeline Bounces between Agendas," *Washington Post*, October 5, 1998, p. A1.

37. Bridas, an Argentine company that invested over $400 million in oil production in Turkmenistan, withdrew after its oil export license was suspended by the Turkmen government. Netherlands-based Larmag Energy Assets faced similar problems albeit with a smaller investment. Petronas of Malaysia had signed a deal to develop oil and natural gas deposits in 1996

but also suspended operations for more than a year because it could not profit under Turkmenistan's export restrictions. American Unocal launched a project in 1994 but abandoned it after 1998.

38. Martha Brill Olcott, "International Gas Trade in Central Asia: Turkmenistan, Iran, Russia and Afghanistan," Working Paper no. 28 (Stanford, CA: Stanford University Program on Energy and Sustainable Development and the James A. Baker III Institute for Public Policy of Rice University, May 2004), available at http://iis-db.stanford.edu/pubs/20605/Turkmenistan_final.pdf.

39. See appendix nine.

40. The consortium consisted of Unocal-Delta Oil with an 85 percent interest, Turkmenistan's Turkmenrosgaz with 5 percent, and Russia's Gazprom with 10 percent. See "Unocal, Delta Sign MOU with Gazprom and Turkmenrosgaz for Natural Gas Pipeline Project," available at Unocal's website: www.unocal.com/uclnews/96htm/081396.htm.

41. Immediately following the U.S. missile attacks, Unocal suspended its pipeline project until the U.S. recognized the Afghan government. Roshan Zamir, "Unocal Withdraws from Pipeline Project," *The Nation*, December 6, 1998. For additional details on Unocal's and other proposed pipeline projects for Turkmen gas, see Martha Brill Olcott, "International Gas Trade in Central Asia: Turkmenistan, Iran, Russia and Afghanistan," Working Paper no. 28 (Stanford, CA: Stanford University and the James A. Baker III Institute for Public Policy of Rice University, May 2004), available at http://iis-db.stanford.edu/pubs/20605/Turkmenistan_final.pdf.

42. Bridas filed a suit against the Government of Turkmenistan for loss of its export license and about $50 million of debt owed by the Turkmenbashi Oil Refinery. The government filed a retaliatory suit against Bridas alleging that the company violated the conditions of the joint venture agreement. "Bridas Likely to Pull Out of Turkmenistan," *Dow Jones via Energy*, vol. 24 (October 18, 2000), in "Company News: Central Asia," *Alexander's Gas & Oil Connections*, vol. 5, no. 21 (November 16, 2000).

43. According to a report by *Deutsche Welle*, Turkmenistan's regime has engaged in systematic narcotics trafficking and has forged ties with poppy producers in Afghanistan. Rustem Safronov, "Turkmenistan's Niyazov Implicated In Drug Smuggling," *Eurasia Insight*, Eurasianet.org, March 29, 2002; also see *Turkmenistan's Political Crisis: Inside the Niyazov Regime; a Discussion with Boris Shikhmuradov* (Washington, DC: Carnegie Endowment for International Peace, April 29, 2002), available at www.ceip.org/files/events/sheikmuradov042902transcript.asp.

44. This author has been told first-person accounts of Niyazov asking for and receiving solid gold Rolex watches from potential investors, just as a "tone setter."

45. All human rights reports on Turkmenistan released by U.S. Department of State can be found at http://dosfan.lib.uic.edu/ERC/democracy.html.

46. For Kyrgyz GDP during this period, see appendix one.

47. On June 29, 2001, Kyrgyzstan's Finance Minister Temirbek Akmataliyev told a meeting of the State Commission on Foreign Aid and Investments that the country's foreign debt reached $2 billion, which was one-third higher than annual GDP. As of January 1, 2000, the country's total foreign debt was estimated at $1.76 billion. RFE/RL, July 2, 2001.

48. Available on the U.S. Department of State's website: www.state.gov/r/pa/ei/bgn/5755.htm.

49. Martha Brill Olcott, *Central Asia's New States* (Washington, DC: U.S. Institute of Peace Press, 1996), p. 102.

50. In May 1998, a Kumtor truck overturned on a mountain road and poured almost two tons of toxins into the Barskoon River, which flows to Lake Issyk Kul, causing several deaths from poisoning. Daphne Biliouri, "The Cyanide Spill in Kyrgyzstan: Measuring Civil Society Development," EurasiaNet.org, January 4, 2000, available at www.eurasianet.org/departments/environment/articles/eav120799.shtml.

51. Available at www.bisnis.doc.gov/BISNIS/COUNTRY/0110overviewch2_kg.htm.

52. For instance, production of meat fell from 254,100 tons in 1990 to 180,000 in 1995; and milk production fell from 1,185,000 tons in 1990 to 864,000 in 1995. International Monetary Fund, *Kyrgyz Republic: Recent Economic Development*, IMF Country Report no. 98/08 (Washington, DC: February 5, 1998). For instance, meat production was 71 percent lower in 1995 than 1990, and milk production 73 percent lower.

53. Sydykova was accused of libeling the president of the state gold company, Kyrgyzaltyn (Dastan Sarygulov, a relative of Akayev's wife) in a series of articles published between 1993 and 1996. She was appointed Ambassador to the United States after Akayev's ouster in March 2005.

54. See appendix twelve on political parties and elections in Central Asia. Akayev won his first presidency in October 1991 in uncontested elections. In the 1995 presidential elections, Akayev ran against former parliament speaker Medetken Sherimkulov and the Communist Party leader Absamat Masaliyev. In 2000, Akayev's opponents were Tursunbek Akunov, Almazbek Atambayev, Tursunbai Bakir Uulu, Melis Eshimkanov, and Omurbek Tekebaev.

55. Office for Democratic Institutions and Human Rights, Election Observation Mission, *Kyrgyz Republic: Parliamentary Elections, 20 February and 12 March 2000, Final Report* (Warsaw: Organization for Security and Cooperation in Europe, April 10, 2000).

56. Office for Democratic Institutions and Human Rights, Election Observation Mission, "Kyrgyz Presidential Election Fails International Standards," press release, Organization for Security and Cooperation in Europe, October 30, 2000.

57. Chinara Jakipova, "The Challenge of Governance in the Central Asian Countries (an Example of Kyrgyzstan)," paper prepared for the International Peace Academy conference on Security in Central Asia, July 2002 (Vienna).

58. Kulov was not released from prison until March 24, 2005, the day Askar Akayev was ousted, and shortly thereafter he had his earlier convictions lifted, which made him eligible to run for president in the June 2005 contest.

59. In 1999, 83 percent of Tajikistan's population lived below the national poverty line, but these statistics are based only on legal, declared income. World Bank and International Monetary Fund, *Poverty Reduction, Growth and Debt Sustainability in Low-Income CIS Countries* (Washington, DC: February 4, 2002), p. 9.

60. International Monetary Fund, "Republic of Tajikistan: Recent Economic Developments," IMF Staff Country Report No. 98/16 (Washington, DC: February 1998), p. 14.

61. The most extensive damage was in the Vakhsh and Bokhtar regions of Katlon oblast.

62. For details, see Nassim Jawad and Shahrbanou Tadjbakhsh, "Tajikistan: A Forgotten War" (Minority Rights Group, February 1995).

63. International Crisis Group, "Tajikistan: An Uncertain Peace," ICG Asia Report no. 30, (Brussels: December 24, 2001).

64. During the late Soviet era, the Uzbek Communist Party elite in Tashkent also dominated political life in the Osh oblast in Kyrgyzstan.

65. The most prominent of these were Akbar Turajonzade and Said Abdullo Nuri of the Islamic Renaissance Party.

66. Tajikistan reorganized its administrative districts. Khujand (formerly known as Leninabad) became Sughd of the Sughd *viloyati* in early 2000. Kulob was combined with Qurgan-Teppe and is now known as Katlon *viloyati*.

67. Muriel Atkin, "Tajikistan: Reform, Reaction, and Civil War," in *New States, New Politics: Building the Post-Soviet Nations*, ed. I. Bremmer and R. Taras (Cambridge, UK: Cambridge University Press, 1997), pp. 602–27.

68. For details, see "Politics of Compromise: The Tajikistan Peace Process," *Accord Report*, eds. Kamoludin Abdullaev and Catherine Barnes, no.10, March 2001, available at www.c-r.org/accord/tajik/accord10/index.shtml.

69. IMU fighters took eight Kyrgyz soldiers and four Japanese geologists hostage in August 1999; the latter are said to have been released only after a $2 million ransom was paid. The IMU returned the next summer and took more foreigners hostage, including four U.S. mountain climbers. See Mark Burgess, *In the Spotlight: Islamic Movement of Uzbekistan* (Washington, DC: Center for Defense Information, March 25, 2002), available at www.cdi.org/terrorism/imu.cfm.

70. Some seventy-three residents of Surkhan Darya were convicted in June 2001 of providing assistance to the IMU, receiving prison sentences ranging from three to eighteen years. EurasiaNet.org, February 14, 2004.

71. For details see appendix thirteen on religious groups in Central Asia.

72. The term *mahalla* broadly translates from Uzbek as neighborhood or local community, which much like today was used during the Soviet period as a tool for local control, through the appointment of a *mahalla* committee of approved elders.

73. Shukhrullo Mirsaidov was a chairman of the Council of Ministers of Uzbek SSR, and from November to January 1992 he served as vice president of Uzbekistan. Shortly after leaving the government, allegations of criminal behavior were made against him. In October 1995, Mirsaidov became a leader of the Democratic Opposition Coordinating Council. For a full profile see www.centrasia.ru/person.php4; and Human Rights Watch, *Human Rights Watch Report 1996* (New York: 1996), available at www.hrw.org/reports/1996/UZBEK.htm.

74. Salih took refuge in Turkey in late 1993. Abdurahim Pulot, cofounder of Birlik, left for the United States in November 1994 after having suffered a near fatal beating in Tashkent. See Olivier Roy, *The New Central Asia* (New York: New York University Press, 1997), pp. 132–3.

75. The most prominent of these were Abduhrali-qori Mirzoev of Andijan and Obid-qori Nazarov of Tashkent. Mirzoev is presumed dead, and Nazarov lives in exile. Martha Brill Olcott and Bakhtiar Babajanov, "The Roots of Radicalism in Central Asia," Carnegie Paper (forthcoming).

76. Following these arrests, IMU leader Tahir Yuldash began styling himself as a spiritual leader, despite his minimal formal training, while Juma Namangani ran the military operations.

77. Critics of President Karimov have repeatedly charged that Uzbek officials planned the bombing to demonstrate the existence of an Islamic threat. These charges have never been substantiated, but it is possible that certain Uzbek security officials collaborated with the IMU, given how close to key government buildings the bombers got.

78. Bureau of Democracy, Human Rights, and Labor, *Uzbekistan, Country Report on Human Rights Practices, 2001* (Washington, DC: U.S. Department of State, March 4, 2002), available at www.state.gov/g/drl/rls/hrrpt/2001/eur/8366.htm. See also Human Rights Watch, *Human Rights*

Watch World Report 2001: Uzbekistan (New York: 2001), available at www.hrw.org/wr2k1/europe/uzbekistan.html.

79. See Ahmed Rashid, *Jihad: The Rise of Militant Islam in Central Asia* (New Haven, CT: Yale University Press, 2002); International Crisis Group, *The IMU and the Hizb-ut Tahrir: Implications of the Afghanistan Campaign*, Central Asia Briefing (Osh and Brussels: January, 30, 2002).

80. RFE/RL NewsLine: Transcaucasia and Central Asia, October 5, 2000.

81. For instance, Uzbek exports to Kyrgyz Republic dropped from $102 million in 1994 to $51.2 million in 1998, while imports decreased from $68 million in 1994 to $19.2 million in 1997; Uzbek exports to Turkmenistan decreased from $174 million in 1994 to $41 million in 1998, and imports decreased from $144 million in 1994 to $10 million in 1998.

82. Small numbers of traders still took advantage of "holes" in the border, such as the stretch of road between Tashkent and Samarkand that passes through Kazakhstan, or the relatively lax Uzbek–Kazakh border on the road between Tashkent and Shymkent, to get goods into Uzbekistan's bazaars.

83. See appendix two for average annual growth rates of GDP in Uzbekistan.

84. In the early 1990s, agriculture accounted for 30 percent of Uzbekistan's GDP, and Uzbekistan was one of the world's five largest producers and exporters of cotton. For instance, cotton exports constituted 41 percent of total exports and 23 percent of total GDP in 1993 and 51 percent of total exports and 26.5 percent of total GDP in 1994.

Chapter Three

1. For a more detailed discussion of the geopolitics of the region during the first five years of independence, see Martha Brill Olcott, *Central Asia's New States* (Washington, DC: U.S. Institute of Peace Press, 1996), pp. 170–9.

2. Stalin deported the Koreans because he feared their potential disloyalty in the face of what he believed to be an impending Japanese invasion. According to the 1989 Soviet census, Uzbekistan had 183,100 Koreans, Kazakhstan had 100,739, Kyrgyzstan had 18,335, Tajikistan had 13,431, and Turkmenistan had 2,800.

3. Andrei Kozyrev served as foreign minister of Russia from 1992 to 1996.

4. The CIS was initially formed on December 8, 1991, by the presidents of Ukraine, Belarus, and Russia, but a second "founding meeting" was held in Almaty on December 21, 1991, at which membership was extended to the remaining eight Soviet republics: Azerbaijan, Armenia, Kazakhstan, Kyrgyzstan, Moldova, Tajikistan, Turkmenistan, and Uzbekistan. Georgia, which refused to join in 1991, decided to join in 1993. For details on its early history, see Martha Brill Olcott, Anders Åslund, and Sherman W. Garnett, eds., *Getting It Wrong* (Washington, DC: Carnegie Endowment for International Peace, 1999).

5. Georgia's first president was a longtime political dissident, Zviad Gamsakhurdia. Abulfaz Elchibey, elected as the president of Azerbaijan in 1992, had been the leader of the Popular Front Party and an activist in the struggle for Azerbaijan's independence.

6. The Russian-led population of the Transdniester region declared independence from Moldova in 1992. The struggle for control of the Karabakh region began in 1988 and became an all-out war in 1993 when Armenia with Russia's tacit support took control of Karabakh and

thus annexed 20 percent of Azerbaijan's territory. The war in Abkhazia broke out in August 1992 when Georgian troops occupied the capital of the independence-seeking region but were pushed back by Russian-supported terrorists, who took control of all of Abkhazia.

7. In the EAU, member states would adopt common policies at an intergovernmental assembly and share a common currency and mutually beneficial foreign economic policies. Each member state would have an equal vote, and decisions would require a four-fifths majority. See Olcott, Åslund, and Garnett, *Getting It Wrong*, p. 24.

8. For more on the customs union, see Olcott, Åslund, and Garnett, *Getting It Wrong*, pp. 170–2.

9. "Russia in Multi-Million Arms Deal with Northern Alliance," *Guardian* (London), October 23, 2001.

10. Russia forced the Kazakhs to accept charged down debt as rent ($115 million) per year for use of Baikonur, the Soviet space center near Leninsk, Kazakhstan. For details of this negotiation, see Martha Brill Olcott, *Kazakhstan: Unfulfilled Promise* (Washington, DC: Carnegie Endowment for International Peace, 2002), p. 45.

11. The Turkmen government owned the company, holding 51 percent of the stock, Gazprom (Russia) held 44 percent, and Itera International Energy Corporation (United States) held 5 percent.

12. Niyazov's concerns were not groundless. Former prime minister Saparmurat Soyunov has lived in Moscow since his dismissal, and Valery Otchertsov (former deputy prime minister of Turkmenistan) is the president of Itera Holding Ltd. (Russian division of Itera Group), a private company that was part of the Itera family that had been heavily involved in trading Turkmen gas.

13. Ukrainians bled off European supplies when their own needs were not being met, and Russia found Georgian debt a very convenient political tool.

14. Gas output was 81.9 billion cubic meters in 1990, 30.1 billion cubic meters in 1995, and 12.4 billion cubic meters in 1998. See James P. Dorian, "Turkmenistan's Future in Gas and Oil Hinges on Certainty for Export Options," *Oil & Gas Journal*, October 12, 2002.

15. For more details, see Martha Brill Olcott and Natalia Udalova, "Drug Trafficking on the Great Silk Road: The Security Environment in Central Asia," Carnegie Working Paper no. 11 (Washington, DC: Carnegie Endowment for International Peace, March 2000).

16. The Kazakh–Chinese and Kyrgyz–Chinese borders were patrolled by Russian border guards from 1992 to 1995 and then by joint forces until 1998. The Russians also patrolled the Turkmen–Iranian border by treaty until 1995 and were said to remain in place afterward.

17. For a while the lobby centered around Vladimir Zhirinovsky. It also included Alexei Mitrofanov and Konstantin Zatulin and Zatulin's Institute of the Commonwealth Countries.

18. The peak years of emigration were the mid-1990s when 75 percent of the total five million Russians from the CIS countries were reported to have left Central Asia and the Caucasus. See International Organization for Migration, "World Migration 2003: Managing Migration Challenges and Responses for People on the Move," IOM World Migration Report Series, vol. 2 (Geneva: 2003), p. 43.

19. Twenty-two were arrested, including twelve Russian citizens. The Kazakhs claimed that the leader, Victor Kazimirchuck of the Rus patriotic movement, was planning to conduct terrorist acts. For more information, see Olcott, *Kazakhstan: Unfulfilled Promise*, pp. 79–80.

20. The Central Bank of Russia decided to withdraw old ruble notes from circulation on July 26, 1993. See U.S. Department of State, *Russia Economic Policy and Trade Practices* (Washington, D.C.: February 1994).

21. This process has not always been a smooth one. Azerbaijan and Turkmenistan both claim ownership of the Serdar–Kyapaz field; and Turkmenistan claims portions of Azerbaijan's Azeri and Chirac fields as well. See Energy Information Administration, "EIA Country Analysis: Caspian Sea Region, July 31, 2002," quoted in *Alexander's Gas and Oil Connections*, News & Trends: Central Asia, vol. 7, no. 16 (August 23, 2002).

22. These agreements were largely negotiated before September 11, although the protocol between Russia and Kazakhstan on the equal division of three oil fields in the northern Caspian (Kurmangazy, Tsentralnoye, and Khvalynskoe) was not signed until May 2002. Each country has a 50-percent stake in developing the deposits. The protocol also defined the median line dividing the two countries' respective sectors of the Caspian Sea. This augmented the 1998 agreement, under which Kurmangazy was in Kazakhstan's sector of the Caspian and the other two fields were in the Russian sector. See *Financial Times*, April 27, 2002; and *Kazakhstan Daily Digest*, Eurasianet.org, May 14, 2002.

23. Kazakh President Nazarbayev visited China in October 1993, September 1995, February 1997, and November 1999; Kyrgyz President Akayev, in 1998 and 2002; Tajik President Rakhmonov, in August 1999, and Tajik Foreign Minister Talbak Nazarov, in June 2001; Uzbekistan President Karimov, in October 1994 and June 2001 (for the Shanghai Summit of Five); and former Turkmen Foreign Minister Shikhmuradov served as ambassador to China from March to November 2001.

24. The intergovernmental agreements include those on trade and economic cooperation, further development of cultural links, and humanitarian assistance. FBIS-SOV-94-080, April 26, 1994.

25. Chinese President Zhiang Zemin also visited Kazakhstan, Kyrgyzstan, and Uzbekistan in July 1996. RFE/RL NewsLine, July 3, 1996.

26. There were large demonstrations in China organized by the Islamic Party of Eastern Turkestan in 1985, in 1989, and again in April 1990. R. Israeli, "A New Wave of Muslim Revivalism in Mainland China," *Issues and Studies*, vol. 33, no. 3 (March 1997), p. 30. For a history of the complicated relationship between Moscow and Muslim separatists in China, see Martha Brill Olcott, "Russian-Chinese Relations and Central Asia," in *Rapprochement or Rivalry? Russia–China Relations in a Changing Asia*, ed. Sherman Garnett (Washington, DC: Carnegie Endowment for International Peace, 2000), p. 371–400.

27. Nine people died and seventy-four were injured. Then in March, a Uighur separatist group, called Eastern Turkestan Liberation Organization–Feddayin of Beijing claimed responsibility for two bombings in Beijing.

28. These rumors began circulating after a series of Islamist groups gathered at a London meeting sponsored by the Syrian-based Harakat al-Mujaharin (the Emigrants Movement) to talk about supporting a *jihad* in China. See Al-Watan Arabi, Paris, May 23, 1997, FBIS-NES-97-102. I have credited it as being true, having found translated Arabic language material in support of this while researching a 1997 article. See Olcott, "Russian-Chinese Relations and Central Asia," in Sherman W. Garnett, ed., *Rapprochement or Rivalry? Russia-China Relations in a Changing Asia* (Carnegie: 2000), p. 384.

29. The SCO was known as the Shanghai Five until its membership was expanded in 2001 to include Uzbekistan, and its organization was a side benefit of the 1996 five-state agreement.

30. The Kazakh and Chinese governments have signed several agreements designed to regularize border arrangements prior to April 1996.

31. According to the agreement, Kazakhstan retained 442 square kilometers in the Zurek Mountains and in the Chogan-Obo River valley and 442 square kilometers in Keregentas. The Chinese border will be moved 187 square kilometers further out. As a result, Kazakhstan retained 56.9 percent of the disputed territory and China retained 43.1 percent. "Kazakhstan Parliament Ratifies Border Agreement with China," Moscow Interfax (in English 1403 GMT), February 3, 1999.

32. The Kazakhstan parliamentary ratification took place in February (by the Majilis) and March (by the Senate) of 1999. The treaty was formally signed at a meeting of foreign ministers held by the Kazakhs and the Chinese on May 10, 2002. In July 2003, President Nazarbayev signed the law, which was approved by Parliament. In May 2002, the Kyrgyz parliament also ratified the Kyrgyz treaty with China. See Necati Polat, *Boundary Issues in Central Asia* (New York: Transnational Publishers, 2002); and "Kazakhstan Ratifies Protocol on Border with China," Interfax News Agency, July 9, 2003.

33. Interview with Azimbek Beknazarov, in Bishkek, Kyrgyzstan, November 2002.

34. Sadji, "An Early Defeat for President Akaev," *Prism*, vol. VIII, no. 4, pt. 4 (April 2002).

35. U.S.-based Access Industries took control of the Kazakh government shares in 2001, in part because of the difficulty that the Kazakh government was having in working with the Chinese in managing the project. In 2003 these shares were restored to the Kazakh government.

36. Interfax, *Central Asia and Caucasus Business Report*, vol. 5, no.16 (April 15–21, 2002).

37. Storage facilities are particularly critical because the Central Asian countries still use a rail gauge different from the standard in most of Europe and Asia, requiring the wheels to be changed or containers reloaded. The absence of storage facilities also crippled the new rail link between Tedjen (Turkmenistan) and Meshed (Iran) on the Turkmen–Iranian border. The latter includes a border crossing at Serakhs, which was opened in May 1996.

38. The Druzhba facilities handled 3.5 million tons of freight in 1999, 5 million tons in 2000, and over 6 million tons in 2001. See Kazakh railways website: www.railways.kz/transit/eng.asp.

39. Traceca envisions the acceleration of free exchange of goods between Europe and Asia and was signed by eight states in 1993 when the borders to Eastern Europe were opened. In the meantime, Traceca consists of thirteen member states: Armenia, Azerbaijan, Bulgaria, Georgia, Kazakhstan, Kyrgyzstan, Moldova, Rumania, Tajikistan, Turkey, Turkmenistan, Ukraine, and Uzbekistan.

40. "Traffic in transit" begins in Almaty (Kazakhstan), goes through Bishkek (Kyrgyzstan) to Kashgar (China), and then on to Khunjera Pass (Pakistan). The total length of the road system is approximately 3,000 kilometers.

41. FREEDOM (Freedom for Russia and Emerging Eurasian Democracies and Open Markets), or the Freedom Support Act, was signed into law on October 25, 1992, endorsing "a range of programs to support free market and democratic reforms being undertaken in Russia, Ukraine, Armenia, and other states of the former Soviet Union."

42. Prior to September 2001, President Nazarbayev made official visits to the United States in 1992, 1994, and twice in 1999. President Akayev came officially in 1993 and unofficially

several times. President Rakhmonov visited in 1999, and President Niyazov came in 1993 but was not received in the White House until 1997. President Karimov traveled to the United Nations twice (1993 and 1995), inaugurated the Uzbek Embassy in Washington on a private visit in 1996, and visited the White House for the first time at the NATO fiftieth anniversary celebrations in April 1999.

43. For the text of this speech, see www.state.gov/www/regions/nis/970721talbott.html.

44. President Bill Clinton used the diplomatically important phrases "multiple pipelines" and "action plan" at a signing ceremony for the Baku-Ceyhan and Trans-Caspian Gas Pipeline protocol. His remarks are available at www.useu.be/ISSUES/casp1118.html.

45. Although for a while it looked as if the Clinton administration might be amenable to a softer attitude toward Tehran, by 1997 it was clear that the U.S. government was unwilling to modify the ILSA (Iran-Libya Sanctions Act), which was adopted in July 23, 1996, and renewed in July 2001. These sanctions effectively barred U.S. firms from shipping Caspian oil and gas through Iran.

46. See appendix eight on major natural resource projects in Central Asia.

47 The author met Giffen at a closed briefing session for newly appointed U.S. Ambassador to Kazakhstan, A. Elizabeth Jones (1995–1998). In fact the ties between Giffen and the government were so close that Giffen claimed that he was a major Central Intelligence Agency asset and should be exempt from prosecution for that reason, a defense that the court rejected.

48. Alexander M. Haig Jr. arrived in Turkmenistan in 1992. He subsequently became President Niyazov's close confidant and helped to arrange his visit to Washington to lobby for increased U.S. investment in Turkmenistan in 1993. David B. Ottaway and Dan Morgan, "Gas Pipeline Bounces between Agendas," *Washington Post*, October 5, 1998, p. A1.

49. Boris Shikhmuradov held various positions in the foreign service of the Soviet Union and later Turkmenistan. He served as deputy foreign minister (1992–1995) and as foreign minister of Turkmenistan (1995–2000). In July 2000 he was appointed Niyazov's special envoy on Caspian affairs to broker peace in Afghanistan. In March 2001, he was appointed ambassador to China. Shikhmuradov left the government and joined the opposition in November 2001.

50. The United States sent cruise missiles to destroy Al Qaeda camps near Khost. See www.cnn.com/US/9808/20/clinton.02/index.html.

51. See Unocal news release available at www.unocal.com/uclnews/98news/082198.htm. The Asian Development Bank in 2005 surprised observers with an announcement that it believed the Trans-Afghan pipeline to be commercially feasible.

52. Bruce Pannier and Zamira Echanova, "Uzbekistan: U.S. Signs Security Agreements in Tashkent," RFE/RL, May 26, 1999.

53. Since Kazakhstan renounced nuclear weapons in 1993, the United States has provided $188 million in assistance. According to the State Department, in 1994, Kazakhstan transferred more than a half-ton of weapons-grade uranium to the United States. See www.state.gov/r/pa/ei/bgn/5487.htm.

54. This program was renewed in May 2002, because Kazakhstan still has six intercontinental ballistic missile (ICBM) silos located at a test range in Leninsk (near Baikonur) in the south of the country. "Kazakh Parliament Prolongs Agreement with U.S. on Destroying Missile Silos," RFE/RL NewsLine, May 17, 2002.

55. Kazakhstan joined the PFP in May 1994, Kyrgyzstan joined in June 1994, Turkmenistan joined in May 1994, and Uzbekistan joined in July 1994. Tajikistan did not join until February 2002.

56. Ambassador Stephen Sestanovich, the State Department special envoy for the Newly Independent States, made this statement at the conclusion of the May 1999 meeting of the U.S.–Uzbek joint commission. See Bruce Pannier and Zamira Echanova, "U.S. Signs Security Agreements with Uzbekistan," RFE/RL, reprinted in Asia Times Online, May 28, 1999, available at www.atimes.com/c-asia/AE28Ag01.html.

57. According to Ted Bridis and John Solomon, eleven drones were sent in during September and October 2000, but the use of drones was discontinued by President George Bush. See the Associated Press, *Washington Dateline*, June 25, 2003.

58. *BBC Monitor*, August 19, 2001, and August 20, 2001.

59. Thousands of Central Asians received scholarships to attend schools of the Nursi movement, which were also opened in Uzbekistan, Kazakhstan, and Kyrgyzstan. These schools were based on a model developed by Fethullah Gullen, a disciple of Said Nursi (1873-1960) who was committed to the goal of Islamization of the spirit and the reinforcement of faith through education, as a means of eventually achieving the Islamization of the state. For details see Bayram Balci, "Fethullah Gullen's Missionary Schools in Central Asia and their Role in the Spreading of Turkism and Islam," *Religion, State and Society*, vol. 31, no. 2 (2003), pp.151–74.

60. The change of alphabet is for the national languages; Russian continues to be written in Cyrillic. The Kyrgyz, Kazakhs, Uzbeks, and Turkmen have all made the switch. The Tajiks have reintroduced the Persian (Arabic) alphabet, with the support of the Iranians.

61. The Twelvers believe that the leadership of the Muslim community rightfully belongs to the descendants of Ali, the son-in-law of the Prophet, through Ali's son Husain. There were twelve such rightful rulers, known as imams, the last of whom, according to the Twelvers, did not die but went into hiding in the ninth century, to return in the fullness of time as the messiah (mahdi) to create the just and perfect Muslim society.

62. Iranian textbooks are more easily adapted to immediate use than the Turkish ones, as written Tajik and Persian are virtually interchangeable, whereas only Turkmen is in the same Turkic-language grouping as Istanbul Turkish.

63. Martha Brill Olcott, *Turkmenistan: Challenges in the Transport of Turkmen Gas* (Stanford, CA: Stanford University Program on Energy and Sustainable Development, May 2004), p. 13.

64. Indian Prime Minister Narasimha Rao made an official trip to Kazakhstan in May 1993; Indian Foreign Minister Salman Hurshid visited Kazakhstan in June 1994; Indian Minister of Oil and Gas V. Ramamurati visited Kazakhstan on March 30, 1999; and Indian Foreign Minister Omar Abdulla visited Uzbekistan in September 17, 2001.

65. Originally called Regional Cooperation for Development, ECO was founded in 1965 by Iran, Pakistan, and Turkey and was later renamed ECO in 1985. The organization extended its membership to Afghanistan, Azerbaijan, and all the Central Asian republics in 1992. The group's general goal is to integrate the Muslim states of the region into a European Union–type structure. For more information, see Olcott, Åslund, and Garnett, *Getting It Wrong*, pp. 191–3.

66. Kyrgyzstan, Tajikistan, and Turkmenistan joined the 56-member ICO in 1992, Kazakhstan in 1995, and Uzbekistan in 1996. Available at www.oic-oci.org.

67. President Nazarbayev visited Saudi Arabia in September 1994. During his trip, he met with King Fahd bin Abdel Aziz. Rakhmonov's trip to Saudi Arabia took place in July 1997, and

he also discussed Saudi–Tajik cooperation with King Fahd. Both presidents attended Mecca to make the *umra* ("little" *Hajj*, or pilgrimage). RFE/RL Newsline, July 2, 1997.

68. Kyrgyzstan President Akayev was the first among the Central Asian leaders to travel to Israel in 1993. Kazakhstan's Nazarbayev visited the country in December 1995, and Uzbek President Karimov traveled there in September 1998. "Israel Emerges as a Player in Central Asia," EurasiaNet.org, August 15, 2001.

69. "Turkmenistan: President Signals New Gas Export Strategy," *RFE/RL Magazine*, April 27, 1998.

70. Some U.S. congressional leaders active in U.S.-Jewish community organizations have served as a pro-Kazakhstan lobbying force. See "Wexler to Travel to Kazakhstan," press release from the Office of Congressman Robert Wexler (D-FL), May 24, 2002.

71. In addition to the EBRD, the European Union provided the Central Asian countries with assistance through the TACIS program: €4,226 million were committed between 1991 and 1999, and €3,138 million will be given out between 2000 and 2006. See http://europa.eu.int/comm/external_relations/ceeca/.

72. "Kyrgyzstan: Militants Test Regional Security," RFE/RL, August 31, 1999.

73. According to the 1989 Soviet census, there were 946,855 ethnic Germans living in Kazakhstan and 101,198 living in Kyrgyzstan.

74. ADB has a total of seventeen projects to improve transport and communications in Central Asian countries, including those that involve rehabilitation and modernization of existing routes, and development of new ones. More details on ADB's projects available on its website: www.abd.org.

75. See appendix nine on major energy projects in Central Asia.

76. See U.S. Department of State, *Overview of Uzbekistan's Mining Industry* (Washington, DC: December 16, 1998).

Chapter Four

1. See Nancy Lubin, *Calming the Ferghana Valley: Development and Dialogue in the Heart of Central Asia* (New York: Century Foundation Press, 1999). Also see the International Crisis Group's ICG Asia Reports, nos. 7, 14, 16, 20, 21, 22, and 38, which concern Central Asia, available at www.crisisgroup.com.

2. For details on economic reforms in Kazakhstan and Kyrgyzstan, see various International Monetary Fund publications, including IMF Staff Country Reports and IMF Working Papers, available at www.imf.org.

3. A diversity of opinion in the United States on the possibility of reform in Central Asia is reflected in the congressional testimonies in the late 1990s and early 2000. By and large, representatives of the U.S. Agency for International Development (USAID) appeared optimistic about reforms in Central Asia, specifically, looking at the achievements of the USAID programs, although the unevenness of reforms and challenges of their implementation were also recognized. Meanwhile, some human rights activists (Cassandra Cavanaugh from Human Rights Watch), journalists (Paul Goble from RFE/RL), and scholars (including this author and Nancy Lubin from JNA Associates) were less assured about reform successes because of the

authoritarian nature of the Central Asian leadership and the continued U.S. disregard of the problems. For details, see the testimonies given by them and others before the House and Senate foreign relations committees between 1997 and 2000.

4. Cheryl Gray, Joel Hellman, and Randi Ryterman, "Anticorruption in Transition 2, Corruption in Enterprise-State Interactions in Europe and Central Asia 1999–2002" (Washington, DC: World Bank, 2002).

5. For Kazakhstan's economic growth rates, see appendix seven. For data on per capita income, see the World Bank's *World Development Report 2005: A Better Investment Climate for Everyone*, Selected World Development Indicators (New York: Oxford University Press, 2004).

6. Local currency, the tenge, was introduced in November 1993. The weighted average exchange rate on the Kazakhstan Stock Exchange was 78 tenge per U.S. dollar in 1998, 112 tenge in 1999, 142 tenge in 2000, 146 tenge in 2001, 153 tenge in 2002, and about 132 tenge as of November 2004. International Monetary Fund, "Republic of Kazakhstan: Selected Issues and Statistical Appendix," IMF Country Report no. 03-211 (Washington, DC: July 2003); and Interfax, March 16, 2004.

7. Kazakhstan's National Bank enjoys a B rating (rating information available at www.kase.kz/eng/kasemembers/). From 2000 until early 2004, the National Bank was headed by a strong reformer, Grigory Marchenko, who earlier served as head of the stock exchange and was responsible for the country's first pension reform. The quality of the banking sector has improved since 1995 when Marchenko introduced a consolidation program. Economist Intelligence Unit, *Country Profile 2003*. The rankings for the "Top 1,000 World Banks" are based on tier one capital as defined by the Bank for International Settlements (BIS). This includes common stock, disclosed reserves, and retained earnings. Available at http://en.kkb.kz.

8. For further details on Kazakhstan's private and state-owned banking structure see Svetlana Voronina, "How Do Companies in Eurasia Finance Their Trade/Investment Deals?" BIS-NIS Finance Survey, Kazakhstan, available at www.bisnis.doc.gov/BISNIS/fq2004/surveys/FinanceSurveyKazakhstan2004.htm.

9. International Monetary Fund, "Republic of Kazakhstan: Selected Issues and Statistical Appendix" (Washington, DC: July 6, 2004), p. 14.

10. The Kazakhstan Stock Exchange (KASE) is primarily an organized place for trade in government securities (81.4 percent of total turnover in 2002), foreign exchange (12.1 percent), and corporate securities (3.1 percent). In 2002 the total KASE turnover amounted to $24.6 billion. See International Monetary Fund, IMF Country Report no. 03/211, p. 61. The equity capitalization was $3.7 billion, the bond capitalization was $4.3 billion, and 1.3 million shares were traded daily. For general information, see www.kase.kz/eng/geninfo/.

11. Economist Intelligence Unit, *Country Profile 2004*, p. 30; and Interfax September 16, 2003.

12. Tasmagambetov was replaced on June 13, 2003, by Daniyal Akhmetov, who pushed through passage of the law.

13. The highest marginal tax rate for individuals and corporations is 30 percent. Economist Intelligence Unit, *Country Profile 2003*.

14. Kazakh pension plans are divided into private pension funds (PPFs) and state pension fund (SPFs), and all are closed joint stock companies. See also Martha Brill Olcott, *Kazakhstan: Unfulfilled Promise* (Washington, DC: Carnegie Endowment for International Peace, 2002), pp. 141–2.

15. Figures for 2003 taken from Interfax, February 2, 2003. The general government budget recorded a surplus equivalent to 0.02 percent of GDP in 2002, compared with a deficit of 0.40 percent of GDP in 2001. See Asian Development Bank, *Annual Report 2002: East and Central Asia* (Manila: 2002), available at www.adb.org/documents/reports/annual_report/2002/kaz.asp. In 2003, the national budget deficit amounted to 40.3 billion tenge, or 0.9 percent of GDP. The budget for 2004 was adopted with a surplus of 92.7 billion tenge, or 1.9 percent of GDP. Interfax Central Asia, February 13, 17, 2004, and March 12, 2004.

16. The Kazakhstan Finance Ministry calculates that GDP in Kazakhstan grew 140.1 percent from 1995 to 2002, controlling for inflation, and the value of the GDP has more than tripled from 1 trillion tenge to 3.7 trillion tenge. In 2003, GDP grew at a 9.2 percent clip to 4.4 trillion tenge. Interfax Central Asia, February 13, 2004.

17. International Monetary Fund, "Republic of Kazakhstan: 2004 Article IV Consultation," IMF Country Report no. 04/339 (Washington, DC: October 28, 2004).

18. According to Kazakhstan's Finance Minister Zeinolla Kakimzhanov, manufacturing accounted for 15 percent of the state budget in 2002; trade and miscellaneous services for 12.9 percent; transportation and communication for 12.2 percent; mining for 7.1 percent; and other sectors for 22.6 percent. These data were presented in a speech at the EBRD annual meeting held in Tashkent in May 2003. Overall industrial output growth in 2004 was stimulated by increased production in the country's mining industry (12.8 percent), processing industry (7.8 percent), and in the production and distribution of electricity, gas, and water (4.4 percent). See International Monetary Fund, IMF Country Report no. 04/339; and Interfax Central Asia, September 6–12, 2004.

19. Energy Information Administration, *Country Analysis Briefs: Kazakhstan* (Washington, DC: U.S. Department of Energy, 2004), available at www.eia.doe.gov/emeu/cabs/kazak.html.

20. Interfax, *Central Asia and Caucasus Business Report*, December 9, 2002. From 1993 to 2003, total foreign direct investment in the Kazakh economy amounted to $25.8 billion. The main investors in the last decade were the United States, Great Britain, Italy, South Korea, and Switzerland. Interfax Central Asia, February 17, 2004; and Interfax Central Asia, September 13–19, 2004.

21. Dinara Sarsenova, "Program to Develop Kazakh Sector of the Caspian Shelf Presented," *Times of Central Asia*, July 16, 2003.

22. RFE/RL, "Focus on Kazakhstan's New Hydrocarbon Behemoth," *Central Asia Report*, vol. 2, no. 8 (February 28, 2002), available at www.rferl.org/centralasia/2002/02/8-280202.asp.

23. *RFE/RL Newsline: Transcaucasia and Central Asia*, vol. 7, no. 48 (March 13, 2003), available at www.rferl.org/newsline/2003/03/2-TCA/tca-130303.asp.

24. The Baku-Tbilisi-Ceyhan pipeline will stretch 1,767 kilometers: 443 kilometers through Azerbaijan, 248 kilometers through Georgia, and 1,076 kilometers through Turkey. The cost of the project is estimated at $2.95 billion. Interfax report, September 23, 2003.

25. In January 2003, the consortium companies agreed to pay Kazakhstan $810 million over the next three years. Steve LeVine, "Oil Companies Settle Flap with Kazakhstan," *Wall Street Journal*, January 29, 2003, p. A16. On September 19, 2003, the shareholders in TengizChevroil signed a formal agreement governing the $3-billion second phase of the project's development. Zaure Kistauova, "Kazakh Tengizchevroil Partners Sign Second Phase Development," Deal Dow Jones Newswire, September 19, 2003.

26. "Kashagan Developer to Pay $150 mln to Kazakhstan Imminently," *525thenewspaper* (Azerbaijan online newspaper), no. 58(1664), March 26, 2004, available at www.525ci.com/2004/03/26/readen.php?m=9&id=13; and Bagila Bukharbayeva, "Kazakh National Oil Company to Pursue More Aggressive Policy to Expand Market Presence," Associated Press, February 23, 2004.

27. Further development phases will raise production to 1.2 million barrels per day. "ExxonMobil Confirms Approval of Kashagan Development Plan," Scandinavian Oil and Gas Magazine, February 26, 2004, available at www.scandoil.com/moxie/news/world_news-/exxonmobil-confirms-appro.shtml.

28. Interviews by author in Almaty in June 2004. See "Kazakhstan's Government to Buy out Part of BG's Stake in Kashagan Project," *RosBusinessConsulting*, March 14, 2005, available at www.rbcnews.com/free/2005314125341.shtml.

29. The second phase of the project, costing $3.5 billion, was completed in August 2003. It involved raising annual liquid hydrocarbon production to 7 million tons and building the Karachaganak Gas Processing Plant, which is designed to process the hydrocarbons. A 650-kilometer pipeline for transportation of liquid hydrocarbons from Karachaganak to Atyrau was launched on the same date. See LUKoil's website: www.lukoil.com/static.asp?id=76 and Alexander's Gas and Oil Connections website: www.gasandoil.com/goc/company/cnc24884.htm.

30. "Kazkommerts Securities," p. 22. The gas field is developed by the British–Italian–U.S.–Russian consortium. See also *Kazakhstan Daily Digest*, EurasiaNet.org, October 31, 2001.

31. International Monetary Fund, "Republic of Kazakhstan: Selected Issues," IMF Country Report no. 04/362 (Washington, DC: November 15, 2004), p.21.

32. Kazakhstan sells gas for around $40 per thousand cubic meters, and the cost recovery price is around $20 per thousand cubic meters. See Economist Intelligence Unit, *EIU ViewsWire*, September 7, 2004.

33. Government of Kazakhstan, "The Innovative Industrial Development Strategy of the Republic of Kazakhstan for 2003-2015" (Astana: 2003); Aggregate Net Resource Flows, Table 2, World Bank, *Report on Global Development Finance 2002* (Washington, DC: 2002).

34. Initially twelve firms were required to turn over their tax revenues to the fund: Aktobemunaigaz Corporation, TengizChevroil Joint Venture, L.L.P., Kazzinc Corporation, Karachaganak Petroleum Operating, B.V., Kazakhmys Corporation, Hurricane Kumkol Munai Corporation, Turgai Petroleum Limited Partnership, Mangistaumunaigas Corporation, Uzenmunaigaz Corporation, and OJSC Karazhanbasmunai. Firms can be added or removed from the list by decision of the government. Open Society Institute, "Caspian Oil Windfalls: Who Will Benefit?" *Caspian Revenue Watch* (New York: 2003), p. 146.

35. Economist Intelligence Unit, *Country Profile for Kazakhstan* (London: August 12, 2003).

36. See discussion of the scandal surrounding James Giffen's role in Kazakhstan's oil industry in chapter two of this volume.

37. Some speculate that Tasmagambetov was appointed to contain the damage from the scandal. Gazeta.kz reported that while addressing parliament on April 4, 2002, he admitted that a secret foreign bank account was established in 1996 containing some $1 billion that the Kazakh government received from the sale of a 20-percent stake in the vast Tengiz oil field.

Eurasia Policy Forum, EurasiaNet.org, May 5, 2002, available at www.eurasianet.org/ policy_forum/crw_news_archiveapril.shtml.

38. RFE/RL, April 18 2002.

39. The Kazakhstan government's Innovative Industrial Development Strategy for 2003–2015 was drafted based on Nazarbayev's address titled "On the Current Situation in the Country and on the Main Trends of Internal and External Policies for 2002" and on discussions at the tenth Forum of Entrepreneurs of Kazakhstan.

40. The Law of the Republic of Kazakhstan no. 373-II "On Investments" of January 8, 2003, was published on January 11, 2003, in *Kazakhstanskaya Pravda* and became effective from January 22, 2003. The new law equalizes the rights of foreign and domestic investors, repealing the 1994 law "On Foreign Investments" and the 1997 law "On State Support for Direct Investments."

41. International Monetary Fund, IMF Country Report no. 03/211, pp. 49–52.

42. In October, Mittal announced that it would acquire U.S.-based LMN Steel for $17.8 billion. See http://msnbc.msn.com/id/6326993/.

43. Tractebel, the Belgian energy group, had acquired a twenty-year concession for Almaty Energy in August 1996, but sold it to KazTransGaz in 2000 for a fraction of its original estimated worth. AES Corporation, an American firm, tried to benefit from Tractebel's problems. The Texas-based AES also bought into Kazakhstan's power sector in 1996 and has had a difficult time managing this investment. *Caspian World News*, August 27, 2003; and Olcott, *Kazakhstan: Unfulfilled Promise*, pp. 164–5.

44. In 2003, $8.4 billion in mineral products were exported. Kazakhstan's main exports are oil products, base metals, food and agricultural goods, and chemicals, while its main imports are machinery, chemicals, and food. Economist Intelligence Unit, *Country Profile 2004*, p. 50.

45. International Monetary Fund, IMF Country Report no. 04/339, pp.16–7.

46. World Bank, *World Development Indicators 2004* (Washington, DC: 2004). The Gini coefficient is a number between 0 and 1, where 0 corresponds with perfect equality (where everyone has the same income) and 1 corresponds with perfect inequality (where one person has all the income, and everyone else has zero income). The Gini index is the Gini coefficient expressed in percentage form, and is equal to the Gini coefficient multiplied by 100.

47. Swiss Agency for Development and Cooperation, *FAST Update, Kazakhstan, Quarterly Risk Assessment (May to July 2003)* (Bern: 2003), p. 5.

48. UN Development Program, *Human Development Report—Kazakhstan: Rural Development in Kazakhstan: Challenges and Prospects* (New York: 2002).

49. The investments by Petronas, Maersk Oil, Dragon Oil, Burren Energy Ltd., and Maitro International Ltd. amount to over $800 million since 1996. John C. K. Daly, *UPI Energy Watch*, United Press International, August 12, 2004.

50. This practice is especially applied in petroleum and textile sectors but only at the last stage of project approval. In addition, all foreign investment must be approved by the State Agency for Foreign Investment.

51. The loans were for the Urban Transport Project, the Water Supply and Sanitation Project, and the Institution-Building Technical Assistance Project and were supposed to be repayable in twenty years, including a five-year grace period, at the Bank's standard rate for the LIBOR-based single currency loans. Turkmenistan's failure to report its external debt is a vio-

lation of the Bank's negative pledge clause, and Turkmenistan does not meet the Bank's minimum public resource management standards.

52. European Bank for Reconstruction and Development, *Strategy for Turkmenistan* (London: June 23, 2004), p. 1.

53. Economist Intelligence Unit, *Country Profile 2002* (London: 2002) and Institute for War and Peace Reporting, "Turkmenbashi Wields the Axe," no. 356, March 11, 2005, available at www.iwpr.net/index.pl?archive/rca2/rca2_356_3_eng.txt.

54. Economist Intelligence Unit, *Country Profile 2002;* European Bank for Reconstruction and Development, *Strategy for Turkmenistan.*

55. "RFE/RL: Report Says Turkmen President Orders Closure of Hospitals, Libraries," available at http://www.eurasianet.org/resource/turkmenistan/hypermail/200502/0008.shtml

56. European Bank for Reconstruction and Development, *Strategy for Turkmenistan*, p. 23.

57. European Bank for Reconstruction and Development, *Strategy for Turkmenistan*, p. 17. The transition indicator index measures small-scale privatization, price liberalization, trade and foreign exchange system, large-scale privatization, governance, enterprise restructuring, competition policy, banking reform, and the securities market.

58. Gazprom chief operating officer Alexei Miller told journalists that this payment arrangement would be in place until 2006. From 2007 forward, Russia and Turkmenistan would then change over to payment for gas at world prices or using a payment formula similar to that used in contracts with Western partners, which is tied to the oil product basket. The agreement calls for Turkmenistan to provide Russia with 2 trillion cubic meters of gas over twenty-five years. Interfax, April 10, 2003.

59. The bartered goods also include the cost of technical assistance provided by Gazprom, and trade as well as the provision of technical assistance is managed by companies affiliated with Gazprom.

60. Under the long-term agreement, Turkmenistan was scheduled to deliver a relatively modest 6-7 billion cubic meters of gas to Russia in 2005. However, the deliveries are due to rise to 10 billion cubic meters in 2006 and to jump to 60-70 billion cubic meters in 2007. It is only for deliveries from 2007 onward that the price is subject to renegotiation. Gazprom counts on cheap Turkmen gas for ensuring windfall profits for Russia. It uses cheap Turkmen gas to supply certain Russian regions, releasing corresponding volumes of Russian gas for sale at high prices in Europe, and, increasingly, reselling Turkmen gas as Russian gas with a high mark-up in Europe. For more, see Vladimir Socor, "Niyazov Unbending on Gas Prices to Russia and Ukraine," Eurasia Daily Monitor, March 24, 2005, www.jamestown.org/edm/article.php?article_id=2369474.

61. International Energy Agency, *Caspian Oil and Gas* (Paris: 1998), pp. 255–7.

62. The author has received two different eyewitness accounts of these cash-for-fuel exchanges.

63. In the first six months of 2004 alone, President Niyazov authorized $4.5 billion in construction projects. International Crisis Group, "Repression and Regression in Turkmenistan: A New International Strategy," ICG Asia Report no. 85 (Brussels: November 4, 2004).

64. Esenov now lives in Sweden, having been deported from Russia in 1994 for allegedly planning a coup against Niyazov. See International Crisis Group, "Repression and Regression in Turkmenistan," p. 18.

65. See Energy Intelligence Group, "Turkmenistan: Seidi Refinery Set for $1 Billion Facelift," *Nefte Compass*, March 23, 2004; and Dun's 100, Israel's Largest Enterprises 2004, available at http://duns100.dundb.co.il/600057061/. Also see Amangeldy Esenov, "Turetski biznesmen Ahmed Calyk–'sery kardinal' turkmenskoi politiki," September 29, 2003, available at www.dogryyol.com/article/3729.html; and "Largest Textile Factory to Be Built in Ashgabat," ITAR-TASS News Agency, October 21, 2003.

66. The total capacity of the lake will be about 140 billion cubic meters, and it will increase irrigated land areas from the present 1.8 million hectares to 2.24 million hectares in the future. The annual intake of the lake will be some 10 billion cubic meters, which will flow from all regions of Turkmenistan. The lake, estimated to cost $4.5 billion, will be completed within the next twenty years. *Turkmenistan Daily Digest*, EurasiaNet.org, May 8, 2003.

67. See Unocal website: www.unocal.com/uclnews/97news/102797a.htm.

68. Turkmenistan has two refineries: one at Turkmenbashi that produces 116,500 bbl per day and the other at Seidi that produces 120,500 bbl per day (note that bbl stands for "blue barrel," the 42-gallon barrel that came to be the standard for oil trade). The Turkmenbashi refinery has been upgraded and modernized at the cost of $1.4 billion with financing from German and Japanese sources. Technip of France was awarded a contract to build a lubricants blending plant with a capacity of 36,150 bbl per day to be completed in 2004. Energy Information Administration, *Report on Turkmenistan Energy Sector* (Washington, DC: U.S. Department of Energy, May 2002).

69. A good example is Toily Kurbanov, a young economist who briefly headed Turkmenistan's energy sector and is now in a mid-career training program in the United States.

70. The use of the Russian language in official life was not banned as a single event and further restrictions on the use of Russian in public life were introduced in 2002. European Institute for the Media, *EIM Media Report from the CIS: Turkmenistan*, Internews Russia, no. 7 (28) (August 2002), available at www.internews.ru/eim/august2002/tme.html.

71. The decree to abolish exit visas in Turkmenistan was signed by President Niyazov in December 2001, and the visas were abolished on January 1, 2002. On February 21, 2003, Niyazov signed a decree reinstating the requirement of an exit visa for Turkmen citizens to leave the country. Starting March 1, 2003, Turkmen citizens were required to obtain exit visas, but exit visa requirements were eased again in 2004, under heavy U.S. pressure. *RFE/RL Turkmen Report*, December 24, 2001, and February 2, 2003.

72. President Niyazov's decree reinstating the exit visa requirement put harsh limits on opportunities to study abroad. According to the decree, most students would not be able to exchange the Turkmen currency, the manat, for convertible currencies. Only students chosen by the education ministry were allowed to convert their manats at the artificially low official rate. See Ina Iankulova, "Presidential Decree Expected to Restrict Turkmen Study Abroad," EurasiaNet.org, March 11, 2003, available at www.eurasianet.org/resource/turkmenistan/hypermail/200303/0021.shtml.

73. In March 2003, President Niyazov signed a decree that lowered the age at which youths could start their national service from 18 to 17 years old. EurasiaNet.org, March 11, 2003.

74. European Bank for Reconstruction and Development, *Turkmenistan at a Glance* (London: August 22, 2003).

75. World Bank, *World Bank Development Indicators 2004*. Note: It is very hard to know for certain what percentage of the population in any of the Central Asian countries live in poverty,

as each international financial institution has its own criteria for calculation, as does the United Nations and each national government, and this results in widely varying estimates.

76. The existence of heavily subsidized communal services also means that there is no economic incentive for investment in the deteriorating infrastructure in these sectors.

77. World Bank, "Linking IDA Support to Country Performance, Third Annual Report on IDA's Country Assessment and Allocation Process" (Washington, DC: April 2002), available at http://worldbank.org/ida.

78. Kyrgyzstan was pledged $700 million over 2003-2005 at the 2002 Consultative Group Meeting of International Donors in October 2002. See "Kyrgyzstan: Is Bishkek Ready to Spend Its Aid Money Wisely?" *RFE/RL Magazine*, October 16, 2002.

79. The European Union Commission has decided to nearly double its assistance to Kyrgyzstan; the UN Development Program has switched from a project-based to a program-based approach; the ADB has signed a new three-year memorandum of understanding with the Kyrgyz government; the World Bank is providing closer supervision through a new regional office in Almaty; the Islamic Development Bank has promised to begin a direct investment program; the EBRD has committed to larger scale projects in agriculture, energy, and telecommunications; and Switzerland, Germany, Japan, and the Scandinavian countries have made commitments to increase bilateral assistance.

80. In June 2004, payment of the third tranche of a World Bank Governance Structural Adjustment Credit was held up because of Kyrgyz failure to meet deadlines for privatization of Kyrgyzenergy, Kyrgyzgaz, and Kyrgyztelecom. These targets were not met partly because of heavy legislative opposition to the privatization of these utility companies. Interfax, September 19, 2004. Kyrgyzstan Development Gateway, "Kyrgyz Leader Says Debt Relief a Vote of Confidence," March 22, 2005, available at http://eng.gateway.kg/cgi-bin/page.pl??id=1&story_name=doc7577.shtml.

81. See appendix one.

82. World Bank, *Kyrgyz National Poverty Reduction Strategy 2003-2005: First Progress Report* (Washington, DC: April 2004), p. 13, available at http://poverty.worldbank.org/files/cr04200.pdf.

83. Kyrgyzstan Development Gateway, "Small and Medium Business in the Year 2002," http://eng.gateway.kg/business_small.

84. See World Bank, *Comprehensive Development Framework of the Kyrgyz Republic to 2010, Expanding the Country's Capacities, National Poverty Reduction Strategy 2003-2005* (Washington, DC: December 9, 2004), available at http://poverty.worldbank.org/files/Kyrgyz_PRSP.pdf.

85. Central Intelligence Agency, *CIA World Factbook: Kyrgyzstan*, available at www.cia.gov/cia/publications/factbook/geos/kg.html#Econ.

86. In Bishkek city and three surrounding oblasts, only 29.2 percent of the population were reported as living in poverty, compared with oblasts in the south (41 percent in Batken, 55 percent in Jalal-abad, 56 percent in Osh, and 67 percent in Talas) and those in the north (55 percent in Issyk Kul and 71 percent in Naryn). This information is based on Government of Kyrgyzstan's *National Poverty Reduction Strategy 2003-2005*. See also World Bank, *Comprehensive Development Framework of the Kyrgyz Republic to 2010*, ch. 4.

87. Based on data from 1996 to 1999, UN Development Program, *Human Development Report 2004: Cultural Liberty in Today's Diverse World* (New York: Oxford University Press, 2004), p. 151.

88. Batken, Osh, Jalal-abad, and Talas oblasts (southern Kyrgyzstan) are all separated from the country's capital city of Bishkek by mountains. The oblasts of northern Kyrgyzstan (Chu, Issyk Kul, and Naryn) are also separated by a series of mountains.

89. Of the roughly 60,000 registered unemployed in 2001, 15 percent were under the age of 21, 55 percent were 22–39, 20 percent were 39–49, and 10 percent were over 50.

90. Uzbekistan reports a slightly ($330) higher per capita gross national income (GNI) ($420 per year) than Kyrgyzstan, but observed conditions there suggest otherwise. See appendix five. The author's own extensive travels in the region bear this out. She has seen hundreds of illegal Uzbek traders and itinerant Uzbek workers in Kyrgyzstan.

91. International Monetary Fund and International Development Association, *Kyrgyz Republic: Joint Staff Assessment of the Poverty Reduction Strategy Paper* (Washington, DC: January 24, 2003), p. 27.

92. In fact, investment in Kyrgyzstan as a share of GDP dropped by 2 percent in 2001. Kyrgyzstan did attract $146 million in foreign direct investment (FDI) in 2003, an increase of 27 percent from 2002 but still less than 10 percent of its GDP. See World Bank, *Comprehensive Development Framework of the Kyrgyz Republic to 2010*, p. 152.

93. Many of these transport links were necessary because Uzbekistan closed access points that connected the principal cities of the southern oblasts of Kyrgyzstan and because transit from north to south in Kyrgyzstan was generally accomplished through roads that passed through both Kazakhstan and Uzbekistan.

94. As well as being a member of the WTO, Kyrgyzstan is also part of the Eurasian Economic Community, a loose customs union with Russia that also includes Kazakhstan, Tajikistan, and Belarus. It was permitted to keep this prior membership as part of its WTO accession terms.

95. The 14 percent figure is low compared with 60 percent between Russia and Tajikistan, 85 percent between Russia and Kazakhstan, and 95 percent between Russia and Belarus. Constantine Michalopoulos, "The Integration of Low-Income CIS Members in the World Trading System," report prepared for the Lucerne Conference of the CIS-7 Initiative, January 20-22, 2003, p. 28, available as a link from the initiative's homepage: http://lnweb18.worldbank.org/ECA/CIS7.nsf

96. Michalopoulos, "Integration of Low-Income CIS Members," p. 44.

97. On May 20, 1998, a truck transporting sodium cyanide for the mine crashed, causing injuries and fatalities. For more details, see "Poisoned Gold, The Kumtor Goldmine in Kyrgyzstan," available at www.zpok.hu/~jfeiler/kumtor/.

98. See Emil Suerkulov's overview of the country's gold industry at http://eng.gateway.kg/gold. Under the conditions of the new agreement, Cameco owns 54 percent of Centerra, Kyrgyzaltyn JSC owns 16 percent, and the International Finance Corporation and EBRD together own 4 percent. For details, see "Gold Mine Reorganization in Kyrgyzstan Spurs Political Controversy," EurasiaNet.org, July 20, 2004; and Larisa Lee, "Jypar Jeksheef: Zoloto pakhnet kriminalom," *Moya Stolitsa-Novosti*, July 13, 2004, www.msn.kg.

99. Despite the June 30, 2003, legislation that any changes to Kumtor's 1992 operating agreement would require parliament's agreement, the government, led by Prime Minister Nikolai Tanaev, reorganized Kumtor in December 2003 by creating a new joint venture between Kyrgyzaltyn and Centerrra Gold Inc., a subsidiary of Cameco,. The outcry from opposition forces that followed this change resulted in three parliamentary committees that determined

Tanayev's decree on Kumtor was a violation of the June 2003 legislative decision; the government, however, announced that the decree would remain and the deal would proceed.

100. See David Stern, "Kyrgyz President Admits Relative Sells to U.S. Base," *Financial Times,* July 22, 2002.

101. Khalida Rakisheva, "Impact of the Internal Migration upon the Poverty Problem," paper delivered at the World Bank Conference on Poverty in Central Asia, Issyk Kul, Kyrgyzstan, June 2003.

102. Based on the World Bank data available at www.worldbank.org/data/countrydata/aag/ tjk_aag.pdf.

103. Tajikistan's external debt was estimated to be $1.2 billion in 2002. About 75 percent of Tajikistan's external debt stock is owed or guaranteed by the public sector. Russia is Tajikistan's single largest bilateral creditor, with other creditors including Kazakhstan, Belarus, and Uzbekistan. Economist Intelligence Unit, *Country Profile,* (London: September 1, 2003); and World Bank, *World Development Indicators 2004,* p. 244.

104. International Development Association and International Monetary Fund, *Republic of Tajikistan: Joint Staff Assessment of the Poverty Reduction Strategy Paper* (Washington, DC: November 13, 2002), p. 4; and Government of Tajikistan, *Poverty Reduction Strategy Paper* (Dushanbe: June 2002), p.12.

105. According to the International Organization for Migration, an estimated 620,000 Tajik seasonal labor migrants travel abroad each year in search of work, primarily to Russia, but also to neighboring Kazakhstan, Kyrgyzstan and Uzbekistan [and] while in 2002 labor migrants sent remittances totaling $80 million through Tajik commercial banks, the combined value of money and goods flowing into the country that year was between $200 million and $230 million." See "Tajikistan: IOM Announces New Programme on Labor Migrant Remittances," IRINnews.org, November 2, 2004.

106. Tajikistan now consists of the Gorno-Badakhshan autonomous oblast, Sughd oblast (formerly Leninabad), Khatlon oblast (formerly Kurgan Tiube and Kulob), and the city of Dushanbe.

107. UN Economic Commission for Europe (UNECE), Committee on Environmental Policy, "Economic Instruments, Environmental Expenditures, and Privatization," in *Draft Environmental Performance Reviews of Tajikstan: First Review* (Geneva: August 2004), ch. 3, available at www.unece.org/env/epr/studies/Tajikistan.

108. Government of Tajikistan, *Poverty Reduction Strategy Paper,* p. 27.

109. See appendix one.

110. The food production index in the late 1990s was 53.8 percent of that of the late 1980s.

111. See UN Economic and Social Commission for Asia and the Pacific, "Foreign Direct Investment in Central Asian and Caucasian Economies: Policies and Issues" (Bangkok: July 22, 2003), available at www.unescap.org/tid/publication/chap3e_2255.pdf.

112. The World Bank has invested $36 million in health and social services since 1996. The UNDP's Reconstruction, Rehabilitation, and Development Program (RRDP) for Tajikistan executed 911 projects worth $25 million on rehabilitation and reconstruction of basic economic and social infrastructure. As of FY2002, total U.S. assistance for the social sector was $12.2 million. The ADB's financial assistance to Tajikistan was worth $15 million at the end of 2003. See

World Bank, "Tajikistan Country Brief" (Washington, DC: September 2002); UN Development Program, "Reconstruction, Rehabilitation and Development Programme in Tajikistan," available at www.undp.tj/programmes/rrdp.html; U.S. State Department, "U.S. Assistance to Tajikistan" (Washington, DC: December 6, 2002), available at www.state.gov/r/pa/prs/ps/2002/15766.htm; and Asian Development Bank, "Tajikistan and ADB" (Manila: December 31, 2003), available at www.adb.org/Documents/Fact_Sheets/TAJ.asp?p=ctrytaj#loans.

113. Government of Tajikistan, *Poverty Reduction Strategy Paper*, p. 21-22.

114. As of July 1, 2003, the Tajiks owe some $40 million to the Uzbeks, $33 million of which is householder debt. See Asia-Plus News Agency, Dushanbe, in Russian: Transmitted at 900 GMT, July 16, 2003.

115. "Over 620 kg of Drugs Seized in Tajikistan for a Week – Government," Interfax, November 25, 2004.

116. For 2003 figures, see UN Office for the Coordination of Humanitarian Affairs, "Tajikistan: Stemming the Heroin Tide," IRINnews.org, available at www.plusnews.org/webspecials/opium/regTaj.asp.

117. See appendix two for more details.

118. The letter of intent promised that 30 percent of the cotton harvest would be purchased from farms at state procurement prices, another 20 percent at negotiated prices, and the remaining 50 percent would be freely disposed of by the farmers at their discretion. The agreed figures for grain production were 25 percent, 25 percent, and 50 percent, respectively.

119. The World Bank and IMF are ready to support the Uzbek economic reforms. The IMF has committed to up to $350 million in the next three years, assuming a rapid pace of reform, or roughly $150 million if there is a slower pace of reform.

120. They promised to simplify the import tariff system in 2002 by limiting the number of items subject to trade restrictions and to eliminate the system of ex ante registration of import contracts by the end of 2002. See the letter of intent signed by Rutam Azimov (deputy prime minister and minister of macroeconomics), Mamarizo Nurmuradov (minister of finance), and Faizulla Mulladjanov (chairman of the Central Bank of Uzbekistan), on January 31, 2001; available at www.imf.org/external/np/loi/2002/uzb/01/index.html.

121. In October, Uzbekistan officially lifted all currency restrictions, including required currency purchases by firms and individuals and the use of multiple exchange rates. The national currency unit became convertible on October 15, 2003. All convertibility restrictions on payments and transfers for current international transactions and deals were canceled starting from October 8, 2003. See *RFE/RL Reports on Central Asia*, 2003.

122. For some discussion of the EBRD decision, see Ron Synovitz, "Uzbekistan: EBRD Freeze on Aid Praised by NGOs," RFE/RL, April 19, 2004; Michael Andersen, "Uzbekistan: EBRD Gets Tough with Tashkent: Credit That Karimov Didn't Deserve," Index for Free Expression, April 7, 2004, available at www.indexonline.org/news/20040403_uzbekistan.shtml. See also the discussion in chapter six of this volume.

123. Figures given in purchasing power parity terms. See UN Development Program, *Human Development Report 2004*, pp. 140–1.

124. European Bank for Reconstruction and Development, *Strategy for Uzbekistan*, approved by the Board of Directors on March 4, 2003, p. 16.

125. According to the most recent World Bank data, in 2000, 21.8 percent of the Uzbek population lived at below $1 a day, and 77.5 percent below $2 per day. World Bank, *World Development Indicators 2004*, p. 56.

126. See World Bank, *World Development Report 2005*, p. 261; and U.S. Department of State, *Country Profile: Uzbekistan* (Washington, DC: October 2004), available at www.state.gov/r/pa/ei/bgn/2924.htm.

127. On November 1, 2004, around 10,000 Uzbeks in the city of Kokand descended on the mayor's office to demand the repeal of new laws that restrict trade by banning the sale of imported goods through intermediaries and demanding vendors obtain a special license to import goods from abroad. During the demonstration, protestors broke into a warehouse and burned police cars. Similar protests took place in other markets in the south—in Kashi where 500 bazaar merchants assembled in front of the city administration and in Ferghana where 1,000 traders blocked the road. Ben Wetherall, "U.S. Authorities Warn of Imminent Terror Attacks in Uzbekistan Following Mass Protests," *World Markets Analysis*, November 5, 2004; and Igor Rotar, "Merchants Protest New Banking Laws in Uzbekistan," *Eurasia Daily Monitor*, vol. 1, no. 123 (November 9, 2004).

128. Russian newspaper *Izvestia* quoted secular Uzbeks who said, "Today in the Ferghana Valley, where there are many religious people, one can buy a prostitute for two dollars. Women are willing to bear this shame, or else their children will remain hungry. In this situation, I am ready to support even Islamists. At least, it will not be bribing and stealing!" See Igor Rotar, "Zhiteli Tashkenta udivlyautsa, chto terakty ne sluchilis' ran'she," *Izvestia*, April 14, 2004, available at www.izvestia.ru/world/article61230.

129. Economist Intelligence Unit, *Uzbekistan Country Profile 2004* (London: 2004), p. 21.

130. European Bank for Reconstruction and Development, *Strategy for Uzbekistan*, p. 17.

131. In Transparency International's 2004 Corruption Perceptions Index, all five Central Asian states were ranked in the rampantly corrupt range, scoring less than 3 on a 10 point scale, where 10 indicates zero corruption. Uzbekistan was tied at 114th place with Sierra Leone, Honduras and Moldova, ahead of Kazakhstan and Kyrgyzstan, which tied with Sudan for 122nd. Turkmenistan and Tajikistan meanwhile scored even lower, coming in at 133rd. www.transparency.org/cpi/2004/.

132. European Bank for Reconstruction and Development, *Strategy for Uzbekistan*, p. 17, 28.

133. In 1999, Russia imported 143,000 tons of cotton (worth $188,000 and 62 percent of its total imported cotton) from Uzbekistan; in 2000, it imported 208,000 tons ($263,000 and 70 percent of total imported cotton). See Interstate Statistical Committee of the CIS, *External Trade of the CIS Countries, Statistical Abstract* (Moscow: 2001).

134. Personal observations of the author.

135. European Bank for Reconstruction and Development, *Strategy for Uzbekistan*, approved by the Board of Directors on March 4, 2003, p. 26.

136. According to the European Commission, SMEs have the following characteristics: Medium-sized enterprises have fewer than 250 employees, their annual turnover should not exceed $40 million, and their annual balance sheet total should be less than $27 million. Small enterprises have between 10 and 49 employees, should have an annual turnover not exceeding $7 million, or an annual balance sheet total not exceeding $5 million. Microenterprises have fewer than 10 employees. See European Commission, *Activities of the European*

Union, Summaries of Legislation, available at http://europa.eu.int/scadplus/leg/en/lvb/n26001.htm.

137. For GDP data, see Andrei Kudryashov, "Business: Private Sector in Uzbekistan Produces over 70% of GDP," Ferghana.ru Information Agency, September 7, 2004. For employment figures, see "Razvitie malogo i srednego predprinimatelstva v Uzbekistane," Radio Tashkent International, June 23, 2003, available at http://ino.uzpak.uz/rus/econom_rus/econom_rus_2406.html.

138. European Bank for Reconstruction and Development, *Strategy for Uzbekistan*, p. 27.

Chapter Five

1. Strobe Talbott emphasized that the U.S. support to the Central Asian countries must be based on several key dimensions, one of them being the respect for human rights, which is "not deeply rooted in the region." See Strobe Talbott, "A Farewell to Flashman: American Policy in the Caucasus and Central Asia" (Washington, DC: U.S. Department of State, July 1997).

2. Testimony before the House International Relations Committee by Ambassador John Tefft, Deputy Assistant Secretary for European and Eurasian Affairs, "Ukraine's Election: Next Steps," December 7, 2004, www.state.gov/p/eur/rls/rm/39542.htm

3. See appendixes five and six.

4. The total requested U.S. foreign assistance to Central Asia for FY2005 is $178.61 million, which is smaller than the budgeted cumulative funds of FY2003 ($306.77 million) and the FY2004 estimate ($208.75 million). Jim Nichol, "Central Asia: Regional Developments and Implications for U.S. Interests," CRS Report for Congress (Washington, DC: Congressional Research Service, November 12, 2004), available at www.fas.org/man/crs/IB93108.pdf.

5. For a breakdown of U.S. foreign assistance by category and year, see appendix five.

6. See appendix eleven.

7. Kazakhstan, Kyrgyzstan, and Uzbekistan experienced a slight increase in funding in 2002 relative to 2001. Aid to Uzbekistan was the highest, almost tripling from $47.3 million in 2001 to $130.4 million in 2002. However, U.S. funding to all Central Asian states except Kazakhstan dropped sharply in 2003. See FY2001, FY2002, FY2003 U.S. Assistance to Eurasia, U.S. State Department, all linked from this web page www.state.gov/p/eur/rls/rpt/c10250.htm.In contrast, total foreign assistance to Egypt was $2.2 billion in 2003 and $1.9 billion in 2004. Israel received an estimated $3.8 billion in 2003 and about $2.7 billion in 2004. See Clyde R. Mark, "Egypt-United States Relations," CRS Issue Brief for Congress (Washington, DC: Congressional Research Service, October 10, 2003); and Clyde R. Mark, "Israel: U.S. Foreign Assistance," CRS Issue Brief for Congress, (Washington, DC: Congressional Research Service, May 14, 2003, and July 12, 2004).

8. The author saw some of this firsthand when she worked as a director of the USAID-funded Central Asian American Enterprise Fund from 1994 to 2000.

9. Such nongovernmental groups include the National Endowment for Democracy (NED), National Democratic Institute (NDI), International Republican Institute (IRI), and International Foundation for Election Systems (IFES), all of which worked in partnership with leg-

islative bodies, political parties, political movements, Central Election Commissions, opposition groups, journalists, and human rights groups of the Central Asian countries.

10. On October 2, 2001, Uzbekistan gave permission for U.S. troops and aircraft to base operations in the country, with a U.S. presence expected to eventually grow to several thousand, including special operations forces. Available at www.globalsecurity.org.

11. Government of Kyzgyzstan, *National Poverty Reduction Strategy*, available at the Kyrgyzstan Development Gateway website: http://eng.gateway.kg/prsp.

12. There were some technical changes introduced to the election process as part of the UN election assistance program, such as placing transparent urns in polling stations, redesigning voting booths to facilitate secret voting, but also allow observers to ensure that nothing untoward is done inside the booth, and to provide indelible ink to mark voters' hands and prevent multiple voting. International Crisis Group, *Political Transition in Kyrgyzstan: Problems and Prospects*, ICG Report (Brussels: August 11, 2004).

13. As part of the poverty reduction strategy, Kyrgyzstan's donors pledged $700 million in foreign aid, much of which has already been disbursed. As much as $1 billion would be needed for the 2005–2010 period. Among other things, the strategy includes political reform projects such as reform of the public administration system, judicial system, local self-government, as well as anticorruption efforts. See World Bank, *National Poverty Reduction Strategy, 2003-2005, First Progress Report* (Washington, DC: April 2004), pp. 16–42, available at http://poverty.worldbank.org/files/cr04200.pdf.

14. The Kyrgyz government bought only enough boxes for northern Kyrgyzstan, which they purchased from China. Interfax, November 24, 2004.

15. Freedom House, "New Printing Press Opening in Kyrgyzstan," press release, available at www.freedomhouse.org/media/pressrel/111403.htm.

16. Alexander Kim, editor in chief of Moya Stolitsa-Novosti (MSN), or My Capital News, an opposition newspaper, began national distribution in January 2005. Opposition candidates in the parliamentary elections bought truckloads of the papers to distribute as campaign literature. Before the press began printing a 200,000-copy special issue of MSN, the power at the press went out. Kyrgyz-language Radio Azattyk, the local U.S government financed franchise of Radio Free Europe/Radio Liberty was also taken off the air, ostensibly because the government was putting its frequency up for auction. The U.S. Embassy sent Freedom House two generators the day after the power went out, allowing the press to print nearly all of the 200,000 copies of MSN's special issue. The power was restored on March 8, and MSN became one of the primary sources of information for the mobilizing opposition. See Craig S. Smith, "U.S. Helped Prepare the Way for Kyrgyzstan's Uprising," *New York Times*, March 30, 2005.

17. The U.S.-sponsored independent media center in Kyrgyzstan also prints the Tajik paper *Ruz-i Nav*. The editor-in-chief of the *Delo No* newspaper, Viktor Zapolskiy, has been accused of the favoritism toward *MSN*, that is, charging it artificially low prices for print runs to keep the cost to consumers low. See Tolkun Namatbayeva, "U.S.-Funded Print Plant Gives Hope to Embattled Central Asian Media," *Agence France-Presse*, November 14, 2003; and "Administrator, Kyrgyz Editor Disappointed with U.S.-Backed Printing House," *Slovo Kyrgyzstana*, October 4, 2004.

18. In September 2003, Ernis Nazalov, a correspondent for the national newspapers *Kyrgyz Ruhu* and *Kyrgyz Ordo*, was found dead in southern Kazakhstan. Nazalov was known to be preparing to publish material on high-level corruption in Kyrgyzstan, and his records appar-

ently have disappeared. Economist Intelligence Unit, *Country Profile 2003* (London, 2003), p. 22; *RFE/RL Newsline*, vol. 7, no. 182 (September 24, 2003). The Osh Media Resource Center (OMRC) was attacked early the morning of February 4, 2004, when two unknown men in masks stole the hard disks, processors, RAMs, and CD drives from all desktop computers as well as a notebook, digital camera, and multimedia projector. The funding for the OMRC comes from the regional UN Educational, Scientific, and Cultural Organization (UNESCO) office and the U.S. Information Service. See "Criminal Attack Was Made on the OMRC Office," CASCFEN, fergana.org, February 4, 2004, available at www.unesco.kz/ci/projects/omrc/omedia.htm.

19. President Akayev and his family, all of whom are either heavily involved in politics or business or both, are blamed for the systemic corruption that makes transition much more difficult. For details see International Crisis Group, "Political Transition in Kyrgyzstan: Problems and Prospects," ICG Report (Brussels: August 11, 2004), pp. 6–7.

20. The government used these accusations to replace Dyryldayev as the chairman of the Kyrgyz Committee for Human Rights on August 25, 2003. In a public statement, he linked all the claims to a campaign by the Kyrgyz authorities to discredit him. RFE/RL Newsline, August 28, 2003.

21. Promptly after declaring his candidacy for the 2000 presidential elections, Feliks Kulov was charged with abuse of power during his 1997–1998 tenure as a national security minister, but acquitted in August 2000. Then, in January 2001, he faced fifteen new charges, including embezzlement while governor of the Chui province in 1993-1997 as well as while serving as mayor of Bishkek in 1998-1999. He was sentenced to seven years in prison, and remained there until his release by supporters in the wake of Akayev's ouster. For details see Venera Jumatayeva, *Kulov Muzzled* (London: Institute for War and Peace Reporting, August 10, 2001). See also the Ar-Namys Party website: www.ar-namys.org/en/view_temp.php?i=140.

22. Akayev's resignation was called for in spring 2001. The actual claims were not well covered in the West, but Beknazarov argued his position with the author in a very convincing fashion during a meeting held in Bishkek in November 2002. Beknazarov also claimed that the 125,000 hectares were not part of Soviet-era land disputes but were offered to the Chinese by the Kyrgyz president as an act of appeasement by a weak state to a strong one. See "Double Standard a Real Danger to Central Asia," State News Service, Washington, DC, March 16, 2002.

23. The Russian government's decision in 1916 to force Central Asians to fight in labor battalions in the Imperial Army led to organized and anomic violence across much of Kyrgyz-inhabited lands. Tens of thousands of people died during the suppression of the violence, and hundreds of thousands fled to China. See Jumadil Baktygulov and Jyrgal Mombekova, "Istoria kyrgyzov i Kyrgyzstana s drevneishikh vremen do nashikh dnei" (Bishkek: Kyrgyzstan–Mektep, 1999), pp. 210–20.

24. Beknazarov was found guilty and given a one-year suspended sentence, losing his seat in the parliament. He was released on May 24, 2002, under a written commitment not to leave the country. In June an appeal court upheld the conviction but annulled the sentence, restoring his parliamentary mandate. Human Rights Watch, *Human Rights Watch World Report 2003 on Kyrgyzstan* (New York: January 2003), available at www.hrw.org/wr2k3/europe9.html.

25. More than 700 protesters engaged in hunger strikes. On February 7, 2002, a famous economist and deputy chairman of the Kyrgyz Human Rights Movement, Sheraly Nazarkulov,

died of a political hunger strike. The Kyrgyz authorities have always claimed that the bulk of the demonstrators came from Beknazarov's extended family, which may be true. But if so, his family is very large because photos taken during the demonstration clearly show several hundred, if not more than a thousand demonstrators in attendance. Yuri Razgulaev, "Aggravation of Political Crisis in Kirghizia," Pravda.ru, February 12, 2002.

26. The special investigators included the prosecutor general (Chubak Abyshakaev) and then the head of the defense and security department in the presidential administration (Myktybek Abdyldayev). See Alisher Khamidov, "Ak-Sui Trial in Kyrgyzstan Causes Rift between President and Law-Enforcement Officials," EurasiaNet.org, October 18, 2002. Note: the spellings Ak-Sui and Aksy are interchangeable.

27. Osmonov's superiors who were removed from office were State Secretary Osmonakun Ibraimov, a former presidential aide named Amanbek Karypkulov, and Minister of the Interior Temirbek Akmataliyev. Karupkulov was subsequently appointed Kyrgyz ambassador to Turkey, and Akmataliyev became the president's deputy chief of staff. Khamidov, "Ak-Sui Trial."

28. Khamidov, "Ak-Sui Trial."

29. This is the author's strong impression, gained through numerous interviews conducted in Bishkek in 2002 and 2003.

30. Several prominent opposition figures serve in the Kyrgyz parliament, including Adakhan Madumarov (Uzgen), Omurbek Tekebaev (Bazar-Korgon), and Major-General Ismail Isakov (Osh).

31. Akayev's address, August 26, 2002.

32. Kyrgyz Committee for Human Rights Report, January 21, 2003. A nationwide constitution referendum approved on February 2, 2003 introduced reforms that included the extension of immunity from prosecution for the first president. It will now be more difficult to impeach the president because four-fifths of the vote is required instead of the two-thirds needed before the amendment.

33. OSCE report, March 14, 2005, "Second Round of Kyrgyz Elections Demonstrates Need for Further Improvement," www.osce.org/item/8980.html

34. Roza Otunbayeva is Kyrgyzstan's leading female politician and leader of the Ata-jurt, or Fatherland, movement. Like Bakiyev, she is a former ally of Akayev who, after being dismissed by him, became very critical of the way he was allegedly taking power into his own and his family's hands. Her main power base is in the north.

35. Kurmanbek Bakiyev, who became interim president upon Akayev's departure, is head of the People's Movement of Kyrgyzstan. An economist, he is experienced in government and draws most of his popular support from the south of the country, where he was born. He served as prime minister until May 2002. He left under a cloud, being forced to resign after an opposition demonstration in the southern district of Aksy turned sour and police shot dead five demonstrators.

36. Akayev's resignation was offered in a videotaped statement prepared in Moscow and accepted by the Kyrgyz parliament on April 11, 2005.

37. For example, the Kazakhstan Institute of Management, Economics, and Strategic Research was formally established on January 1, 1992, by Nazarbayev's resolution. Available at www.kimep.kz.

38. See Anders Åslund, Building Capitalism: The Transformation of the Former Soviet Bloc (New York: Cambridge University Press, 2002).

39. Antoine Blua, "Kazakhstan: Movement Elects to Transform Itself into a True Opposition Party," RFE/RL, December 5, 2003. The DMK held its founding congress in Almaty on February 21, 2004, with 180 delegates attending. The congress adopted a party program and a charter, both of which will be submitted with other registration documents to the justice ministry. RFE/RL, February 23, 2004.

40. See also Martha Brill Olcott, *Kazakhstan: Unfulfilled Promise* (Washington, DC: Carnegie Endowment for International Peace, 2002), p. 228.

41. Criminal charges were also brought against *Karavan*'s chief editor, Aleksandr Shukhov, in April 2002. EurasiaNet.org, April 22, 2002.

42. RFE/RL, August 26, 2003.

43. Zhandosov served as first deputy economy minister, chairman of the Kazakh National Bank from 1996 to1998, and then first deputy prime minister and chairman of the State Committee on Investment. RFE/RL, January 30, 2003. Abilov joined the political council of Democratic Choice of Kazakhstan (DMK) in November 2001, and cochairs Ak Zhol. www.dpkakzhol.kz/eng/leaders_cv/abilov_cv.htm.

44. The platform of the Democratic Party of Kazakhstan, or Ak Zhol, states: "Our goal is a sovereign, prosperous, democratic Kazakhstan, and a life of dignity for each citizen of our country." The entire platform of Ak Zhol is available at www.dpkakzhol.kz/eng.

45. According to the new law, parties were required to have at least 700 members in each of the country's 14 oblasts and 50,000 signatories, up from 3,000 signatories before. As a result, pro-Nazarbayev parties, which have official backing, comfortably met the requirements, whereas most opposition parties either failed or had difficulty registering. This law allows political parties to seek funds through entrance and membership fees, donations by Kazakh citizens, Kazakh NGOs, and local businesses. It stipulates that taxes on donations must be paid and that documentary evidence of donations must be provided. There were nineteen registered parties before the new law was passed and now there are only seven. Economist Intelligence Unit, *Country Profile 2003* (London: August 12, 2003).

46. See also Martha Brill Olcott, "Ceremony and Substance: The Illusion of Unity in Central Asia," in *Central Asia and the World*, ed. Michael Mandelbaum (New York: Council of Foreign Relations, 1999), pp. 18–19.

47. Michael Wines, "Bruised, but Still Jabbing Kazakh Heavyweights" *New York Times*, July 13, 2002.

48. See University of Southern California's Annenberg School for Communication *Online Journalism Review*, available at www.ojr.org/ojr/world_reports/1031248269.php.

49. Commission for Security and Cooperation in Europe, press release, May 2, 2003, available at www.csce/gov/press_csce.cfm?press_id=291.

50. Duvanov wrote an article titled "Silence of the Lambs" on May 6, 2002, after which he was prosecuted for "harming the honor and dignity" of President Nazarbayev. Available at www.ojr.org/ojr/world_reports/1031248269.

51. Duvanov's supporters continue to push for his full release and exoneration. RFE/RL, January 30, 2004.

52. Interfax-Kazakhstan, September 23, 2003; and BBC Monitoring, September 23, 2003.

53. This was established by the law on local and state governance passed in April 2003.

54. Addressing the ninth session of the Assembly of Peoples of Kazakhstan on November 15, 2002, Nazarbayev said that this consultative body, consisting of representatives from the

parliament, government, administration, political parties, and NGOs, would draft proposals to further develop democracy in the country. EurasiaNet.org, November 18, 2002.

55. The new electoral law passed its first reading in the Kazakh parliament on January 26, 2004. The parliament approved a series of amendments to the existing election legislation on February 20, 2004. The commissions are now to be formed by regional *maslikhats* (local assemblies) based on proposals from political parties participating in the elections. Local *akims* will be required to present voter lists to election commissions no later than twenty days in advance of balloting. Persons under criminal sentence will be prohibited from running for parliament. The third reading of the changes passed on March 15, 2004. Both houses of parliament voted in favor of the bill. The bill was then sent to the president for his consideration and eventual signing. IRINnews Asia, January 29, 2004; and RFE/RL, February 23, 2004.

56. The text of the new media law is available in Russian at www.government.kz. In their reports on the media law, members of the European Parliament concluded that it fails to respect international standards regarding freedom of expression of media. See CASCFEN.org, February 4, 2004. The International Press Institute also released a report in July 2003 criticizing the draft of the media law, which is available at www.freemedia.at/Kazakhstanreport.htm. On March 17, 2004, the Majilis approved amendments to the new media bill (RFE/RL, March 18, 2004).

57. Abilov was found guilty of slander on July 27, 2004, and received an 18-month suspended sentence. Bruce Pannier, "Kazakhstan: Opposition Party Sees Fortunes Rise and Fall," EurasiaNet.org, July 31, 2004, available at www.eurasianet.org/departments/rights/articles/pp073104.shtml.

58. Official election figures from Ibragim Alibekov, "Kazakhstan: Election Results Harden Opposition," EurasiaNet.org, September 29, 2004, available at www.eurasianet.org/departments/insight/articles/eav092704a.shtml. Exit poll figures from "Open Society Foundation Sums Up Results of Election in Almaty," September 21, 2004, available at www.cascfen.org/news.php?nid=408&cid=12

59. "Kazakh Election Commission Nixes Opposition Referendum Proposal," EurasiaNet.org, November 19, 2004.

60. Institute for War and Peace Reporting, "Kazak Heavyweight Takes on President" (London: April 30, 2004), available at www.iwpr.net/index.pl?archive/rca/rca_200404_281_1_eng.txt.

61. Among those supporting Tuyakbai's candidacy are Ghalymzhan Zhakqiyanov and Akezhan Kazhegeldin. See Kazakhstan Daily Digest, March 21, 2005, at www.eurasinet.org/resource/kazakhstan/hypermail/2005030024.shtml.

62. For photographs of a January 29, 2005 rally in Almaty see "Kazak Opposition Protest," http://www.iwpr.net/index.pl?centasia_photoessay_01.html.

63. See Nazarbayev's February 18, 2005, address,"Kazakhstan on the Road to Accelerated Economic, Social and Political Modernization," on his official website: www.president.kz/main/mainframe.asp?lng=en.

64. See Nazarbayev's address to the people of Kazakhstan on domestic and foreign policy for 2003, delivered in April 2002, and Nazarbayev's address to the people of Kazakhstan on domestic and foreign policy for 2004, delivered in April 2003.

65. Bagila Bukharabaeva, "Kazakstan Politics Could Turn Dynastic," *Seattle Post-Intelligencer*, January 31, 2004.

66. The intent of Asar was to stimulate the younger generation, those 18 to 35 years of age, to participate in the political system. In Kazakh *asar* is the term for communal obligation to provide service or aid to one's neighbors, and the organization of the party on the local level was designed to provide a forum for people to come with their complaints or grievances against local authorities.

67. Female demonstrators are subject to arrest when they are protesting the arrest of their relatives, but female demonstrators protesting social conditions often are not.

68. There were two attacks on police that resulted in the death of three policemen during the night of March 28-29 and March 30, 2004; two suicide bombings at the main Chorsu bazaar in Tashkent, killing three policemen and a child on March 29; and an explosion that killed 10 people at a house used by an extremist in Bukhara on March 28. Ordinary Uzbeks' reactions to these attacks are reported by Bagila Bukharbaeva, "Poor, Enraged, Fated to Die: Militant Islamists Find a Fertile Recruiting Ground in Bleak Uzbekistan," Associated Press-*Times Union* (Albany, NY), April 4, 2004.

69. In early November 2004, several thousand people in Kokand took to the streets to protest against the government's new trade laws that imposed new barriers to import goods. Protesters threw stones, burnt police cars, and broke the windows of a government building. See "Protests in Uzbekistan over Trade Law," available at www.uzland.info/2004/november/04/02.htm.

70. The State Department declared that the authoritarian regime of Karimov has failed to make progress toward international standards on human rights. Available at the State Department website: www.state.gov/p/eur/rls/prsrl/2003/27665.htm. Also Peter Slevin, "U.S. Gives Uzbekistan Failing Grade on Rights," *Washington Post*, January 11, 2004, p. A18.

71. For a copy of the complete text of the United States–Uzbekistan Declaration on the Strategic Partnership and Cooperation Framework, see www.state/gov/r/pa/prs/ps/2002/8736pf.htm.

72. See www.state/gov/r/pa/prs/ps/2002/8736pf.htm.

73. According to the National Information Agency of Uzbekistan, turnout in the January 27, 2002, referendum that amended the constitution of Uzbekistan was 13.26 million, or 91.58 percent of the total electorate, although Human Rights Watch called the vote fatally flawed. Human Rights Watch, "Uzbekistan: President Rigs Extended Term of Office" (New York: January 25, 2002).

74. Parties registered to compete in the 2004 parliamentary elections were the Liberal Democratic Party, the People's Democratic Party, the Social-Democratic Party Justice, the Democratic Party of National Revival, and the Self-Sacrificing National-Democratic Party. "Uzbekistan Starts Preparations for Parliamentary Elections," Interfax, July 14, 2004, available at www.interfax.com/com?id=5740185&item=Uzb.

75. Erk, Birlik, Ozod Dekhkanlar Partiyasi (Agrarian Party), and the Party of Farmers and Entrepreneurs were denied registration. For details, see Andrei Kudryashov, "Opposition in Uzbekistan Misses Another Chance to Participate in the Parliamentary Election," Fergana.ru, June 28, 2004. Unregistered parties may sponsor unaffiliated candidates for single member districts. See Freedom House, "Uzbekistan," in Nations in Transit (New York: 2003), p. 634. Birlik's experience underlines that political parties need to meet several other important criteria, such as having a local branch in the northern Autonomous Republic of Karakalpakstan, providing information on party members' dates of birth and places of employment, and making

sure the head of the party does not lead two organizations simultaneously. Despite the Birlik party's argument that it meets all these criteria, the Justice Ministry did not budge. See "Uzbek Opposition Party's Registration Bid Rejected," BBC Monitoring International Reports, January 5, 2004.

76. On December 6, 2003, the Agrarian Party held its constituent meeting in Tashkent, bringing 150 participants from across Uzbekistan; the Erk party held a convention on October 22, 2003, and a board meeting on January 7, 2004 in Uzbekistan; and the Birlik party's branch in Shahrikhon district of Andijan region (eastern Uzbekistan) held a constituent conference on January 11, 2004, attended by twenty-two delegates.

77. In 2003 alone, numerous journalists were beaten or arrested. For example, RFE/RL correspondent Khusniddin Qutbiddinov and Voice of America correspondent Yusuf Rasulov working for the Uzbek broadcasting services were beaten on March 7, 2003, while covering a protest by a group of about forty women at a Tashkent market. One of the attackers later admitted that the beatings of the journalists were ordered by the anticorruption department of the Uzbek interior ministry (RFE/RL, March 10, 2003). On February 20, 2003, Uzbek police arrested Tokhtomurad Toshev, editor-in-chief of the newspaper *Adolat* published by the Social-Democratic Party. Ruslan Sharipov, an independent journalist and human rights defender, was arrested on May 26, 2003. Police also arrested Sharipov's colleagues Oleg Sarapulov and Azamat Muamnkulov. Matluba Azamatova, a reporter for the BBC, was attacked on August 20, 2003, while attending a rally against the conduct of local law-enforcement officials in the Ferghana Valley. And finally, an independent journalist, Shahnazar Yormatov, was beaten and arrested after heroin was allegedly planted in his car. EurasiaNet.org, September 10, 2003, available at http://usinfor.state.gov; and *Times of Central Asia*, February 22, 2003.

78. On March 5, 2002, Uzbekistan's ministry of justice registered the Independent Human Rights Organization of Uzbekistan (IHROU) after five years of the group's attempts to gain official recognition. The IHROU has lobbied heavily on behalf of Uzbekistan's prisoners of conscience. Ezgulik, a human rights group, was registered in March 2003. See Human Rights Watch website: www.hrw.org/press/2003/12/uzbek120603.htm.

79. Mutabar Tajibaeva, the leader of human rights group Ot Yuraklar, was attacked on August 20, 2003, while attending a rally against the conduct of local law-enforcement officials in the Ferghana Valley (EurasiaNet.org, September 20, 2003). Mothers Against the Death Penalty and Torture, a local civil society group, was not allowed to hold a conference in Tashkent in December 2003, and earlier in 2002, the ministry of justice denied the group's registration application. Available at www.hrw.org/press/2003/12/uzbek120603.htm.

80. On January 30, 2002, a Tashkent court convicted four Uzbek police officers who tortured a man to death in detention. Each of the officers was sentenced to twenty years imprisonment. The victim, 32-year-old Ravshan Haitov, died from torture just hours after police took him into custody on October 17, 2001, for alleged membership in Hizb ut-Tahrir. Authorities returned his bruised and battered corpse to his family the next day. The official cause of death was given as a heart attack. Human Rights Watch, "Uzbek Court Convicts Police for Beating Death" (New York: January 25, 2002).

81. Boven visited Uzbekistan in December 2003 for two weeks and submitted a report to the UN Human Rights Committee. He met with the justice and interior ministers, the prosecutor general, the Supreme Court chair, and NGOs. Boven expressed concern about the fact that guilty pleas are often obtained through torture. Interfax Central Asia, December 6, 2003.

82. The investigations were organized by the Freedom House's rule-of-law program in Tashkent.

83. The state-sponsored National Center of Uzbekistan for Human Rights headed by Akmal Saidov has been instrumental in buying televisions, bedding, and even new underwear for some of the facilities in which political and religious prisoners are incarcerated.

84. Elver Ramazanov, "Fresh Allegations Continue Pattern of Repression in Uzbekistan," EurasiaNet.org, May 1, 2002. The prison system's current population is about 30,000 people, of which about 3,400 are jailed for religious and political beliefs. There are 47 penitentiaries including 11 remand facilities in Uzbekistan. Interfax Central Asia, December 6, 2002.

85. For detailed accounts of the systematic abuse of religious activists, see Human Rights Watch, "Creating Enemies of the State: Religious Persecution in Uzbekistan," in *Human Rights Watch Report* (New York: March 2004), available at www.hrw.org/reports/2004/uzbekistan0304/index.htm.

86. On July 30, 2003, virtually simultaneous explosions (by suicide bombers) went off in front of the U.S. embassy, the Israeli embassy, and the Uzbekistan general procurator's office.

87. On November 22, 2004, the court issued a guilty verdict for the thirteen defendants accused of involvement in the March-April attacks, sentencing eight of them to prison for five and a half years, two for six years, one for ten years. The remaining two defendants received probation. Human rights groups doubt the presence of due process and claim that the March attacks were triggered by a government crackdown on Muslims who worshipped outside state-run mosques. "Terror Trial Jails 13 in Uzbek Capital," BBC Monitoring, November 23, 2004; and "Uzbek Court Convicts Five Alleged Terrorists amid Torture Allegations," Associated Press, November 11, 2004.

88. From 1997 to 2004, 199,000 prisoners have been released under different official amnesties, including many religious activists. EurasiaNet.org, February 2, 2004.

89. Arrests in these neighboring countries are based on the suspicion of membership in Hizb ut-Tahrir. Other charges include possession of unsanctioned religious literature and attempted encroachment on the constitutional order. EurasiaNet.org, February 17, 2004.

90. Hizb ut-Tahrir is able to raise money locally through trading activities of its members, as well as by charitable donations. For details, see Martha Brill Olcott, "Financing Islamic Groups in Uzbekistan," unpublished manuscript

91. Returned properties include Shah-i-Zinda in Samarkand and a shrine in Termez, both sites with historical significance. Shah-i-Zinda is a large medieval burial complex built around the tenth century under Tamerlane.

92. This was not an abstract question, as Soviet internal passports included a line on nationality that was obligatory to fill in.

93. Tajiks in Uzbekistan make up less than 5 percent of the population according to official figures, but the true number is believed to be much higher. Uzbekistan had a large Russian population at the time of independence, but today estimates are that only 5.5 percent of Russians remain in the country, compared with 8.3 percent in 1989. The Kazakh population has also diminished, as most Kazakhs who can have relocated to Kazakhstan, where economic opportunities are greater.

94. After Uzbek security forces reportedly drove IMU militants out of the region that summer, local officials established minefields among the border. Tajik experts also say that Uzbek security forces forcibly removed some 5,000 residents from border villages. Most of those

removed were Tajiks, who were resettled about 100 miles away in Sherabad. EurasiaNet.org, February 14, 2003.

95. The Jackson-Vanik Amendment to Title IV of the 1974 Trade Act was adopted after the Soviet Union had placed severe restrictions on emigration in 1972. The main goal was to penalize the Soviet government for blocking the exodus of Soviet Jews, but the amendment later expanded its scope covering all "nonmarket economy" countries.

96. U.S. General Accounting Office, "Foreign Assistance: U.S. Economic and Democratic Assistance to the Central Asian Republic" August 1999, available at www.gao.gov/archive/1999/ns99200.pdf. Freedom Support Act funds in Turkmenistan projects supported various grant providers including the Eurasia Foundation, which channeled funds to the development of private enterprises, civil society, and public administration; the Community Action Investment Program (CAIP), which promotes citizen dialogue and participation in community development activities; and USAID's technical assistance programs, which target areas relevant to transition to democracy and a free market economy. See USAID Program Data Sheet on Turkmenistan, available at www.usaid.gov/pubs/cbj2003/ee/tm/120-0420.html.

97. The Open Society Institute's project on Turkmenistan is aimed at promoting civil society as well as supporting arts, culture, access to information, and public health. In addition, there are opposition groups active in Sweden, some of which are privately funded by commercial interests, including those of Saparmurat Yklymov, Murad Esenov of the *Central Asian Journal*, and Shikhmuradov's son in the United States (and United Arab Emirates), who runs the Gundogar website. See Open Society Institute, "OSI Launches Turkmenistan Project," December 16, 2002, available at www.soros.org/initiatives/cep/news/turkmenistan_20021216.

98. In June 2004, President Niyazov hinted that "he might unveil plans for elections of the new president of Turkmenistan during the next session of Halk Maslahaty in autumn of 2004," arguing that one person cannot be in power forever. When he brought up these plans in November 2004 before the People's Council, the most powerful body in Turkmenistan, the audience rejected his proposal and urged him to stay in power. "Niyazov May Announce Presidential Election Plans in Autumn," News Central Asia, June 22, 2004, available at www.newscentralasia.com/modules.php?name=News&file=article&sid=675; and "Turkmen Leader Bows to Calls not to Hold Elections," BBC Monitoring Central Asia, October 26, 2004.

99. Antoine Blua, " Turkmenistan: Observers Denounce Sentencings as Pretext for Crackdown" January 4, 2003. www.eurasianet.org/departments/rights/articles/eav010403_pr.shtml

100. Before taking U.S. citizenship, Leonid Komarovsky was a Russian TV journalist. He was visiting Turkmenistan as a guest of a local businessman and old friend Guvanch Jumayev when he was arrested. In an interview, he confirmed the attempted coup, of which Jumayev was a part, and it was to be carried out without the use of firearms. "Turkmenistan—One Year after the Botched Coup," News Central Asia, available at www.newscentralasia.com/modules.php?name=News&file=article&sid=365.

101. There is speculation by those who believe Shikhmuradov was framed that disgruntled supporters of former security chief Muhammad Nazarov were responsible or even Niyazov himself.

102. Some close to Shikmuradov even claim that there was no gunfire, but U.S. diplomats, speaking off the record, confirmed that there were shots fired and several of the attackers were wounded and one person killed, as the official Turkmen reports maintain. "Turkmen President

Niyazov Survives Assassination Attempts," EurasiaNet.org, November 25, 2002, available at www.eurasianet.org/departments/insight/articles/eav112502.shtml.

103. This is in sharp contrast to the actions of Feliks Kulov, who both inside and outside the country professed support for Akayev completing his elected term.

104. Shikhmuradov gave a presentation at the Carnegie Endowment for International Peace in Washington on April 29, 2002. His talk was entitled "Turkmenistan's Political Crisis: Inside Niyazov's Regime." The transcript is available at www.ceip.org/files/events/sheikmu-radov042902transcript.asp.

105. For example, according to the presidential decision, January is renamed Turkmenbashi (the second name for President Niyazov), February is Baidag (the month of the banner), March is Novruz (a spring Muslim holiday), April is Gurbansoltan Edzhe (after the president's mother), and so on. See Pravda.ru, August 12, 2002.

106. The author met with Boris Shikhmuradov four times during the period of his exile.

107. Bruce Pannier, "Turkmenistan: Former Minister Wanted on Criminal Charges," RFE/RL, November 2, 2001. See also Ariel Cohen, "Defection Shakes Tyrant," *Johnson's Russia List*, November 8, 2001, pp. 5,531–2.

108. See Shikhmuradov's website at www.gundogar.org.

109. One of the reasons generally given for this was that Shikhmuradov's father (who was Turkmen by nationality) had held a prominent post in the late Stalin-era KGB in Turkmenistan, and had been responsible for the arrests of many prominent people, whose families were said to continue to view Shikhmuradov as having been tainted.

110. Interfax, May 7, 2002.

111. Interfax, May 7, 2002

112. RFE/RL, May 16, 2002.

113. Amnesty International, "Concerns in Europe and Central Asia, July–December 2002," available at www.erkin.net/chronicle2/news207.html.

114. This was certainly the author's impression when she heard it, and the content was repeated in a December 2003 document attributed to Shikhmuradov, which offered a lengthy account of his assassination plot against President Niyazov in a book entitled "My Associates and I: Terrorists." For details, see "Turkmenistan Publishes 'Confession' in Presidential Assas-sination Plot," *Agence France-Presse*, February 26, 2004.

115. This rarely used instrument, adopted in Moscow in 1991, provides for the deployment of expert missions to examine human rights concerns in OSCE countries. It was invoked in December 2002 with strong U.S. support. See www.osce.org.

116. Bureau of International Information Programs, U.S. Department of State, "U.S. at OSCE: Human Rights Violations Unabated in Turkmenistan," press release, available at www.usinfo.pl/releases/docs/text_212.htm.

117. Although the Uzbek foreign minister did not admit to this, in a public statement he noted that Shikhmuradov, as long-time Turkmen foreign minister, had many friends in the Uzbek government. Also, in a virtual admission of guilt, the Uzbeks did not declare the Turk-men minister to be persona non grata after the Uzbek ambassador in Ashgabat was forced to leave the country. RFE/RL, December 23, 2002

118. Also, in June 2003, the education ministry passed a general decree that stated that the higher education degrees received by Turkmen state workers from schools outside the coun-

try after 1993 will no longer be recognized. RFE/RL, *Central Asia Report*, vol. 4, no. 19 (May 11, 2004).

119. UN Office for the Coordination of Humanitarian Affairs, "Turkmenistan: Religious Leader Arrested and Imprisoned," March 18, 2004, available at www.irinnews.org/print.asp?ReportID=40133.

120. Ekaterina Grigoryeva, "25 Years of Happiness," *Nezavisimaya Gazeta*, no. 64, p. 3.

121. On June 27, Russian mass media reported that officials of the Turkmenistan National Security Ministry confiscated apartments of people holding dual citizenship. Russian citizens who were deprived of their apartments organized mass protest actions. Pravda.ru, June 30, 2003.

122. President Niyazov and Gazprom CEO Alexei Miller agreed during talks in Moscow in April 2005 that Gazprom would switch to exclusively cash settlements, and would no longer pay for Turkmen gas in kind, that is, with technical equipment. RIA Novosti, April 15, 2005.

123. Niyazov has defined and divided the ages of man into nine segments, each of which is a dozen or so years. This lifetime calendar has stretched the potential life span to 109 years, with the age of the prophet beginning at 49 and lasting until 62 years old, the age of inspiration beginning at 63 and lasting until 73. Then comes the age of the white-bearded elder, still leaving room for a role for Niyazov in his waning years. Gary Graves, "The Age of Reason: A Liberal Interpretation," CBC News Online, September 23, 2003.

124. The constitution states that "if the president is not capable of meeting his or her obligations, until the election of a new president, his or her powers are transferred to the Chair of the Parliament. In such situation, a presidential election should be conducted no later than two months from the day of transfer of powers to the chair of the parliament. A person meeting the obligations of the president may not be a candidate in the presidential election."

125. The authors of a November 2004 report by the International Crisis Group speculated that Niyazov might give the presidency to a weak candidate but continue to rule as head of the Halk Maslahaty at the same time. Another possibility is an emergence of a new dictator with Niyazov-like methods after a bout of infighting. Furthermore, in light of the strong clan identity of the Turkmen society and Niyazov's targeting of large minority groups, the possibility of a contest between clan leaders in a post-Niyazov environment is not farfetched. See International Crisis Group, "Repression and Regression in Turkmenistan: A New International Strategy," ICG Report (Brussels: November 4, 2004), p. 21.

126. For a discussion of this outcome, see ICG reports on Tajikistan: "Tajikistan: A Roadmap for Development," Asia Report no. 51, April 24, 2003; and "Tajikistan: An Uncertain Peace," Asia Report no. 30, December 24, 2001, available at www.crisisweb.org.

127. Khujand (known in Soviet times as Leninabad) is now renamed Sughd, and Kulob is now part of the renamed Katlon province.

128. Thirty percent of posts at all levels of administration were reserved for former UTO. International Crisis Group, "Tajikistan: Uncertain Peace"; and www.un.org/Depts/DPKO/Missions/unmot/prst9757.htm.

129. Details available at www.un.org/Depts/DPKO/Missions/unmot/UnmotB.htm#general.

130. The U.S. ambassador to Tajikistan was not formally resident in the country from 1998 to 2003, choosing instead to make weekly trips from his base in Almaty, Kazakhstan. But within a week of September 11, he was permanently resident in Dushanbe. Available at http://usembassy.state.gov/dushanbe/wwwhcons.html. The European Union's Technical Assis-

tance to Commonwealth of Independent States (TACIS) program withdrew its mission entirely from December 1997 to 2003, after the death of the TACIS expert's wife. Available at http://europa.eu.int/comm/external_relations/tajikistan/intro/.

131. Roger McDermott, "Border Security in Tajikistan: Countering the Narcotics Trade?" (Camberley, UK: Conflict Studies Research Centre, August 2003).

132. See NATO website: www.nato.int/docu/update/2003/03-march/e0325a.htm.

133. See U.S. Department of State website: www.state.gov/p/eur/ci/ti/c7013.htm.

134. In 2003, the UN estimate of a 6 percent increase in opium production to 3,600 metric tons differed from the U.S. estimate of 2,865 metric tons. Reuters, "U.S.: Afghan Poppy Production Doubles," November 28, 2003.

135. Zafar Abdullaev and Said Nazarova, "Tajikistan: Referendum Result Controversy" (London: Institute for War and Peace Reporting, June 28, 2003).

136. Interfax Central Asia, June 23, 2003.

137. Interfax, June 23, 2003.

138. Due to its low levels of foreign direct investment (FDI) and humble privatization, external borrowing and grants were main sources of funding of fiscal and current-account deficits in Tajikistan, which resulted in a massive debt of about $1 billion in 2003. In 1998, Tajikistan concluded bilateral agreements on debt relief with Kazakhstan, Kyrgyzstan, Turkey, Uzbekistan, and Russia, and in 2002 similar negotiations were signed with Kazakhstan, Uzbekistan, and Belarus. In mid-2003, the Tajik parliament ratified an intergovernmental accord with Russia to restructure Tajikistan's debt worth $300 million to Russia, its single largest bilateral creditor. United Nations Economic and Social Commission for Asia and the Pacific, "Country Reports on Investment Climate: Tajikistan," in *Foreign Direct Investment in Central Asian and Caucasian Economies: Policies and Issues* (Bangkok: 2003), available at www.unescap.org/tid/publication/chap3e_2255.pdf.

139. Two independent newspapers were forced to suspend publication in 2004, but the closure of *Ruz-i Nav* for nonpayment of taxes points to the difficulty of outside observers rendering judgement in these cases, because the editors of that publication admitted to not paying all the taxes due. They complained that most papers underreported circulation due to high taxes, but that they were penalized for this because of their editorial line. RFE/RL, January 11, 2004. *Ruz-i Nav* later began using the Kyrgyz media center press to publish but encountered periodic problems getting their newspapers into the country. For example, in November 2004, the Tajik state revenues and tax collection ministry seized 15,000 copies of the newspaper claiming that these materials violate the Tajik law, which the journal is subject to as the weekly is registered with the Justice Ministry of Tajikistan. See "Tajik Opposition Weekly Seized for Being Printed in Kyrgyzstan," *BBC Monitoring International Reports*, November 9, 2004.

140. For example, IRP member Mirzo Zioev serves as the minister of emergency situations in Rakhmonov's cabinet. See www.cia.gov/cia/publications/chiefs/chiefs174.html. A prominent IRP member, Davlat Usmon, served as minister of the economy until he was removed in 2000. International Crisis Group, "Tajikistan: An Uncertain Peace."

141. An example from this camp is Muhiddin Kaburi, the deputy chairman of the Islamic Renaissance Party of Tajikistan.

142. Two IRP members face criminal charges, and very serious allegations involving party leader Said Abdullo Nuri emerged in the fall of 2003. Senior IRP member Kasym Rakhimov was arrested in July 2003 on rape charges. In October 2003 charged were filed against IRP

Deputy Chairman Shamsuddin Shamsuddinov, who is accused of high treason, forming an illegal armed group, illegally crossing the border, and bigamy. Available at www.muslimuzbekistan.com/eng/ennews/2003/10/ennews25102003.html.

143. The government officials carried out training for all *imams* (religious community leaders) of the region in July 2003. Two *imams* were removed, and two mosques were closed for improper registration. U.S. State Department, *Country Report on Human Rights Practices in Tajikistan, 2003* (Washington, DC: 2003).

144. For more on Prince Aga Khan and his family, see www.amaana.org/agakhan/profile.htm.

145. Jean-Christophe Peuch, "Central Asia: Charges Link Russian Military to Drug Trade," RFE/RL, June 8, 2001, available at www.rferl.org/features/2001/06/08062001111711.asp.

146. International Crisis Group, "Central Asia: Drugs and Conflict," ICG Asia Report no. 25 (Brussels: November 21, 2001). Also, Reuter Peter, Emil Pain, and Victoria Greenfield, "The Effects of Drug Trafficking on Central Asia," unpublished manuscript.

147. Institute for War and Peace Reporting, "Tajikistan: Fall of Praetorian Guardsman" (RCA no. 306, August 10, 2004), available at www.iwpr.net/index.pl?archive/rca2/rca2_306_1_eng.txt.

Chapter Six

1. See appendix five.

2. In addition to U.S. Defense Secretary Donald Rumsfeld's February 2004 trip to Uzbekistan, there were a few other visits by U.S. delegates. For example, there were visits by congressmen, diplomats, and military officials. In August, 2004, General Richard Myers paid a two-day visit to Uzbekistan, resulting in the United States increasing its financing of joint projects by $21 million to help Uzbekistan deal with the threat of the spread of biological weapons still stored in the Central Asian region. See www.usembassy.uz/home/index.aspx?&=&mid=327; John Hendren, "Head of Joint Chiefs Reassures Uzbekistan amid Aid Cutoff; Gen. Richard Myers Says the Central Asian Nation Is a Key Ally in the Fight against Terrorism," *Los Angeles Times*, August 13, 2004; and "US Helps Uzbekistan Fight Spread of Bio Weapons," *Agence France-Presse*, August 12, 2004.

3. There was also a resolution submitted to the Committee on International Relations in February 11, 2003, entitled "Expressing the Sense of Congress with Respect to Human Rights in Central Asia." Availabe at www.hrw.org/reports/2002/usmil/USass0202-01.htm.

4. President Bush issued a waiver of restrictions on assistance to Uzbekistan under the Cooperative Threat Reduction Act of 1993 and Title V of the Freedom Support Act on December 20, 2003. Available at www.state.gov/p/eur/rls/prsrl/2003/27665.htm.

5. His decision was announced by U.S. Department of State official spokesman Richard Boucher on July 13, 2004.

6. See remarks from Rumsfeld's press conference in Tashkent on February 24, 2004, available at www.state.gov/p/eur/rls/rpt/23724.pf.htm.

7. Jacquelyn Davis and Michael Sweeney, "Central Asia in U.S. Strategy and Operational Planning" (Cambridge, MA: Institute for Foreign Policy Analysis, February 2004,) p. 51.

8. Rumsfeld visited Uzbekistan to discuss basing rights with President Karimov in October 2001. See www.defenselink.mil/transcripts/2001/t10082001_t1005uz.html. Despite their eagerness to cooperate with the United States, Uzbek authorities were nonetheless said to have been tough negotiators on the exact terms of the Status of Forces Agreement (SOFA).

9. See appendix five.

10. Bureau of Democracy, Human Rights, and Labor, "Country Reports on Human Rights Practices 2003," U.S. Department of State, February 25, 2004, available at www.state.gov/g/drl/rls/hrrpt/2003/27873.htm; and Human Rights Watch, "Creating Enemies of the State: Religious Persecution in Uzbekistan," in *Human Rights Watch Report* (New York: March 30, 2004), available at www.hrw.org.

11. "Judicial Reform Index for Kyrgyzstan, June 2003," Central European and Eurasian Law Initiative, 2003.

12. IMU leader Tahir Yuldash is presumed to still be hiding in either Afghanistan or Pakistan. See RFE/RL, *Central Asia Report*, vol. 4, no. 14 (April 7, 2004); and Seth Mydans, "Uzbeks' Anger at Rulers Boils Over," *New York Times*, April 8, 2004.

13. The bomb detonated at the gates of the U.S. embassy, killing a local security employee.

14. A survey conducted by the Ijtimoiy Fikr public opinion center in Uzbekistan in October 2001 showed about 90 percent approval for the antiterror campaign and support for Uzbekistan's close cooperation with the United States. A follow-up survey in July 2002 found that approval for Uzbekistan's support for antiterrorism operations fell to about 60 percent. In 2003 testimony to the Senate Foreign Relations Committee, Andrew Kohut from the Pew Research Center said that public polls in Uzbekistan indicate an 85 percent support of the U.S.-led war on terror. Zamira Eshanova, "Uzbekistan: Survey Shows Waning Support for War on Terrorism," RFE/RL, July 26, 2002.

15. Karimov's foreign trips in 2003 included visits to Spain, Bulgaria, and Poland. For details of visits of Western leaders to Uzbekistan, see www.press-service.uz/eng/pressa_eng/pressa_eng.htm..

16. International Crisis Group, "The Failure of Reform in Uzbekistan: Ways Forward for the International Community," Asia Report no. 76 (Brussels: March 11, 2004).

17. Such criticisms were noted in unpublished manuscripts of deceased IMU members from the mid-1990s collected by the author. For more on the appeal of these groups, see various publications published by International Crisis Group: "The Failure of Reform in Uzbekistan: Ways Forward for the International Community," Asia Report no. 76, March 11, 2004; "Uzbekistan's Reform Program: Illusion or Reality?" Asia Report no. 46, February 18, 2003; "Central Asia: Uzbekistan at Ten–Repression and Instability," Asia Report no. 21, August 21, 2001.

18. See "Pentagon Studies Central Asia Forces," Associated Press, April 30, 2002. Initially the base was home to 1,800 troops, half from the United States, and it housed FA-18 fighter planes and French Mirage jets, which were being deployed in Afghanistan. Unlike the Uzbek air base at Khanabad, restricted solely to search-and-destroy missions, the air base in Kyrgyzstan can be used for combat forays. However, with the opening of the U.S. base in Bajram, Albania, the need for combat forays from Kyrgyzstan was obviated.

19. The base is home to about 1,100 troops (rotated in without their families), KC-135 refueling jets, and C-130 transport planes. By August 2004, some 18,000 missions had been flown

328 | Notes to Chapter Six

from this base. See Ann Scott Tyson, "New U.S. Strategy: 'Lily Pad' Bases," *Christian Science Monitor*, August 10, 2004, available at www.csmonitor.com/2004/0810/PO6s02-wosc.html.

20. This highly mountainous country shares a border with China, but not with Afghanistan, to which it is linked through Tajikistan at a high mountain border. As a result, humanitarian assistance going into Afghanistan through Kyrgyzstan had to be trucked on a highway with six mountain passes at over 6,500 feet. The Kyrgyz–Tajik border has been a source of "leakage" into Kyrgyzstan, serving as a conduit for the drug trade, and it was along this route that the IMU gained access to Kyrgyzstan's Batken region in 1999 and 2000.

21. See appendix five.

22. The base is named after the chief of the New York City Fire Department who was killed in the attack on the World Trade Center.

23. The Kyrgyz government was reported to receive $7,000 for each takeoff. See Edmund L. Andrews, "Bustling U.S. Air Base Materializes in the Mud," *New York Times*, April 27, 2002. According to Alexander Kim, a former *Vecherny Bishkek* journalist who was forced out of the country, Toigonbayev and his associates control numerous enterprises, including a television and print media empire, a vodka business, the largest Kyrgyz sugar refinery, a cement business, and a big jet fuel business that is making millions selling fuel to allied air forces using the Manas air base. Robert Kaiser, "Difficult Times for a Key Ally in Terror War, Kyrgyzstan's Politics, Economy in Turmoil," *Washington Post*, August 5, 2002, p. A9.

24. Interfax Central Asia, March 4, 2003, and March 20, 2003.

25. "The opposition now has to shoulder a lot of responsibility, especially with regard to the maintenance of law and order," OSCE representative Alojz Peterle said in Bishkek on March 24, 2005. He expressed concern about reports of looting in some parts of the country and called on all sides to behave in a peaceful and responsible manner. See press release at www.osce.org/item/9014.html.

26. Kazakhstan's parliament authorized the sending of its troops to Iraq in May 2003 for one year. The troops were deployed there in August 2003 and were replaced in February 2004. In April 2004 Kazakhstan's foreign and defense ministers stated that the country will not resume sending troops to Iraq after May 2004. Ewen MacAskill, "A Coalition Showing Signs of Fracture," *The Guardian*, April 9, 2004.

27. President Nazarbayev held talks with President Bush during a working visit to the United States on December 20 and 21, 2001.

28. Kazakhstan's total proven hydrocarbon reserves have been estimated to be between 9 and 17.6 billion barrels. In 2003 the Kazakh government announced that it expects the country will produce 2.4 million barrels per day by 2010 and 3.6 million barrels per day by 2015. Energy Information Administration, *Kazakhstan Country Analysis Brief* (Washington, DC: U.S. Department of Energy, July 2003).

29. An agreement allowing Kazakhstan to export oil from Kashagan via the Baku-Tbilisi-Ceyhan pipeline will be signed by September 2005, the managing director of Kazakhstan's state oil and natural gas company KazMunayGaz, Kairgeldy Kabyldin, said in April. The president of Azeri state oil company Socar, Natik Aliyev, said new infrastructure necessary to connect Kazakhstan to the BTC pipeline would include 700 kilometers of pipeline. Marketwatch.com, April 18, 2005.

30. See www.defenselink.mil/news/Apr2002/t04282002_t0428kzk.html.

31. Embassy of the Republic of Kazakhstan, *Kazakhstan News Bulletin*, vol. 2, no. 16 (May 8, 2002); and Interfax Central Asia, September 27, 2002.

32. See www.defenselink.mil/transcripts/2004/tr20040225-secdef0494.html; and "Statement of the Ministry of Foreign Affairs of Kazakhstan," *Kazakhstan News Bulletin*, vol.1, no. 14 (March 18, 2003).

33. RFE/RL, *Central Asia Report*, vol. 2, no. 30, August 8, 2002; and Interfax Central Asia, August 5, 2002.

34. Antoine Blua, "Central Asia: Rumsfeld Wraps Up Visit to Uzbekistan, Kazakhstan," RFE/RL, February 26, 2004.

35. See appendix five for a list of CTR projects in Kazakhstan. See also www.fas.org/nuke/control/ctr/provisions.htm.

36. For example, in November 2002, the Government of Turkmenistan signed a contract valued at $8.3 million with the U.S.-based Case Corp. for the supply of 70 tractors with ploughs. See Interfax, *Central Asia and Caucasus Business Report*, November 18–24, 2002.

37. *Krasnaya Zvezda*, January 25, 2002, p. 3.

38. Turkmenistan signed the partnership document on May 10, 1994, in Brussels. See www.newscentralasia.com/modules.php?name=News&file=article&sid=555.

39. See appendix five.

40. The advanced training program was conducted by the U.S. Drug Enforcement Administration in Ashgabat from February 9–20, 2004. In December 2002 Turkmenistan was the only Central Asian country that did not attend the third antinarcotics regional training exercise for police and customs officers held in Tehran by the UN Office on Drugs and Crime.

41. Interfax Central Asia, March 3, 2003; and Victoria Panfilova, "Dvoynaya Igra Turkmenabashi," *Nezavisimaya Gazeta*, March 12, 2003.

42. The UNODC pledged $17 million in June 2003 for this multiyear initiative. Ted Weihman, "U.S. Focus on Interdiction in Central Asia Is Inadequate to Meet Drug Trafficking Challenge," EurasiaNet.org, September 23, 2003.

43. According to the State Department, the United States earmarked $22 million in 2002 for antitrafficking initiatives in Central Asia. See Weihman, "U.S. Focus on Interdiction"; and Nancy Lubin, Alex Klaits, and Igor Barsegian, "Narcotics Interdiction in Afghanistan and Central Asia" (New York: Open Society Institute, 2002).

44. Moscow has offered some free or low-cost equipment to the Kyrgyz in 2003 and 2004, and U.S. funds have also occasionally been made available to allow for the purchase of Russian equipment. In 2003, Russia handed over to Kyrgyzstan military equipment worth $3 million, and the Russian–Kyrgyz military and technical cooperation continued in 2004. The improved relations between Russia and Uzbekistan in June 2004 led to the creation of joint defense-industrial enterprises, repair of Tashkent's Chkalov aviation plant, training of Uzbek military personnel, and transfer of Russian military equipment to Uzbekistan. See various *BBC Monitoring International Reports*. See also "Tashkent Will Settle Accounts with Russian Weapon by Shares of Its Enterprises," *Nezavisimaya Gazeta*, June 18, 2004; and Vladimir Muhin, "Tashkent protiv 'besplatnoi pivatizatsii,'" *Nezavisimaya Gazeta*, May 13, 2004.

45. Vladimir Socor, "Kyrgyzstan's Hosting of U.S. Forces Irritates Moscow," *Monitor 26* vol. VIII, no. 82 (April 2002), p. 2.

46. Tom Shanker, "Russian Official Cautions U.S. on Use of Central Asian Bases," *New York Times*, October 10, 2003; and Interfax Central Asia, August 5, 2003.

47. "Zasedaniya Vyshykh Organov SNG," *Diplomatichskii Vestnik*, no. 7 (July 2000), pp. 47–8. The force was set up in spring 2002 on the basis of the Russian 201st Motorized Rifle Division from Tajikistan. Lena Jonson, "Russia and Tajikistan in a New Regional Context: Post September 11, 2001" (Stockholm: Swedish Institute for International Affairs, October 2002), p. 7.

48. During his May 2004 visit to Uzbekistan, Russian Defense Minister Sergei Ivanov said that the Collective Security Treaty Organization will hold large-scale antiterrorism exercises in Kazakhstan and Kyrgyzstan, with China and Uzbekistan attending as observers. Interfax Central Asia, May 12, 2004.

49. The base hosts ten military aircraft (Sukhoi-27 fighter jets and Sukhoi-24 bombers), two military transport vehicles, and thirteen training aircraft and helicopters. "Russia Opens Airbase in Kyrgyzstan," *Russia Journal*, October 23, 2003. For a more detailed list, see EurasiaNet.org, February 13, 2003; and Interfax Central Asia, February 24, 2004.

50. Kambiz Arman, "Russia and Tajikistan: Friends Again," EurasiaNet.org, October 28, 2004, available at www.eurasianet.org/departments/insight/articles/eav102804.shtml.

51. The Tajiks owed the Russians approximately $300 million and received another $50 million in debt credit through the deal between Russia's Unified Energy Systems (RAO-UES) and the Tajik government for the development of the Sangtuda hydroelectric station.

52. During his May 2004 visit to Uzbekistan, Russian Defense Minister Sergei Ivanov said that Uzbekistan and Russia would conduct joint military exercises in 2005. RFE/RL, *Central Asia Report*, vol. 4, no. 16, April 19, 2004, and May 3, 2004; and Interfax Central Asia, May 12, 2004.

53. RFE/RL, *Central Asia Report*, vol. 4, no. 18, May 3, 2004.

54. The May 12, 2004, visit of Russia's Defense Minister Sergei Ivanov resulted in a bilateral agreement that allows Russia to continue to train Uzbek air defense specialists and to prepare pilots, as well as to help Uzbekistan modernize its military planes. Vladimir Muhin, "Tashkent protiv 'besplatnoi pivatizatsii,'" *Nezavisimaya Gazeta*, May 13, 2004.

55. Available at www.muslimuzbekistan.com/eng/ennews/2003/09/ennews17092003.html.

56. Gulnara lives there with her two children and is in violation of a New Jersey court that granted her husband custody rights. Richard Lezin Jones, "Immigrant Wins Custody of Children, Who Are with Mother in Uzbekistan," *New York Times*, February 11, 2003; and "*Maqsudi v. Karimova-Maqsudi*, New Jersey Superior Court, Chancery Division," *New Jersey Law Journal*, August 11, 2003. For more on her role in the politics of Uzbekistan and Russia, see Mary Dejevsky, "Interviews with Gulnara Karimova," *Independent*, January 7, 2004.

57. More than 10,000 people, 60 warships, and 30 reconnaissance and fighter jets participated in the exercises. During the first international Caspian forum in Astana, Kazakhstan, in April 2004, Russian Deputy Foreign Minister Viktor Kalyuzhny, speaking of Caspian Sea security, said that "the external factor [the United States] will only cause problems." He also said that it was necessary for the Caspian states to agree that there should be no troops of other countries in the Caspian region and that Russia sees itself as a key guarantor of national security in the region. See "Russia against Demilitarized Caspian Region," *Russia Journal*, April 28, 2004.

58. In 2002 Kazakhstan bought armaments and military hardware from the Russian defense industry. Interfax Central Asia, April 22, 2004.

59. See Uzbekistan Information Directory, "Military Forces and Military and Political Direction of the Republic of Uzbekistan," January 31, 2003, available at www.uzland.uz.

60. RFE/RL, *Central Asia Report*, March 23, 2004.

61. For example, Uzbek officers have been training at NATO facilities in Spain and Germany. See Uzbekistan Information Directory, "Military Forces."

62. Sergei Blagov, "Kazakhstan Looks to Russia amid Hail of Western Criticism," EurasiaNet.org, February 19, 2003.

63. "Putin, Nazarbayev Set to Bring Two Countries Closer Together," ITAR-TASS News Agency, February 18, 2003; and "President Putin Pleased with Russian-Kazakh Relations," *RIA Novosti*, February 18, 2003.

64. Trade with Russia accounted for 15.5 percent of Kazakhstan's exports and 39 percent of its imports in 2002. International Monetary Fund, *Direction of Trade Statistics Yearbook 2003* (Washington, DC: 2003), pp. 290–1. See also appendix one on Central Asia's main trading partners.

65. For example, Duma Deputy Dmitri Rogozin, a nationalist politician, proposed an international organization to protect the rights of ethnic Russians. The most dissatisfied Russians, however, have already left. There were 6,062,000 ethnic Russians in Kazakhstan in 1989 and only 4,479,600 a decade later. See also www.eisenhowerinstitute.org.

66. Kazakhstan initially acquiesced to Russia's continued use of the Baikonur cosmodrome, but then moved in the late 1990s to restrict Russian launches, hoping to renegotiate the terms of the Russian lease, as well as to protest the environmental damage sometimes caused by launches. The current agreement allows Kazakhstan to purchase Russian goods worth the debt amount that Russia owes for leasing the cosmodrome. Russia has been leasing Baikonur since 1994 under a twenty-year agreement. Putin and Nazarbayev negotiated the prolongation of the lease in 2002, and then in January 2004, they signed a lease that extends the agreement to 2050. Interfax Central Asia, July 30, 2003; "Russia Extends Space Site Lease," BBC Reporting, January 9, 2004.

67. See appendix one on main trading partners in Central Asia.

68. Russia, Belarus, Kazakhstan, Kyrgyzstan, and Tajikistan signed a treaty for a Customs Union and the Common Economic Space in February 1999 with three primary objectives: (1) collaborating on efforts to join the WTO, (2) harmonizing customs tariffs, and (3) developing common guidelines on border security. See *Alexander's Gas and Oil Connections*, October 17, 2003; and the Eurasian Economic Community Chronology, available at www.photius.com/eaec.

69. Kazakhstan's President Nazarbayev has proposed that the "altyn," meaning gold, be made the common currency unit in the Common Economic Space. Nazarbayev wants a free trade zone and state uniform tariffs on freight haulage. Interfax Central Asia, April 1, 2003.

70. Kazakhstan officially applied for WTO entry in 1996 and expects to join the WTO only after Russia. In March 2004, Kazakh Prime Minister Daniyal Akhmetov stated that Kazakhstan plans to join the WTO at the end of 2005 or early 2006. Interfax, *Central Asia and Caucasus Business Report*, March 22–28, 2004.

71. "Russia, Iran, Kazakhstan, Azerbaijan, Turkmenistan Still Negotiating Caspian," BBC Monitoring, April 14, 2004; "Legal Status of the Caspian Sea to Be Discussed in Baku," Gazeta.kg, March 15, 2004; and "Five Countries to Discuss Legal Status of Caspian Sea in Tehran," Pravdaonline, December 4, 2003.

72. The most recent meeting on the legal status of the Caspian Sea took place in April 2004 in Kazakhstan. The next summit, set for Tehran in January 2005, was postponed for undisclosed reasons.

73. LUKoil is currently participating in three Kazakh oil and gas projects. It holds a 15 percent share in Karachaganak Integrated Organization, which is developing the Karachaganak field, a 50 percent share in the joint venture Turgai Petroleum, which is developing the Kumkol field in the Kzyl-Orda region of central Kazakhstan, and has a share in the Russia–U.S. joint venture LUKArco, which in turn owns a 5 percent share in the Tengiz field. LUKoil also owns a 12.5 percent share in the Caspian Pipeline Consortium, which exports oil from Tengiz to Novorossiisk. Interfax Central Asia, February 10, 2003.

74. Kazakhstan and Russia signed a protocol in May 2002, which declares Kazakh jurisdiction over the Kurmangazy oil field and Russian jurisdiction over the Tsentralnoye and Khvalynskoye fields in the north of the Caspian Sea. See Interfax Central Asia, October 2, 2002; and "Kazakhs Turn Up Heat on Rosneft," Reuters, April 14, 2004.

75. Interfax, *Central Asia and Caucasus Business Report*, March 22–28, 2004.

76. This, of course, is a highly complicated thing to negotiate, as it involves the Karachaganak joint venture partners, the Kazakh government, the Russian gas industry, as well as the Russian government, which stands behind them. LUKoil Overseas started talks with Gazprom in 2003 over increasing the price of gas produced in Karachaganak field. Gazprom has been paying only about $14.5 per thousand cubic meters, one-third of what it pays for Turkmen and Uzbek gas. Interfax Central Asia, August 28, 2003.

77. According to Western companies operating in the Central Asian region, Gazprom buys Kazakh gas at less than $40 per thousand cubic meters. See www.capitallinkrussia.com/press/companies/50010088/6619.html. With the creation of the KazRosGaz, it was decided that about 3 billion cubic meters of Kazakh gas will be annually sold in European countries. *Alexander's Gas and Oil Connections*, July 12, 2002. In April 2004, Gazprom and Kazakhstan's energy and natural resources minister were negotiating on admission of additional gas from Kazakhstan to the European markets. In exchange, the Kazakh government offered to finance the program worth $2 billion to broaden the capacity of the Kazakh gas pipelines to meet the needs of Gazprom for transit of gas from Turkmenistan. See *Kommersant*, April 6, 2004.

78. Kazakhstan plans to increase its natural gas production to 70 billion cubic meters by 2015, of which 40-45 billion cubic meters is planned for export. The country extracted 14 billion cubic meters of gas in 2002. Energy Information Administration, *Kazakhstan Country Analysis Brief* (Washington, DC: U.S. Department of Energy, July 2003).

79. The agreement on gas imports and strategic cooperation from 2003 to 2012 between Gazprom and Uzbekneftegaz was signed on December 17, 2002. Available at www.uzland.uz.

80. Kyrgyzstan and Gazprom signed the agreement on May 15, 2003, to promote joint efforts to explore and develop oil and gas deposits, to transport gas to Kyrgyzstan, and to overhaul and build future gas pipelines. Under this agreement, Gazprom is supposed to buy gas from Turkmenistan and Uzbekistan and then sell it to Kyrgyzstan with payments made to Gazprom rather than the Uzbek government. Interfax Central Asia, May 16, 2003.

81. Maya Nobatova, "Gazprom Lays Down the Rules for Gas Business in Central Asia," *Russian Petroleum Investor*, March 2003, p. 76.

82. Nobatova, "Gazprom Lays Down the Rules," p. 78.

83. In April 2004 Zarubezhneftegaz and Uzbekneftegaz signed a fifteen-year 50/50 production sharing agreement to develop Uzbekistan's Shakhpakhty gas field. Gazprom pledged to invest $15 million upgrading the field's infrastructure to bring annual gas production to 500 million cubic meters. Then in June 2004 the Uzbeks and Russians agreed to Russian development of the Kandym gas field, with a reserve of 150 billion cubic meters, in a consortium agreement in which the Russians own 90 percent of what is slated to be 9 billion cubic meters of annual production. "Lukoil to Launch Uzbekistan Gas Project This Week," Interfax, November 24, 2004.

84. In addition to isolating Turkmenistan within the Central Asian gas system, Gazprom has also sought to cut off Turkmenistan's efforts to export its gas directly to Ukraine, through Itera, which was transporting Turkmen gas from 1999 to 2003. In December 2002 Gazprom signed a contract with Eural Transgas, putting it in charge of transporting 36 billion cubic meters of gas annually to Ukraine, which led to allegations that Eural Transgas was a private daughter company of Gazprom. Catherine Belton, "Gazprom Gives Away Turkmenistan-Ukraine Gas Sales," *The Moscow Times*, February 28, 2003.

85. The construction of the Central Asia and Center System (CAC) pipelines began after a discovery of the Dzharkak field, and the first section was completed in 1960. The second section reached Tashkent in 1968 and was extended to Bishkek in 1970 and to Almaty in 1971. By the mid-1970s, the 13,750-kilometer CAC transmission system had been completed, including four parallel lines from the junction point of Beyneu in northwest Kazakhstan, two lines going northwest to Moscow, and two others proceeding westward across the Volga river to the North Caucasus-Moscow transmission system. Leslie Dienes, *The Soviet Energy System: Resource Use and Policies* (Washington, DC: Wiley and Sons, 1979), pp. 79–80. The 2,300-kilometer Bukhara–Ural pipeline system also originates in Central Asia, reaching from northern Turkmenistan to the Urals. It was laid in 1963–1965, following a discovery of a major gas field in Gazli, Uzbekistan. Bukhara–Ural also moves gas to Bashkiria and Tatarstan, west of Orenburg. Energy Information Administration, *Country Analysis Brief on Turkmenistan Energy Sector* (Washington, DC: U.S. Department of Energy, May 2002). See also www.gazprom.com.

86. In June 1999 RAO-UES created a new transnational energy company, Uraltek, with Kazakhstan, in which it owns 25 percent of the shares. RAO-UES subsidiaries owned 45 percent, and Access Industries owned 30 percent. *RIA Oreanda Economic News*, June 11, 1999; and *Finansoviye Izvestia*, June 10, 1999.

87. See www.cawater-info.net/news/11-2004/04_e.htm.

88. Before independence, Soviet central planners arranged for Kyrgyzstan to use its water to supply the cotton fields of Uzbekistan and Kazakhstan, and these two republics sent a portion of their oil and gas resources to Kyrgyzstan in the winter. RusAl, one of the world's three biggest aluminum companies, will provide $560 million to get the project, stalled since the 1980s, off the ground. In addition to its Rugun investment, RusAl will also spend $600 million over the next five years for construction of an aluminum smelter in southern Tajikistan. All told, the company plans to invest more than $10 billion in the Tajik economy within the next decade. See Kambiz Arman, "Russia and Tajikistan: Friends Again," EurasiaNet.org, October 28, 2004.

89. "Energy and Environmental Security in Central Asia: The Syr Darya," CSIS briefing by Keely Lange, United States Department of Energy, February 20, 2001. www.csis.org/ruseura/cs010220lange.htm.

90. The most notable agreement regulating the use of water and energy resources was signed in March 1998 by Kazakhstan, Kyrgyzstan, and Uzbekistan. Uzbekistan uses 51 percent and Kazakhstan 37 percent of the water from the Syr Darya, whereas most Amu Darya water is consumed by Uzbekistan and Turkmenistan. The quotas for Tajikistan and Kyrgyzstan are 15 percent each. International Crisis Group, Asia Report no. 34 (Brussels: May 30, 2002), pp. 9, 12; and "Tajikistan Calls for More Cooperation in Water Management," Transitions Online, September 9, 2003.

91. Turkmenistan started building a $4.5 billion lake called the Lake of the Golden Century in Karakum desert in 2000. According to the plan, it will take twenty years to complete. The lake is expected to have a surface area of 3.5–4 thousand square kilometers and has a maximum depth of between 70 and 100 meters. Once completed, the lake would contain some 132 to 150 cubic kilometers of water. Drainage water is derived to the lake from five Turkmen provinces as well as the Uzbek province of Khorezm through two major collector canals. Some experts argue that the lake will not be sustainable solely from drainage water and that eventually it will either disappear or draw on the Amu Darya River. Daniel Linette, "Water Resources Management in Central Asia: Addressing New Challenges and Risks," *Central Asia and Caucasus Analysis*, August 15, 2001; International Crisis Group, ICG Asia Report no. 34, pp. 25–6; and EurasiaNet.org, May 12, 2003.

92. Addressing water usage in Central Asia was a pet project of British Foreign Minister Robin Cook. Various international organizations have been working with small water projects, including the Global Energy Facility with World Bank funding, the Special Program for the Economies of Central Asia in cooperation with the UN Economic Commission for Europe, the UN Economic and Social Commission for Asia and the Pacific, and USAID.

93. East Turkestan Islamic Movement (ETIM), an Uighur separatist group, is the most militant of the various Muslim groups operating in China's western Xinjiang province. Its members demand separation from China and the creation of an independent state called East Turkestan. Center for Defense Information, "In the Spotlight: East Turkestan Islamic Movement," December 9, 2002, available at www.cdi.org/terrorism/etim.cfm. The United States added the ETIM the list of terrorist organizations in 2002. Zamira Eshanova, "China: Uighur Group Added to U.S. List of Terrorist Organizations," EurasiaNet.org, September 1, 2002.

94. In 2003 Kyrgyzstan's Supreme Court banned four groups branded as terrorist and extremist organizations, three of which were linked to China's Uighurs: the Organization for the Liberation of Turkestan, the Islamic Party of Turkestan, and the East Turkestan Islamic Movement. Also in 2003 the Chinese government published an official document that listed the World Uighur Youth Congress and the East Turkestan Information Center as terrorist organizations. Antoine Blua, "Kyrgyz Rights Activists Call for End to Deportation of Uighurs to China," EurasiaNet.org, January 25, 2004.

95. Faruk Turaey, "Prickly Uzbekistan Comes Closer to Russia," *Transitions Online*, August 19, 2003.

96. The prime ministers of the member countries agreed to move the center to Tashkent in Uzbekistan on September 24, 2003. See Ferghana.ru, September 24, 2003.

97. In the fall of 2002 Kyrgyz and Chinese troops had joint military exercises. It was the first time Chinese troops had ever participated in maneuvers abroad. Kazakhstan and China also planned to hold joint antiterrorism exercises along their border in 2003. They decided to train together in the inaugural counterterrorism exercises of the SCO in the summer of 2003.

98. China is reported to have provided a total of $4.2 million in 2002 in military aid to Central Asia. Alyson J. K. Bailes et al., "Armament and Disarmament in the Caucasus and Central Asia" (Stockholm: Stockholm International Peace Research Institute, July 2003), p. 20.

99. India, Pakistan, Mongolia, and Iran are all candidates for eventual membership in the SCO. See WPS: Defense and Security, April 26, 2004, available at www.wps.ru.

100. Heads of government of the six member states held the first meeting in Almaty on September 14, 2001, to discuss regional economic cooperation.

101. See appendix one on main trading partners of Central Asian states.

102. In the early years China was the source of goods for a large shuttle trade with Kazakhstan and Kyrgyzstan, and to a lesser extent Tajikistan and Uzbekistan, which was used by local residents to accumulate capital, and in each case this trade has been subject to strict government regulation as part of the process of creating a fiscally responsible government.

103. Interfax Central Asia, September 26, 2003.

104. The U.S.-based Access Industries took control of the Kazakh government's shares in March 2001, in part because of the difficulty that the Kazakh government was having in working with the Chinese in managing the project. Access Industries received management of the state shares for five years. Interfax Central Asia, March 31, 2003.

105. Interfax, *Central Asia and Caucasus Business Report*, vol. 5, no.16 (April 15–21, 2002); and RFE/RL, *Central Asia Report*, vol. 4, no. 12, March 23, 2004.

106. "China Inks Historic Kazakh Oil Pact," *The Moscow Times*, May 19, 2004.

107. CNOOC North Caspian Sea Ltd. and Sinopec failed in their bid to purchase British Gas's rights to Western companies, like ENI and Royal Dutch/Shell, which have exercised their preemptive rights to block deals for these two Chinese oil companies in May 2003. See "Kashagan Project Participants Exercise Preemption Rights," *Alexander's Oil and Gas Connections*, vol. 8, no. 11 (June 3, 2003).

108. Kazakhstan and, to a lesser extent, Kyrgyzstan fear for the security of their water supply. The two main rivers that China proposes to divert, the Ili and the Irtysh, flow into Kazakhstan and on to Russia. The rivers feed important agricultural and industrial regions in central and eastern Kazakhstan. For details, see Eric Hagt, "China's Water Policies: Implications for Xinjiang and Kazakhstan," *The Central Asia–Caucasus Analyst* (Washington, DC: Central Asia–Caucasus Institute, or CACI, July 30, 2003).

109. More than 7,000 students are at the Turkish–Kazakh International Hoca Ahmet Yesevi University in Kazakhstan, founded in 1992. About 1,700 students are at the Turkish–Kyrgyz Manas University. About 10,000 Central Asian students are training in Turkey.

110. The volume of trade with Central Asian countries is approximately $7 billion since 1992. Turkey is a main export partner for Turkmenistan and a leading importer for Tajikistan. Economist Intelligence Unit, *Country Profiles 2003* (London: 2003). See also appendix one on trade.

111. For example, Turkish Prime Minister Recep Tayip Erdogan had a four-day tour of Kyrgyzstan and Tajikistan in October 2003. The summits of Turkish-speaking states as multilateral forum of cooperation bring together Azerbaijan, Kazakhstan, Kyrgyzstan, Turkey, Turkmenistan, and Uzbekistan. The seventh summit was held in April 2001.

112. Paul Starobin, "The Next Oil Frontier," *Business Week*, May 27, 2002.

113. The OIC, an intergovernmental organization with fifty-seven members, was established in 1969 in Morocco. Kyrgyzstan, Tajikistan, and Turkmenistan joined in 1992, and Kazakhstan and Uzbekistan joined in 1995.

114. See the Islamic Development Bank website: www.isdb.org/.

115. For Mashkevich's biography, see http://eajc.org/pers_bio_e.php?idpers=1.

116. Wexler's policy statements are available at www.wexler.house.gov/. Also see *Kazakhstan Daily Digest*, EurasiaNet.org, May 29, 2002; and "Reaction of Some Kazakh Intellectuals to Robert Wexler's Statement on Democratic Achievement in Kazakhstan," RFE/RL, May 30, 2002.

117. For details of the meeting, see www.kazakhstanembassy.org.uk/cgi-bin/index/87?id=76.

118. Pope John Paul II chose to come to Astana because a considerable Polish population was forcibly resettled and imprisoned in Kazakhstan after the Soviet seizure of western Ukraine in 1941.

119. Kyrgyzstan has sought to enhance its reputation as an Asian nation, with rather less success, given its modest economic circumstances. Among Akayev's recent trips to Asia are visits to Japan in April 2004, to Iran in December 2003, and to India in November 2003. Kyrgyzstan has embassies in India, Malaysia, China, Turkey, and the United Arab Emirates.

120. The Conference on Interaction and Confidence-Building Measures in Asia (CICA) includes sixteen member states: Afghanistan, Azerbaijan, China, Egypt, India, Iran, Israel, Kazakhstan, Mongolia, Russia, Kyrgyzstan, Pakistan, Palestine, Tajikistan, Turkey, and Uzbekistan (FBIS, June 4, 2002).

121. Nazarbayev and India's Prime Minister Vajpayee signed a joint declaration on February 12, 2002. The full text of the document is available at www.meadev.nic.in/foreign/jt-decl-indo-kazakh.htm.

122. Sudha Ramachandran, "India, Iran, Russia Map Out Trade Route," *Asia Times*, June 29, 2002, available at www.atimes.com/ind-pad/DF29Df02.html; and Rahul Bedi, "India and Central Asia," *Frontline*, vol.19, no.19 (September 14–27, 2002), available at www.frontlineonnet.com/fl1919/19190600.htm.

123. Alec Appelbaum, "EBRD Annual Meeting in Tashkent: No Showcase for the Uzbek Government," EurasiaNet.org, May 2, 2003.

124. In 2003, EBRD allocated $2.3 million for the reconstruction of Tashkent Airport. The same year the EBRD opened credit facilities worth $2 million for equipment and transport leasing to small businesses in Uzbekistan. The EBRD announced in April 2004 that it was cutting financial aid to Uzbekistan because of the poor human rights situation in the country. A new EBRD strategy for Uzbekistan is planned for spring 2005. Interfax Central Asia, April 7, 2003; Uzbekistan Information Directory–Uzland website: www.uzland.uz; FBIS, May 5, 2003, April 7, 2004, and April 8, 2004.

125. At the Berlin Donors' Conference on March 31–April 1, 2004, Afghanistan received $8.2 billion in pledges for the next three years. Afghanistan, China, Iran, Pakistan, Tajikistan, Turkmenistan, and Uzbekistan signed a regional cooperation agreement to step up the fight against the drug trade in the region. Esfandiari Golnaz, "Afghanistan Donors Conference Focuses on Security," RFE/RL, April 1, 2004. For European commitments, see http://europa.eu.int/comm/external_relations/afghanistan/intro/memo_04_33.htm.

Chapter Seven

1. U.S. Deputy Assistant Secretary of State Lynn Pascoe is responsible for Central Asia, the Caucasus, and Southeast Europe. He was appointed to this position in 2001.

2. For responsibilities of USAID field offices, see www.usaid.gov/policy/ads/100/103.pdf.

3. The Central Asian Economic Community was transformed into the Central Asian Cooperation Organization in February 2002.

4. Niyazov interprets positive neutrality to preclude Turkmenistan from joining the CACO and the SCO yet allow for Turkmen membership in the Economic Cooperation Organization (headquartered in Iran) or the Organization of the Islamic Conference.

5. There is an extensive literature about efforts to transform narco-states, which focuses particularly on cocaine production in Latin America. For more information, see Bruce Michael Bagley and William O. Walker, "Drug Trafficking in the Americas" (Miami: North/South Center Press, December 1, 1994); Menno Vellinga, "The Political Economy of the Drug Industry: Latin America and the International System" (Gainesville: University Press of Florida, 2004); and Jose Cristy, "Colombia: A Risk-Prone Democracy" (Monterey, CA: Naval Post-Graduate School, 1998).

6. For figures on opium cultivation, see UN Office on Drugs and Crime, available at www.unodc.org/unodc/en/world_drug_report.html.

7. See also UN Office on Drugs and Crime, *The Opium Economy in Afghanistan: An International Problem*, 2nd ed. (Vienna: 2003); UN Drug Control Program, *Afghanistan Opium Survey 2002* (Vienna: October 2002); International Monetary Fund, "Islamic State of Afghanistan: Rebuilding a Macroeconomic Framework for Reconstruction and Growth," IMF Country Report no. 03/299 (Washington, DC: September 2003).

8. The two strongest proponents of this were U.S. Ambassador to Afghanistan Zalmay Khalilzad and then Afghan Minister of Finance Ashraf Ghani (a former World Bank economist). For details see John Lancaster, "Karzai Urges War on Opium Trade: Leader Says Cultivation Imperils Attempt to Rebuild Afghanistan," *Washington Post*, December 10, 2004; Stephen Graham, "Karzai Urges Afghans to Give Up Lucrative Opium Trade, Says Taliban Profiting," Associated Press, December 9, 2004; and Ashraf Ghani, "Where Democracy's Greatest Enemy Is a Flower," *New York Times*, December 11, 2004.

9. The full text of the Berlin Declaration on Counter-Narcotics is available at http://bglatzer.de/aga/berlinantidrugs.htm.

10. Drug Policy Alliance, "Opium Cultivation Continues to Rise in Afghanistan" (New York: February 13, 2004).

11. Washington had long viewed Afghanistan's drug problem as a primarily European concern because over 90 percent of all heroin and opium consumed in Europe came from Afghanistan. As a result, the United Kingdom was the coalition partner to take primary responsibility for drug trafficking and drug eradication programs. But this did not satisfy the United States because the U.S. preferred military-style raids of poppy storage facilities, given the bad timing of the eradication campaign. Claudio Franco, "Afghanistan's Anti-Poppy Drive Off to Shaky Start," EurasiaNet.org, June 3, 2004.

12. Golnaz Esfandiari, "Afghanistan: Donors Conference Focuses on Security," RFE/RL, April 1, 2004.

13. See appendix eleven on ONDCP spending on programs related to Central Asia. See also the National Drug Control Strategy, released by the White House in February 2002, available at www.whitehousedrugpolicy.gov/policy/index.html.

14. This is the author's strong impression, gained through interviewing representatives of security forces in the region, as well as some Western specialists who were involved in training exercises.

15. RFE/RL, *Central Asia Report*, vol. 4, no. 19, May 11, 2004.

16. Robert Charles, the assistant secretary who heads the State Department's Bureau for International Narcotics and Law Enforcement Affairs, told Congress that CIA figures showed Afghanistan's opium poppy cultivation approaching 250,000 acres in 2004, up more than 60 percent from the 2003 level. T. Christian Miller, *Los Angeles Times* "Post-Invasion Chaos Blamed for Drug Surge," October 4, 2004.

17. For details on drug seizures in 2004 and a local press roundup on drug-related articles, see "Afghan Heroin Engulfs Central Asia," RFE/RL, *Central Asia Report*, vol. 4, no. 45, December 17, 2004.

18. Owais Tohid, "Bumper Year for Afghan Poppies," *Christian Science Monitor*, July 24, 2003.

19. For more information, see International Crisis Group, "Central Asia: Drugs and Conflict," Asia Report no. 25 (Brussels: November 26, 2001); Tamara Makarenko, "Crime, Terror, and the Central Asian Drug Trade," Caspian Brief no. 25 (Bromma, Sweden: Cornell Caspian Consulting, July 2002); and Roger McDermott, "Border Security in Tajikistan: Countering the Narcotics Trade?" (Surrey, UK: Conflict Studies Research Centre, October 2002).

20. The U.S. Centers for Disease Control/Central Asia office has operated since 1995. For its activity on HIV/AIDS, see www.cdc.gov/epo/dih/centralasia.html. See also UN Development Program, *HIV/AIDs: Reversing the Epidemic* (New York: 2004), pp. 21–3, available at http://rbec.undp.org/hiv/?english. Kazakhstan seems to have the most accurate data, reporting the highest incidence of HIV/AIDS: 0.1–0.3 percent as compared to under 0.1 percent elsewhere in the region.

21. See the account of the talk given by former ambassador Craig Murray to the Royal Institute of International Affairs on November 4, 2004, available at www.riia.org.

22. If the technical and command and control standards of NATO's Partnership for Peace Program, the CIS collective security organization, and the SCO cannot be made compatible, then the Central Asians could opt out of participation in NATO-supported structures since CIS and SCO structures seem certain to be made compatible.

23. This view has been expressed in private meetings with officials from all three countries. In fact, there are many in the decision-making elite in Uzbekistan who are very critical of the way the Karimov government has treated Islamic extremists and are even more critical of its economic policies.

24. "Traditional" Christian groups long present in the region, such as the Russian Orthodox or the (Polish) Catholics in Kazakhstan, are treated well, but Protestant minority groups have frequently been denied registration throughout the region and have been openly persecuted in Turkmenistan. For details, see the Bureau of Democracy, Human Rights, and Labor, *Country Reports on Human Rights Practices* (Washington, DC: U.S. Department of State), available at www.state.gov/g/drl/rls/hrrpt/. The treatment of Christian evangelicals has been particularly harsh in Turkmenistan, where not only were they denied registration, but also a church

was raided in 2001 and several members of the Protestant community were fined and detained. See Felix Corely, "Tortured Baptist Prisoner Near Death in Turkmenistan," *ChristianityToday.com*, available at www.christianitytoday.com/ct/2001/106/35.0.html.

25. The chief of Tajikistan's Mine Action Center said that Uzbek mines have caused over 120 Tajik casualties since 2000, 62 of whom have died. EurasiaNet.org, February 25, 2004.

26. Uzbek plans to start de-mining were announced on August 13, 2004, at a council meeting by Uzbekistan's minister of defense. This follows a June 18, 2004 statement made before the OSCE. Interfax, August 13, 2004.

27. The agreement on border demarcation for 690 kilometers was signed between Kyrgyzstan and Uzbekistan in 2001. See www.uzland.uz. Uzbekistan has assailed Kyrgyzstan for supposedly delaying the implementation of this agreement. Kyrgyz officials want to define a separate 256-kilometer stretch of frontier before the new border takes effect. EurasiaNet.org, February 25, 2004.

28. Uzbekistan has two enclaves—Sokh and Shahimardan, Iordan—in southern Kyrgyzstan. Tajikistan has two as well: Vorukh in Kyrgyzstan and one in the Altynken area near the highway passage into Ferghana Valley in Uzbekistan.

29. In July 2002, 70 percent of the Tajik–Uzbek border was demarcated. The border is 1,300 kilometers long. Interfax Central Asia, July 30, 2002. Also See Aleksei Malashenko and Martha Brill Olcott, eds. *Multi-Dimensional Borders of Central Asia* (Moscow: Carnegie Moscow Center, 2000).

30. In September 2002 Nazarbayev and Karimov signed a bilateral agreement finalizing the border demarcation between the two countries. In November 2001, a document was signed defining 96 percent of the 2,440-kilometer shared border. The remaining four percent was defined in the September 2001 agreement. RFE/RL Newsline, September 10, 2002; RFE/RL, *Central Asia Report*, vol. 2, no. 35, September 13, 2002; and EurasiaNet.org, January 5, 2002.

31. One of the spring 2004 bombs went off in a village in Ferghana Valley that is nestled against the Kazakh and Kyrgyz border. There is also some speculation that the Uzbek terrorists had some training facility secreted on Kazakh territory as well. On November 11, 2004, the Kazakh security forces dismantled a terrorist cell named Mujahadeen Jamaat, affiliated with Al Qaeda, and arrested seventeen members of the group, including Kazakh and Uzbek citizens, among them four women. Government officials claimed that the group was rooted out in Kazakhstan. For details see, "Al-Qa'idah-Linked Group Detained in Kazakhstan," BBC News, November 11, 2004.

32. For details, see "Nizayov-Karimov Press Conference–Transcript of Tape," November 21, 2004, available in the archive of Turkmen news agency NewsCentralAsia.com.

33. See UN Development Program, "Tapping the Potential: Improving Water Management in Tajikistan" and "Water as a Key Human Development Factor Kazakhstan," in *National Human Development Report 2003* (New York: 2003).

34. In the case of Kyrgyzstan, the author was able to substantiate some of these rumors.

35. The author spent five years as a director of the Central Asia American Enterprise Fund (CAAEF), which gave her the opportunity to see a number of U.S. assistance projects and European Bank for Reconstruction and Development (EBRD) projects up close. It also provided extensive exposure to the kinds of petty corruption that existed in many small loan projects in particular.

36. See Mohsin S. Khan and Sunil Sharma, "IMF Conditionality and Country Ownership of Programs," IMF Working Paper no. WP/01/142 (Washington, DC: September 2001). (At the time the paper was written, Mohsin S. Khan was head of the IMF Research Institute; he is now Director of the IMF's Middle East and Central Asia Department.)

37. The EBRD has a subscribed capital of 20 billion euros, of which 2 billion is provided by the United States. This compares to sums of $32-$70 billion dollars that the Reagan administration sought for the Strategic Defense Initiative, which was designed to protect the United States from the threat of communism.

38. The failure of the Central Asian countries to meet the MCA requirements mainly has to do with poor performance in government effectiveness and demonstrations in voting. Kazakhstan is not poor enough to be eligible for MCA funds. See the Millennium Challenge Corporation, which manages the account, available at www.mcc.gov.

39. Nicolas Van de Walle and Timothy Johnston, *Improving Aid to Africa*, Policy Essay no. 21 (Washington, DC: Overseas Development Council, 1996), pp. 3–4.

40. Interviews in the region conducted from 1998 to 2004.

41. Van de Walle and Johnston, *Improving Aid*, p. 5.

42. Constantine Michalopoulos, "The Integration of Low-Income CIS Members in the World Trading System," January 2003, p. 13, available at through the World Bank's website. Michalopoulos uses 2000 trade data.

43. See Martha Brill Olcott, *Kazakhstan: Unfulfilled Promise* (Washington, DC: Carnegie Endowment for International Peace, 2002), p. 81.

44. For example, many Russian speakers gathered around the Russian Embassy in April 2003 to protest the new citizenship law (RFE/RL, June 11, 2003). Russian citizens in Turkmenistan who were deprived of their apartments after the June 22 deadline also protested near the Russian embassy, throwing their Turkmen passports across the embassy fence (Pravda.ru, June 27, 2003).

45. One long public protest held in Uzbekistan lasted most of the day on August 20, 2002, in which human rights activists picketed the justice ministry to complain about living conditions in Uzbekistan. On August 27, 2002, the nongovernmental human rights organizations of Uzbekistan staged another protest to demonstrate against alleged state corruption and police abuse. RFE/RL, *Central Asia Report*, vol. 2, no. 33 (August 29, 2002). According to Human Rights Watch, to stop protest gatherings, Uzbek authorities would usually detain several dozen women with their children and hold them for fifteen days on minor charges. See Human Rights Watch, *Human Rights Watch World Report 2003 on Uzbekistan* (New York: 2003). Turkmenistan also witnessed protests, organized separately on April 11, 15, 16, and 18, by several hundred citizens and by the National Democratic Movement of Turkmenistan, against Niyazov's rule as well as against the state security services' alleged abuse of power. See EurasiaNet.org, *Turkmenistan Daily Digest*, April 18, 2002; and RFE/RL, *Central Asia Report*, August 16, 2002.

46. See also Martha Brill Olcott, "Ceremony and Substance: The Illusion of Unity in Central Asia," in *Central Asia and the World*, ed. Michael Mandelbaum (New York: Council of Foreign Relations, 1999), pp. 18–9. For information on the history of Kyrgyz statehood, see www.eurasianet.org/resource/kyrgyzstan/hypermail/200212/0034.shtml.

47. For example, the long-lived Soviet Communist Party General Secretary Leonid Brezhnev was called Ak Padyshah, the White Supreme Ruler, in much of rural Central Asia, and today's presidents are themselves still referred to as *padyshah*.

48. Forty-four percent of Kazakhs say their country is primarily not a democracy. Most define a democracy as a society that observes human rights and permits personal freedoms and the freedom of choice. Forty-one percent say the country's election laws are "in need of reform," but they do not have detailed preferences concerning the specific kind of electoral reform they want. Among Kyrgyz surveyed, 41 percent prefer democracy, while only 23 percent feel Kyrgyzstan is a fully democratic country. Fifty percent feel it is partially democratic, 17 percent do not feel it is a democracy at all, and 9 percent cannot say whether it is a democracy or not. Fifty-eight percent define democracy as rights and freedom. Forty-one percent are dissatisfied with the practice of democracy in the country. The primary reasons for dissatisfaction are both political and economic: no democracy (11 percent), low living standards (6 percent), unemployment (3 percent), lack of social protection (3 percent), economic recession (3 percent), and inflation (2 percent). Vladimir Pilototskii and Rakesh Sahrmi, *IFES Surveys in Kazakhstan and Kyrgyzstan* (Washington, DC: International Foundation of Electoral Studies, May 2002).

49. Respondents of the IFES poll give a low rating to the government's performance on job creation, reduction of inflation and income inequality, and reduction of crime and corruption. The government performs better in handling terrorism (47 percent well, 43 percent not well) and resolving issues between the northern and southern parts of the country (29 percent well, 39 percent not well).

50. The 1992–1997 civil war in Tajikistan claimed an estimated 50,000 to 100,000 lives and forced close to a million people to flee their homes. Economist Intelligence Unit, *Country Profile 2003* (London: September 1, 2003).

51. The first parliamentary elections in Kazakhstan were held in 1999. The most recent local elections to regional, district, and city councils were held on September 20, 2003. In Kyrgyzstan, President Akayev signed a special decree to fix the date of the local elections in the country. RFE/RL, *Reports 2001–2003*.

52. These leaders included poets such as Muhammad Salih in Uzbekistan, Olzhas Suleimenov in Kazakhstan, or Bozor Sobirin in Tajikistan. Bozor Sobir himself was jailed in 1992–1993, charged with inciting interethnic hatred and provoking the seizure of members of parliament in April 1992. He was convicted in December 1993 and given a four-year suspended sentence. He now lives in voluntary exile in the United States. See U.S. Department of State, "Tajikistan Human Rights Practices, 1992" (Washington, DC: January 31, 1994).

The groups started by these leaders include Erk, Birlik, Nevada Semipalatinsk (an international antinuclear movement), and the Democratic Party of Tajikistan. For example, the Democratic Party of Tajikistan was founded by the philosopher academic Shadman Yusuf in August 1990. Banned in early 1993, it moved its headquarters from Tehran to Moscow in 1995 and was a signatory to an agreement of national reconciliation in 1957. Federal Research Division, *Country Studies on Kazakhstan, Kyrgyzstan, Tajikistan, Turkmenistan, and Uzbekistan* (Washington, DC: U.S. Library of Congress, 1997), p. 275; and Shireen Hunter, *Central Asia since Independence* (Washington, DC: Center for Strategic and International Studies, 1996), p. 53.

53. See appendix twelve on political parties in Central Asia.

54. Thomas Carothers, *Aiding Democracy Abroad: The Learning Curve* (Washington, DC: Carnegie Endowment for International Peace, 1999), p. 88.

55. For a critique of the functioning of NGOs in Central Asia, see Erika Weinthal and Pauline Jones Luong, "Environmental NGOs in Kazakhstan: Democratic Goals and Non-democratic Outcomes," in *The Power and Limits of NGOs*, ed. Sarah E. Mendelson and John H. Glenn (New York: Columbia University Press, 2002), pp. 152–76; and Fiona B. Adamson, "International Democracy Assistance in Uzbekistan and Kyrgyzstan: Building Democracy Assistance from the Outside?" in *The Power and Limits of NGOs*, ed. Mendelson and Glenn pp.177–206.

56. For example, see the OSCE Charter on Preventing and Combating Terrorism, the Charter of Paris for a New Europe, and the Charter for European Security, available at www.osce.org.

Selected Bibliography

Aaron, Sushil J. *Straddling Faultlines: India's Foreign Policy toward the Greater Middle East*. New Delhi: Centre de Sciences Humaines, 2003.

Abazov, Rafis. "Struggling for Recognition," April 2, 2004. www.ciaonet.org/atlas/countries/kz_data_tol.html.

Adamson, Fiona B. "International Democracy Assistance in Uzbekistan and Kyrgyzstan: Building Democracy Assistance from the Outside?" In *The Power and Limits of NGOs*, edited by Sarah Elizabeth Mendelson and John K. Glenn. New York: Columbia University Press, 2002.

Abdullaev, Kamoludin and Catherine Barnes, eds. "Politics of Compromise—The Tajikistan Peace Process," Accord Report no. 10. March 2001. Conciliation Resources, London, England. www.c-r.org.

Ahmedova, Fatimakhon, and Keith A. Leitich. "Ethnic and Religious Conflict in the Ferghana Valley." *Journal of Central Asian Studies*, vol. VI, no. 1 (Fall/Winter 2001).

Akbarzadeh, Shahram. "Keeping Central Asia Stable." *Third World Quarterly*, vol. 25, no. 4 (2004).

Akcali, Pinar. "Islam as a 'Common Bond' in Central Asia: Islamic Renaissance Party and the Afghan Mujahidin." *Central Asian Survey*, vol. 17, no. 2 (1998): 237–84.

Akiner, Shirin. *The Caspian: Politics, Energy and Security*. London: Routledge Curzon, 2004.

———. *The Formation of Kazakh Identity: From Tribe to Nation-State*. London: Royal Institute of International Affairs, 1995.

Akiner, Shirin, and Sander Tideman. *Sustainable Development in Central Asia*. London: Curzon Press, 1998.

343

Alaolmolki, Nozar. *Life after the Soviet Union: The Newly Independent Republics of Transcaucasus and Central Asia.* Albany: State University of New York Press, 2001.

Alexander's Gas and Oil Connections. "EIA Country Analysis: Caspian Sea Region, July 31, 2002." *News and Trends: Central Asia*, vol. 7, no. 16 (August 23, 2002).

―――. "Kashagan Project Participants Exercise Pre-emption Rights," vol. 8, no. 11 (June 3, 2003). www.gasandoil.com/goc/company/cnc32386.htm.

Alma-Ata Yegemendi Qazaqstan. "Kazakhstan Census, 12 January 1989." Translated in *FBIS Daily Report*, USR-92-144, November 11, 1992.

Alibekov, Ibragim. "Kazakhstan: Election Results Harden Opposition." EurasiaNet.org, September 29, 2004. www.eurasianet.org/departments/insight/articles/eav092704a.shtml.

Allison, Roy. "Regionalism, Regional Structures and Security Management in Central Asia." *International Affairs*, vol. 80, no. 3 (2004).

Allison, Roy, and Christoph Bluth, ed. *Security Dilemmas in Russia and Eurasia.* London: Royal Institute of International Affairs, 1998.

Amirahmadi, Hooshang, ed. *The Caspian Region at a Crossroad: Challenges of a New Frontier of Energy and Development.* New York: St. Martin's Press, 2000.

Amnesty International. "Concerns in Europe and Central Asia, July–December 2002." www.erkin.net/chronicle2/news207.html.

Andersen, Michael. "Uzbekistan: EBRD Gets Tough with Tashkent: Credit That Karimov Didn't Deserve." Index for Free Expression, April 7, 2004. www.index-online.org/news/20040403_uzbekistan.shtml.

Anderson, John. *The International Politics of Central Asia.* Manchester and New York: Manchester University Press, 1997.

―――. *Kyrgyzstan: Central Asia's Island of Democracy.* London: Taylor and Francis, 1999.

Anderson, Kathryn H., and Richard W. T. Pomfret. *Consequences of Creating a Market Economy: Evidence from Household Surveys in Central Asia.* Northampton, MA: Edward Elgar Publishing, 2003.

Andrews, Edmund L. "Bustling U.S. Air Base Materializes in the Mud." *New York Times*, April 27, 2002. www.nytimes.com/2002/04/27/international/27KYRG.html.

Appelbaum, Alec. "EBRD Annual Meeting in Tashkent: No Showcase for the Uzbek Government." EurasiaNet.org, May 2, 2003.

Arman, Kambiz. "Russia and Tajikistan: Friends Again." EurasiaNet.org, October 28, 2004. www.eurasianet.org/departments/insight/articles/eav102804.shtml.

Armanini, A. J. *Politics and Economics of Central Asia*. New York: Novinka Books, 2002.

Asian Development Bank. *Fiscal Transition in Kazakhstan*. Manila: 1999, pp. 47–97. www.adb.org/Documents/Books/Fiscal_Transition_in_Kazakstan/4_Chap_1.pdf.

———. *Tajikistan and ADB*. Manila: December 31, 2003. www.adb.org/Documents/Fact_Sheets/TAJ.asp?p=ctrytaj#loans.

———. Environment Division. *Central Asian Environments in Transition*. Manila: 1997.

Åslund, Anders. *Building Capitalism: The Transformation of the Former Soviet Bloc*. New York: Cambridge University Press, 2002.

Associated Press. "Pentagon Studies Central Asia Forces." April 30, 2002. www.nytiimes.com/aponline/national/AP-US-Central Asia.html.

Atal, Subodh. "Central Asia Geopolitics and U.S. Policy in the Region: The Post-11 September Era." *Mediterranean Quarterly*, vol. 14, no. 2 (2003).

Atkin, Muriel. *The Subtlest Battle: Islam in Soviet Tajikistan*. Philadelphia: Foreign Policy Research Institute, 1989.

———. "Tajikistan: Reform, Reaction, and Civil War." In *New States, New Politics: Building the Post-Soviet Nations*, edited by I. Bremmer and R. Taras. Cambridge: Cambridge University Press, 1997.

Babajanov, Bakhtiar. "Islam v Obshestvenno-politicheskoi zhizni Uzbekistanna." *Tsentralnoaziatskii Jurnal*. www.ctaj.elcat.kg/e000.shtml.

Babus, Sylvia, and Judith Share Yaphe. *U.S.–Central Asian Security: Balancing Opportunities and Challenge*. Washington, DC: National Defense University, Institute for National Strategic Studies, 1999.

Baev, Pavel. *Challenges and Options in the Caucasus and Central Asia*. Carlisle Barracks, PA: Strategic Studies Institute, U.S. Army War College, 1997.

Bagley, Bruce Michael, and William O. Walker. *Drug Trafficking in the Americas*. Miami: University of Miami, North/South Center Press, December 1, 1994.

Balci, Bayram. "Fethullah Gulen's Missionary Schools in Central Asia and Their Role in the Spreading of Turkism and Islam." *Religion, State and Society*, vol. 31, no. 2 (2003).

Baran, Zeyno. *The Challenge of Hizb-ut Tahrir: Deciphering and Combating Radical Islamist Ideology*. Washington, DC: Nixon Center, September 2004.

———. *Understanding Sufism and Its Potential Role in US Policy*. Washington, DC: Nixon Center, March 2004.

Bedi, Rahul. "India and Central Asia." *Frontline*, vol. 19, no. 19 (September 14–27, 2002). www.frontlineonnet.com/fl1919/19190600.htm.

Benard,Cheryl. "Hizb ut Tahrir—Bolsheviks in the Mosque." *Journal of Central Asian Studies*, vol. VI, no. 1 (Fall/Winter 2001).

Bensmann, Marcus. "IMU in Retreat." London: Institute for War and Peace Reporting, July 19, 2002. www.iwpr.net./index.pl?archive/rca/rca_200207_130_7_eng.txt#.

Berryman, Sue E. *Hidden Challenges to Education Systems in Transition Economies*. Washington, DC: World Bank, 2000.

Bertsch, Gary K. *Crossroads and Conflict: Security and Foreign Policy in the Caucasus and Central Asia*. New York: Routledge, 2000.

Birdsall, Nancy, John Williamson, and Brian Deese. *Delivering on Debt Relief: From IMF Gold to a New Aid Architecture*. Washington, DC: Center for Global Development, 2002.

Bissell, Tom. *Chasing the Sea*. New York: Vintage Books, 2003.

Bjornlund, Eric C. *Beyond Free and Fair: Monitoring Elections and Building Democracy*. Washington, DC: Woodrow Wilson Center Press, 2004.

Blagov, Sergei."Kazakhstan Looks to Russia amid Hail of Western Criticism." EurasiaNet.org, February 19, 2003.

Blank, Stephen. "Radical Islamic Challenges in Central Asia." Testimony before the House Committee on International Relations, October 2003. wwwc.house.gov/international_relations/108/90361.pdf

Blank, Stephen, and Alvin Z. Rubinstein. *Imperial Decline: Russia's Changing Role in Asia*. Durham, NC: Duke University Press, 1997.

Blua, Antoine. "Central Asia: Rumsfeld Wraps up Visit to Uzbekistan, Kazakhstan." RFE/RL, February 26, 2004.

———. "Kazakhstan: Movement Elects to Transform Itself into a True Opposition Party." RFE/RL, December 5, 2003.

———. "Kyrgyz Rights Activists Call for End to Deportation of Uighurs to China." EurasiaNet.org, January 25, 2004.

Bohr, Annette. "Regional Cooperation in Central Asia: Mission Impossible?" *Helsinki Monitor*, vol. 14, no. 3 (2003).

———. "Regionalism in Central Asia: New Geopolitics, Old Regional Order." *International Affairs*, vol. 80, no. 3 (2004).

———. *Uzbekistan Politics and Foreign Policy*. London: Royal Institute of International Affairs, 1998.

British Broadcasting Corporation. "Uzbek Opposition Party's Registration Bid Rejected." *BBC Monitoring International Reports*, January 5, 2004.

Buckley, Mary. *Post-Soviet Women from the Baltic to Central Asia*. Cambridge: Cambridge University Press, 1997.

Bukharabayeva, Bagila. "Kazakh National Oil Company to Pursue More Aggressive Policy to Expand Market Presence." Associated Press, February 23, 2004.

———. "Kazakstan Politics Could Turn Dynastic." *Seattle Post-Intelligence*, January 31, 2004.

Burgess, Mark. *In the Spotlight: Islamic Movement of Uzbekistan*. Washington, DC: Center for Defense Information, March 25, 2002. www.cdi.org/terrorism/imu.cfm.

Burghart, Daniel L., and Theresa Sabonis-Helf, eds. *Central Asia's Path to the 21ˢᵗ Century*. Washington, DC: National Defense University–Center for Technology and National Security Policy, 2004.

Burles, M. "Chinese Policy toward Russia and the Central Asian Republics." *Peace Research Abstracts*, vol. 38, no. 1 (2001).

Camdessus, Michel. "Challenges Facing the Transition Economies of Central Asia." Address at "Challenges to Economies in Transition" conference, Bishkek, Kyrgyz Republic, May 27, 1998.

Carnegie Endowment for International Peace. "Turkmenistan's Political Crisis: Inside the Niyazov Regime: A Discussion with Boris Sheikmuradov." Washington, DC: April 29, 2002. www.ceip.org/files/events/sheikmuradov042902transcript.asp.

Carothers, Thomas. *Aiding Democracy Abroad: The Learning Curve*. Washington, DC: Carnegie Endowment for International Peace, 1999.

———. *Critical Mission: Essays on Democracy Promotion*. Washington, DC: Brookings Institution Press, 2004.

———. "Promoting the Rule of Law Abroad: The Problem of Knowledge," Carnegie Working Paper no. 34. Washington, DC: Carnegie Endowment for International Peace, 2003.

Castets, Rémi. *The Uyghurs in Xinjiang—The Malaise Grows*. Hong Kong: Universities Service Centre for China Studies, Chinese University of Hong Kong, 2003. www.usc.cuhk.edu.hk/wk_wzdetails.asp?id=3033.

Center for Defense Information. *In the Spotlight: East Turkestan Islamic Movement*. Washington, DC: December 9, 2002.

Cernea, Michael M., and Ayse Kudat, eds. *Social Assessments for Better Development: Case Studies in Russia and Central Asia*. Washington, DC: World Bank, 1997.

Chufrin, Gennady, ed. *The Security of the Caspian Sea Region*. Stockholm: Stockholm International Peace Research Institute, 2001.

Cohen, Ariel. "Defection Shakes Tyrant." *Johnson's Russia List* (November 8, 2001):5531–2.

————. "Radical Islam and U.S. Interests in Central Asia." Testimony before the Subcommittee on Middle East and Central Asia, Committee on International Relations, U.S. House of Representatives, October 2003. Washington, DC: Heritage Foundation, 2003.

————. Testimony before House International Relations for Asia and Pacific, U.S. Policy toward Central Asia Republics, March 17, 1999.

Commercio, Michele E. "Exiles in the Near Abroad: The Russian Minorities in Latvia and Kyrgyzstan." *Problems of Post-Communism*, vol. 51, no. 6 (November/December 2004).

Coll, Steven. *Ghost Wars: The Secret History of the CIA, Afghanistan and Bin Laden, from the Soviet Invasion to September 10, 2001*. New York: Penguin, 2004.

Collins, Kathleen. "Clans, Pacts, and Politics in Central Asia." *Journal of Democracy*, vol. 13, no. 3 (July 2002).

————. "The Political Role of Clans in Central Asia." *Comparative Politics* (January 2003).

————. "Tajikistan: Bad Peace Agreements and Prolonged Civil Conflict." In *From Promise to Practice: Strengthening UN Capacities for the Prevention of Violent Conflict*, edited by Chandra Lekha Sriram, Karin Wermester, and International Peace Academy. Boulder, CO: Lynne Rienner, 2003.

Cooley, Alexander, and James Ron. "The NGO Scramble: Organizational Insecurity and the Political Economy of Transnational Action." *International Security*, vol. 27, no. 1 (Summer 2002).

Coppieters, Bruno, and A. Zverev, eds. *Commonwealth and Independence in Post-Soviet Eurasia*. Portland, OR: F. Cass, 1998.

Corely, Felix. "Tortured Baptist Prisoner Near Death in Turkmenistan." ChristianityToday.com. www.christianitytoday.com/ct/2001/106/35.0.html.

Craft, Cassady, Gary K. Bertsch, Scott A. Jones, and Michael Beck, eds. *Crossroads and Conflict Security and Foreign Policy in the Caucasus and Central Asia*. New York: Routledge, 2000.

Craner, Lorne W. "Uzbekistan: Stifled Democracy, Human Rights in Decline." Testimony at a hearing of the Commission on Security and Cooperation in Europe, Washington, DC, June 24, 2004.

Craumer, Peter. *Rural and Agricultural Development in Uzbekistan*. London: Royal Institute of International Affairs, 1995.

Cristy, Jose. *Colombia: A Risk-Prone Democracy*. Monterey, CA: Naval Post-Graduate School, 1998.

Critchlow, James. *Nationalism in Uzbekistan: A Soviet Republic's Road to Sovereignty*. Boulder, CO: Westview Press, 1991.

Cronin, Patrick M. "Towards a U.S. Foreign Aid Strategy." Testimony before the Committee on International Relations, U.S. House of Representatives, Washington, DC, February 26, 2004.

Csáki, Csaba, and Laura Tuck. *Rural Development Strategy: Eastern Europe and Central Asia*. Washington, DC: World Bank, 2000.

Cummings, Sally N. *Oil, Transition and Security in Central Asia*. London and New York: RoutledgeCurzon, 2003.

————. *Power and Change in Central Asia*. London and New York: Routledge, 2002.

Curtis, Glenn E. "Kazakhstan, Kyrgyzstan, Tajikistan, Turkmenistan, and Uzbekistan: Country Studies." Washington, DC: Federal Research Division, Library of Congress, 1997.

Dadmehr, Nasrin, ed. "Tajikistan: Regionalism and Weakness." In *State Failure and State Weakness in a Time of Terror*, edited by Robert I. Rotberg. Washington, DC: Brookings Institution Press, 2003.

Dalpino, Catharin E. *Deferring Democracy*. Washington, DC: Brookings Institution Press, 2000.

Daly, John C. K. *UPI Energy Watch*. United Press International, August 12, 2004.

Dani, Ahmad Hasan. *Central Asia Today*. Lahore, Pakistan: Sang-e-Meel Publications, 1996.

Dannreuther, Roland. "Can Russia Sustain Its Dominance in Central Asia?" *Sage Family Studies Abstracts*, vol. 28, no. 4 (2002).

Davis, Jacquelyn, and Michael Sweeney. *Central Asia in U.S. Strategy and Operational Planning*. Cambridge, MA: Institute for Foreign Policy Analysis, February 2004, p. 51.

Degnbol-Martinsussen, John, and Poul Engberg-Pedersen. *Aid: Understanding International Development Cooperation*. London: Zed Books, 2003.

Dejevsky, Mary. "Interviews with Gulnara Karimova." *Independent*, January 7, 2004.

Dekmejian, R. Hrair, and Hovann H. Simonian. *Troubled Waters: The Geopolitics of the Caspian Region*. London: Great Britain: I. B. Tauris, 2001.

Demko, George. *Population Under Duress: The Geodemography of Post-Soviet Russian*. Boulder, CO: Westview, 1999.

Denison, Michael. "Identity Politics in Central Asia." *Asian Affairs*, vol. 34, no. 1 (2003).

Donovan, Jefferey. "Kyrgyzstan: U.S. Congressmen Concerned about Rights Abuse." EurasiaNet.org, December 14, 2001. www.eurasianet.org/departments/insight/articles/pp121401.shtml.

Dorian, James P. "Turkmenistan's Future in Gas and Oil Hinges on Certainty for Export Options." *Oil & Gas Journal* (October 12, 2002).

Drug Policy Alliance. *Opium Cultivation Continues to Rise in Afghanistan.* Washington, DC: February 13, 2004.

Dudoignon, Stéphane A. "Devout Societies v. Impious States? Transmitting Islamic Learning in Russia, Central Asia and China through the Twentieth Century." Proceedings of an international colloquium held in the Carré des Sciences, French Ministry of Research, Paris, November 12–13, 2001. Berlin: Schwarz, 2004.

Dudoignon, Stéphane A., and Komatsu Hisao. *Islam in Politics in Russia and Central Asia: Early Eighteenth to Late Twentieth Centuries.* London: Kegan Paul, 2001.

Dwan, Renata, and Oleksandr Pavliuk, eds. *Building Security in the New States of Eurasia: Subregional Cooperation in the Former Soviet Space.* Armonk, NY: M. E. Sharpe, 2000.

Ebel, Robert E., and Rajan Menon, eds. *Energy and Conflict in Central Asia and the Caucasus.* Lanham, MD: Rowman & Littlefield Publishers, 2000.

Economist Intelligence Unit. *Country Forecast.* London: November 3, 2004. www.economist.com/countries/Kazakhstan/profile.cfm?folder=Profile-Forecast.

Efegil, Ertan. "Iran's Interests in Central Asia: A Contemporary Assessment." *Central Asian Survey,* vol. 20, no. 3 (2001).

Eicher, Sharon. "When Does a Transition Economy Become a Market Economy? The Example of Kazakhstan." *Journal of Central Asian Studies,* vol. VI, no. 1 (Fall/Winter 2001).

Eickelman, Dale F. *The Middle East and Central Asia: An Anthropological Approach.* New York: Prentice-Hall, 1998.

Eizenstat, Stuart E., John Edward Porter, and Jeremy M. Weinstein. "On the Break: Weak States and US National Security." Report of the Commission on Weak States and US National Security. Washington, DC: Center for Global Development, May 2004.

Eizenstat, Stuart. Testimony for the Senate Foreign Relations Committee on U.S. Policy toward Caucasus and Central Asia, July 22, 1997.

Elebaeva, A. "The Osh Incident: Problems for Research." *Post-Soviet Geography,* vol. 33, no. 2 (1992): 70–8.

Energy Information Administration. *Country Analysis Briefs: Kazakhstan.* Washington, DC: U.S. Department of Energy, November 4, 2004. www.eia.doe.gov/emeu/cabs/kazak.html.

Esfandiari, Golnaz. "Afghanistan: Donors Conference Focuses on Security." RFE/RL, April 1, 2004. www.rferl.org/featuresarticle/2004/04/9ca24011-a853-4225-b074-b99f9f994ed0.html.

Eshanova, Zamira. "China: Uighur Group Added to U.S. List of Terrorist Organizations." Eurasianet.org, September 1, 2002.

———. "Uzbekistan: Survey Shows Waning Support for War on Terrorism." RFE/RL, July 26, 2002.

EurasiaNet.org. "Gold Mine Reorganization in Kyrgyzstan Spurs Political Controversy." July 20, 2004.

———. "Turkmen President Niyazov Survives Assassination Attempts." November 25, 2002. www.eurasianet.org/departments/insight/articles/eav112502.shtml.

Falkingham, Jane. *Household Welfare in Central Asia*. New York: Palgrave Macmillan, 1997.

Fleming, Alexander, and Lajos Bokros. *Financial Transition in Europe and Central Asia: Challenges of the New Decade*. Washington, DC: World Bank, 2001.

Forsythe, Rosemarie. *The Politics of Oil in the Caucasus and Central Asia: Prospects for Oil Exploitation and Export in the Caspian Basin*. Oxford: Oxford University Press, 1996.

Fox, Louise M., and Ragnar Gotestam. *Changing Minds, Policies and Lives: Improving Protection of Children in Eastern Europe and Central Asia: Redirecting Resources to Community-Based Services*. New York: UNICEF, 2003.

Frantz, Douglas. "Central Asia Braces to Fight Islamic Rebels." New York Times Online, May 3, 2001.

Franco, Claudio. "Afghanistan's Anti-Poppy Drive Off to Shaky Start." EurasiaNet.org, June 3, 2004. www.eurasianet.org/departments/insight/articles/eav060304.shtml.

Freedom House. *Freedom House Report on Uzbekistan 2003*. New York: 2003, p. 634. www.freedomhouse.org/research/nitransit/2003/uzbekistan2003.pdf.

———. "New Printing Press Opening in Kyrgyzstan." Press release. www.freedomhouse.org/media/pressrel/111403.htm.

Garnett, Sherman W. *Rapprochement or Rivalry: Russia–China Relations in a Changing Asia*. Washington, DC: Carnegie Endowment for International Peace, 2000.

Garnett, Sherman W., Alexander G. Rahr, and Koji Watanabe, eds. *The New Central Asia: In Search of Stability: A Report to the Trilateral Commission*. New York: Trilateral Commission, 2000.

Ghani, Ashraf. "Where Democracy's Greatest Enemy Is a Flower." *New York Times*, December 11, 2004.

Gibb, H. A. R. *The Arab Conquests in Central Asia*. New York: AMS Print, 1970.

Gill, Bates, and Matthew Oresman. *China's New Journey to the West: China's Emergence in Central Asia and Implications for U.S. Interests.* Washington, DC: Center for Strategic and International Studies, August 2003.

Gleason, Gregory. *The Central Asian States: Discovering Independence.* Boulder, CO: Westview Press, 1997.

―――. "Inter-State Cooperation in Central Asia from the CIS to the Shanghai Forum." *Europe–Asia Studies*, vol. 53, no. 7 (2001).

―――. *Markets and Politics in Central Asia: Structural Reform and Political Change.* London: Routledge, 2003.

Glenn, John. *The Soviet Legacy in Central Asia.* New York: Palgrave, 1999.

Godinho, Joana. *HIV/AIDS and Tuberculosis in Central Asia: Country Profiles.* Washington, DC: World Bank, 2004.

Golnaz, Esfandiari. "Afghanistan Donors Conference Focuses on Security." RFE/RL, April 1, 2004.

Gorshkov, Teimuraz. "TRACECA: Restoration of Silk Route." *Japan Railway and Transport Review*, no. 28 (September 2001).

Graham, Stephen. "Karzai Urges Afghans to Give Up Lucrative Opium Trade, Says Taliban Profiting." *Associated Press*, December 9, 2004.

Gray, Cheryl Williamson, Joel S. Hellman, and Randi Ryterman. *Anticorruption in Transition 2, Corruption in Enterprise-State Interactions Europe and Central Asia, 1999-2002.* Washington, DC: World Bank, 2004.

―――. *Anticorruption in Transition 2, Corruption in Enterprise-State Interactions in Europe and Central Asia 1999-2002.* Washington, DC: World Bank, 2002.

Gray, John. *Kazakhstan: A Review of Farm Restructuring.* Washington, DC: World Bank, 2000.

Graves, Gary. "The Age of Reason: A Liberal Interpretation." *CBC News Online*, September 23, 2003.

Haggard, Stephan, and Robert R. Kaufman. *The Political Economy of Democratic Transitions.* Princeton, NJ: Princeton University Press, 1995.

Haghayeghi, Mehrdad. *Islam and Politics in Central Asia.* New York: St. Martin's Press, 1996.

Hagt, Eric. "China's Water Policies: Implications for Xinjiang and Kazakhstan." *The Central Asia–Caucasus Analyst.* Washington, DC: Center for Strategic and International Studies, July 30, 2003.

Hartung, William D. "War without End? The Costs of the New Military Buildup." In *The Hidden Costs of War*, report commissioned by Howard S. Brembeck and the Fourth Freedom Forum. Goshen, IN: Fourth Freedom Forum, 2003.

Herzig, Edmund. "Regionalism, Iran and Central Asia." *International Affairs*, vol. 80, no. 3 (2004).

Herzig, Edmund, and Neil Melvin. "Central Asia: Aspects of Security and Stability." *Helsinki Monitor*, vol. 14, no. 3 (2003).

Heyneman, Stephen P., and Alan DeYoung. *The Challenge of Education in Central Asia*. Greenwich, CT: Information Age Publication, 2004.

Hill, Fiona. "Central Asia: Terrorism, Religious Extremism, and Regional Stability." Testimony before the House Committee on International Relations, Subcommittee on the Middle East and Central Asia, October 29, 2003. wwwc.house.gov/international_relations/108/90361.pdf

Hoelsher, David. "Banking System Restructuring in Kazakhstan." IMF Working Paper no. 98/96. Washington, DC: June 1, 1998.

Höynck, Wilhelm. "The OSCE in Central Asia—On the Right Track?" *Helsinki Monitor*, vol. 14, no. 3 (2003).

Human Rights Watch. *Creating Enemies of the State: Religious Persecution in Uzbekistan*. www.hrw.org/reports/2004/uzbekistan0304/index.htm.

———. *Human Rights Watch World Report 2001: Uzbekistan*. New York: 2001. www.hrw.org/wr2k1/europe/uzbekistan.html.

———. *Human Rights Watch World Report 2003 on Kyrgyzstan*. New York: 2003.

———. *Republic of Uzbekistan, Crackdown in the Ferghana Valley: Arbitrary Arrests and Religious Discrimination*. Washington, DC: 1998.

———. *The Rise of Xenophobia in Russia*. New York: 2003. www.hrw.org/reports98/russia/srusstest-03.htm.

———. *Uzbek Court Convicts Police for Beating Death*. New York: January 25, 2002.

———. *Uzbekistan: President Rigs Extended Term of Office*. New York: January 25, 2002.

Hunter, Shireen. *Central Asia since Independence*. Westport, CT: Praeger, 1996.

Iankulova, Ina. "Presidential Decree Expected to Restrict Turkmen Study Abroad." EurasiaNet.org, March 11, 2003. www.eurasianet.org/resource/turkmenistan/hypermail/200303/0021.shtml.

Ingram, George M. Testimony of George M. Ingram, Deputy Assistant Administrator for Newly Independent States, House International Relations Aid to Russia, June 9, 1999.

Intercon Daily Report on Russia, Washington DC, February 23, 1999.

Interfax. "Industry in Tajikistan," 2004.

Interfax Central Asia. September 6–12, 2004.

———. August 5, 2003.

———. August 5, 2002.

International Crisis Group. "The Curse of Cotton: Central Asia's Destructive Monoculture." ICG Asia Report no. 93. February 28, 2005.

———. "Repression and Regression in Turkmenistan: A New International Strategy." ICG Asia Report no. 85. Osh/Brussels: November 4, 2004.

———. "Political Transition in Kyrgyzstan: Problems and Prospects," ICG Asia Report no. 81. Osh/Brussels: August 11, 2004.

———. "The Failure of Reform in Uzbekistan: Ways Forward for the International Community," ICG Asia Report no. 76. Osh/Brussels: March 11, 2004.

———. "Youth in Central Asia: Losing the New Generation," ICG Asia Report no. 66. Osh/Brussels: October 31, 2003.

———. "Central Asia: Islam and the State," ICG Asia Report no. 59. Osh/Brussels: July 10, 2003.

———. "Radical Islam in Central Asia: Responding to Hizb-ut Tahrir," ICG Asia Report no. 58. Osh/Brussels: June 30, 2003.

———. "Tajikistan: A Roadmap for Development," ICG Asia Report no. 51. Osh/Brussels: April 24, 2003.

———. "Uzbekistan's Reform Program: Illusion or Reality?" ICG Asia Report no. 46. Osh/Brussels: February 18, 2003.

———. "Cracks in the Marble: Turkmenistan's Failing Dictatorship," ICG Asia Report no. 44. Osh/Brussels: January 17, 2003.

———. "Central Asia: The Politics of Police Reform," ICG Asia Report no. 42, Osh/Brussels: December 10, 2002.

———. "Ferghana Valley, Kyrgyzstan and Tajikistan," ICG Asia Report no. 38. Osh/Brussels: September 11, 2002.

———. "Central Asia: Water and Conflict," ICG Asia Report no. 34. Osh/Brussels: May 30, 2002.

———."Central Asia: Border Disputes and Conflict Potential," ICG Asia Report no. 33. Osh/Brussels: April 4, 2002.

———. "Tajikistan: An Uncertain Peace," ICG Asia Report no. 30. Osh/Brussels: December 24, 2001.

———. "Central Asia: Drugs and Conflict," ICG Asia Report no. 25. Osh/Brussels: November 26, 2001.

———. "Kyrgyzstan at Ten: Trouble in the Island of Democracy," ICG Asia Report no. 22. Osh/Brussels: August 28, 2001.

———. "Uzbekistan at Ten—Repression and Instability," ICG Asia Report no. 21. Osh/Brussels: August 21, 2001.

———. "Fault Lines in the New Security Map," ICG Asia Report no. 20. Osh/Brussels: July 4, 2001.

———. "Incubators of Conflict: Central Asia's Localized Poverty and Social Unrest," ICG Asia Report no. 16. Osh/Brussels: June 8, 2001.

———. "Islamist Mobilisation and Regional Security," Asia Report no. 14. Osh/Brussels: March 1, 2001.

———. "Crisis Conditions in Three States," ICG Asia Report no. 7. Osh/Brussels: August 7, 2000.

———. "Tajikistan's Politics: Confrontation or Consolidation?" Asia Briefing. Dushanbe/Brussels: May 19, 2004.

———. "The IMU and the Hizb ut-Tahrir: Implications of the Afghanistan Campaign," Asia Briefing. Osh/Brussels: January 30, 2002.

———. "Recent Violence in Central Asia: Causes and Consequences." Asia Briefing. October 18, 2000.

International Energy Agency. *Caspian Oil and Gas*. Paris: 1998, pp. 254–7.

International Helsinki Federation for Human Rights. *Turkmenistan: The Making of a Failed State*. Vienna: April 2004.

International Monetary Fund. "Islamic State of Afghanistan: Rebuilding a Macroeconomic Framework for Reconstruction and Growth," IMF Country Report no. 03/299. Washington, DC: September 2003.

———. "Kazakhstan: Recent Economic Developments," IMF Country Report no. 98/84. Washington, DC: 1998.

———. "Kazakhstan: Selected Issues and Statistical Appendix," IMF Country Report no. 02/64. Washington, DC: March 2002.

———. "Kyrgyz Republic: Selected Issues and Statistical Appendix," IMF Country Report no. 00/131. Washington, DC: October 30, 2000.

———. "Kyrgyz Republic: Statistical Appendix," IMF Country Report no. 01/224, December 19, 2001.

———. "Republic of Kazakhstan," IMF Country Report no. 01/20. Washington, DC: January 25, 2001.

———. "Republic of Kazakhstan: 2004 Article IV Consultation—Staff Report; and Public Information Notice on the Executive Board Discussion," IMF Country Report no. 04/339. Washington, DC: October 28, 2004.

————. "Republic of Kazakhstan: Recent Economic Developments," IMF Country Report no. 98/94. Washington, DC: September 23, 1998.

————. "Republic of Kazakhstan: Selected Issues and Statistical Appendix," IMF Country Report no. 04/362. Washington, DC: November 2004.

————. "Republic of Kazakhstan: Selected Issues and Statistical Appendix," IMF Country Report no. 03/211. Washington, DC: July 2003.

————. "Republic of Kazakhstan: Selected Issues and Statistical Appendix," IMF Country Report no. 00/29. Washington, DC: March 6, 2000.

————. "Republic of Tajikistan: Recent Economic Developments," IMF Country Report no. 98/16. Washington, DC: February 1998.

————. "Turkmenistan: Recent Economic Developments," IMF Country Report no. 99/140. Washington, DC: December 1999.

International Monetary Fund and International Development Association. *Kyrgyz Republic: Joint Staff Assessment of the Poverty Reduction Strategy Paper.* Washington, DC: January 24, 2003, p. 27.

International Organization for Migration. *Migration Trends in Eastern Europe and Central Asia.* Geneva: 2002.

————. "World Migration 2003: Managing Migration Challenges and Responses for People on the Move," IOM World Migration Report Series no. 2. Geneva: 2003, p. 43.

International War Peace and Reporting. "Kazak Heavyweight Takes on President." London: April 30, 2004. www.iwpr.net/index.pl?archive/rca/rca_200404_281_1_eng.txt.

Iran Press Service. "Caspian Sea States to Discuss the Sea's Status." April 5, 2004. www.iran-press service.com/articles_2004/Apr_04/caspian_sea_meeting_5404.htm.

IRIN News. "Tajikistan: IOM Announces New Programme on Labour Migrant Remittances." November 2, 2004, www.plusnews.org/report.asp?ReportID=43966&SelectRegion=Central_Asia&SelectCountry=TAJIKISTA.

————. "Turkmenistan: Religious Leader Arrested and Imprisoned." March 18, 2004. www.irinnews.org/print.asp?ReportID=40133.

Islamov, Esmer. "Bombings and Shootings Rock Uzbekistan." EurasiaNet.org, March 30, 2004.

Ismael, Tareq Y., and Mustafa Aydin. *Turkey's Foreign Policy in the 21st Century: A Changing Role in World Politics.* Burlington, VT: Ashgate, 2003.

Jakipova, Chinara. "The Challenge of Governance in the Central Asian Countries (an Example of Kyrgyzstan)." Paper prepared for the International Peace Academy conference on Security in Central Asia, Vienna, Austria, July 2002.

Jalalza'I, Musa Khan. *The Pipeline War in Afghanistan: Oil, Gas and the New Energy Great Game in Central Asia*. Lahore: Sang-e-Meel Publications, 2003.

Jawa, Nassim, and Shahrbanou Tadjbakhsh. "Tajikistan: A Forgotten War." *Minority Rights Group* (February 1995).

Johnsrud, Cristy, Ryan P. Theis, and Maria Bezerra. *Business Incubation: Emerging Trends for Profitability and Economic Development in the U.S., Central Asia, and the Middle East*. Washington, DC: Office of Technology Policy, U.S. Department of Commerce, and Pathfinder Research, 2003.

Jones, Richard Lezin. "Immigrant Wins Custody of Children, Who Are with Mother in Uzbekistan." *New York Times*, February 11, 2003.

Jonson, Lena. *Russia and Central Asia: A New Web of Relations*. London: Royal Institute of International Affairs, Russia and Eurasia Programme, 1998.

———. *Russia and Tajikistan in a New Regional Context: Post September 11, 2001*. Stockholm: Swedish Institute for International Affairs, October 2002, p. 7.

———. *Vladimir Putin and Central Asia: The Shaping of Russian Foreign Policy*. London: I. B. Tauris, 2004.

Jumataeva, Venera. "Kulov Muzzled." London: Institute for War and Peace Reporting, August 10, 2001. www.iwpr.net/index.pl?archive/rca/rca_200108_64_3_eng.txt.

Kaiser, Robert. "Difficult Times for a Key Ally in Terror War, Kyrgyzstan's Politics, Economy in Turmoil." *Washington Post*, August 5, 2002, p. A9.

Kalyuzhnova, Yelena, and Dov Lynch. *The Euro-Asia World: A Period of Transition*. New York: St. Martin's Press, in association with the Centre for Euro-Asian Studies, 2000.

Karimov, Islam, and William Perry. Memorandum for correspondence on a meeting of June 26, 1996. www.defenselink.mil/news/jun1996/m062696_m144-96.html.

Kaser, Michael. *The Economies of Kazakhstan and Uzbekistan*. London: Royal Institute of International Affairs, 1997.

Kasymova, Nazokat. *Uzbekistan and the Challenges of Creating a Regional Security System within Central Asia*. Washington, DC: Kennan Institute and Woodrow Wilson Institute, 2001.

Kempton, Daniel R., and Terry D. Clark. *Unity of Separation: Center-Periphery Relations in the Former Soviet Union*. Westport, CT: Praeger, 2002.

Khalid, Adeeb. *The Politics of Muslim Cultural Reform Jadidism in Central Asia*. Berkeley: University of California Press, 1998.

―――――. "A Secular Islam: Nation, State, and Religion in Uzbekistan." *International Journal of Middle East Studies*, vol. 35, no. 4 (2003).

Khamidov, Alisher. "Ak-Sui Trial in Kyrgyzstan Causes Rift between President and Law-Enforcement Officials." EurasiaNet.org, October 18, 2002.

Khan, Mohsin S., and Sunil Sharma. "IMF Conditionality and Country Ownership of Programs," IMF Working Paper no. WP/01/142. Washington, DC: September 2001.

Khazanov, Anatoly. *After the USSR: Ethnicity, Nationalism, and Politics in the Commonwealth of Independent States.* Madison: University of Wisconsin Press, 1995.

King, Charles, and Neil J. Melvin, eds. "Nations Abroad: Diaspora Politics and International Relations in the Former Soviet Union." *Peace Research Abstracts*, vol. 39, no. 2 (2002).

Kistauova, Zaure. "Kazakh Tengizchevroil Partners Sign Second Phase Development Deal." Dow Jones Newswires, September 19, 2003.

Kleveman, Lutz. *The New Great Game: Blood and Oil in Central Asia.* New York: Atlantic Monthly Press, 2003.

Kobori, Iwao, and Michael H. Glantz. *Central Eurasian Water Crisis: Caspian, Aral, and Dead Seas.* Tokyo: United Nations University Press, 1998.

Koening, Daniel J., and Dilip K. Das, eds. *International Police Cooperation: A World Perspective.* Lanham, MD: Lexington Books, 2001.

Kuchins, Andrew C., ed. *Russia after the Fall.* Washington, DC: Carnegie Endowment for International Peace, 2002.

Kudryashov, Andrei. "Opposition in Uzbekistan Misses Another Chance to Participate in the Parliamentary Election." Fergana.ru, June 28, 2004. http://enews.ferghana.ru/detail.php?id=478&code_phrase=.

Kuti, Eva. "Civic Service in Eastern Europe and Central Asia: From Mandatory Public Work toward Civic Service." *Nonprofit and Voluntary Sector Quarterly*, vol. 33, no. 4, supplement 1 (2004).

Kyrgyzstan Development Gateway. "Small and Medium Business in the Year 2002." http://eng.gateway.kg/business_small.

Lancaster, Carol. *Transforming Foreign Aid.* Washington, DC: Institute for International Economics, 2000.

Lancaster, John. "Karzai Urges War on Opium Trade; Leader Says Cultivation Imperils Attempt to Rebuild Afghanistan." *Washington Post*, December 10, 2004.

Landau, Jacob M., and Barbara Kellner-Heinkele. *Politics of Language in the Ex-Soviet Muslim States: Azerbayjan, Uzbekistan, Kazakhstan, Kyrgyzstan, Turkmenistan, Tajikistan.* London: Hurst, 2001.

Laruelle, Marlène, and Sébastien Peyrouse. *Les Russes du Kazakhstan: Identités nationales et nouveaux États dans l'espace post-soviétique.* Paris: Maisonneuve & Larose, 2003.

Lazreg, Marnia. "Making the Transition Work for Women in Europe and Central Asia." *Sage Family Studies Abstracts,* vol. 24, no. 1 (2002).

Lee, Larisa. "Jypar Jeksheef: Zoloto pakhnet kriminalom." *Moya Stolitsa Novosti,* July 13, 2004.

Legvold, Robert. *Thinking Strategically: The Major Powers, Kazakhstan, and the Central Asian Nexus.* Cambridge, MA: MIT Press, 2003.

Lenczowski, George. *American Presidents and the Middle East.* Durham, NC: Duke University Press, 1990.

Lerman, Zvi, and Karen McConnell Brooks. *Turkmenistan: An Assessment of Leasehold-Based Farm Restructuring.* Washington, DC: World Bank, 2001.

LeVine, Steve. "Oil Companies Settle Flap with Kazakhstan." *Wall Street Journal,* January 29, 2003.

Lewis, David C. *After Atheism: Religion and Ethnicity in Russia and Central Asia.* New York: Palgrave Macmillan, 2000.

Linette, Daniel. "Water Resources Management in Central Asia: Addressing New Challenges and Risks." *Central Asia and Caucasus Analysis* (August 15, 2001).

Lorie, Henri. "Priorities for Further Fiscal Reforms in the Commonwealth of Independent States," IMF Working Paper no. WP/03/209. Washington, DC: International Monetary Fund, European II Department, October 2003.

Loukoianova, Elena, and Anna Unigovskaya. "Analysis of Recent Growth in Low-Income CIS Countries," IMF Working Paper no. WP/04/151. Washington, DC: International Monetary Fund, Monetary and Financial Systems Department, August 2004.

Lovei, Laszlo. *Energy in Europe and Central Asia: A Sector Strategy for the World Bank Group.* Washington, DC: World Bank, 1998.

Lubin, Nancy. Testimony of Nancy Lubin, President of JNA Associates, INC., House International Relations for Asia and Pacific, U.S. Policy toward Central Asia Republics, March 17, 1999.

Lubin, Nancy, Keith Martin and Barnett R. Rubin. *Calming the Ferghana Valley: Development and Dialogue in the Heart of Central Asia.* New York: Century Foundation Press, 1999

Luong, Pauline Jones. *Institutional Change and Political Continuity in Post-Soviet Central Asia: Power, Perceptions, and Pacts.* Cambridge: Cambridge University Press, 2002.

———. *The Transformation of Central Asia: States and Societies from Soviet Rule to Independence*. Ithaca, NY: Cornell University Press, 2004.

Lynch, Dov. *Russian Peacekeeping Strategies in the CIS: The Cases of Moldova, Georgia and Tajikistan*. New York: Palgrave Macmillan, 2000.

MacAskill, Ewen. "A Coalition Showing Signs of Fracture." *Guardian*, April 9, 2004.

MacFarlane, Neil. "International Organisations in Central Asia: Understanding the Limits." *Helsinki Monitor*, vol. 14, no. 3 (2003).

———. "The United States and Regionalism in Central Asia." *International Affairs*, vol. 80, no. 3 (2004).

———. *Western Engagement in the Caucasus and Central Asia*. London: Royal Institute of International Affairs, 1999.

Magnus, Ralph H. *Afghanistan: Mullah, Marx and Mujahid*. Boulder, CO: Westview Press, 2002.

Makarenko, Tamara. "Crime, Terror, and the Central Asian Drug Trade," Caspian Brief no. 25. Bromma, Sweden: Cornell Caspian Consulting, July 2002.

Malashenko, Aleksei. "Islam, Politics and the Security of Central Asia." *Russian Politics and Law*, vol. 42, no. 4 (2004).

Malashenko, Aleksei, and Martha Brill Olcott, eds. "Multi-Dimensional Borders of Central Asia." April 2000. Moscow, Russia: Carnegie Moscow Center.

Malik, Hafeez. *The Roles of the United States, Russia, and China in the New World Order*. New York: St. Martin's Press, 1997.

Manz, Beatrice Rorbes. "Tamerlane's Career and Its Uses." *Journal of World History*, vol. 13, no. 1 (2002).

Marketos, Thrassy. "Shanghai Cooperation: A Political / Military Coalition in the Making?" *Journal of Central Asian Studies*, vol. VI, no. 1 (Fall/Winter 2001).

McCauley, Martin. *Afghanistan and Central Asia: A Modern History*. Harlow, UK: Longman Books, 2002.

McDermott, Roger. *Border Security in Tajikistan: Countering the Narcotics Trade?* Camberley, UK: Conflict Studies Research Centre, August 11, 2003.

———. *Countering Global Terrorism Developing the Antiterrorist Capabilities of the Central Asian Militaries*. Carlisle, PA: Strategic Studies Institute, U.S. Army War College, 2004. http://purl.access.gpo.gov/GPO/LPS47654.

McKee, Martin, and Judith Healy. *Healthcare in Central Asia*. Buckingham, PA: Open University, 2002.

Melvin, Neil J. *Uzbekistan: Transition to Authoritarianism on the Silk Road*. London: Taylor and Francis, 2000.

Mendelson, Sarah E., and John H. Glenn. *The Power and Limits of NGOs*. New York: Columbia University Press, 2002.

Menzel, Marcus. *Doomed to Cooperate? American Foreign Policy in the Caspian Region.* Frankfurt: Peter Lang, 2003.

Mercy Corps Central Asia. *Ferghana Valley Field Study: Reducing the Potential for Conflict through Community Mobilization.* Portland, OR: May 2003.

Mesbahi, Mohiaddin. "Iran's Foreign Policy toward Russia, Central Asia, and the Caucasus." In *Iran at the Crossroads*, edited by John L. Esposito and R. K. Ramazani. New York: Palgrave Macmillan, 2001.

Metcalf, Barbara D. *Islamic Revival in British India*. Princeton, NJ: Princeton University Press, 1982.

———. *Traditionalist Islamic Activism: Deoband, Tablighis, and Talibs.* New York: Social Science Research Council, 2001.

Michalopoulas, Constantine. "The Integration of Low-Income CIS Members in the World Trading System." Paper prepared for the CIS-7 Conference in January 2003, Lucerne Switzerland, p. 44.

Micklin, Philip P. *Managing Water in Central Asia*. London: Royal Institute of International Affairs, 2000.

Mikesell, John L., and Daniel R. Mullins, eds. "Reforming Budgetary Processes and Procedures in Countries of the Former Soviet Union: Experiences in Azerbaijan and the Central Asian Republics." *Sage Public Administration Abstracts*, vol. 29, no. 1 (2002).

Misra, Amalendu. "Shanghai 5 and the Emerging Alliance in Central Asia: The Closed Society and Its Enemies." *Central Asian Survey*, vol. 20, no. 3 (2001).

Miyamoto, Akira. *Natural Gas in Central Asia: Industries, Markets and Export Options of Kazakhstan, Turkmenistan and Uzbekistan.* Washington, DC: Brookings Institution, 1997.

Mommer, Bernard. *Global Oil and the Nation State*. New York: Oxford University Press, 2002.

Montgomery, John D., and Dennis A. Rondinelli, eds. *Beyond Reconstruction in Afghanistan: Lessons from Development Experience.* New York: Palgrave Macmillan, 2004.

Morgounov, A., and L. W. Zuidema. *The Legacy of the Soviet Agricultural Research System for the Republics of Central Asia and the Caucasus.* The Hague, Netherlands: International Service for National Agricultural Research, 2001.

Morningstar, Richard L. Testimony of Richard L. Morningstar, Special Adviser to the President and Secretary of State, House International Relations, Foreign Policy in Caucasus, Central Asia, April 30, 1998.

Moscow Times. "China Inks Historic Kazakh Oil Pact." May 19, 2004.

Motyl, Alexander, and Amanda Schnetzer, eds. *Nations in Transit 2004: Democratization in East Central Europe and Eurasia.* Lanham, MD: Rowman & Littlefield, 2004.

Muhin, Vladimir. "Tashkent protiv 'besplatnoi pivatizatsii.'" *Nezavisimaya Gazeta,* May 13, 2004.

Murrell, Peter. *Assessing the Value of Law in Transition Economies.* Ann Arbor: University of Michigan Press, 2001.

Mydans, Seth. "Uzbeks' Anger at Rulers Boils Over." *New York Times,* April 8, 2004.

Nahaylo, Bahdan, and Victor Swoboda. *Soviet Disunion: A History of the Nationalities Problem in the USSR.* London: Hamish Hamilton, 1990.

Naumkin, Vitaly V. "Militant Islam in Central Asia: The Case of the Islamic Movement of Uzbekistan." Berkeley Program in Soviet and Post-Soviet Studies, Institute of Slavic, East European, and Eurasian Studies, University of California, Berkeley, CA, Spring 2003.

New Jersey Law Journal. "*Maqsudi v. Karimova-Maqsudi,*" New Jersey Superior Court, Chancery Division, August 11, 2003.

News Central Asia. "Turkmenistan—One Year after the Botched Coup." www.news-centralasia.com/modules.php?name=News&file=article&sid=365.

Nichol, James P. "Central Asia: Regional Developments and Implications for U.S. Interests," CRS Report for Congress. Washington, DC: Congressional Research Service, November 12, 2004. www.fas.org/man/crs/IB93108.pdf.

———. *Central Asia's New States: Political Developments and Implications for U.S. Interests.* Washington, DC: Congressional Research Service, 2001.

Nobatova, Maya. "Gazprom Lays Down the Rules for Gas Business in Central Asia." *Russian Petroleum Investor,* March 2003, p. 76.

Norris, Era-Dabla, Jorge Martinez-Vazquez, and John Norregaard. *Making Decentralization Work: The Case of Russia, Ukraine, and Kazakhstan.* Washington, DC: International Monetary Fund, November 20, 2000.

Norsworthy, Alexander L. *Rural Development, Natural Resources, and the Environment: Lessons of Experience in Eastern Europe and Central Asia.* Washington, DC: Environmentally and Socially Sustainable Development, Europe and Central Asia Region, World Bank, 2000.

Odom, William. Testimony of Lieutenant General William E. Odom for the Senate Foreign Relations Committee on U.S. Policy toward Caucasus and Central Asia, July 22, 1997.

Olcott, Martha Brill. "Caspian Sea Oil Exports." Testimony before the U.S. Senate Foreign Relations Committee, Subcommittee on International Economic Policy, Export, and Trade Promotion, Washington DC, July 8, 1998. www.ceip.org/people.olccaspw.htm.

———. "Central Asia's Catapult to Independence." *Foreign Affairs*, vol. 71, no. 3 (Summer 1992):118–28.

———. *Central Asia's New States*. Washington, DC: USIP Press, 1996.

———. "Central Asia: Terrorism, Religious Extremism, and Regional Stability." Testimony before the U.S. House of Representatives, Committee on International Relations, Subcommittee on the Middle East and Central Asia, October 29, 2003. wwwc.house.gov/international_relations/108/90361/pdf.

———. "Ceremony and Substance: The Illusion of Unity in Central Asia." In *Central Asia and the World*, edited by Michael Mandelbaum. New York: Council on Foreign Relations, 1999, pp. 18–9.

———. "Democracy in the Central Asian Republics." Testimony before the U.S. House of Representatives, Committee on International Relations Subcommittee on Asia and the Pacific, April 12, 2000. www.ceip.org/files/Publications/Housetestimony.asp?from=pubtype.

———. "Facing the Future: Twelve Myths about Central Asia." Paper presented at the Central Asian Conference on Regional Cooperation, Bishkek, Kyrgyzstan, 1995.

———. *The Kazakhs*, 2nd edition. Stanford, CA: Hoover University Press, 1995.

———. *Kazakhstan: Unfulfilled Promise*. Washington, DC: Carnegie Endowment for International Peace, 2002.

———. "Politics of Economic Distribution in the Caspian Sea States." Testimony before the U.S. Senate Foreign Relations Committee, Subcommittee on International Economic Policy, Export, and Trade Promotion, Washington DC, April 12, 2000. www.ceip.org/files/Publications/housetestimony.asp?from=pubtype.

———. "Russian–Chinese Relations and Central Asia." In *Rapprochement or Rivalry? Russia–China Relations in a Changing Asia*, edited by Sherman Garnett. Washington, DC: Carnegie Endowment for International Peace, 2000.

———. "Shifting Sands in Central Asia?" *Helsinki Monitor*, vol. 14, no. 3 (2003).

———. Testimony before the U.S. Congress Commission on Security and Cooperation in Europe on the Challenge of Building Democracy in Kazakhstan, May 6, 1999. www.eurasianet.org/resource/kazakhstan/links/olcott.html.

———. *Turkmenistan: Challenges in the Transport of Turkmen Gas*. Stanford, CA: Stanford University Program on Energy and Sustainable Development, May 2004.

Olcott, Martha Brill, Anders Åslund, and Sherman Garnett, eds. *Getting It Wrong: Regional Cooperation and the Commonwealth of Independent States*. Washington, DC: Carnegie Endowment for International Peace, 1999.

Olcott, Martha Brill, and Natalia Udalova. "Drug Trafficking on the Great Silk Road: The Security Environment in Central Asia," Carnegie Working Paper no. 11. Washington, DC: Carnegie Endowment for International Peace, March 2000.

Oliker, Olga, and Thomas S. Szayna, eds. *Faultlines of Conflict in Central Asia and the South Caucasus: Implications for the U.S. Army*. Santa Monica, CA: Rand, 2003.

Open Society Institute. "Caspian Oil Windfalls: Who Will Benefit?" *Caspian Revenue Watch*. New York: Open Society Institute, 2003, p. 146.

———. "Open Society Foundation Sums Up Results of Election in Almaty." New York: September 21, 2004. www.cascfen.org/news.php?nid=408&cid=12.

Organization for Economic Cooperation and Development. *Financing Strategies for Water and Environmental Infrastructure*. Paris: 2003.

Organization for Security and Cooperation in Europe, Office for Democratic Institutions and Human Rights, Election Observation, *Kyrgyz Republic: Parliamentary Elections, 20 February and 12 March 2000, Final Report*. Warsaw: April 10, 2000.

———. "Kyrgyz Presidential Election Fails International Standards." Press release, October 30, 2000.

Otsuka, Shigeru. "Central Asia's Rail Network and the Eurasian Land Bridge." *Japan Railway and Transport Review*, vol. 28 (September 2001).

Ottaway, David B., and Dan Morgan. "Gas Pipeline Bounces between Agendas." *Washington Post*, October 5, 1998, p. A1.

Ottaway, Marina, and Thomas Carothers. "Toward Civil Society Realism." In *Funding Virtue: Civil Society Aid and Democracy Promotion*, edited by Marina Ottaway and Thomas Carothers. Washington, DC: Brookings Institution Press, 2000.

Panfilova, Victoria. "Dvoynay Igra Turkmenabashi." *Nezavisimaya Gazeta*, March 12, 2003.

Pannier, Bruce. "Kazakhstan: Opposition Party Sees Fortunes Rise and Fall." EurasiaNet.org, July 31, 2004. www.eurasianet.org/departments/rights/articles/pp073104.shtml.

———. "Kyrgyzstan: Former Prime Minister to Run for President." RFE/RL, June 16, 2004. www.rferl.org/featuresarticle/2004/06/74fed59e-7f21-41c9-9e76-98410de9c4b3.html.

———. "Turkmenistan: Former Minister Wanted on Criminal Charges." RFE/RL, November 2, 2001.

Pannier, Bruce, and Zamira Echanova. "Uzbekistan: U.S. Signs Security Agreements in Tashkent." RFE/RL, May 26, 1999. Reprinted in *Asia Times Online*, May 28, 1999. www.atimes.com/c-asia/AE28Ag01.html.

Parra, Francisco. *Oil Politics: A Modern History of Petroleum.* London: I. B. Tauris, 2004.

Peck, Anne E. *Economic Development in Kazakhstan: The Role of Large Enterprises and Foreign Investment.* London: Routledge Curzon, 2004.

Peimani, Hooman. *Regional Security and the Future of Central Asia: The Competition of Iran, Turkey, and Russia.* Westport, CT: Praeger, 1988.

Peterson, D. J. *Troubled Lands: The Legacy of Soviet Environmental Destruction.* Boulder, CO: Westview Press, 1993.

Peuch, Jean-Christophe. "Central Asia: Charges Link Russian Military to Drug Trade." RFE/RL, June 8, 2001. www.rferl.org/features/2001/06/08062001111711.asp.

Pirseyedi, Bobi. *The Small Arms Problem in Central Asia: Features and Implications.* Geneva: United Nations Institute for Disarmament Research, 2000.

Polat, Necati. *Boundary Issues in Central Asia.* New York: Transnational Publishers, 2002.

Pomfret, Richard. *Central Asia Turns South? Trade Relations in Transition.* London: Royal Institute of International Affairs, 1999.

———. *The Economies of Central Asia.* Princeton, NJ: Princeton University Press, 1995.

Pressley, Donald L. Testimony of Donald L. Pressley, Acting Assistant Administrator for Europe and the Independent States, House International Relations Foreign Policy in Caucausus, Central Asia, April 30, 1998.

———. Testimony of Donald L. Pressley, Assistant Administrator, Bureau for Europe and Eurasia, U.S. Agency for International Development, April 12, 2000.

Prosterman, Roy L., and Timothy M. Hanstad. *Legal Impediments to Effective Rural Land Relations in Eastern Europe and Central Asia.* Washington, DC: World Bank, 1999.

Radio Free Europe/Radio Liberty (RFE/RL). "Afghan Heroin Engulfs Central Asia," *Central Asia Report*, vol. 4, no. 45 (December 17, 2004).

———. "Kyrgyzstan: Is Bishkek Ready to Spend Its Aid Money Wisely?" *RFE/RL Magazine*, October 16, 2002.

———. "Report Focus on Kazakhstan's New Hydrocarbon Behemoth." *Central Asia Report*, vol. 2, no. 8 (February 28, 2002). www.rferl.org/centralasia/2002/02/8-280202.asp.

————. "Transcaucasia and Central Asia." March 13, 2003. www.rferl.org/centralasia/2002/02/8-280202.asp.

Rakisheva, Khalida. "Impact of the Internal Migration upon the Poverty Problem." Paper presented at the World Bank conference on poverty in Central Asia, Issyk-Kul, Kyrgyzstan, June 2003.

Ramachandran, Sudha. "India, Iran, Russia Map Out Trade Route." *Asia Times*, June 29, 2002.

Rashid, Ahmed. *Jihad: The Rise of Militant Islam in Central Asia*. New Haven, CT: Yale University Press, 2002.

————. *Taliban: Militant Islam, Oil, and Fundamentalism in Central Asia*. New Haven, CT: Yale University Press, 2000.

Rasulova, Aigul. "Opposition Leaders Make Unity Effort as Kyrgyzstan Prepares for Election Season." EurasiaNet.org, May 26, 2004.

Razgulaev, Yuri. "Aggravation of Political Crisis in Kirghizia." *Pravda.ru*, February 12, 2002.

Rechel, Bernd, Laidon Shapo, and Martin McKee. *Millennium Development Goals for Health in Europe and Central Asia: Relevance and Policy Implications*. Washington, DC: World Bank, 2004.

Redo, Slawomir. "Organized Crime and Its Control in Central Asia." Office of International Criminal Justice (OICJ), Sam Houston State University, Criminal Justice Center, Huntsville, Texas, 2004.

Reusse, Eberhard. *The Ills of Aid*. Chicago: University of Chicago Press, 2002.

Ro'I, Yaacov. *Democracy and Pluralism in Muslim Eurasia*. London: Frank Cass, 2004.

————. *Islam in the CIS: A Threat to Stability?* London: Royal Institute of International Affairs, 2001.

————. "Islam, State and Society in Central Asia." *Helsinki Monitor*, vol. 14, no. 3 (2003).

Rose, Richard. *Can Muslims Be Democrats? Evidence from Central Asia*. Glasgow: Centre for the Study of Public Policy, University of Strathclyde, 2002.

Rotar, Igor. "Merchants Protest New Banking Laws in Uzbekistan." *Eurasia Daily Monitor* (Jamestown Foundation), vol. 1, no. 123 (November 9, 2004). www.jamestown.org/publications_details.php?volume_id=401&issue_id=3134&article_id=2368818.

Rotberg, Robert I. "Failed States, Collapsed States, Weak States: Causes and Indicators." In *State Failure and State Weakness in a Time of Terror*, edited by Robert I. Rotberg. Washington, DC: Brookings Institution Press, 2003.

Roy, Olivier. *The New Central Asia*. New York: New York University Press, 2000.

Rubin, Barnett R. *Blood on the Doorstep: The Politics of Preventive Action.* New York: Century Foundation Press, 2002.

———. "Central Asia Wars and Ethnic Conflicts—Rebuilding Failed States," UNCP Occasional Paper no. 2004/11. New York: United Nations Development Program, Human Development Report Office, 2004.

———. "Situation in Afghanistan." Testimony before the U.S. Senate Committee on Foreign Relations, Washington, DC, October 8, 1998. www.cfr.org/public/pubs/rubin3.html.

Ruffin, M. Holt, and Daniel Waugh, eds. *Civil Society in Central Asia.* Seattle, WA: Civil Society International, 1999.

Rumer, Boris. *Central Asia: A Gathering Storm?* New York: M. E. Sharpe, 2002.

———. *Central Asia and the New Global Economy.* New York: M. E. Sharpe, 2000.

———. *Central Asia in Transition Dilemmas of Political and Economic Development.* New York: M. E. Sharpe, 1996.

Rumer, Eugene B. *Flashman's Revenge: Central Asia after September 11.* Washington, DC: Institute for National Strategic Studies, National Defense University, 2002.

Rumsfeld, Donald H. "Secretary Rumsfeld Interview with Reuters TV and Wire." News transcript, March 4, 2004. www.defenselink.mil/transcripts/2004/tr20040325-secdef0564.html.

"Sadji" (the pen-name of a Bishkek journalist for the newspaper *Respublika*). "An Early Defeat for President Akaev." *Prism*, vol. VIII, no. 4, part. 4 (April 2002).

Safronov, Rustem. "Turkmenistan's Niyazov Implicated in Drug Smuggling." *Eurasia Insight*, EurasiaNet.org, March 29, 2002.

Sagdeev, Roald, and Susan Eisenhower, eds. "Islam and Central Asia: An Enduring Legacy or an Evolving Threat?" Washington, DC: Center for Political and Strategic Studies, 2000.

Sampson, Paul. "Kazakhstan—Ten Years and Counting." *Energy Compass*, January 4, 2002.

Saralaeva, Leila. *Changing Sides in Kyrgyzstan.* London: Institute for War and Peace Reporting, June 1, 2004. www.iwpr.net/index.pl?archive/rca/rca_200406_289_2_eng.txt.

Saroyan, Mark, and Edward W. Walker. *Minorities, Mullahs, and Modernity: Reshaping Community in the Former Soviet Union.* Berkeley: University of California, International and Area Studies, 1997.

Schatz, Edward. *Modern Clan Politics: The Power of 'Blood' in Kazakhstan and Beyond.* New York: University of Washington Press, 2004.

Schendel, William van, and Erik Jan Zürcher. *Identity Politics in Central Asia and the Muslim World: Nationalism, Ethnicity and Labour in the Twentieth Century.* New York: St. Martin's Press, 2001.

Sestanovich, Stephen. Testimony of Stephen Sestanovich, Ambassador to New Independent States, House International Relations, Asia and Pacific, U.S. Policy toward Central Asia Republics, March 17, 1999.

———. Testimony of Stephen Sestanovich, Special Adviser, Department of State, Senate Foreign Relations International Economic Policy, Export and Trade Promotion, Caspian Sea Oil Exports, July 8, 1998.

Shanker, Tom. "Russian Official Cautions U.S. on Use of Central Asian Bases." *New York Times,* October 10, 2003.

Shams-ud-Din. *Geopolitics and Energy Resources in Central Asia and Caspian Sea Region.* New Delhi: Lancer's Books, 2000.

Sharma, Raghuveer, Loup Brefort, Marat Iskakov, and Peter Thomson. *Uzbekistan, Energy Sector: Issues, Analysis, and an Agenda for Reform.* Washington, DC: World Bank, June 2003.

Sievers, Eric. *The Post-Soviet Decline of Central Asia: Sustainable Development and Comprehensive Capital.* London: Routledge Curzon, 2003.

Skagen, Ottar. *Caspian Gas.* London: Royal Institute of International Affairs, 1997.

Slevin, Peter. "U.S. Gives Uzbekistan Failing Grade on Rights." *Washington Post,* January 11, 2004.

Smillie, Ian. "NGOs and Development Assistance: A Change in Mindset?" *Third World Quarterly,* vol. 18, no. 18 (1997).

Socor, Vladimir. "Kyrgyzstan's Hosting of U.S. Forces Irritates Moscow." *Monitor 26,* vol. VIII, no. 82 (April 2002): 2.

Sokolsky, R., and T. Charlik-Paley. "NATO and Caspian Security: A Mission Too Far?" *Peace Research Abstracts,* vol. 38, no. 1 (2001).

Staines, Verdon. *A Health Sector Strategy for the Europe and Central Asia Region.* Washington, DC: World Bank, 1999.

Stalenheim, Peter, and Dmitri Trofimov. *Armament and Disarmament in the Caucasus and Central Asia.* Stockholm: Stockholm International Peace Research Institute, July 2003, p. 20.

Starr, Frederick S. Testimony of Frederick Starr, Chairman of the Central Asia-Caucasus Institute, Senate Foreign Relations, Extremist Movements, November 2, 1999.

———. *Xinjiang: China's Muslim Borderland.* Armonk, NY: M. E. Sharpe, 2004.

Starobin, Paul. "The Next Oil Frontier." *Business Week,* May 27, 2002.

State News Service, "Double Standard a Real Danger to Central Asia." Washington, DC: March 16, 2002.

Stern, David, "Kyrgyz President Admits Relative Sells to U.S. Base." *Financial Times*, July 22, 2002.

Suerkulov, Emil. "Gold Production." Kyrgyzstan Development Gateway, http://eng.gateway.kg/gold.

Synovitz, Ron, "Uzbekistan: EBRD Freeze on Aid Praised by NGOs." RFE/RL, April 19, 2004. www.rferl.org/featuresarticle/2004/04/bf3f3488-8010-43c2-9ea0-89e8e774c756.html.

Tabyshalieva, Anara. *The Challenge of Regional Cooperation in Central Asia: Preventing Ethnic Conflict in the Ferghana Valley*. Washington, DC: U.S. Institute of Peace, 1999.

Talbott, Strobe. "A Farewell to Flashman: American Policy in the Caucasus and Central Asia," Address delivered at the Johns Hopkins School of Advanced International Studies, Washington, DC., July 1997.

Tang, Shiping. "Economic Integration in Central Asia: The Russian and Chinese Relationship." *Asian Survey*, vol. 40, no. 2 (March–April 2000).

Tarnoff, Curt. "The Former Soviet Union and U.S. Foreign Assistance," CRS Issue Brief for Congress. Washington, DC: Congressional Research Service, September 16, 2003.

Tart, William M. *Ethnic Conflict and U.S. Central Command Policy for the Central Asian Republics*. Maxwell Air Force Base, Alabama: Air Command and Staff College, Air University, 2001.

Tazmini, Ghoncheh. "The Islamic Revival in Central Asia: A Potent Force or a Misconception?" *Central Asian Survey*, vol. 20, no. 1 (2001).

Thorvaldur, Gylfason. "Nature, Power, and Growth," CESifo Working Paper no. 413. Munich: Center for Economic Studies and Ifo Institute for Economic Research (CESifo), January 2001.

Thrower, James. *The Religious History of Central Asia from the Earliest Times to the Present Day*. Lewiston, NY: Edwin Mellen Press, 2004.

Tolipov, Farkhod. "On the Role of the Central Asian Cooperation Organization within the SCO." *Central Asia and Caucasus*, no. 3 (2004).

Tsalik, Svetlana. "Caspian Oil Windfalls: Who Will Benefit?" New York: Open Society Institute, 2003.

Turaey, Faruk. "Prickly Uzbekistan Comes Closer to Russia." *Transitions Online*, August 19, 2003.

Tyson, Ann Scott. "New U.S. Strategy: 'Lily Pad' Bases." *Christian Science Monitor*, August 10, 2004.

United Nations. *Generating Employment for Rural Women: Studies from Selected Central Asian Republics*. New York: 2001.

———. *Land Transport Corridors between Central Asia and Europe*. New York: 1997.

United Nations Development Program. *Central Asia 2010: Prospects for Human Development*. New York: Regional Bureau for Europe and the CIS, UNDP, 1999.

———. *Human Development Report 2004: Cultural Liberty in Today's Diverse World*. New York: Oxford University Press, 2004, pp. 140–1, 151.

United Nations Development Program in Tajikistan. *Reconstruction, Rehabilitation and Development Programme*. Dushanbe, Tajikistan: July 2000.

United Nations Drug Control Program. *Afghanistan Opium Survey 2002*. Vienna: 2003.

United Nations Economic and Social Commission for Asia and the Pacific. *Foreign Direct Investment in Central Asian and Caucasian Economies: Policies and Issues*. Bangkok: July 22, 2003. www.unescap.org/tid/publication/chap3e_2255.pdf.

United Nations Economic Commission for Europe. *Economic Instruments, Environmental Expenditures and Privatization*. Geneva: 2004. www.unece.org/env/epr/studies/Tajikistan/chapter03.pdf.

Upton, Barbara, Bill Bradley, and John R. Kasich. "The United States and the Multilateral Development Banks." In *Report of the CSIS Task Force on the Multilateral Development Banks*. Washington, DC: CSIS Press, 1998.

U.S. Bureau of Democracy, Human Rights, and Labor. *Annual Report on International Religious Freedom 2000: Uzbekistan*. Washington, DC: U.S. Department of State, September 5, 2000.

———. *Country Report on Human Rights Practices 2003: Uzbekistan*. Washington, DC: U.S. Department of State, February 25, 2004. www.state.gov/g/drl/rls/hrrpt/2003/27873.htm.

———. *Country Report on Human Rights Practices 2001: Uzbekistan*. Washington, DC: U.S. Department of State, March 4, 2002. www.state.gov/g/drl/rls/hrrpt/2001/eur/8366.htm.

U.S. Central Intelligence Agency. *The Caucasus and Central Asia*. Langley, VA: 2003.

———. *CIA World Factbook on Kyrgyzstan*. Langley, VA: May 11, 2004. www.cia.gov/cia/publications/factbook/geos/kg.html#Econ.

———. "Heroin Movement Worldwide." Langley, VA: 2000. http://purl.access.gpo.gov/GPO/LPS18491.

U.S. Department of State. *Country Profile: Uzbekistan*. Washington, DC: October 2004. www.state.gov/r/pa/ei/bgn/2924.htm.

———. *Overview of Uzbekistan's Mining Industry*. Washington, DC: December 16, 1998.

———. *U.S. Assistance to Tajikistan*. Washington, DC: December 6, 2002. www.state.gov/r/pa/prs/ps/2002/15766.htm.

U.S. General Accounting Office. *Central and Southwest Asian Countries: Trends in U.S. Assistance and Key Economic, Governance, and Demographic Characteristics*. Washington, DC: 2003.

———. *Foreign Assistance: U.S. Economic and Democratic Assistance to the Central Asian Republics*. Washington, DC: August 1999. www.gao.gov/archive/1999/ns99200.pdf.

———. "International Efforts to Aid Russia's Transition Have Had Mixed Results." Report to the Chairman and to the Banking Minority Member, Committee on Banking and Financial Services, House of Representatives, (GAO-01-8) Washington, DC: November 2000.

Van de Walle, Nicolas. *African Economies and the Politics of Permanent Crisis*. Cambridge, UK: Cambridge University Press, 2001.

Van de Walle, Nicolas, and Timothy Johnston. *Improving Aid to Africa*, Policy Essay no. 21. Washington, DC: Overseas Development Council, 1996, pp. 3–4.

Vellinga, Menno. *The Political Economy of the Drug Industry: Latin America and the International System*. Gainesville: University Press of Florida, 2004.

Voronina, Svetlana. "How Do Companies in Eurasia Finance Their Trade/Investment Deals?" BISNIS Finance Survey, Kazakhstan, www.bisnis.doc.gov/BISNIS/fq2004/surveys/FinanceSurveyKazakhstan2004.htm.

Wetherall, Ben. "U.S. Authorities Warn of Imminent Terror Attacks in Uzbekistan Following Mass Protests." *World Markets Analysis*, November 5, 2004.

Whitehead, Laurence. *Democratization: Theory and Experience*. Oxford: Oxford University Press, 2002.

Whitlock, Monica. *Land Beyond the River: The Untold Story of Central Asia*. New York: Thomas Dunne, 2003.

Wegren, Stephen K. *Land Reform in the Former Soviet Union and Eastern Europe*. London: Routledge, 1998.

Weihman, Ted. "U.S. Focus on Interdiction in Central Asia is Inadequate to Meet Drug Trafficking Challenge." EurasiaNet.org, September 23, 2003.

Weinthal Erika. *State Making and Environmental Cooperation: Linking Domestic and International Politics in Central Asia*. Cambridge, MA: MIT Press, 2002.

Weinthal, Erika, and Pauline Jones Luong. "Environmental NGOs in Kazakhstan: Democratic Goals and Non-democratic Outcomes." In *The Power and Limits of NGOs*, edited by Sarah Elizabeth Mendelson and John K. Glenn. New York: Columbia University Press, 2002.

Weisbrode, Kenneth. *Central Eurasia: Prize or Quicksand?* New York: Oxford University Press, 2001.

Winrow, Gareth. *Turkey in Post-Soviet Central Asia*. London: Royal Institute of International Affairs, 1995.

World Bank. *Comprehensive Development Framework of the Kyrgyz Republic to 2010, Expanding the Country's Capacities, National Poverty Reduction Strategy 2003–2005*. Washington, DC: January 2003. p. 152.

———. *First Progress Report, Kyrgyz Republic National Poverty Reduction Strategy 2003-2005*. Washington, DC: April 2004, p. 13. http://poverty.worldbank.org/files/cr04200.pdf.

———. *Non-Payment in the Electricity Sector in Eastern Europe and the Former Soviet Union*. Washington, DC: Energy Sector Unit, Europe and Central Asia Region, 1999.

———. *Rural, Environment, and Social Development Strategies for the Europe and Central Asia Region*. Washington, DC: World Bank, 2000.

———. *Tajikistan Country Brief*. Washington, DC: World Bank, September 2002.

———. *Third Annual Report on IDA's Country Assessment and Allocation Process*. Washington, DC: April 2002. http://worldbank.org/ida.

———. "Uzbekistan-Country Economic Memorandum," Economic Report. Washington, DC: World Bank, 2003.

———. *World Bank Development Indicators, 2003*. Washington, DC: 2003, table 26, survey year 1998.

———. *World Development Report 2005: A Better Investment Climate for Everyone*. Washington, DC: 2004.

Zanca, Russel. "Explaining Islam in Central Asia: An Anthropological Approach for Uzbekistan." *Journal of Muslim Minority Affairs*, vol. 24, no. 1 (2004).

Zardykhan, Zharmukhamed. "Russians in Kazakhstan and Demographic Change: Imperial Legacy and the Kazakh Way of Nation Building." *Asian Ethnicity*, vol. 5, no. 1 (2004).

Zettelmeyer, Jeromin. "The Uzbek Growth Puzzle." *IMF Staff Papers*, vol. 46, no.3 (September/December 1999). Washington, DC: International Monetary Fund, 1999.

Zhovtis, Yevgeny. "11th September: Consequences for Human Rights in Central Asia." *Helsinki Monitor*, vol. 13, no.1 (2002).

Zviagelskaia, Irina. *The Russian Policy Debate on Central Asia.* London: Royal Institute of International Affairs, 1995.

Index

Freedom House: democracy indicators of, 269–270; printing press in Kyrgyzstan a, 132

Freedom Support Act (FSA): allocation of funding for, 127; expenditures for, 259–262; explanation of, 67

Gaidar, Yegor, 60

Ganci air base (Kyrgyzstan), 180–181

Gazprom, 38, 58, 92–93, 99, 100, 111, 162, 191, 194, 195

GDP. *See* Gross domestic product (GDP)

Georgia: CIS and, 55; natural gas and, 58; revolution in, 1

Germany, 80, 184

Giffen, James, 34, 69, 146–147

Gold mining, in Kyrgyzstan, 110

Gorbachev, Mikhail, 45, 211

Gore, Al, 67–68

Great Britain, energy interests and, 81–82

Gross domestic product (GDP): by country, 264; in Kazakhstan, 86–88, 96, 118; in Kyrgyzstan, 106, 109, 118; in Tajikistan, 118; in Turkmenistan, 118; in Uzbekistan, 118, 119

Haig, Alexander, 37, 69

Hanafi legal tradition, 153

Healthcare systems, 8

HIV/AIDS, 215

Hizb-ut Tahrir, 19, 29, 49–50, 108, 152, 153, 168, 282

Human rights issues: in Kazakhstan, 144; in Kyrgyzstan, 7; in Turkmenistan, 162; in Uzbekistan, 125–126, 149, 151–152, 154, 176, 178

Human Rights Watch, 178

Hussein, Saddam, 124, 206

Hyatt Corporation, 111–112

Hydroelectric industry: China and, 200; in Kyrgyzstan, 111, 195, 196; Russia and, 195–196, 220; in Tajikistan, 116, 195; water resources and, 195–196. *See also* Electricity production; Energy sector

Ibadullah, Nasrullah ibn, 162

Imam Shamil of Dagestan, 25

IMU. *See* Islamic Movement of Uzbekistan (IMU)

Independence: early years of, 11–13; ethnic identities and, 24–26; extremist ideologies and, 28–29; interest of international community and, 21–24; in Kazakhstan, 30–36; in Kyrgyzstan, 41–44; overview of, 20–21; in Tajikistan, 44–47; in Turkmenistan, 37–41; in Uzbekistan, 47–51; water shortages and, 26–28

India, relations with Central Asian states, 76, 203

Indo-Europeans, 24, 25

Indonesia Petroleum, 103

International Development Association (IDA), 105

International financial institutions (IFI), 222, 223, 225, 227, 228

International Foundation for Electoral Studies (IFES), 236

International Monetary Fund (IMF), 227; Kazakhstan and, 33, 94, 97, 98; Kyrgyzstan and, 23, 41, 110; Tajikistan and, 44; U.S. policy and, 67; Uzbekistan and, 117, 118, 224

Internet use, in Uzbekistan, 148

Iran: cultural ties with, 14–15; hydroelectric power and, 195; relations with Central Asian states, 53, 74–76; Turkmenistan and, 37; war on terror and, 201

Iraq: democracy building in, 176; present state of, 206

Iraq war: cost of, 206; Kazakhstan and, 182; Turkmenistan and, 184; Uzbekistan and, 177–178

Islam: relations between state and, 28–29, 152–153; self-government limitations and, 25. *See also* Muslims

Islamic Development Bank, 201

Islamic extremist groups: in Afghanistan, 13, 17; border security and, 217;

About the Author

Martha Brill Olcott, a specialist in Central Asian and Caspian affairs and interethnic relations in the Soviet successor states, joined the Carnegie Endowment in 1995. She is also a professor of political science at Colgate University. Olcott codirects the Carnegie Moscow Center's Project on Ethnicity and Politics in the former Soviet Union, which organizes seminars and conferences, and creates publications on problems of state building in multiethnic Soviet successor states and on regional and ethnic conflicts within Russia. She has previously served as a special consultant to Acting Secretary of State Lawrence Eagleburger and as director of the Central Asian American Enterprise Fund.

Olcott received her graduate education at the University of Chicago and has been a member of the faculty at Colgate University since 1975. A prolific author on Central Asian affairs, her books include *Kazakhstan: Unfulfilled Promise* (Carnegie Endowment, 2002); *Getting It Wrong: Regional Cooperation and the Commonwealth of Independent States*, coauthored with Anders Åslund and Sherman Garnett (Carnegie Endowment, 1999); and *Russia after Communism*, edited with Anders Åslund (Carnegie Endowment, 1999).

Carnegie Endowment for International Peace

The Carnegie Endowment is a private, nonprofit organization dedicated to advancing cooperation between nations and promoting active international engagement by the United States. Founded in 1910, its work is nonpartisan and dedicated to achieving practical results.

Through research, publishing, convening, and, on occasion, creating new institutions and international networks, Endowment associates shape fresh policy approaches. Their interests span geographic regions and the relations between governments, business, international organizations, and civil society, focusing on the economic, political, and technological forces driving global change. Through its Carnegie Moscow Center, the Endowment helps to develop a tradition of public policy analysis in the states of the former Soviet Union and to improve relations between Russia and the United States. The Endowment publishes *Foreign Policy*, one of the world's leading magazines of international politics and economics.

OFFICERS
Jessica T. Mathews, *President*
Paul Balaran, *Executive Vice President and Secretary*
George Perkovich, *Vice President for Studies*
Carmen MacDougall, *Vice President for Communications*

BOARD OF TRUSTEES

James C. Gaither, *Chairman*
Gregory B. Craig, *Vice Chairman*
Bill Bradley
Robert Carswell
Jerome A. Cohen
Richard A. Debs
Susan Eisenhower
Donald V. Fites
Leslie H. Gelb
William W. George
Richard Giordano

Jamie Gorelick
Stephen D. Harlan
Donald Kennedy
Robert Legvold
Stephen R. Lewis, Jr.
Jessica T. Mathews
Zanny Minton Beddoes
Olara A. Otunnu
William J. Perry
W. Taylor Reveley III

WIDENER UNIVERSITY
WOLFGRAM
LIBRARY
CHESTER, PA

389